THE

RESULTS OF EMANCIPATION.

BY

AUGUSTIN COCHIN,

EX-MAIRE AND MUNICIPAL COUNCILLOR OF PARIS.

WORK CROWNED BY THE INSTITUTE OF FRANCE
(*ACADÉMIE FRANCAISE*).

TRANSLATED BY

MARY L. BOOTH,

TRANSLATOR OF COUNT DE GASPARIN'S WORKS ON AMERICA, ETC.

BOSTON:
WALKER, WISE, AND COMPANY,
245 WASHINGTON STREET.
1863.

CAMBRIDGE:
WELCH, BIGELOW, AND COMPANY,
PRINTERS.

TRANSLATOR'S PREFACE.

THE stranger, visiting Paris and admiring its monuments of art, turns aside to examine its more noble monuments of public charity. He visits the Hôtel-Dieu, founded by an Archbishop of Paris, endowed by Philip Augustus and St. Louis, enlarged by Henri IV., and enriched by the benefactions of a long line of monarchs. He then, in the Faubourg-Saint-Jacques, visits another hospital, more airy, neater, more commodious, and better ordered, with a smaller proportional mortality than the Hôtel-Dieu, giving annual relief to more than 2,000 patients, founded during the last century by a single man, whose name it still bears, the Hôpital-Cochin.* Its founder, the Curate of Saint-Jacques-du-Haut-Pas, was one of a family distinguished for its services in the French magistracy, for its administrative ability, and for its beneficence. Two generations later a member of the same family, Augustin Cochin, produces a work which, in far-reaching conse-

* This hospital was commenced in 1780 and finished in 1782, in the Rue du Faubourg-Saint-Jacques, by the venerable M. Cochin, Curé of Saint-Jacques-du-Haut-Pas, who, to rescue his poor parishioners from the dangers to which they were exposed at the Hôtel-Dieu, over-crowded, ill-ventilated, and malarious, where 5,000 patients were huddled together in 1,400 beds, disposed of all his property, and even his books, to furnish them a safer and more comfortable asylum. It was first called the Hôpital de Saint Jacques-du-Haut-Pas; the name of its founder has since been appropriately bestowed on it by the *Conseil des Hospices*, who have placed his marble bust in the principal hall. The hospital contains some 150 beds, and is under the supervision of the Sisters of St. Martha.

quences, generous purpose, and practical utility, stands in noble rivalry with the earlier labors of his progenitors.

The possessor of an ample fortune, independent, frank, averse to intrigue, and unpretending withal, M. Cochin has persistently held aloof from all office, only accepting a municipal councillorship and the *mairie* of one of the arrondissements of Paris, a position furnishing him an opportunity to do much good in an unostentatious way as almoner to its needy population. From his earliest youth M. Cochin has been identified with the cause of liberty in France. A Legitimist in principle, the fast friend and ally of Count de Montalembert in his efforts to raise up a Catholic liberal party for the development of republican sentiments and institutions, the ardent coadjutor of Père Lacordaire, Monseigneur d'Orleans, Viscount de Melun, Prince de Broglie, and a host of other reformers, he has long been distinguished for his efforts and zeal in behalf of freedom. He is well known as a publicist, has been for years an able contributor to the *Journal des Débats*, one of the most enlightened and influential journals in Europe, where his articles on American affairs have lately attracted much attention, and is at present editor-in-chief of *La Correspondance*, the organ of the party represented by Count de Montalembert, Monseigneur d'Orleans, and Prince de Broglie, in opposition to Louis Veuillot and the Napoleonic party.

M. Cochin is now in the prime of life, — scarcely forty years old. His wife is the daughter of the well-known Legitimist, Viscount Benoist d'Azy, one of the most clear-sighted and practical men of France, who, possessed of immense fortune, an extensive land-owner and proprietor of iron-forges, has done more perhaps than any other man to advance the material interests of his country, by railway building, mining, and agricultural improvements. M. Cochin is himself an eminently practical man, with rare administrative ability, and his work, which is here offered to the public, is no enthusiastic theory based on mere visionary speculation, but an array of clear and well-digested facts, presented in a calm, unprejudiced manner, and drawn from official sources to which few men could have had so full access, and which few men would have studied so diligently and minutely. Indeed, the published and unpublished papers and records of every ministry of Europe have been placed at his disposal during the preparation of his work; in England he has had all the unpublished documents of the Board of Trade, and the sagacious Nassau Senior, one of the wisest counsellors of the British government, has rendered him constant aid. The reliability of his facts and conclusions cannot, therefore, be contested, and in this respect the work is of the utmost value to the American public, as there is no work extant in the English language which sums up so fully and incontestably the practical results of emancipation.

The present volume comprises the first volume of the original work, *L'Abolition de l'esclavage*, and is wholly distinct from the second volume, the Results of Slavery. It has been thought advisable, having the author's consent, to publish this volume separately, trusting that the public demand may justify us erelong in issuing the second, the greater part of which is devoted to the United States and its present condition. M. Cochin is a warm advocate of the cause of the North, and of emancipation. In a recent letter he writes: "With what anxious and sympathizing emotion we follow the painful trials which the United States are enduring! European opinion has great need of being sustained. On the one hand, the material interests which are suffering, on the other, the passion of the English journals, delighted with the misfortunes of so powerful a rival, and through which alone your news reaches Europe, — these are the two causes which stifle the voices of the friends of justice and human liberty. I thank God for having permitted me opportunely to take a humble part in this great cause. I firmly hope that, whatever may be the issue of the war, slavery will be dishonored and stricken down; — this would be the most glorious crown of the nineteenth century; it deserves the warmest efforts. Count on my perseverance in acting within the narrow limits that I can, and on my gratitude to the unknown but much loved friends who do my work more honor than I had hoped for it."

The estimation in which this work is held in Europe may be judged from the fact that the French Academy, at its last annual meeting, July 3, 1862, on the report of its illustrious Perpetual Secretary, M. Villemain, decreed it the first prize, 3,000 francs. In his report M. Villemain says: —

"Obliged to limit itself in its choice, the Academy has designated the works which, through talent and presumed influence, have appeared to answer best to the idea of its founder and the varied destinations of its work. It has placed first of all two books full of laborious knowledge and generous ardor. The one is a study of religious history, philosophy, and eloquence (that of M. de Pressensé). The other, recommended to us by the interests of moral study as well as by the present lesson of events, is deserving the choice of the Academy. This is *L'Abolition de l'esclavage*, by M. Cochin, former *maire* and municipal councillor of the city of Paris. The distinctive feature, the eminent merit of the author, is that of uniting scientific precision and philanthropic ardor, of demanding with eloquent zeal the abolition of slavery in the name of God and humanity, and of demonstrating in minute detail all the advantages of this useful moral reform. The author is at once an apostle and an economist. This double power of fervor and of science marks the Introduction, addressed to the Duke de Broglie as the first promoter of the intervention of France in the suppression of the slave-trade, and the constant and enlightened defender of emancipation in all the stages through which this cause has passed, to the complete abolition of slavery, abruptly proclaimed in the French colonies in 1848, and even then as salutary as irrevocable.

"Setting out from this too much disputed example, M. Cochin shows what has been done for humanity in the colonies of two powerful nations, and of two others no less civilized; and also how many slaves still remain in the Christian world, — more than 4,000,000 in a portion of the republican States of America, where appears at this moment that great civil war, that convulsion of an empire substituted for a question of philanthropy, as if to attest how great peril and calamity are comprised in social injustice. We read the eloquent summary of facts prior to the war, the fatal symptoms, the aggravated difficulties which preceded the formidable crisis, the greatness of which retards the catastrophe, without ceasing to render it inevitable. The heart of the author does not falter, but, in the face of the vicissitudes of war, while invoking peace, he counsels, he demands, he predicts, the abolition of slavery; then, turning from a land desolated by war, he more forcibly repeats the course that policy as well as humanity should hasten to adopt where slavery is not yet attacked and defended by arms, where it is still at peace, and where it only risks drawing on the masters the dangers of foreign conquest, and tempting other slave states by calculations of ambition or solidarity.

"After this review of slavery in the Christian world of our day, we take up with the author the question on its own merits, according to the Mosaic law, philosophy, and the Gospel. We see religion unceasingly active in the lightening of this scourge. If, after having labored to destroy it in antiquity and the Middle Ages, it sees it spring up anew in modern times, it more than ever belongs to it to second policy and science united in rendering it impossible under the latest form which it has assumed.

"Such is this plea against slavery. Full of generous sentiments and exact researches, a blending of moral and statistical philosophy, this book is one of the best that can be brought to the support of the great reform which the genius of Modern Europe has begun in its colonies, and which its mediation and example should extend throughout the world.

"The Academy decrees to each of these works a prize of 3,000 francs."

Besides this flattering testimonial, the Pope has conferred an order of knighthood on the author in recompense for his work, and the most illustrious of the French bishops, Monseigneur d'Orleans, has addressed him a letter in eulogy of its merits.

Its value in this country can hardly be estimated, appearing as it does on the eve of a crisis of emancipation, caused abruptly, as in the French colonies, by revolution, and which, as in these, will wreck for a time the prosperity of the States in which it is wrought, or lead them without suffering to a more prosperous condition, according as we profit by the experience of our neighbors. This experience M. Cochin has lucidly summed up, proving beyond dispute that emancipation by itself alone has caused less disturbance than a hail-storm or a year of drought would have done. He has shown more, — that, in the British West India Islands, with the single exception of Jamaica, the result of emancipation has been to increase the progress and wealth of the islands, and that in Jamaica itself, while its general results have been most beneficent, any apparent failure in the prosperity of the island is to be traced to local causes and the home legislation upon sugar, the details and results of which are fully explained.

Thanks are due, in conclusion, to Messrs. Orestes A. Brownson and George Sumner, the friends and correspondents of the author, who have kindly furnished the facts relating to his personal history.

MARY L. BOOTH.

BOSTON, December 1, 1862.

CONTENTS.

CHAPTER VI.

CHAPTER VII.

CHAPTER VIII.

CHAPTER IX.

CHAPTER X.

CHAPTER XI.

CHAPTER XII.

CHAPTER XIII.

CHAPTER XIV.

CHAPTER XV.

CHAPTER XVI.

BOOK SECOND.

ENGLISH COLONIES.

CHAPTER I.

CHAPTER II.

CHAPTER III.

CHAPTER IV.

BOOK THIRD.

COLONIES OF DENMARK, SWEDEN, AND HOLLAND.

APPENDIX.

FRENCH COLONIES.

ENGLISH COLONIES.

INTRODUCTION.

TO M. LE DUC DE BROGLIE.

Monsieur le Duc: —

If I did not dedicate this book to you, I should think myself doubly ungrateful.

I should forget that you had approved my designs, aided my researches, encouraged my perseverance.

I should forget, above all, that to you belongs the question to which I devote my efforts. Your hand has contributed more than any other to break at length, by repeated blows, the heavy and unjust bond which held, under the shadow of the French flag, in the face of Christian altars, in the midst of the nineteenth century, two hundred and fifty thousand human beings in slavery.

You it was that, March 28, 1822, proposed to the Chamber of Peers an address to the king, demanding that he should prescribe measures suited better to secure the entire abolition of the traffic in slaves.

You it was that, January 24, 1827, on the occasion of Article I. of the projected law for the suppression of the negro slave trade, pronounced a memorable speech, the memory of which has not perished with time.*

You it was that, March 26, 1840, was called to the pres-

* See the learned Memoir of M. Charles Giraud to the Institute upon Negro Slavery, *Comptes rendus de l'Académie des Sciences morales*, 1861, p. 194.

idency of the celebrated commission charged with drawing up the plan of emancipation for the colonies, and their political constitution.

You it was that, in March, 1843, after an immense investigation, and prodigious labors, presented to the Minister of the Marine the report of this commission.

You it was that, May 29, 1845, signed, after negotiating the agreement concluded with her Britannic Majesty for the suppression of the negro slave-trade, an agreement which reconciled the interests of humanity with the just national susceptibilities aroused by the treaties of 1831 and 1833 and the agreement of 1841.

You it was that, July 7, 1845, supported, by a speech in the Chamber of Peers, the bills designed to favor the redemption, education, and well-being of slaves.

You it was that, January 13, 1846, defended the agreement of May 29, attacked in the Chamber of Peers.

After the abolition of slavery (March 4, 1848), when it became imperative to establish in our distant possessions the order endangered by the Revolution, it was you who was called upon, November 22, 1849, to preside over the commission charged with framing the new régime of the colonies.

Ten years later, when a new colonial commission examined the difficult questions raised by the enlistment of negroes on the African coast, it was again to you, in 1858, that this commission turned, believing itself unable to dispense in such a matter with the authority of your incomparable experience.

What would it be, if I were to add to the enumeration of so many public acts the results of your influence, constantly occupied during the past forty years with the obscure interests of the humble clients of whom Providence has made you counsel?

You have encountered in this struggle obstinate opponents, but also indefatigable allies. One need not complain when he can associate in the defence of the same cause the practical reason of MM. Passy and de Tracy, the authors of the first plans of emancipation, the admirable language of MM. de Remusat and de Tocqueville, the supporters of these projects, the eloquence of M. Guizot, M. de Lamartine, or M. Berryer, the zeal of M. de Gasparin, the knowledge of M. Wallon, the democratic ardor of M. Schoelcher, in a word, the co-operation of the various and numerous soldiers of that vast army which justice has power to raise up in France on every side.

There has not been a twelvemonth, scarcely a day, for the last forty years, in which, in concert with these generous auxiliaries, you have not kept awake the authorities by interpellations, public opinion by publications, authors by rewards, travellers by questions, France and Europe by continual discussion, the wide-spread and peaceful agitation of mercy which England had already witnessed, and which, growing by degrees and at length raising its voice above the clamors of interest, has ended by inscribing in the depths of every conscience the irrepressible condemnation of slavery. By your memorable report of 1843, you wrote the sentence, you pronounced the condemnation; the Republic of 1848 had the honor of carrying it into effect.

It is to you that emancipation in the French colonies is chiefly due. After the fatigues of a long career, interspersed with triumphs and disappointments, "there is not a drop of sweat upon the brow," in the beautiful language of M. Guizot, "which such a palm-wreath cannot dry." *

Nevertheless, moved by the noise of the violent agitations of the United States, you follow, with an anxious glance, slavery in its new aspects, no longer afflicting only a few little second-rate communities, but aggrandized, envenomed, menacing the peace, the very existence, of one

* *Vie de Washington.*

of the first nations possessed by earth and known in history. You ask yourself whether in this sad life, in which one bewails his affections, one by one, he must in the same manner wear mourning for his hopes ; whether he must renounce emancipation ; what is the present position, what the future, of this great question, one of the passions of your soul. Where do we stand after a century of effort ?

I.

More than half a century ago, at the time when Mr. Wilberforce was soliciting of the British Parliament the abolition of the slave-trade, Mr. Pitt exclaimed : "Mankind is now likely to be delivered from the greatest practical evil that has ever afflicted the human race, from the severest and most extensive calamity ever recorded in the history of the world." This crown, which the eighteenth century failed to gain, the nineteenth, already inclining towards its closing years, does not yet hold in its hands, for the great work of the emancipation of slaves in the bosom of Christian nations is far from being accomplished.

The *slave-trade,* to say nothing of the special laws of each country, has been condemned by three Congresses, a Papal bull, twenty-six treaties, and more than a hundred agreements with the petty African sovereigns. Glorious days have witnessed the birth to freedom of eight hundred thousand slaves emancipated by England,* two hundred and fifty thousand by France,† and several thousand by Denmark and Sweden.

But the slave-trade is still carried on ; it defies laws, it braves cruisers. The United States possess by themselves alone more than four million slaves ; Brazil, at least two million ; the Dutch colonies, more than a hundred thou-

* Exact number, 770,390, without including India and Ceylon.

† Exact number, 248,560, including Senegal, Nossi-bé, and St. Mary.

sand; the Spanish colonies, six hundred thousand. There remain, therefore, upon Christian territory, without speaking of the heathen world, nearly seven million baptized slaves!

Why, then, is the voice of the illustrious men who have carried the work of emancipation so far, and to whom reverts the immortal honor of having insured one of the most glorious triumphs which human communities have ever won over themselves, — why is it extinct or silent?

It seems that this century, so quickly enthused by, and so soon weary of, so many generous causes, again stands still; is it to repose or to repent?

The silence of public opinion and its masters has another cause. There is silence, because there is nothing more to say.

The unlawfulness of servitude belongs, in fact, to the few truths which the Gospel, science, and political liberty have rendered rulers of the human conscience throughout all Europe.

Philosophy accords to all slaves a soul equal to our own, perhaps refused them by Aristotle.* Physiology declares the white and black, despite important differences, members of the same family. History discovers between the possessors and the possessed no trace of lawful conquest. The law no longer recognizes any validity to a pretended contract whose title has no existence, whose object is illicit, and whose parties are, the one without free will, the other without good faith.† Ethnology raises to the height of an admirable law the radical difference, which places in the first rank on earth the races that work, like the Northern Europeans, and in the last rank the races that are served, like the Turks. Political economy affirms

* Wallon, *Histoire de l'Esclavage dans l'Antiquité*, Tom. I. Chap. XI. p. 356. Moehler, *Abolition de l'Esclavage par le Christianisme dans les quinze premiers Siècles*, Chap. II., translation, Symon de Latreiche, 1841, p. 199.

† *Du Droit industriel*, by M. Renouard, Part I. Chap. V. Paris, 1860.

the superiority of free over forced labor, and condemns everything that deprives man of the essential condition of his moral and material life, — the family. Policy and charity, from different stand-points, accept the same conclusion; charity, more tender, detests slavery because it oppresses the inferior race; policy, more elevated, condemns it especially because it corrupts the superior race.

Like sciences, parties, and faiths are in unison.

All nations, free or despotic, monarchical or republican, all clergies, Catholic or Protestant, have been accomplices of slavery. The nations which continue such are the Southern United States and Holland, two Protestant nations; Spain and Brazil, two Catholic monarchies. But England and France, the Northern United States and Peru, Sweden and Portugal, have renounced the participation. The Anglicans, Baptists, and Wesleyans share as largely as the Catholics in this salutary repentance. So great a question is a happy ground where tolerance and union are acquired properties and necessary forces. This remarkable harmony is the triumph of our age: it is complete in the domain of ideas; the principal nations of Europe have conformed their conduct to their conviction; they are silent, persuaded that time will do the rest.

Unhappily, it is the nature of slavery unceasingly to spring up anew; when stifled on one point of the earth, it breaks forth and spreads on another.

It springs up anew — a thing wellnigh incredible! — in purely theoretical discussions; it is not even entirely expelled from reasoning. In America whole libraries are composed of books in favor of slavery. A school is formed for its defence, which M. de Gasparin pungently styles the school of *cottony* theology.* In England, men dare write: "Our grandfathers committed the crime, our fathers repented it, to us belongs reflection; we may perhaps be

* The Uprising of a Great People, p. 76.

mistaken." * In France they repeat, without examination, that emancipation has killed the colonies. Public opinion suffers itself to be influenced more than is believed by this repentance for a good action. It is in the nature of the human mind to doubt on the morrow its deeds of yesterday. The inconveniences of every infant act disturbs the vision and revives objections; errors the most thoroughly uprooted have a speedy reaction, a second season, as it were, a dangerous moment, when it is necessary to begin again to justify evidence, and to demonstrate the commonplace.

Moreover, among the most grievous consequences of a wrong is the weariness, the indifference, induced by the reiterated exposition of its evils. Declamation and satiety have rendered the cause of the slaves fastidious, almost suspicious, before it is won. There are those who have the same contempt for the question of slavery as for the slave himself. Insensible to these difficulties, I content myself with repeating what Mr. Canning said to Mr. Dundas more than half a century ago: "So long as there are no clear and positive refutations of the old arguments, I shall continue to use them." †

But new arguments abound, for slavery springs up anew much more in facts than in ideas.

It is generally admitted that slavery almost entirely disappeared from Europe, under the influence of the Catholic Church, about the twelfth century.‡ In the fifteenth and sixteenth, it again revived. In the seventeenth century kings encouraged it by treaties, and aided it by premiums. In the eighteenth century it was attacked; in the nine-

* London Times, 1861.

† Speech on the motion of Mr. Wilberforce, March 1, 1799.

‡ Michelet, *Rapport à l'Académie des Sciences morales*, August 31, 1839. Naudet, *Mémoires sur la Condition des Personnes.* Wallon, *Histoire de l'Esclavage dans l'Antiquité*, 1840. Édouard Biot, *De l'Abolition de l'Esclavage ancien en Occident*, 1840. Yanoski, *De l'Abolition de l'Esclavage ancien au Moyen Âge*, 1860.

teenth, it is effaced from the laws of England and France; at the same moment it is spreading, at a rate hitherto unknown, in the two most powerful states of America, — the vast and flourishing empire of Brazil, and the young, free, and great republic of the United States.

I write in 1861, which, during the same month, has seen the Emperor of Russia (March 19) proclaim the emancipation of more than twenty million serfs, and, on another continent, has witnessed the installation of the President of the republic of the United States (March 4) greeted by the separation of the slaveholding States, which have risen in arms to save their living property at the expense of the country.

In the face of such events, it is impossible to dispute either the novelty, or the abundance, or the terrible opportuneness of arguments.

Only, it is fitting to present them from a new stand-point.

As the systems invented by the human mind appear on the scene of history in a certain regular order, as demonstrated by M. Cousin, so in a long-continued debate do arguments also present themselves in a certain order, and demonstrations, without changing their object, change form. It is usual to begin with the extremes. Between feelings and interests, between emotion and menaces, no agreement is possible. By degrees, they are drawn nearer by reasoning, facts are taken as arbiters, and harmony is established on practical grounds.

The arguments of a hundred years ago *for* and *against* slavery are no longer wholly in place.

In 1778, Sir Peter Parker, Governor of Jamaica, declared that the abolition of the slave-trade would deprive England of her colonies, half her commerce, and her rank as a maritime power.*

* "The abolition of the African slave-trade would cause a general despondency among the negroes, and gradually decrease population, and consequently the

The Abolitionists of the same epoch (1792) proclaimed, in a sort of stupidly pious crusade, universal abstention from the use of sugar.*

In France, during this time, the Minister of the Marine wrote to the Governor of St. Domingo (1771): —

"*His Majesty thinks that it is important to good order not to lessen in any degree the humiliation attached to the species, a prejudice the more useful as it exists in the hearts of the slaves themselves, and contributes mainly to the repose of the colonies.*" †

On the other side, the Abolitionists, braving evidence and history, accorded to the black race the most brilliant intellectual destinies, and Grégoire composed a work on *Negro Literature.*

We are no longer a prey to these exaggerations. Feeling keeps its place, reason has taken its stand, prejudice has lost what did not belong to it. We are in the presence of facts, in the presence of practical realities. It would be too easy to enter into a pathetic appeal; we must turn aside from tears, and consult figures.

Let us institute an inquiry, therefore, *on the comparative results of emancipation in the countries which have proclaimed it, and of slavery in the countries where it is maintained.* ‡

produce of our islands, and must in time destroy nearly one half our commerce, and take from Great Britain all pretensions to the rank she now holds, of being the first maritime power in the world."

* An Address to his Royal Highness, the Duke of York, against the Use of Sugar, 1792: — "As the slavery of the negroes is owing to the cultivation of sugar, all the enemies of this slavery, all who wish its abolition, should altogether abstain from the use of this commodity till such time as effectual measures shall be taken to prevent the further importation of slaves, and proper measures be adopted to procure their freedom for such as are now in our plantations." (*Bibliothèque de l'Arsenal, Papiers de Grégoire,* Vol. II.)

† May 27, 1771. (*Histoire de la Guadeloupe,* by M. Lacour, 1855 - 1860, p. 392.)

‡ The present volume, which is complete in itself, gives the results of emancipation wherever effected. The following volume, the translation of which is not as yet published, depicts slavery in the countries where it still exists, treats briefly of Africa and the slave-trade, and concludes with a chapter on Christianity and Slavery. — Tr.

II.

The outline of this inquiry is as follows.*

1. What has been the fate of the nineteen slave colonies of England since the Emancipation Bill of 1834? Have

* The results of the English experiment have been fully set forth in the Parliamentary documents, translations, and reports, published in 1840, 1841, and 1842, by our Minister of the Marine and the Colonies; lastly, and above all, in the memorable report of the President of the Colonial Commission, the Duke de Broglie. We have only to continue the inquiry to our own time, — an easy task, as England publishes all that she does, and lives in the midst of a perpetual investigation. I owe my acquaintance with the Parliamentary documents to my honorable friend Mr. Monsell, member of Parliament, to two of the sons of William Wilberforce, and lastly to the indefatigable and universal kindness of Mr. Senior.

The results of the French experiment are more recent and less known. Thanks to the permission of the Count de Chasseloup-Laubat, Minister of the Colonies, I have been admitted to researches throughout all the departments of the ministry, and I owe the warmest thanks to the Minister, to the Baron de Roujoux, the Director of the Colonies, to the continual encouragement of one of the persons best acquainted with all colonial questions, M. Jules Delarbre, Director of the Cabinet, and, lastly, to the helpful assistance of MM. Beau, Guiraud, du Chayla, Roy, Farcy, Éguyer, Avalle, etc.

In the colonies I have consulted with the utmost profit M. Husson, Director of the Interior at Martinico, M. Constant Mourette, and inhabitants of the various French possessions. Outside the ministry, the excellent writings of MM. Jules Duval and Lepelletier Saint-Remy, who, more than any other, possess the merit and talent of interesting France in her too often forgotten colonies, Galos, Baudrillart, Lacour, de Chazelles, Legoyt, Richelot, Chemin-Dupontès, etc., have been of no less service to me than the reports to the Chambers, old and new, presented by superior men like MM. Dumon, Passy, de Tocqueville, Rossi, Beugnot, Benoist-d'Azy, Béhic, Mestro, Kolb-Bernard, Ancel, Hubert-Delisle, Caffarelli, etc., without forgetting the memorable speeches of MM. de Montalembert, de Gasparin, de Lamartine, de Tracy, de Rémusat, de Lasteyrie, d'Haussonville, or the books and labors of MM. Schœlcher, Castelli, Lechevalier, Bayle-Mouillard, Barbaroux, Layrle, d'Avrainville, and so many other enlightened adversaries of slavery, or intelligent defenders of colonial prosperity, industry, the navy, and national greatness. I owe thanks, lastly, to Mgr. Desprez, formerly Bishop of the Isle of Bourbon, now Archbishop of Toulouse, to the venerable Abbé Jean de la Mennais, founder of the brothers de Plœrnel, who conduct nearly all the colonial schools, to the Abbé Sénac, to R. P. Gratry, to the Abbé Perreyve, and to the Abbé Gaduel, who have kindly furnished me with valuable information, or revised and approved the chapters relating to the influence of Christianity.

As to historical documents, the archives of the Colonial Ministry have been opened to me, with inexhaustible liberality, by M. Pierre Margry, those of the

they progressed, or declined, since this epoch, in morals, wealth, and happiness?

Has France to repent of the law. of 1848? Has she sacrificed to vain humanitarian Utopias the last remnants of her colonial grandeur? or, on the contrary, has she

Ministry of Foreign Affairs by M. Prosper Faugère, those of the Seminary du Saint Esprit, so rich and curious, by the R. P. Schwindenhammer, the R. P. Levavasseur, the Library of the Institute by M. de Landresse, and that of the Arsenal by M. Paul Lacroix.

American documents superabound. Without speaking of the great book of M. de Tocqueville, and the celebrated works of our writers and travellers, MM. de Beaumont, Michel Chevalier, Ampère, de Gasparin, Marmier, de Witte, etc., I have collected a considerable number of wholly special works. In the choice of these I have been guided by the Count de Montalembert, an illustrious and obliging friend, who knows, reads, and learns without parallel, with passionate curiosity; by M. Jules Carron, editor of foreign affairs; by the eloquent emancipationist, Charles Sumner; by the learned writer, Brownson; and by a devout French missionary of the diocese of Natchez, M. Buteux; and I have been enabled to draw from other sources, thanks to M. Bailly, in the rich and too little known collection of American books procured by M. Vattemare to the library of the City of Paris.

Ignorance of the Spanish language, and the rarity of official publications of the governments of Madrid, Lisbon, and Rio, have annoyed me, and will, I fear, render somewhat incomplete, despite the obligingness of M. Fournier, First Secretary of the Embassy at Madrid, the information which I have been able to gather on slavery in Cuba, the Portuguese possessions, and Brazil.

More fortunate here, I owe to M. de Frezals, Secretary of the French Legation in Holland, M. Lux of Haye, and Professor Ackersdyk of Utrecht, abundant documents on the state of the question in the Netherlandic colonies.

For twenty years the *Revue Coloniale* has collected all the facts relative to the suppression of the slave-trade, and the exploration of Africa. This precious collection, with the published accounts of the extensive travels of Livingstone, Barth, etc., the excellent compends of M. Malte-Brun, the *Bulletins de la Société de Géographie*, the correspondence addressed by the Catholic missionaries to the *Société de la Propagation de la Foi*, the principal writings of the Protestant missionaries, — such are the sources of the too brief pages devoted to the last part of the inquiry which I have undertaken.

I owe, lastly, deep gratitude to the *Académie des Sciences morales*, which has kindly listened to a fragment of my work; to its Perpetual Secretary, M. Mignet, who has aided, counselled, and encouraged me; to its President, M. Giraud, who has been pleased to approve this work publicly in his learned *Mémoire sur l'Esclavage des Nègres*, 1861; to M. Albert de Broglie, whose friendship has been so helpful to me from the beginning; to two members of the Institute, M. Cousin and M. Saint-Marc Girardin, who have repeatedly accorded to me their valuable opinion.

opened to these outside provinces of her empire, which aspire to, and are bordering on, commercial freedom, a purer and happier future?

Has the abolition of slavery annihilated, or enriched, the little colonial possessions of Denmark, Sweden, and Portugal? *

2. On the other hand, what is the state of religion, of politics, of morals, of justice, of literature, of wealth itself, in the countries which preserve slavery?

By what steps has the republic of the United States descended to the situation which threatens it? Whence comes it that, less than a century after the Revolution that was so fruitful only because it was so just, we are forced to tremble lest this great work should fail, and lest a young, vigorous, and powerful nation should be on the point of abandoning civilization? Whence comes it, — to use the words of the eloquent William H. Seward, — whence comes it that thirty million men, European by origin, Christian by faith, have not known how to combine prudence with humanity in this perturbing question of slavery, in such a manner as to preserve their admirable institutions, and to preserve them in peace and harmony?

In the bosom of the flourishing Catholic monarchy of South America, Brazil, what are the results of slavery? What is the scope of the emancipation movement which is manifesting itself there? Will the Latins of South America have the honor of setting an example to the Saxons of North America?

What is the economical position of the Spanish possessions, — of Cuba, doubly privileged, loaded with gifts from Heaven, and also enriched by the trials of the neighboring

* To this part of the inquiry might be attached the abolition of serfdom in Russia. But the results of the memorable measure, which is being executed without disturbance, cannot yet be appreciated, and so vast a subject should not be treated incidentally.

colonies, — of Porto Rico, a country almost entirely cultivated, despite the climate, by a free white race?

By what means has Holland been able to avoid establishing slavery in her magnificent East Indian possessions? By what experience has this intelligent and prudent people been brought, at this very moment, to suppress it in its colonies of Guiana and the Antilles?

In an inquiry already so overburdened, I shall not enter upon slavery in the Mussulman or heathen countries. Christians might find there more than one example. There, at least, slavery is in its place among other plagues, since these nations have not received the Gospel. Progress has its natural boundaries on the atlas; it grows where shines the torch of Christianity, and barbarism extends its darkness over the rest of mankind.

3. A new series of questions is connected with the suppression of the traffic in slaves. What has been the effect of the memorable efforts made by Europe for the abolition of the slave-trade?

What is the condition of Africa? What is taught us of its future by missionaries and travellers, — Livingstone, Baikie, Burton, Overweg, Barth, Raffenel, Faidherbe, — all the great explorers, the great benefactors of this unhappy continent?

In short, is slavery an indispensable, economical system? Is it an instrument of useful education? Has emancipation brought back the slaves to barbarism while leading the colonies to ruin? Is the African race really incapable of labor without constraint? Is it devoted to irredeemable inferiority? May what is morally wrong be materially necessary?

I have endeavored to gather a few facts which may aid in preparing the reply to these questions.

I may be reproached with not having observed these facts by myself, and I do not conceal that herein is an imperfection of my labor. I have made the tour of the world only in books. But, under penalty of not treating such a subject as a whole, one must indeed be resigned to see with the eyes of those who have seen; and if I am accused of having visited neither Timbuctoo nor Cayenne, nor even Senegal or Mississippi, I can answer that the authors who write the history of the thirteenth century have not apparently lived in it; that every day men refer the decision of the gravest interests to judges whose opinion rests on the impartial confrontation of the testimony of others. I dare say, at least, that I have neglected nothing to collect, verify, and compare the most abundant information and the most authentic documents.

You now know, Monsieur le Duc, the programme of my work and its instruments. What are its general results?

III.

This voyage around the world, from Africa to Asia, from Europe to America, in search of freemen, — how grievous is it at first!

One third of the terrestrial globe is uninhabited; it is still on the fifth day of creation, — it awaits man.

Two thirds of the inhabitants of the rest of the world are where Europe was nineteen hundred years ago, — they await God.

By an inexplicable mystery, the sun, whose hottest rays call forth in tropical lands the most luxuriant vegetation, repels man thence. There is an intelligent race which might form in these lands a civilized community; it cannot live there and labor. There is a vigorous race which might inhabit and cultivate them; it develops therein no civilization. At least, these two races might draw nearer together; from their united efforts might spring progress with labor;

from their mixed blood might spring an intermediate race, predestined to possess and people these regions, — a race providentially made for this climate by Him who made the climate for it. No! Slavery intervenes.

Slavery is, before everything, the negation of the family. Now man is endowed with an astonishing capacity for suffering. He knows how to live under ground or on the water; an Indian in the forests, a Chinaman in his boat, a Laplander in his darkness; but on condition of being able to say, My wife, my child, my mother, my boat, my cabin, my tools. The slave is without family; he is not sure of keeping his wife or of knowing his father, his canoe is not his own, and when he lays his hand on his breast, he cannot say, "This skin is mine." Now, without these rights, the man is not a man, nature is violated in his person.

Instead of families, slavery forms herds. It pens up captives, under the guard of jailers, in a little corner of one of the most magnificent lands of creation; this land will not be peopled. For the relation of brother to brother it substitutes that of drover to ox and master to cattle; this land will not be civilized. It inspires the races with mutual horror and aversion for each other; if ties are formed between them, they are criminal; the two races live together without mingling; the race of heirs predestined to these countries will not be founded. We shall see the inferior race suffer, revolt or submit, never rise, become brutalized, then die out. We shall see the superior race grow hardened, become corrupt, become infatuated with crime, seek wealth therein, prefer it to everything, and find in it debasement, dishonor, then ruin. On beginning to write, I was moved by the fate of the oppressed, by the fate of that unhappy race which has made the fortune of those who perpetuate its misery; on ending, I am seized with pity for the oppressors, I conjure them to have pity on themselves, and to put an end to their evil-doing.

Follow slavery under all latitudes, in all regions, whatever the institutions, nations, or creeds, everywhere you find the same origin, the same progress, the same law, the same result; as monotonous and horrible as the life of the slaves. The history of slavery knows no change. It is in all places, it has been at every epoch, an obstacle to the systematic peopling of the earth, an obstacle to the propagation of the Gospel, an obstacle to the modest elevation of the inferior races, an obstacle to the progressive civilization of the superior races. The moralist calls it a crime, the historian and economist a scourge.

Yes, but what is to be done? The evil is the work of the past. To destroy it rashly would be another evil. Slavery corrupts communities, but emancipation destroys them. What is to be done?

The experiment of both systems has been made; we may therefore compare them. This comparison is the whole scope of my work.

Assuredly, emancipation was the occasion of losses and deplorable misfortunes. "The punishment of faults," says M. Thiers, "would be too light, indeed, if to cease persisting in them sufficed to abolish the consequences."* These troublesome consequences are not all ended. We are in great haste, indeed! We demand of twenty years of liberty to repair the results of two hundred years of slavery; we cannot endure the idea of laboring without the hope of contemplating the result of our efforts.

Nevertheless, our impatience has already wherewith to satisfy itself; after ten years, the fears for the colonies of France and England have been dissipated. It seems as though each colony had received the mission of representing a distinct experience. We shall see in the investigation which is outlined in this book the success of emancipation depend,—in Antigua, on religious education; in Barbadoes,

* *Histoire du Consulat et de l'Empire*, Tom. XVII. Liv. LI. p. 80.

on the numbers of the population; in Martinico, on the intelligent activity of the colonists; in St. Thomas, on commercial freedom; in the Isle of Bourbon, on the precautions taken from the beginning to maintain labor; in English Guiana, on the progress of small estates; in Mauritius, on the facility of procuring laborers. We shall see, on the contrary, long sufferings caused in Guadaloupe by political disturbances; in Jamaica, by the ill-will of the former masters; in French Guiana, by the scarcity of capital and the insufficiency of population on a vast territory. But whatever may be these difficulties, we shall see all these little communities finally uprise, emerge from the old system of the *colonial compact,* confront commercial freedom, become more moral as well as happier, and emancipation thus keep all its promises.

Slavery, alas! keeps all its promises also.

In Cuba, amidst an exceptional prosperity, the causes of which we shall analyze, the gross profits do not liquidate the debts; the presence of a strong power does not preserve the laws; the reign of a uniform religion does not purify morals; the great number of slaves does not secure the progress of the population; the mildness of the relation does not prevent insurrections; the facility of redemption does not advance liberty.

The same embarrassments, the same results, are found in the well-managed colonies of prudent Holland.

But it is in the United States, above all, that facts demolish the systems of the partisans of servitude.

In the United States, strange moralists affirm that slavery elevates the intelligence of the possessing race, and, freeing it from all cares, devotes it to the pursuit of noble mental labors, communicates to it the governing qualities, and expands the heart, constantly moved by the spectacle of weak and imperfect beings, whilst, discharging society from the burden of these weak beings, it places them under the patronage of the best citizens, who rear, guide, and assist them ; a beneficent and productive organization, superior to every combination of relations between rich and poor presented in the history of the world! Experience, pitiless experience, replies, that the master becomes hard, indolent, and sensual; that the habit of command takes away all cordiality even towards free working-men; that it leads to confounding in the same contempt the labor and the laborer; that the plus value of lands cultivated by free labor exceeds the capital represented by slaves; that the human intellect is developed only through activity, — that passive, it slumbers, — constrained, it becomes soured or degraded. In a word, in this detestable system, the owner becomes a beast of prey, the owned a beast of burden, the master is without calculation, the workman without progress; time, far from ameliorating this position, aggravates it; with time, instruction, the pretext of slavery, is interdicted by law; affranchisement, the hope of the slave, is interdicted by law; the separation of classes widens and becomes envenomed; prejudice, created by slavery, survives it to the degree that the North refuses equality to the black, while the South refuses him liberty; the pretended political superiority of the South is only the unanimous and persevering resolution to sacrifice to the maintenance of the *peculiar institution*, everything, even honor, even peace, even country. The sacrifice is made, the war declared, — not a war between slave and master, but between whites, between brethren, between fellow-citizens, — war against justice and nature, — civil war!

Servitude is a poisoned river, flowing into evil from which it takes its rise. Whilst its fatal consequences are rending America, another continent, Africa, suffers from its criminal origin.

The efforts of England and France to abolish the *slave-trade* have been persevering and prodigious.

International treaties; special laws by each country; agreements with the native chiefs; establishment of offices and stations; enlistment of free laborers; correspondence with ambassadors and consuls; decisions of courts and mixed commissions established by treaties; — such is the part of politics, diplomacy, and justice.

The exercise of the mutual right of search; systems of permanent cruising; seizures and confiscations; military expeditions; — such is the part of the navy.

Incontestable facts prove that immense results have been obtained, and that the law which prohibits the slave-trade has not, as foretold by the traveller Jacquemont,* condemned the colonies to perish. The principal result has been the rise in price of servile labor, which by degrees, producing less than free labor, is coming to cost more. The day when this result shall be evident will be the last of slavery. Until this time, so long as it shall live, the slave-trade will not be dead, and a most legitimate, most desirable operation, the engagement of free blacks for the European colonies, will remain equivocal and dangerous. It is necessary, in order to destroy the slave-trade, to abolish, or at least diminish, two evils, — slavery in America, barbarism in Africa.

The frightful state of an entire continent, condemned from the beginning of the world to be never civilized, never free, never elevated to the love of labor and of the arts, reduced beneath the level of all the others, destined to furnish negro slaves to the rest of the earth, as a mine produces charcoal, — such is the first and last consequence of slavery. By degrees, commerce teaches the chiefs that it is more profitable to employ men than to sell them; travellers teach Europe what incalculable wealth and abundant population have fallen on this continent from the hands of the Creator; missionaries, striving to efface the traces of

* *Correspondance,* Vol. I.

blood and scandal spread by Christians, plant the cross on these dreaded shores. Europe is beginning to pay its debt. It ends where it should have begun ; instead of exploiting Africa, it thinks of exploring and civilizing it. Perhaps the following century, happier than our own and succeeding to its labors, will witness the re-establishment between Africa and better known and analogous climates of those systematic and free migrations of inhabitants and products which people the world and mingle men, obedient to the laws of Providence, the inevitable course of which may be suspended by their faults, but not forever checked.

Two of these august laws are evolved from these complicated and distant facts, — the great law of solidarity among men, the great law of the fundamental harmony of interests with duties.

The memorable example given by England and France honors all humanity ; the obstinacy of America and Spain dishonors it ; — here is moral solidarity. The slavery in these nations threatens, by unequal competition, the prosperity of our colonies ; it eternizes the slave-trade ; it fetters regular emigration ; it exposes Europe, through the reaction of the crises which it excites, to formidable misfortunes ; it perpetuates the degradation of Africa ; nothing is done when all is not done ; — here is material solidarity.

It was once exclaimed, "Perish the colonies, rather than a principle !"

The principle has not perished, the colonies have not perished.

It is not correct that interests should yield to principles ; between legitimate interests and true principles, harmony is infallible ; this is truth. Those who look only to interests are sooner or later deceived in their calculations ; those who, exclusively occupied with principles, are generous without being practical, cease to be generous, for they lead the cause which they serve to certain destruction. It is the will of God that realities should mingle with ideas, and that material obstacles should compel the purchase of progress by toil. Let us not be surprised, therefore, behind every moral question to encounter a question of budget and tariff, nor indignant if the arguments of philosophers seem checked by sugar or cotton.

An obscure workman of the United States has effected more against the slaves, by the invention of a machine for picking cotton, than all the slave-traders. Cotton in America is slavery; cotton in Africa would perhaps be liberty; slavery will cease when we go to buy things where we are accustomed to buy persons, and the progress of the culture of peanuts and the traffic in palm-oil on the coast of Africa will do more for emancipation, than numerous meetings, speeches, and works like mine. Speeches and books are efficacious in their turn; while arousing in the soul respect for eternal principles, they may at the same time establish, by certain facts, that, while the evils of slavery have surpassed everything foretold by the most sinister predictions, even the material advantages of emancipation have risen in a few years above all that the most partial hopes had conceived for them.

Before this glorious conclusion, interest, the last but solid rampart of the peoples not yet persuaded by religion and reason, crumbles to dust. France and England have not to repent; science and morality have not to bow their heads; the lowest race of men has not lost the inheritance of freedom; slavery is not a necessary evil; always censurable, it ends by not being even useful. Once more, it remains proven that God has established unison between all things, that the science of political economy holds the same language as morality, and that a steadfast harmony intertwines with the phenomena of the world of matter the sublime laws of the moral world.

IV.

These conclusions, Monsieur le Duc, will indicate to you the spirit of this work.

I owe to Christianity the horror with which slavery inspires me. My work would have seemed incomplete to me, therefore, had I not concluded it by a chapter on Christianity and Slavery, designed to demonstrate in the sequel, and by the aid of so many learned writings, not that Christianity has destroyed slavery by itself alone, but that it would not have been, will not be, abolished without it.

Let those who speak, let those who write, never forget that emancipation in the nineteenth century was and will be the work of the Gospel, the rostrum, and the press.

The power of evil in this world is formidable. Centuries after centuries pass over China and India without shaking their empire. But, thanks to Christianity, the conscience knows how to listen ; thanks to liberty, the conscience can speak. Under the reign of this holy alliance, evil is not easily surmounted, but it is unceasingly restless, it is forbidden to make itself a tranquil domain in the bosom of a regular community.

In 1773, ten years after the odious treaty of 1763, which secured to England the monopoly of the slave-trade, William Wilberforce, then on the benches of the school at Poklington,* wrote for the first time against this infamous traffic, the very name of which was an English word,† and which a council held in the city of London in 1102, under the presidency of St. Anselm, had interdicted eight hundred years before the same object was debated in the same city

* The Life of William Wilberforce, by his Sons Robert and Samuel. London: Murray. 1838.

† *Traite*, from Trade.

before Parliament.* In 1780, Thomas Clarkson proposed to abolish the slave-trade. In 1787, Wilberforce renewed the proposition. Seven times presented from 1793 to 1799, the bill seven times failed. Successively laid over, it triumphed at length in 1806 and 1807. All the Christian nations followed this memorable example. At the Congress of Vienna, all the powers pledged themselves to unite their efforts to obtain *the entire and final abolition of a traffic so odious and so loudly reproved by the laws of religion and nature.*† The slave-trade was abolished in 1808 by the Northern United States; in 1811, by Denmark, Portugal, and Chili; in 1813, by Sweden; in 1814 and 1815, by Holland; in 1815, by France; in 1822, by Spain. In this same year, 1822, Wilberforce attacked slavery after the slave-trade, and won over public opinion by appeals and repeated meetings, while his friend Mr. Buxton proposed emancipation in Parliament. The Emancipation Bill was presented in 1833. On the 1st of August, 1834, slavery ceased to sully the soil of the English colonies. In 1846, Sweden, in 1847, Denmark, Uruguay, Wallachia, and Tunis, obeyed the same impulse, which France followed in 1848, Portugal in 1856, and which Holland promised to imitate in 1860. An earnest movement agitated Brazil.

Lastly, in 1861, the last form of servitude disappeared in Russia; Spain, in retaking a part of the island of St. Domingo, promised never to re-establish slavery there, and the antislavery cause obtained the majority in the general elections which raised Abraham Lincoln to the Presidency of the United States.

In a century, the initiative of Wilberforce has put slavery to rout, or at least called it in question over the whole surface of Christianity.

* Rémusat, *Vie de Saint-Anselme*, p. 163.

† Declaration of February 4, 1815, and additional article of the agreement of November 20, 1815.

The destinies of servitude and liberty are at once at stake in the crisis which is shaking the New World. This combat is the rudest of all, but it will be the last. Instead of suffering one's self to be overwhelmed by the inconceivable slowness of moral progress, it is precisely because the last effort is difficult that it is necessary to enter into it with all one's might, full of faith in the sure triumph of the Christian religion, justice, and perseverance over the conspiracy of interests, the obstinacy of prejudices, the despotic torpor of habits. When Wilberforce begun, the struggle was less advanced and the cause more desperate.

So memorable an example is worthy forever to strengthen perseverance. The most obscure of men has his duty, and this is my excuse for associating with great minds in sending forth a protest against evil, as a child does his duty in joining with strong men to cast a drop of water upon a conflagration.

"The eternal laws bind us to take the side of the injured. On this point we have no liberty. To embody and express this great truth is in every man's power, and thus every man can do something to break the chain of slavery." *

You, Monsieur le Duc, have comprehended this duty; be pleased to permit me to dedicate and refer to you the humble enterprise undertaken to follow the example which you have set me.

AUGUSTIN COCHIN.

* Channing.

BOOK FIRST.

FRENCH COLONIES.

CHAPTER I.

EMANCIPATION BY THE CONVENTION, AND THE RE-ESTABLISHMENT OF SLAVERY BY THE CONSULATE.

1794 - 1802.

The history of the French colonies is well known, yet it is so sad that we would gladly forget it. But the wrecks remain to us of our ancient splendor. The war of the Spanish Succession cost us Canada, Newfoundland, Acadia, and Hudson's Bay (1713); the Seven Years' War, Louisiana (1763), for an instant retroceded to France (1800), then sold by her (1803); the Revolution cost us St. Domingo; the wars against Europe, St. Lucia, Tobago, the Sechelles, the Isle of France, and the territory of our East Indian possessions.

Since its occupation (1635), Martinico has been ceded to two companies; taken in 1762, surrendered in 1763; taken in 1794, surrendered in 1802; taken in 1807, retaken in 1815. Guadaloupe has passed through the hands of three companies (1626 – 1642); was sold for sixty thousand livres, Tours currency, and a rent of six hundred pounds of sugar, to the Marquis de Boisseret, redeemed for one hundred and twenty-five thousand livres by Colbert; attacked unsuccessfully three times by the English (1666, 1691, 1703); taken in 1759, surrendered in 1763; retaken in 1794, and erelong valiantly recovered; lost anew in 1810, ceded to Sweden in 1813, surrendered in 1814, retaken in 1815. More fortunate, Bourbon, remaining a century in the hands of the East India Company, then reunited to the state (1767), succeeded in governing itself independently during the Revolution, but was taken in 1810 with Mauritius, and surrendered alone in 1815.

Since this epoch, since the moment when the mother country regained on the same day liberty and peace, a better directed anxiety for the national greatness, a more eager emulation of foreign strength, the living power of complaints borne by the press and rostrum to the ear of kings, have contributed, no less than the development of means of communication and the progress of the navy, to restore to the colonies some degree of favor and prosperity. We owe to the constitutional government Algeria, the fairest province of the world ; we owe to it our possessions of the Mozambique Channel, Mayotte, Nossi-bé, and St. Mary of Madagascar, and those of Oceanica, Tahiti, the Marquesas, and New Caledonia, points useful for our stations, exchanges, and missions. The continuance of the same policy will procure us the occupation of Touranne and Saigon in the empire of Annam, and the consolidation of our power in Senegal. We are lastly indebted to the same régime for a series of measures which have developed what remains to us of our American colonies, *Martinico, Guadaloupe, Guïana,* and the beautiful African colony, the *Isle of Bourbon,* to which is left, without reason, the inexact and insignificant name *Reunion.*

Despite all this progress, our maritime possessions are trifling. England possesses thirty-seven colonies, without counting the East Indies, inhabited by nearly 4,000,000 subjects. France, Algeria apart, possesses fourteen colonies and fourteen secondary stations, occupied, over an extent of less than 250,000,000 acres, by less than 600,000 inhabitants, — in all, the territory of three great departments and the population of three small ones.

The internal history of these possessions offers a no less mournful aspect than the annals of their conquests. The colonial theory is beautiful, — daughters of the greatest nations, fulcrums of their influence, entrepôts of universal commerce, landmarks of civilization planted in the bosom of the seas, scattered beacons of religion and progress, the modern colonies, the stations of our fleets, are themselves, as it were, fleets at anchor, displaying to the farthest limits of the world the flag of Europe and the standard of Christianity! Alas! facts do not faithfully reproduce this enchanting vision of the political mind. At the origin of the colonies we find, in general, two men, — a filibuster and a missionary. To go so far, one must either have the Devil in his body or God in his heart. When to these two men is joined a third, — a ruler, — all goes well; the first subjugates, the second converts, the third organizes. But this organizer may be long in coming. Thus, the beginning of settlements is a mixture of heroism and disorder, of sublime devotion and savage cupidity. A heroic navigator was D'Énambuc, a younger son of Picardy, who was the founder of the colonization of the Antilles. A brave soldier was Captain l'Olive, who, with M. du Plessis, in 1633, demanded of the Lords of the West India Company a commission to occupy Guadaloupe. But it is well known with what barbarity, after the death of his companion, he fell upon the peaceful Caribs, declaring against them, says the unpublished account of a missionary,* *a war as unjust as shameful, and thus hindering our principal design, which was no other than the promulgation of the Gospel and the education of this poor people.* A saint was this Father Raymond, a Dominican like Las Casas, who did his best *to thwart this detestable design, and finally*

* A curious MS. purchased by the author at the sale of the Erdevin Collection, pp. 32, 40. See also the *Histoire générale des Antilles*, by the Rev. Father du Tertre, of the Frères-Prêcheurs, 1654.

so far won over M. l'Olive that he promised, and even swore, to do no harm to the savages unless he were first set upon; then, seeing himself deceived, *went to find the governor, and to insist with him, with a zeal that was not relished, that it was no more lawful to make war without reason on a free nation, than to wrest its property from it unjustly.* But the soldier triumphed over the missionary.

The extermination of the natives is almost everywhere the first page of colonial occupation. The rapacious exploitation of the soil by the occupants, by companies, and by governors, is generally the second page.

Happy these distant possessions, when the mother country does not exploit them in turn, like a selfish owner of distant estates, who extracts from them all he can, complains of what they cost, and is represented thereon by a relentless steward; happy when they receive a veritable administrator, such as were M. de Poincy at the Antilles, M. de la Bourdonnaye, M. Poivre, and M. Desbassayns de Richemont at Bourbon, M. de la Barre and M. Malouet at Guiana, with humane and intelligent inhabitants! * But the greater part come so far from home only to make a fortune at any price. Thus we see the colonies, by the side of respectable and intelligent families, serve as nests for corsairs enriched by rapine, or as prisons without walls, — for centuries detestable manufactories for the production of tobacco, cotton, and sugar, and the consumption of slaves.

Like England, Holland, Spain, and Portugal, like all nations, almost as soon as she had colonies, France had slaves. Like all nations, she kept up the supply by the infamous practice of the slave-trade. This traffic was not only tolerated, but favored, encouraged, sanctioned by treaties. On the 27th of August, 1701, his *Most Christian* Majesty received from his *Most Catholic* Majesty

* Archives of the Ministry of Foreign Affairs.

the monopoly of the slave-trade for ten years, and both sovereigns took a personal interest of one fourth in the business. In 1784, a premium was accorded to the slave-trade by an order of the Council.

Let us pass quickly over these shameful details, and over the history of slavery in the French colonies, since it is abolished, since good has triumphed over evil. Humanity, which, without greatly advancing, marches onward with rapid strides, does not willingly pause at details; when a degree of progress is accomplished, it closes the account, as it were, and passes on to a new chapter. It looks at results, rather than means; thus too often causing the unjust popularity of despots, and the false greatness of powers judged from a distance. To mankind, the missionary and the slave-trader repose in the bosom of equal oblivion. Doubtless, humanity needs to believe that crime and virtue have received their wages; but, knowing that this distribution is not intrusted to its hands, it forgets, and passes on. History, like all sciences, supposes God; without God, it would have no conclusion, no morality. In its eyes nothing is small, nothing forgotten. It knows, it has seen, it has numbered on the African coasts, under the decks of ships, behind silent walls, the crimes of the trader, the tears of the slave, the severities of the master, as well as the prayers of unknown souls, the paternal kindness of numerous masters, the zeal of an obscure missionary, the outcry of a free conscience, the gift of a generous heart, the humble labor of the writer, the courageous perseverance of the statesman.

Let us leave the whole past of this lamentable history with God, and recount only the event which concluded, and the consequences which survive it.

The first laws in Europe which assailed slavery came from France; they were the work of the Revolution,* — a

* Noble examples were given before these laws. In 1785, General Lafayette

work which bears the mark of the greater part of the acts of this period; a work at first too long deferred, then too much precipitated; the decree of justice executed by violence.

The Constituent Assembly dared do nothing, the Legislative Assembly could do nothing, the Convention risked everything; * the timidity of the first was as disastrous as the ardor of the last. The colonies received from the mother country their destinies ready made; too great indecision or too great violence were translated there into like calamities.

Before slavery, the Constituent Assembly, so abundant, moreover, in noble souls burning for justice, only recoiled as from an abyss. It feared to meddle with these strange, far-off communities, which were spoken of only with terror. To hear Malouet, Maury, and Barnave, freedom was civil war, with the skin for cockade; it was, through the defeat of the white race, the disruption of the tie which united the colonies to the mother country. Divided between justice and fear, the Assembly decided by a decree, March 8, 1790, and instructions, March 28, that the colonies should continue to live *under the régime of special laws*, and should make known their voice by the organ of the Colonial Assemblies, to which alone belonged the initiative of laws concerning the *condition of persons*. Article 4 of the instructions reads: —

"*All persons*, who have attained the full age of twenty-five, owners of real estate, or, in default of such property, domiciliated for two years in the parish, and subject to

sent a M. de Richepray to Cayenne to purchase an estate and divide it among the negroes, for which purpose he conferred with the missionaries of Saint-Esprit. A letter from the Marshal de Castries, dated June 6, 1785, proves that Louis XVI. ordered similar experiments.

* See the excellent work published in the *Revue coloniale*, 1850, Tom. IV. Series II. p. 149, under the title, *Les Colonies et les Assemblées de la Révolution* (1789-1802), by M. Maurel-Dupeyré.

taxation, will unite to form the parish assembly." This was styled the Colonial Assembly.

Abbé Grégoire asked whether the words *all persons* included persons of color. Charles de Lameth hastened to urge the Assembly to close the debate on this *indiscreet* interrogation, which was done.

Bloody disturbances in the colonies were the result of this ambiguity, which the whites interpreted against the free negroes, and which the latter invoked in their favor. The Assembly was troubled. In the name of the committee of the colonists, Barnave proposed that a Congress of twenty-nine Commissioners, appointed by the Colonial Assembly, should meet in the little island of St. Martin to settle the question. This was to remit the rights of the blacks to the decision of a congress of whites. From this incidental proposition sprung a passionate discussion, which lasted three days. Before closing, under the influence of a speech of the Abbé Maury, which dimly predicted the loss of the colonies on the day that the domination of the whites should cease, the Assembly decreed the following article: —

"The Assembly decrees, as a constitutional article, that no law on the condition of *persons not free* may be made for the colonies, except on the *formal and spontaneous* demand of the Colonial Assemblies."

Moreau de Saint-Méry, deputy from Martinico, proposed to say clearly, the condition of *slaves;* Robespierre opposed it; the Assembly hesitated between *cultivators, those charged with culture,* and *those employed in culture,* then returned to the words, *persons not free.*

A like silence had disarmed, four years before, upon another continent, the scruples of the framers of the Constitution of the United States. They dared not say that there were no slaves, and they dared not say that there should be none thenceforth. They abolished the word, they did not abolish the thing.

Reassured, the Constituent Assembly resumed the deliberation on the rights of free men of color, and, after several days, adopted, May 15, 1791, the following article : —

"The Assembly decrees that it shall never deliberate on the condition of persons of color, *which have not been born of free parents on both sides,* without the preliminary, free, and spontaneous petition of the colonies; . . . . . but that persons of color, *born of free parents on both sides,* shall be admitted into all the future parish and colonial assemblies, if they possess the requisite conditions besides." At St. Domingo the whites resisted; at Paris the deputies of the colonies declared that they would thenceforth absent themselves, and that the decree of March 8, 1790, was violated. The Assembly, troubled at its decision, decreed that it should be explained by instructions, and these instructions, framed by the Duke de Nemours, with cowardly and hypocritical timidity, declared that the decree of May 15, far from violating that of March 8, restricted its application to men of color *born of free parents on both sides.* The instructions were adopted on the 29th of May, and were despatched to bear to the colonies the wishes of the mother country and civil war. They were destined to cost France St. Domingo.*

* Hostilities commenced anew. In 1792, the Convention put in force the decree of May 15, 1791, and sent the Commissioners Santhonax and Polverel to St. Domingo. The island was stained with blood in 1790, 1791, and 1792, by reason of the conflict between the whites and the *free* colored men, aided on both sides by their slaves, but before there had been any question of freeing these last. It was to prevent the effervescence from drawing in the slaves, it was to re-establish tranquillity, that Polverel determined to announce emancipation by a proclamation, Oct. 30, 1793. This was confirmed by the decree of 1794. No excesses thence resulted during the years 1795 and 1796, nor from 1796 to 1802, under the strict and intelligent administration of Toussaint l'Ouverture. (See the Memoirs of Clarkson and Macaulay on the events in Hayti.) Thus the disturbances in St. Domingo broke out from 1790 to 1792, while emancipation was not decreed there till the end of 1793; it is an error, therefore, to attribute the disorder to the abolition of slavery.

Five months after, the Constitution being finished, the Constituent Assembly turned its attention again to the colonies, and by the decree of September 24, 1791, reserved to the Legislative Assembly the right of deciding *exclusively* on the *external* régime of the colonies (Art. I.), abrogating the decree of May 15, and leaving the *internal* régime to the Colonial Assemblies, the propositions of which were to be carried *directly to the king for sanction,* without any anterior decree having power to throw obstacles in the way of the full exercise of the right preserved to the Colonial Assemblies.

Strange arrangement! by which the Assembly stripped itself with its own hands of power. It had well deserved it.

But it bequeathed, in dying, an impossible position; — to the colonies, divisions; to the Legislative Assembly, powerlessness of intervention. Happily, while this intolerable state of things called forth fiery but sterile debates in the Assembly, in the colonies a better spirit prevailed, and, January 20, 1792, a Congress of Commissioners from Guadaloupe, Martinico, St. Lucia, and Mary Galante assembled at Port Royal, and resolved that, contrary to the last decree of the Constituent Assembly, men of color should be admitted, by the same right as whites, into the electoral assemblies. The same compromise was accepted at St. Domingo. The Legislative Assembly received the example from the colonies, instead of setting it them, and abrogated the decree of the Constituent Assembly by another decree, March 24, 1792, which accorded political rights to all free colored men, without distinction.

By a law of August 11, 1792, the *Legislative* Assembly suppressed the premium accorded, by virtue of a decree of the Council of 1784, to the *negro slave-trade.* The Convention renewed this suppression by a decree, July 27, 1793, rendered without opposition, on the proposal of Grégoire.

But slavery still subsisted in the colonies.

Not only did slavery subsist, but, far from ameliorating the lot of the slave, the superior agents of the Republic endeavored to stifle and extinguish all that might prepare him to become a freeman. Read the unpublished instructions * of the Captain-General of Martinico and St. Lucia, dated at Fort de France, 19th Brumaire, Year II.†

"THE CAPTAIN-GENERAL OF MARTINICO AND ST. LUCIA,

To the Commissioner of Government at the Court of Appeals in Session at Fort de France.

"The French government has perceived, Citizen Commissioner, that the philosophical systems on the necessity of extending and generalizing instruction, suited, without doubt, to the education of a free people, are incompatible with the existence of our colonies, which reposes on slavery and the distinction of color. In preserving to Martinico the régime and laws of 1789, it has implicitly proscribed everything that may tend to overthrow the ancient colonial organization, whether by physical force or by public opinion. Now a deplorable experience has proved that the abuse of enlightenment is often the principle of revolutions, and that ignorance is a necessary bond for men fettered by violence or blighted by prejudice.

"It would, therefore, be dangerous imprudence to continue to tolerate in the colony schools for negroes and persons of color. What will they learn in these establishments? They will not draw thence the higher acquirements which make of the enlightened man the most absolute slave of the law; and their intellect, inflated by an imperfect and gross education, will unceasingly represent to them the colonial régime as the code of tyranny and oppression.

* Communicated by M. Margry, Keeper of the Colonial Archives.

† The seal of the document bears France with a palm-tree at her side, behind which is the sun; she is surrounded by divers attributes, and carries a balance in her hand, one side of which is weighed down.

"These ideas, long diffused by perverse or mistaken men, have sufficed to destroy our most flourishing settlements, and the wisdom of a reparative government, which watches over the prosperity of Martinico, cannot suffer the continuance there of a deceitful spark, which will, sooner or later, light up the flames of a revolution.

"I have therefore judged it necessary, and I order you expressly, citizen commissioner, to *close all the public schools in which negroes and persons of color are admitted.* I shall inform the colonial prefect of the order which I give you in this respect, and concert with him on the measures to be taken to insure and legalize the execution.

"I have the honor to salute you.

VILLARET."

This most curious document is dated the 19th Brumaire,* Year II. On the 16th Pluviose† of this same year, almost at the same moment, the abolition of slavery was decreed in the midst of the National Convention, by acclamation, but by surprise.

On the 4th of February, 1794 (16th Pluviose, Year II.), a deputy from St. Domingo, a colored man, came to set forth to the representatives of the people the sufferings and reclamations of the slaves.

"I ask," cried LEVASSEUR (de la Sarthe), "that the Convention, without yielding to an impulse of enthusiasm, however natural under such circumstances, but faithful to the eternal principles of justice and equality which it has consecrated, faithful to the declaration of the rights of man, decree from this moment that slavery is abolished over all the territory of the Republic."

* The second month of the Republican Calendar, from October 25 to November 21.

† The fifth month of the Republican Calendar, from January 20 to February 18 or 19.

Lacroix (d'Eure-et-Loire). "In laboring on the Constitution of the French people, we failed to cast our eyes on the unhappy men of color who are groaning in slavery in America, and posterity may reproach us for this forgetfulness, which, involuntary as it is, is none the less culpable *in the sight of philosophy.* It is in vain to say that we know no slaves in France; is it not true that we leave in *slavery sensible and brave men,* who have reconquered their rights? Vainly shall we have proclaimed liberty and equality, if there remain on the territory of the Republic a single man who is not free as the air he breathes, — if there remain a single slave! Let us proclaim the liberty of men of color!

"Let this great example to the universe, let this principle, solemnly consecrated, re-echo in the hearts of the Africans in chains under English dominion; let them feel all the dignity of their being, let them *arm themselves* and come to augment the number of our brothers and *votaries of universal liberty!*"

Levasseur attempted to proceed to enlarge upon his motion: "President," exclaimed Lacroix, "do not suffer the Convention to dishonor itself by a long discussion."

Levasseur asked that his proposition should be put to vote upon the spot.

The whole Assembly rose, and voted by acclamation.

The President pronounced THE ABOLITION OF SLAVERY.

Immediately, shouts of *Long live the Republic! Long live the National Convention!* broke forth throughout the hall. The deputies from St. Domingo were led by Lacroix to the President, who gave them the fraternal kiss in the name of all the French; they then received it from each representative. The scene was repeated in the galleries; the colored citizens were embraced by their new brethren; tears of joy were in every eye, *Long live liberty!* on every lip.

A member requested that an advice-boat should be at once despatched to bear the happy news to the colonics.

Danton rose: "Representatives of the French people, hitherto we have decreed liberty only as egotists, for ourselves alone; but to-day we proclaim it in the face of the universe, and future generations will find their glory in this decree, — we proclaim universal liberty. The National Convention has done its duty.

". . . There exists between slavery and liberty a passage, delicate and difficult to leap over. It is proposed to you to send an advice-boat, on the spot, to make known the beneficent law which you have decreed. I oppose this, and request that the proposition be referred to the Committee of Public Safety, which will present to you its views, but that the report be made promptly, and that liberty be borne to the colonies with the means to make it fruitful. . . . . .

"Citizens, *to-day the Englishman is dead!* (Loud applause.) Pitt and his plots are foiled! The English behold their commerce annihilated! France, which to this day had, as it were, truncated her glory, at length resumes, in the eyes of astonished and submissive Europe, the preponderance which is due her through her principles, her energy, her soil, and her population! Activity, energy, generosity — but generosity directed by the *torch of reason*, and steered by the *compass of principles*, — will insure you forever the gratitude of posterity."

Lacroix proposed the following formula: —

The National Convention declares slavery abolished throughout all the colonies: consequently it decrees that all men, without distinction of color, domiciliated in the colonies, are French citizens, and entitled to the enjoyment of all the rights secured by the Constitution.

Referred to the Committee of Public Safety for it to report unceasingly on the measures to be taken for the execution of the decree.

The decree was unanimously adopted.*

Take away from this page, torn from the *Moniteur*, the odious or ridiculous features, and the emphatic bad taste habitual to the violent orators of the Convention and the whole epoch, — take away the *sensible and brave men*, the *culpable forgetfulness in the sight of philosophy*, the *appeal to arms*, the *votaries of universal liberty*, the *compass of principles and torch of reason*, — and there remains in this outburst of noble passions, mingled with grosser ones, a scene everywhere touching and grandiose. I do not say grand, since God does not appear therein, and since, when the men embrace as brothers, they do not see the hand of their common Father, or utter his name.

The Englishman is dead! exclaimed Danton. He mingled, therefore, a war-cry with an emotion of humanity. In fact, it had been announced to the Convention that the English had just possessed themselves of Martinico and Guadaloupe, a somewhat premature announcement, for the English attacked Martinico on the 3d of February, the day before the session of the Convention, and rendered themselves masters of it, bravely defended by General Rochambeau, on the 22d of March; and of Guadaloupe, on the 21st of April, 1794.

It is well known that Martinico remained eight years under English rule, until the peace of Amiens, in 1802; the decree of emancipation was not even introduced there.

The Isle of Bourbon and Isle of France, on the contrary, did not fall into the hands of the English until 1810. To diminish the chances of disturbance, the Colonial Assembly of Bourbon had, from August 8, 1794, forbidden the introduction of negroes by the slave-trade. The decree of the Convention was known at the same epoch, but it was not even published; and in 1796, the executive power of the

* *Choix de rapports, opinions et discours prononcés à la tribune nationale depuis* 1789, (Paris, 1821,) Tom. XIV. p. 425.

Republic having sent two agents, Citizens Bacot and Burnel, to promulgate the decree of emancipation, the whole population opposed their landing. They were no better received at Port Louis than at Bourbon, and were forced to renounce their mission ; and for six years, until the arrival of General Decaen in the name of the Consuls (1803), the two islands, with alternations of calmness and agitation, of prosperity and suffering, governed themselves without ceasing to be faithful to France,* without the whites having to suffer any violence on the part of the blacks, who were organized into companies designed to maintain order.† Now, to speak only of Bourbon, there were but 16,000 whites against 44,807 blacks.

Guiana was more unfortunate. No attempt at colonization had succeeded for two centuries in this colony, so vast but always deserted, despite its magnificent elements, where sixteen thousand men inhabited eighteen thousand square leagues. It had prospered, or at least caught a glimpse of the hope of prosperity, at the close of the seventeenth century, under M. de la Barre, and at the close of the eighteenth, under M. Malouet. But since 1778 it had lost, with this able administrator, the best element of an always tardy future, when the Revolution, represented by a nephew of Danton, Jeannet, threw its slaves into vagrancy, its priests into prison and exile, ‡ its proprietors into bankruptcy, and brought it, instead of capital, nothing but political offenders condemned to deportation. It is again and again repeated that Guiana was then ruined by the aboli-

* In 1810 a party proposed to proclaim independence and demand protection from the English. This project was vigorously and triumphantly combated by a young officer destined one day to become President of the Ministerial Council in France, M. Joseph de Villèle.

† *Revue coloniale*, 1844, Tom. IV. p. 324, Notice by M. Voiart; 1846, Tom. VIII. p. 20, Notice by M. Pajot; 1858, Tom. XX. p. 47, Notice by M. Roy.

‡ *Mémoire inédit sur l'histoire des missions aux colonies*, p. 286. Archives of the Seminary du Saint-Esprit.

tion of slavery,* proclaimed without circumspection by Jeannet on the day after the arrival of the frigate that brought the decree. The only survivor, in 1834, of the persons deported without trial on the 18th Fructidor, V., the Marquis de Barbé-Marbois, has given us the true reasons of the ruin of the colony in which he then dwelt (1797).

"All the expenses of the government of French Guiana were defrayed under the monarchy by funds sent annually from France. . . . . . Cayenne was beginning to shake off her languor, when suddenly the emancipation of the slaves checked this flight. *France having ceased at the same epoch to pay the subsidy,* these two causes concurred in plunging the nation into distress. The colonists had renounced the labors necessary to the prosperity of young colonies." †

From 1800 to 1809, the colonists enriched themselves as corsairs. In 1809, Guiana, attacked by an Anglo-Portuguese expedition, fell, and remained for eight years in the hands of the Portuguese.

While the blacks at Bourbon, far from revolting in order to seize the liberty inscribed in the law, aided in the defence of those who concealed this law from them, at Guadaloupe they poured out their blood for the independence of the national territory. On the 21st of April, 1794, the English took possession of the island. On the 2d of June, the agents of the Convention, Victor Hugues and Pierre Chrétien, appeared in sight of the shores of Guadaloupe, with two frigates, a brig, five transports, and twelve hundred men. Being able to communicate with the land, they sent forth the decree of the abolition of slavery, ‡ with a fiery

* See the testimony of M. Vidal de Lingendes, who quotes a writing of M. Armand Aubert, which we have been unable to find (*Procès-verbaux de la commission de* 1839, p. 135). See also *Observations sur la colonie de la Guyane et sur les nègres,* by J. J. Aymé, ex-legislator, Hamburg, 1800.

† *Journal d'un déporté non jugé,* Didot, 1834, Tom. II. Chap. VI. p. 103.

‡ *Revue coloniale,* 1844, Tom. II. p. 416; 1850, 2 Series, Tom. IV. p. 164.

proclamation. On the 7th of June, the slaves flocked to their aid, and, after seven months of heroic struggle, the English were forced to yield before this fifteenth army of the Convention. The colony was saved, but ruined; for with liberty entered revolution,* accompanied with all the excesses produced by the double intoxication of independence and victory; Pointe-à-Pître had its revolutionary tribunal. When liberty has reached this point, dictatorship is not far off, and with it terror, violent absolutism, and the burden of those innumerable laws which dictatorship invents and multiplies, without success, to constrain the only force which resists, and ends by overcoming it, — the force of realities. Chrétien having succumbed to the yellow-fever, Hugues, left sole master of an island blockaded by the English, deserted by its inhabitants, and uncultivated, heaped proclamations upon proclamations, ordinances upon ordinances. The first spoke only of liberty and happiness; then it became necessary to forbid thefts and the forcible seizure of provisions, under penalty of death (June 13, 1794), to prescribe labor under the same penalty (June 18), to brigade the negroes, and man privateers with them to capture on the seas the food which the land no longer produced; yet, by these violent means, to postpone famine without resuscitating labor, and to compel the labors of these pretended freemen (August 28, 1795). In 1796, cultivators and culture, vessels and cattle, were wellnigh annihilated, and Victor Hugues, his energy and hope exhausted, refused to proclaim the Constitution. He wrote (August 9) a sad and sensible letter to the Colonial Minister, in which were these words: —

"What can restrain ninety thousand strong, robust per-

* I point out the dates and principal facts without writing the history of the Revolution in the Colonies. See the remarkable, complete, and curious work, entitled, *Histoire de la Guadeloupe*, by M. A. Lacour, Councillor of the Imperial Court, and especially Tom. II. Liv. VI. Chap. VI. (Basse-Terre, 1855 - 1860.)

sons, imbittered by long misfortunes? What can hinder the baleful effects of the ignorance and brutishness into which they have been plunged by slavery? Can three thousand persons, two thousand of whom detest the present state of things as much as the Republican government? The Constitution, far from being a benefit to the colony, will be its destruction. . . . . . It is only by degrees that these unfortunates can be brought to the state to which the government wishes to call them."

A new Governor, General Desfourneaux, succeeded in reanimating labor by a happy application of the system of renting the lands for a portion of their produce (Order of February 10, 1798), and the institution of inspectors of culture. Replaced at the end of the year by divers agents of the Directory, he left the colony in a more prosperous state, prices higher, the national property more secure, the Constitution effective. With the Consulate began the régime of military dictatorship, preceded by the provisory government of an intelligent and firm colored man, Pélage (1801). An insurrection of outlaws and negroes * was the occasion of proclaiming martial law in Guadaloupe. The insurgents were judged by a council of war. General Richepanse arrived as a conqueror, took military possession of the colony,† and from the beginning, by reserving to the whites alone the title of citizens (Order of July 16, 1802), disarming the blacks, and obliging them to return to their former habitations, clearly preluded the re-establishment of slavery.

Slavery, and even the slave-trade, were re-established, in fact, by the law of the 30th Floreal, X.

We seek in vain in the immortal *Histoire du Consulat et de l'Empire*, by M. Thiers, for a trace of this odious law. We

* *Moniteur*, Year X., p. 291; Report of Rear-Admiral Lacrosse.

† *Moniteur*, Year X., p. 22, and 25 Messidor; Report of 5 and 9 Prairial, of General Richepanse.

‡ *Moniteur* of the 28th Floreal, Year X., p. 970.

would gladly efface it from this great year, 1802, which saw the Concordat, the Consulate for life, the peace of Amiens. We cannot comprehend that slavery and the slave-trade should have been written anew in the laws of France by the same victorious and wise hand which, at that very moment, restored liberty to its country, peace to land and sea, commerce to Martinico, St. Lucia, Tobago, the Isle of France, Bourbon, and the East Indian possessions. But the veracious and pitiless *Moniteur* contains this mournful page. This informs us that in the course of the session extraordinary convoked on the occasion of the peace of Amiens, and which lasted from the 15th Germinal to the 30th Floreal, — a session the memory of which was consecrated by a medal solemnly struck, a session rendered illustrious by the peace, the Concordat, the Legion of Honor, the University, and the framing of the Civil Code and the Code of Commerce, — in this session of the legislative body, the 27th Floreal, X., the Councillors of State, Dupuy, Bruix, and Dessoles, preceded by a message from the Consuls, presented the following bill: —

Art. I. In the colonies restored to France, in the execution of the treaty of Amiens, dated 6th Germinal, year X., slavery shall be maintained conformably to the rules and regulations anterior to 1789.

Art. II. The same shall be done in the other French colonies beyond the Cape of Good Hope.

Art. III. The traffic in negroes, and their importation into the aforesaid colonies, shall take place conformably to the rules and regulations existing before the said epoch of 1789.

Art. IV. The colonial régime shall be subject for ten years to the regulations made by the government, all anterior laws notwithstanding.

"It is well known," said the government orator, Dupuy, "what illusions of liberty and equality have been propagated with respect to these distant countries, where the remarkable difference between the civilized and uncivilized man, the difference of climates, of colors, of inhabitants, and, above all, the safety of European families, imperatively exact great differences in the civil and political condition of persons. . . . . . The accents of a philanthropy falsely applied have affected our colonies like the song of the siren; with them have come evils of every kind, despair and death."

But we must read the report of the tribune Adet to the session of the 29th Floreal, as a model of hypocritical declamation.*

"It is," says he, "with slavery as with war. Long have philosophers mourned the fury which inspires nations with a thirst for blood. . . . . . Notwithstanding, all peoples make war. What would be the condition of that people which, abjuring war, should renounce the manufacture of arms, their use, the support of an army ready for its protection? *In breaking the equilibrium of the forces which counterbalance it,* would it not become *accountable* to other nations for the evils which its *renunciation of common usage* might draw upon them, and would it not be itself exposed to scourges of every kind?

"What I have just said of war may be applied to slavery. Whatever may be the horror with which it inspires philanthropy, useful in the present organization of European communities, no people can renounce it without thereby endangering the interests of other nations. It may be regarded as one of the institutions which one is bound to respect, even when wishing to free himself from them, *because they interest the safety of his neighbors.*"

The tribune Adet next expatiated on the interests of the colonists, and of the negroes themselves. He rejected progressive as well as immediate emancipation, because

* *Moniteur* of the 30th Floreal and 1st Prairial, Year X., pp. 988, 989.

this would be the signal for a bloody insurrection: "Leave *to time alone* the care of paving the way for, and effecting in the colonial organization, the changes demanded by humanity. . . . . .

"I am now about to speak, my colleagues, of the importation of negroes into the colonies. If you carry your thoughts to the coasts of Africa; — if you consider the blacks attached to the soil which has witnessed their birth, separated from those whom Nature has bid them cherish, bending their eyes, bathed in tears, on the shores which they are about to quit forever, tormented by anxiety for the future, rent by memories of the past, and erelong enclosed in a floating prison to breathe a burning air, — your hearts will be wrung, and, listening only to pity, you will instantly proscribe the slave-trade as the most barbarous of institutions.

"But should you suffer yourselves to be persuaded, *as magistrates,* by a sentiment which does honor to you *as men?* Alas! no. If, at the moment of giving battle, a general yields, at the sight of blood, to the impulse of his soul, though excusable in the eyes of the private man, he will not be so in the sight of his fellow-citizens, who will reproach him for ill-timed sensibility. You would sacrifice to the blacks the interests of your country, by destroying an institution necessary to the colonies, themselves become necessary to our existence.

"Let us content ourselves with *forming wishes* that Europeans may wisely conciliate their interests with the duties of humanity in the slave-trade. However limited may be the intelligence of the Africans *relatively to our own,* whatever may be the difference between their species *and ours,* let us never forget that they are men.

"As to the colonial régime, let us repose with confidence on the government. Each colony will erelong become by its care a great family, all the parts of which will thenceforth offer to the philosopher, to the friend of humanity, only those touching scenes of patriarchal life *on which the mind and heart of the good man repose with so much delight.*"

The bill was adopted by the Tribunate, by a majority of fifty-four votes against twenty-seven, on the same day that the institution of the Legion of Honor was proposed.

In the meeting of the Legislative Corps of the 30th Floreal,* Jaubert (de la Gironde), the orator of the Tribunate, was more summary than his colleague.

"Experience teaches us," said he, "what hands can alone be employed in culture in the colonies. It tells us what are the beings to which liberty is but a poisonous fruit. *Let us turn aside our eyes* from the pictures which these ideas recall to us, ... let us obey the great law of empires, necessity. *Let us not trouble the world with theories.*"

"Liberty in Rome," continued Bruix, "surrounded itself with slaves. Milder with us, it banishes them afar. The difference of color, of manners, of habits, might excuse the domination of the whites ; but policy, the care of our greatness, *and perhaps of our preservation,* binds us not to break the chains of the blacks."

Regnaud de Saint-Jean-d'Angély resumed : "Humanity is unwilling that we should condescendingly pity the lot of a few men, and procure them *doubtful* good by exposing a part of the human race to certain and terrible evils. . . . . . By the aid of the law which you have just passed, you may be sure of the duration of the peace of the world."

The bill was adopted by two hundred and eleven votes against sixty-three. It restored to the colonies† three things, slavery, the slave-trade, and absolutism.

* *Moniteur*, p. 1015.

† The Archives of the Colonies contain the circulars which accompanied the despatch of the decree to the Colonies. They are of the same style as the speeches which preceded the vote. They style emancipation a *philanthropic error*, an *indiscreet measure.*

We would have gladly had the liberty of the negroes borne to the tomb without the accompaniment of the false and sentimental phrases which eight years before had resounded at its cradling. We are forced to blush once more at encountering the same jargon in the service of other ideas; we comprehend, we share, the contempt of the First Consul for these tribunes turned courtiers. We would gladly suppress this law in history, but above all its commentaries; we would willingly exclaim, *The slave-trade, but no phrases!*

The law at least had some political reasons for its motive.

The public mind was deeply moved by the example of St. Domingo, which it was sought to reconquer, and the *Moniteur* at this very moment was publishing the first reports of General Leclerc and Admiral Villaret-Joyeuse. But why forget that the insurrection was due, not to emancipation, which it had preceded, but to the law which gave the same rights to freemen of every color? Why forget that the first blood that flowed was the blood of whites, shed by whites? The law of the Constituent Assembly commenced the destruction of St. Domingo; the law of the Consulate consummated it; emancipation did not cause, and might have prevented it.

The orators of the government regarded slavery as necessary *to the safety of families, to their preservation;* affranchisement, even progressive, as being necessarily *the signal for an insurrection.* We have seen that in Bourbon and the Isle of France the blacks had not even availed themselves of their liberty; at Guadaloupe they had fought for the independence of the island. All these reproaches were calumnious.

The example of the Constituent Assembly was alleged, which had shrunk from emancipation. Sad example! All the disorder of the colonies and the ruin of St. Domingo arose from this wavering of the Constituent Assembly. It was, unhappily, more just to plead the laws of the Constituent Assembly in excuse for confiding to the government the right of ruling the colonies by simple regulations, a right which this Assembly had given to the king with respect to all the internal régime, reserving to the legislative power the commercial régime. The Convention had exercised in the colonies, as everywhere, absolute power. The Constitution of the year III. had completely assimilated the colonies to the French territory, and subjected their existence to the same laws as that of the Republic. Wiser, the Constitution of VIII. declared that these colonies should be regulated by special laws, — but *laws*, not *regulations*.

The example of England was no more just. Doubtless this great country entertained no thought of destroying slavery; but Pitt sustained the persevering efforts of Wilberforce for the abolition of the slave-trade, and Regnaud de Saint-Jean-d'Angély was wrong in saying that the postponement voted in 1800 was a dismissal, the limit of which would be known alone to posterity; for this limit, as is and might have been seen, was not far off.

The truth is, that, among the colonies we had retained and those which had been restored to us, some had preserved slavery, others had abolished it; it was difficult to choose. To accept the chances of complete abolition was perhaps to risk the return of commercial activity to which we were so ardently aspiring; it was to charge ourselves with a distant, burdensome, complex question, the mere thought of which was calculated to weary the impatience of the impetuous genius who had espoused a Creole, who detested ideologists, was irritated by petty difficulties, and did not like to be distracted from the continent by interests beyond the sea. Seduced for a moment by the great thought of restoring the colonial and commercial power of France,* he nevertheless soon came to prefer the Continental and manufacturing system; he would one day sell Louisiana,

* Thiers, *Histoire du Consulat*, Liv. XVI. Vol. IV.

for which he had recently bartered Etruria, and already he had just ceded Trinidad. He sent Leclerc to St. Domingo, Richepanse to Guadaloupe. He re-established slavery by force and by law; had he abolished it, posterity would have placed the anniversary above that of Marengo.

England was unwilling that the example should be prematurely set her colonies which she reserved later for ours. The Convention, in emancipating, had intended to injure England; on re-establishing peace, slavery was re-established to please her.

Thus the work of the Convention was defeated by the Consulate; the law of 1794 marks a sombre epoch with a luminous spot; the law of 1802 sullies with a stain an incomparable moment.

The signal of new disorders and new severities in the colonies, this law came to recommence the evil at the moment when it was wellnigh repaired; it closed once more the lamentable circle which men fatally follow from oppression to revolt, and from revolt to oppression; it punished the slaves for not having known how to be free, it punished the masters for not having known how to be just, yet left unscathed another criminal, the law, by whose faults those of men had been caused. Soldiers, threats, and severities were needed to re-establish the order, which had not been disturbed by liberty, let us not forget, in Bourbon or Martinico; it could not be re-established in St. Domingo, forever lost to France.*

Guadaloupe had nearly shared the same fate. Taken, in

* The chief of brigade, Navery, wrote from St. Domingo to the Minister of the Marine, 2 Ventose, XI.: —

"I informed General Dugua that, although the negroes had returned to their labor, they appeared to me fully resolved not to suffer themselves to be disarmed, because we sought to deceive them with respect to their liberty. . . . . . Even to the women, who, taking their children by the feet and drawing the limbs apart, said to me, 'See what we will do: we will rend our children asunder rather than suffer them to become slaves!'" — *Archives coloniales*, unpublished letter.

1810, by the English, ceded to the Swedes (1813), given up to France, retaken, it was finally restored, July 25, 1816; three months after Martinico, given up in 1802, retaken in 1807, restored by the treaties of 1815. The same treaties restored to us Bourbon, which, taken in 1810, returned to us in 1815, but without the Isle of France, after having sustained a blockade during the Hundred Days rather than place themselves under English protection.

But it was with the liberty of the slaves as with so many other principles proclaimed at the moment of the Revolution. Once diffused through the world, principles will not die, but their triumph will be disputed and laborious; they seem condemned to expiate by long compromises the excess of a too hasty outburst, and to become purified by a sort of penitence; we return to them with slow steps; we stretch our hand to them tremblingly; not until two generations have buried in the tomb the suspicions and memories of melancholy days does time finally efface from the brow of justice the stains which still rob the next half-century of a portion of its beauty.

To England thenceforth passed the honor of the initiative in the movement, of which France, let us not forget, had given the signal.

CHAPTER II.

FROM THE RE-ESTABLISHMENT OF SLAVERY BY THE CONSULATE (1802) TO ITS SECOND ABOLITION BY THE REPUBLIC OF 1848.

WE are not to ask of the end of the Consulate, after the too speedy rupture of the peace of Amiens, nor of the Empire, new hopes in behalf of colonial progress. The St. Domingo expedition took away all remaining interest in the cause of the slaves; it was forsaken, and, as it were, a prisoner with Toussaint. In France, in Europe, the war occupied the governments too constantly for them to have time to think of acts of virtue; on the seas, instead of chasing slave-ships, it armed privateers; before dreaming of reforming the colonies, it soon became necessary to ask whether it were possible to preserve them. The moment seemed near when all commerce with them would be interrupted; the government encouraged the culture of the beet-root to replace by indigenous sugar the sugar of the colonies, and asked of M. Parmentier instructions for this new culture, the future progress of which it was far from foreseeing.

Doubtless, public opinion might still have been moved In the midst of national anxieties, the permanent interests of humanity did not cease for a moment to occupy England. It was from 1780 to 1799, from 1800 to 1805, that the persevering agitation of Wilberforce and Clarkson occurred; it was in 1806 and 1807 that it triumphed. But in France, at this epoch, public opinion was itself a slave awaiting emancipation.

We may, therefore, pass quickly, in our present study, over the beginning of the nineteenth century, and content ourselves with pointing out, as an echo of the Christian thought, Article 1780 of the Civil Code, which reads: *"All persons are forbidden to let their services, except for a limited time."*

Overthrown by the excesses of the Revolution, restored by the excesses of war, it was the wish of the Bourbons, as well as their mission, to bring to France, wearied with agitation, strife, and despotism, order, peace, and deliverance. It was their glory to proclaim the principle of liberty, despite the memory of the crimes committed in its name; it was their inclination to seek in the past the image of authority. The ocean does not separate two continents and two peoples more entirely than the torrent of the Revolution had separated the past from the present to all Frenchmen, except to themselves alone. In the eyes of contemporaries, everything was beginning; to them, everything was continuing. Belonging to the nineteenth century by their loyal intentions, but very pardonably drawn towards the institutions of another age by the weight of illustrious traditions, we see them thus stamp the greater part of their acts with a twofold character, according as they obeyed the spirit of their times or their origin. This double influence made itself particularly felt in the government of colonial affairs, left by the Charter *to the régime of special laws and regulations.*

Thus, as soon as the government had retaken possession of Martinico, Guadaloupe, Guiana, and Bourbon, the new governors-general re-established there the institutions anterior to 1789. The Court of Appeals resumed the name of *Superior Council;* the courts of first instance, those of *Seneschal's* and *Admiralty Courts;* and the edict of 1681 was again put in force. The old colonial policy, which consisted, as is well known, in establishing between the mother country and the colonies, as between a freeholder and his country-house, a free privileged exchange of products, re-established the so-called *duty of the West Indian demesne*, the import and export duties, and the interdiction to foreigners of all ports, with a few exceptions.* "If we examine into the circumstances in which the government found itself placed at this epoch," says M. Rossi † with truth, "we shall frankly admit that it could neither think of abandoning the colonies which had just been restored to France by treaties, nor of applying to them at first sight any other than the ancient colonial system." But, at the same time with the edict of 1681, the duty of the West Indian domain, and the Seneschal's Courts, to the Restoration belongs the credit, from 1805, of maintaining the Civil Code, which was in force in the colonies, with the exception of the clause of forced expropriation.‡ (Tit. XIX. Liv. III.) The same government extended to Martinico the code of civil procedure, introduced into Guadaloupe and Bourbon subsequent to 1808, and regulated its application in these two colonies. § It established in all the observance of the penal code and the code of criminal instruction, || and the judicial organization of France.¶ It regulated the mode of procedure before the privy councils ;** enlarged the permitted relations between the colonies and foreign countries ; ††

* Ordinance of December 12, 1814. A decree of the Council of State, August 30, 1814, declared the port of St. Pierre alone open in Martinico to foreigners. (See the proclamations of the Marquis de Vaugiraud, Governor of Martinico; of Baron Boyer de Piereleau, Governor *pro tem.* of Guadaloupe, until the arrival of Admiral Linois. *Moniteur*, February 14, 1815.)

† Report to the Chamber of Peers on the bill of the Sugar Law, June 20, 1843.

‡ Martinico, Nov. 7; Guadaloupe, Nov. 9; Bourbon, Oct. 7 and 25; Guiana, Sept. 23, 1805. The Code of Commerce, applied to Guadaloupe and Bourbon subsequently to 1808 and 1809, was not introduced into Martinico until after the law of Dec. 7, 1850.

§ Ordinances of Dec. 19 and 30, 1827; Oct. 12 and 29, 1828; Feb. 15 and May 10, 1829.

|| Sept. 30, 1827; Sept. 24, 1828; Oct. 10, 1829.

¶ Aug. 31, 1828. ** Feb. 5, 1826. †† Aug. 30, 1826; Aug. 26, 1827.

fixed the monetary régime ; * introduced the metrical system,† registration, and hypothecation.‡ There was no idea of assimilating the colonies to the mother country, nor of re-establishing therein the *Colonial Assemblies;* the example of the Revolution deprecated these two systems. Nevertheless, in 1820, *consultative committees* were created.§ By the ordinance of January 26, 1825, the *expenses of administration* were separated from the expenses of *protection;* the one being left to the charge of the colonies, the other to that of the budget of the state. By the ordinance of August 17, the local revenues of the estates of the domain were made over to the colonies to defray their internal expenses. But, above all, the colonies owe to the Restoration the three great ordinances of 1825, 1827, and 1828 ; || which, modified by that of August 22, 1833, and by the senatus-consultum of May 3, 1854, continue, notwithstanding, to be the veritable basis of the legal and administrative régime in our trans-oceanic possessions. At the same time, nothing was neglected by ministers such as MM. Portal, de Chabrol, and Hyde de Neuville to impart a lively impulse to the commerce and agriculture of the colonies. Banks created, premiums accorded to improvements of every kind, numerous shipments of seeds and animals, revision of the legislation of customs,¶ innumerable ameliorations of details, make of the period of the Restoration, despite disasters generously repaired and petty insurrec-

* 1820, 1825, 1828.

† Dec. 31, 1828; June 14, 1829. The stamp was not in existence in Bourbon till 1804.

‡ June 14, Nov. 22, 1829.

§ Ordinance of Nov. 22, 1821; *Moniteur*, 1821, p. 1447.

|| Bourbon, ordinance of Aug. 21, 1825; Martinico and Guadaloupe, Feb. 9, 1827; Guiana, Aug. 27, 1828. The first, in 195 articles, and the second, in 211 articles, were the work of M. de Chabrol; the third, in 196 articles, was signed on the report of M. Hyde de Neuville.

¶ Ordinance of Oct. 25, 1829.

tions without serious consequences, an era to the colonies of great development and good administration.

The emancipation of the slaves was thought of, — how could it have been otherwise? — but it was not attempted. They remained outside all the preceding laws. The ancient monarchy had not abolished slavery; the Revolution had done so, but at the ill-omened date of 1794, a few days before the President, Molé de Champlâtreux, and the first magistrates of the Parliaments of Paris and Toulouse, mounted the scaffold. It had been re-established at the same time with public order. The events of St. Domingo — even after the king had sent Baron de Mackau to recognize the Presidency of General Boyer, and the independence of the island (July 17, 1825) — had left in the public mind great pity for the colonists, whose indemnity was being laboriously effected, and great animosity against the negroes. The colonists had suffered so much, that men dreaded for their progress the mere announcement of a moral agitation. The Restoration had so much to pay, that they feared for its finances the demand of a new indemnity.

At length, the Congress of 1815, thanks to the initiative of Lord Castlereagh, and the solicitations of the Sovereign Pontiff, despite the opposition of Spain, abolished the slave-trade. It was erroneously supposed that slavery, unable longer to recruit its forces from Africa, was about to die.

These fears, these memories, these reasons, these illusions, united to postpone anew the liberty of so many unfortunate beings who, rebellious or submissive, had shown for so many years the facility of their race to suffer guidance.

In short, under the Restoration the colonies received from the government two precious boons, — order and repose.

We may judge by statistics of the prosperity that thence

resulted :* in 1816, the total production of colonial sugars was but 17,677,475 kilogrammes; in 1826, it reached 73,266,291 kilogrammes; in 1829, 80,996,914 kilogrammes. But the movement for emancipation was not carried forward during this epoch by the French government; it belonged to England and to public opinion.

After having generously lent herself to the abolition of the slave-trade, France did little towards practically executing the solemn pledges of the Congress of Vienna; and it must be confessed that, despite the statutes of April 15, 1818, and April 25, 1827, the slave-trade, diminished, watched over, and sometimes repressed, was not interrupted until 1830. Mr. Clarkson repaired to the Congress of Aix-la-Chapelle,† to demand that the crime of the slave-trade should be assimilated to piracy, and that the powers should unite to obtain of Portugal and Spain the cessation of this odious traffic. The Emperor Alexander, the Duke of Wellington, and Lord Castlereagh, were in favor of both measures. In the discussion of the law on *piracy* and *barratry*, (statute of April 12, 1825,) M. Benjamin Constant‡ asked why the slave-trader was not assimilated to the pirate, and consequently punished with death, or hard labor for life? "Whoever carries on or commands the slave-trade," exclaimed he, energetically, "is a criminal, an armed brigand, often an assassin. He is, besides, as cowardly as ferocious; he has not even the courage of the pirate; he deserves no less hatred, and greater contempt." But this measure failed to become law.

* Let us quote separately the statistics of Bourbon, the most prosperous of the colonies since the loss of St. Domingo. In 1825, the product of the cultures was 17,783,900 francs; thirty years after, with a population of 153,000, instead of 63,000, it amounted to but 28,278,795 francs; in 1855, the joint imports and exports amounted to 32,982,225 francs, while in 1825 the same sources already amounted to 20,723,041 francs. (*Essai statistique sur l'île de Bourbon*, by M. Thomas, 1826. *Notices sur les colonies*, by M. Roy, 1856.)

† *Moniteur*, Jan. 14, 1819.

‡ Session of April 5, *Moniteur*, April 6, p. 507.

In vain, by reference to the budget of the Marine, or by petitions, was the question of the slave-trade, and that of slavery, carried before the public authorities. A last time, in 1829, M. de Tracy mounted the rostrum to denounce the continuance of the slave-trade,* and to demand the establishment in the colonies of a regular civil state, so often promised, which should permit the verification of the right to slaves. But all these manifestations only ended in references to government, or, rather, in less sterile references to public opinion, which did not cease for a single day, by journals, books, academical prizes, societies, sermons, and speeches, to raise to God the prayer which men had rejected.

The Revolution of 1830, in bringing into public affairs a number of the political personages who had solicited emancipation, imposed on them the duty, and furnished them the means, of remaining faithful to themselves. Preoccupied from its first steps with this noble end, the government of July did not cease a single day to think upon and promote it. It did for the internal reform of the colonies what the Restoration had done for their repose and prosperity; it prepared them, in spite of all opposition and predictions, to live and to grow without slaves, and without monopolies. What the government of July did for the queen of our colonies, Algeria, the last gift of the Restoration to France, is well known. We owe to it also in Africa the entrepôts of Sedhiou (1837), Grand Bassam (1842), the Marquesas (1842), Gabon (1842), Assynia (1843), the islands of Nossi-bé and Mayotte in the Mozambique Channel (1843), and the Tahitian Archipelago (1842–1846). A great political thought, then strongly contested, had conceived the project of thus securing to France settlements, planted at regular intervals around the globe, to

* *Moniteur*, p. 1221.

serve as a shelter to her flag, as stations to her commerce, and as fulcrums to her influence.

Without setting forth here how much the government of July expended, besides money, efforts, and perseverance, and despite the most ardent opposition, to co-operate earnestly with England for the suppression of the slave-trade, which it hastened to abolish by the statute of March 4, 1831, let us limit ourselves to examining rapidly its acts for paving the way to the abolition of slavery, as numerous as the years of its duration.

The Charter of 1830, like that of 1814, placed the colonies under a special régime, but indicated that it should be regulated by *laws*, without adding *and by regulations*. All the public authorities were thus more nearly associated in this important task. They united in inscribing in the two statutes of April 24, 1833, the equal rights of men born free and those emancipated, the re-establishment of *colonial councils* and *delegates*, and the apportionment of matters to be regulated by the law, by ordinances, or by local decrees.

We shall see that the government knew how to make an able and diligent use of the part assigned to it.

The ordinances of March 1 and July 12, 1832,* suppressed the tax on emancipations, and simplified their form. The penalties of branding and mutilation were abolished by the ordinance of April 30, 1833. Two ordinances of April 29, 1836, sanctioned the liberation, and created the civil state, of emancipated slaves brought to France; and another ordinance, June 11, 1839, established cases of emancipation by law.

Two ordinances, August 4, 1833, and June 11, 1839, obligated the regular registration and returns of the births, marriages, and deaths of slaves.

* Codicil A to the *procès-verbal* of the colonial commission, meeting of June 4, 1840.

An ordinance of January 5, 1840, regulated the primary and religious instruction of the slaves, and placed them under the patronage of public magistrates, charged with examining regularly into the condition of their workshops and plantations.

Two memorable facts — emancipation in all the English colonies (1834), and the publication of a bull by Pope Gregory XVI. (1839), condemning the slave-trade and slavery — had finally given an irresistible impetus to public opinion. Ardent Democrats,* by force of believing in the rights of man, zealous Catholics and sincere Protestants, by force of believing in duties toward man, were of one mind. The preparatory measures of the government were taxed with insufficiency and slowness, and the interpellations addressed to M. de Rigny in 1833, in 1835 to the Duke de Broglie and Admiral Duperré, and renewed almost every year by M. Isambert, followed by solemn and sincere promises, were not prompt enough to content the public mind.

M. Hippolyte Passy had the honor first directly to attack the subject of emancipation, by presenting to the Chamber, February 10, 1838, the following bill: † —

Art. I. From the date of the promulgation of the present law, all children born in the French colonies shall be free, whatever may be the condition of their parents.

Art. II. Children born of slave parents shall remain under the care of their mother, and an indemnity of fifty francs per head for each child shall be awarded to the owners of the mothers for ten consecutive years. This indemnity shall cease to be paid in case the child from

* *L'Abolition*, by M. Schœlcher; *Christianisme et Esclavage*, by l'Abbé Thérou, etc.; *l'Esclavage colonial*, by M. Castelli, apostolic prefect; *Esclavage et Traite*, by M. Agénor de Gasparin, 1838; *Réflexions sur l'affranchissement des esclaves aux colonies françaises*, by M. Lacharrière, President of the Court of Guadaloupe.

† *Moniteur*, p. 271.

whose birth the right to it arises shall die before attaining the full age of ten years.

ART. III. All slaves shall have the right to purchase their freedom, at a price fixed by arbiters, designated in advance by the metropolitan authority.

The indemnity due to owners, for children born of slave mothers, shall revert of right to such of the mothers as may purchase their freedom.

Wedded slaves shall not be separated in case of sale. Husbands or wives who buy their liberty shall pay but two thirds of the price fixed by the arbiters ; the remaining third shall be paid by the state.

ART. IV. Royal ordinances, which shall be communicated to the Chambers in the session following their promulgation, shall decide on the measures to be taken for the registration and protection of children born of slave mothers, for the distribution and choice of arbiters charged with regulating the conditions of redemption of freedom, for the establishment of savings banks, and for all that concerns the amelioration of the condition of the slaves, and the execution of the present law.

This clear and complete bill deserved to be taken into consideration, and was so, in fact. Its author sustained it by eminently practical arguments (see meeting of February 15), and MM. de Lamartine, Guizot, and Barrot united in supporting it. In vain the government declared the bill *inopportune,* because of the condition of the English and French colonies ; *iniquitous,* because it did not propose a preliminary and sufficient indemnity; and *inhuman,* because it broke all bonds between the master and child. The Chamber unanimously deemed it time to bring to light what M. de Lamartine eloquently called "this great expropriation for the cause of public morality."*

The bill of M. Passy was only a plan of incomplete

* Meeting of Feb. 15, 1838, *Moniteur,* Feb. 16, p. 317.

emancipation. He opened three broad doors to freedom; children received it with life, men attained to it through property, families received it through the aid of the state. It was an excellent programme for the gradual abolition of slavery under two conditions,—little money, and plenty of time; the one was suited to please the mother country, the other, the colonies. A report*—one of the best—penned by one of our first writers, M. de Rémusat, was the eloquent commentary on the proposition of M. Passy. It had been preceded by a profound study and serious and prolonged inquiry on the legal condition of the slaves, the economical condition of the colonies, and the first results of the English experiment.† As firm in principle, the commission tempered the conclusions of M. Passy, and, yielding also to the thought of consulting the colonies, and the desire of receiving a more complete lesson from the example of the English colonies, limited itself to proposing,—

1. That the costs to which the measures destined to pave the way for emancipation should give rise should be at the expense of the state; which was, by accepting a charge, to reclaim a right.

2. That, in consequence, *each year* the finance law should include in the budget the sums necessary to co-operate in the extension of religious service, and the propagation of primary instruction.

3. That, *in three months*, the government should make ordinances on the forms, civil effects, and authorization of marriage of persons not free.

4. That other ordinances should regulate the right of the slaves to acquire money, and obligatory redemption.

5. That a bureau of inspection of the measures taken should be created at the expense of the state.

* *Moniteur*, June 19, 1838, p. 1746.

† Members of the Commission, MM. Guizot, Croissant, Berryer, de Rémusat, Baron Roger, Laborde, H. Passy, Isambert, and Galos.

6. That an *annual* account of the execution of the law should be rendered to the Chambers.

At the present time, these conclusions seem very timid; they simply say to the state: "You shall demand money of us to do as you like, you shall charge inspectors with watching over what you have done, and when they have rendered you an account of it, we shall render you an account of it ourselves."

The dissolution of the Chamber of 1837 brought to naught the proposition of M. Passy. But, reproduced in exactly the same terms by M. de Tracy, June 7, 1839, discussed on the 12th,* the very day after the ordinances for the registration of slaves, and supported this time in the name of the government by M. Passy himself, Minister of Finance, the proposition was taken into consideration by an immense majority, and referred to a commission, which chose for its chairman M. de Tocqueville.

With that measure of sagacity and profundity which stamps all his writings, M. de Tocqueville clearly demonstrated why the commission preferred the system of general and simultaneous to that of gradual emancipation,—the one, necessitating the intervention of the law, indemnity, and administration, at once transforms, under the influence of a vigorous, uniform, and far-seeing impulse, the whole colonial society; the other disorganizes labor, takes from the colonists their best slaves, the love of work from these last, and patience from those who remain captives, and continues long to disturb, without emancipating. The commission proposed a bill of three articles, which obliged the government to produce a bill of complete emancipation *during the session* of 1841. The report, presented July 24, 1839, had not been discussed at the end of the session, and January 27, 1840, M. de Tocqueville demanded that the proposition should be resumed.

* *Moniteur* of 1839, pp. 896, 950.

The government, stimulated by this generous pressure, had commissioned the Governors of the colonies * to consult the Colonial Councils with respect to the report of M. de Rémusat. After that of M. de Tocqueville, which was also sent to the Governors,† the Cabinet Council,‡ on the report of Admiral Duperré, declared itself ready to adhere to the basis of the plan set forth by the commission, and instituted in the colonies a special council, composed of the Governor, the Ordainer, the Director of the Interior, the Attorney-General, and the Colonial Inspector, to furnish the documents necessary to the presentation of a bill.

At the same time it proposed, and the Chambers voted to the budget of 1840 and 1841, an appropriation of 650,000 francs to increase the clergy, chapels, schools, and number of magistrates, whom the ordinance of July 5 designated as the protectors of the slaves. (*Ordinance of November* 6, 1839.)

We were advancing slowly, but surely. What were the colonies doing meanwhile? It would have been supposed that, warned by the progress of the movement of public opinion aroused in France against slavery, warned, above all, by the example of the English colonies, and pressed by the solicitations of the government, our colonial possessions would have prepared themselves by degrees for emancipation. Nothing of the sort; they prepared only for resistance. To believe interested theories, servitude is the novitiate of liberty, but it is a novitiate which never ends, and the sole result of which, on the contrary, is to destroy in the slave all hope, and in the master the very conception of liberty.

When the government intervened, it found minds closed to all enlightenment, interests leagued together against the least concession.

The ordinance of August 4, 1833, which prescribed the

* Aug. 21, 1838. † Aug. 9, 1839. ‡ Dec. 16, 1839.

general registration of the slaves, was considered as a means of establishing a civil state for the blacks at Martinico; the Royal Court, by thirty-eight decrees, refused to pronounce the penalties declared against the delinquents, and these decrees, annulled by the Court of Cassation, were sent back to the Court of Guadaloupe, which again acquitted all the prisoners.*

On being consulted, in 1835, on redemption, and the means of facilitating the acquirement of money by slaves, the Colonial Council replied, that the mother country had no right to concern itself with these questions.

On the communication of the bill of M. Passy, all the councils replied by demanding the rejection of the bill, and even of the modest conclusions of the commission.

To the last appeal made by the government, in 1840, it was replied: —

By the Council of Martinico (March 2, 1841), that the intervention of the mother country was *illegal,* and that it protested against *any* emancipation at any epoch whatsoever; —

By the Council of Guadaloupe, that slavery was a *benefit,* and that voluntary emancipation and the blending of the races would by degrees resolve the question; —

By the Council of Bourbon, that slavery was the *providential and permanent instrument of civilization;* that it would be absurd and unjust to deprive the black of a *benefit;* that this would be moreover to tread under foot the rights of the colonies; —

By the Council of Guiana, that the work could only result from time and patience; that it was necessary to postpone *indefinitely* all legislative measures.

What are we to think of this *benefit* which was to be

* Official proceedings of the commission of the Chamber of Deputies, 1838, for the examination of the proposition of M. Passy. I am indebted to the Duke de Broglie for access to these reports.

gradually transformed by *time* and *patience?* Where were the colonies after two centuries of a patience assuredly unequalled? Had the *blending of the races* been wrought? Had civilization advanced?

In 1855, there was at Martinico * one marriage in 137 whites, one in 221 free blacks, *one* in 5,577 *slaves.*

At Guadaloupe, 198 marriages in 31,252 freemen, *and* 14 *marriages in* 96,803 *slaves.*

At Bourbon, 284 marriages in 36,803 freemen, and 0 *marriage in* 69,296 slaves.

At Guiana, a commission appointed in the Colonial Council, about the same epoch, to examine a projected ordinance on emancipation, Article 4 of which prescribed that fathers or mothers should not be emancipated without their children, nor husbands without their wives, had rejected the article for this reason: —

"The quality of father, among slaves, is till now *a fact* indicated by no proof, unless by the allegation of whoever may choose it, since no legal bond exists between the man and woman. The benediction given by the Church to a few unions formed among them, *often without the consent or knowledge of the masters,* likewise demonstrates nothing certain, and cannot produce on the slave an effect which it does not produce on the freeman." (The slave not being authorized, like the freeman, to contract marriage before the officer of civil state.) "Otherwise," says the speaker, "in virtue of his *pretended* ties of parentage, a slave might claim *his companions as his children* or his progenitors, his father and mother, and thus procure them their liberty, despite the master."

Aristotle is again stigmatized, for he supposed, three thousand years ago, that there might be inequality of soul between the races; this is what Christians voted in the nineteenth century of the Christian era.

* *De l'Esclavage,* by M. Castelli, apostolic prefect of Martinico, 1844.

Such language was well calculated to make it the right and duty of the mother country to go on and interfere openly, without expecting anything of the blindness which inspired these base and selfish words. This part was taken resolutely by the new minister, March 1, 1840, and was announced by him, in answer to an interrogation, on the 13th of May, to the Chamber of Deputies.

On the proposition of Admiral Roussin, a commission was named, March 26, 1840, to look in the face the question of the abolition of slavery. This was composed of the Duke de Broglie, Count de Saint-Cricq, Marquis d'Audiffret, and Rossi, peers of France; Count de Sade, MM. Wustemberg, de Tracy, Hippolyte Passy, de Tocqueville, Bignon, Reynard, and Galos, deputies; Vice-Admiral de Mackau, Rear-Admiral de Moges, MM. Jubelin, de Saint-Hilaire, and Mestro. The Duke de Broglie was president and framer of the report. Interrogating facts with the most scrupulous minuteness, without ceasing firmly to maintain principles, unravelling justice and injustice through interests, it attained decisive and practical conclusions, which it embodied in two distinct bills, the one of progressive emancipation, the other of simultaneous emancipation. The superior statesman who directed these long labors, M. de Broglie, has summed them up in a celebrated report. The learning of the jurisconsult, the experience of the economist, the far-sightedness of the political legislator, the talent and method of the finished writer, and everywhere, above all, the tone of the upright man and Christian, make of this great work a masterpiece which forever honors the author and France.

The commission and the framer of the report have merited much of humanity.

The assemblage of the official proceedings, the vast collection of reports and documents gathered together by the commission, form a precious repertory, like unto those monuments of learning and jurisprudence raised up by the hands of our great jurisconsults to serve as a mine and guide to all legislation.

The following is a brief summary of the labor of the commission, the report, and the proposed bill.

From the beginning, M. de Broglie lighted the torches that were to illumine his course, — Christian philosophy and practical experience. He united in a few pages, as in a solid phalanx, all the great motives of religion, of conscience, of reason, and of right, that condemn slavery; * then, passing rapidly on, so simple is the cause and so certain the victory before God and the modern mind, he went straight to facts, and painted with a bold hand the acquired results of the English experiment.† He concluded this preamble by demonstrating that so great an example was decisive, but above all inevitable; that, from day to day, flight might give our slaves to the emancipated possessions of England, and war might give them our colonies themselves. Moreover, compromises would not enlighten the colonists, but ruin them; they would not elevate the slaves, but agitate them. The time had come to have done with these.

Before all things, it was necessary to take care that emancipation did not disturb the moral and material order of the colonies. ‡ Now, in conferring rights on the slaves, we took away duties from the masters; the liberty of the one involved the liberty of the other. It was important that the authority of the state should replace both the watchfulness and the kindness of the masters; their watchfulness, by increasing the number of courts of justice, § garrisons, ‖ and prisons,¶ and by preparing new regulations of order and police; ** their kindness, by multiplying schools and hospitals.†† It was important, above all, to develop moral order, and to this end to organize worship more

* Pp. 4 – 8. † Pp. 8 – 70. ‡ P. 71. § P. 84.
‖ P. 78. ¶ P. 91. ** P. 103. †† P. 125.

completely, to obtain the erection of bishoprics, to have recourse, in fine, to a wider diffusion of those divine principles of Christianity which are precisely fitted to emancipate man from servitude of all kinds, by teaching him voluntarily to impose on his reconquered liberty the light and easy burden of moral duties.

These objects fill the first part of the work. The second part is devoted to the interest of the slaves.*

There was to choose between three systems, — *immediate* emancipation, *deferred but simultaneous* emancipation, and *progressive* emancipation.

Immediate liberty was objectionable in that it delivered without transition the child to abandonment, the adult to idleness, the aged to destitution. Liberty preceded by an apprenticeship left the slave in an uncertainty as to his fate, which he might be tempted to abuse, as it might be abused against him. This intermediate system had been attempted in the English colonies, but had not been persisted in to the end. To emancipate children and the aged, and to leave adults to emancipate themselves by their economy, was to create mixed families, children without parents and parents without children ; to choose for adults an interminable path, as was proved by the example of Spain ; to disorganize labor by mingling slaves and freemen together on the plantations, and securing to the latter only their worst workmen. The majority of the commission found it preferable to fix a delay of ten years, after which freedom would be universal, and during which all measures would be taken among the slave population to prepare the family by marriage, property by savings, savings by the institution of one free day in the week, morality by religion, and intelligence by instruction.

The third part of the report considers emancipation in its relations with the interests of the colonists.†

* Pp. 235 - 343. † Pp. 130 - 235.

These interests were reduced to soliciting,—1st, a delay; 2d, protective duties; 3d, measures securing labor.

1. Why a delay? The slaves had already waited two centuries, and the burdens of the transition would be borne by the state. The necessity of effecting the liquidation of numerous colonial estates was the reply. How pay wages without money, and where was money to be found? In savings? The colonists had none. In loans? The plantations were almost all hypothecated. In indemnity? It would remain in the hands of the creditors. In order that the colonists or their creditors, regularly in possession of the liquidated property, might be able to devote the indemnity or new capital to labor, a law was needed that should apply to Martinico and Guadaloupe the forced expropriation which was practised only at Bourbon. This law was to be prepared, adopted, then executed. A delay was therefore indispensable.

2. The commission likewise regarded as equitable a provisory increase of the protective duties on colonial products, in order to maintain the price of the latter, especially of sugar, already so much threatened by the rivalry of native sugar, and evidently exposed to the danger of a diminution in the quantity produced.

3. As to indemnity, it was based upon no right. More limited, more variable, more onerous, more precarious than other kinds of property, even in the eyes of those who recognized it, this right was held as naught by the commission. But the good faith of owners, above all, the interests of labor, and also the complicity of the laws and the state, permitted the admission of an indemnity which should partake of the nature of a fine and a tax. Upon what basis should this be fixed? Not in the arbitrary setting up of indirect damages involved by the measure, but upon the average value of the slaves during ten years,—a value nearly the same in our different colonies,—and estimated

largely at 1,200 francs per head,* which exacted, for 250,000 slaves, a sum of 300,000,000 francs. How was this to be paid? It was somewhat shrewdly calculated, that, by immediately paying half to the colonists, the state would also become co-proprietor of the slaves, and would be consequently entitled to half their labor during the two years preceding emancipation; whence it was concluded that giving up this half to the colonists would be paying them a value equal *in kind* to half the indemnity, and would thus release the state from it. It sufficed, therefore, to enter to the indebtedness of the state the interest of a capital of 150,000,000 at four per cent, or 6,000,000† francs, which interest was to be left in deposit from 1853 to the moment of emancipation, through precaution, for the sake of the creditors, whose claims might not be liquidated, of the slaves, whose lot would be sad indeed if their masters, ceasing to have any care in the matter, should no longer find it for their interest to preserve them, and, lastly, of the state, which would have indemnified to no purpose if, before ten years, some unforeseen event should modify the law. In short, it was to make the slaves themselves pay in part for their liberty, and to exonerate the state, as the family of a child pays for his apprenticeship by giving time in default of money. The indemnity was to be apportioned among the colonies by the *pro rata* of their population; then again apportioned among the colonists, not per head, but, as was more just to the small proprietors, according to age, sex, etc., in accordance with detailed regulations to be established by royal ordinances. Invalids already a burden on their masters were to continue such.

* In the English colonies, they were valued at 1,400 francs a head; but this did not include children under six years old, who were declared free without indemnity. This difference brings back the sum to about the same amount.

† M. de Broglie calculated that the saving from the sinking fund, pledged till 1853 for previous deficits and for the public works, would permit the reimbursal in two years of the capital of the indemnity.

4. The experience of England proved the necessity of taking measures in advance to secure labor after emancipation. The indemnity was designed that labor should not lack wages. What should be done that wages should not lack labor, or that wages, becoming exaggerated, should not swallow up capital, two paths leading equally to the same abyss, — absolute ruin?

"In no country does man labor beyond his wants; in no country does man labor willingly for another, when he can labor for himself." Now there was reason to fear that the negro, having few wants, easily satisfied in this beautiful climate, would labor but little. In the English colonies this anxiety had not been, in general, confirmed; the negro had shown himself active, industrious, a lover of comfort and luxury, or avaricious, much rather than idle or lazy. But having to choose between field-labor, so toilsome to him and so truly irksome, and labor in the city, offering, with better wages, the attraction of novelty, — having to choose between labor on the property of another, and the easy acquirement of a portion of the uncultivated lands found in almost all the colonies, with the joy of being at home, and living there for himself, — would not the negro fly the land, the mere aspect of which filled his memory with all the terrors of slavery? The abandonment of the plantations in all the colonies of extended territory, the emigration from one colony to another in search of better wages, such were the two perils which the commission proposed to conjure down by suspending emancipation for five years, and imposing on the freed slaves an obligation to enter into a written engagement for the same length of time, leaving them, moreover, the free choice of master, proper occupation, and conditions; the freed slave who found no engagement was to be employed on the public works, and he who refused to make one was threatened with forced labor under surveillance. These conditions, borrowed from the code of Hayti, effected a prudent transition, which the commission deemed sufficient to maintain labor, without forcing an exaggerated rise of wages, the minimum and maximum rates of which it empowered government to fix in privy council, and perhaps without having recourse to the costly and complicated system of immigration.

To give sanction to the proposed measures, it had appeared indispensable to prepare a new statute on the *judicial organization of the colonies.* To this statute, which remained to be made, as well as the law on forced expropriation, the commission added a statute on *the political constitution of the colonies,* the text of which it proposed, excluding all freed slaves from political rights. Before possessing the quality of a citizen, it wished them always to have exercised the rights and duties of a man.

Lastly, with the bill of *simultaneous* emancipation adopted by the majority, the commission presented the bill of *progressive* emancipation, preferred by the minority. Of the forty-one articles which composed it, twenty-three were the same as those of the majority. It differed, —

1. In extending from ten to twenty years the duration of the intermediate régime ;

2. In allowing a premium to adult slaves who should contract marriage during this delay, to aid in their redemption ;

3. In freeing infirm slaves, not all at once, after the expiration of the delay, but in proportion as their incapacity for labor should be proved, and according an alimentary pension to the colonist chargeable with their support ;

4. In freeing immediately all children born and under the age of seven, or to be born, estimating at five hundred francs the indemnity to be paid the master for the price of the child and his education ; these children to be reared at the expense of the state, and, when old enough to work, apprenticed to their mothers' masters, or placed in the public establishments.

More favorable to the slaveholders than the first bill, and less onerous to the state, since it estimated the sacrifices which it demanded of the treasury at 80,000,000 francs only, apportioned over twenty years, this second bill was objectionable in that it retarded emancipation almost a quarter of a century, and thus subjected it to unforeseen events, and during this time transformed all children into foundlings, pledging them to an apprenticeship strongly resembling servitude, and giving them for a mother a slave woman, scarcely free to love them, scarcely worthy their respect, and for a father the state, a far-off tutor, thinking little of their youthful age and liberty.

The bill of the majority had also the defect of but half accomplishing the work, and leaving it for ten years face to face with the impatience of the slaves and the disquietude of the masters. But this transition seemed indispensable, and it was impossible to manage it with more justice, intelligence, and prudence.

It may be said that the commission of 1840 was the tribunal which decided the abolition of slavery beyond appeal. After its sentence, the thing was judged, and naught remained but to execute the decree.

Why was this execution retarded ?

This question was put to the government January 23, 1844,* and it was replied, that the bill would be taken up in the course of a few weeks. The same day, a petition, signed by 7,126 workmen of Paris and 1,704 workmen of Lyons, in all 8,830 persons, for the immediate abolition of slavery, was brought before the Chamber of Deputies. The session of May 4, when it was presented, showed clearly how far the report of M. de Broglie had reanimated the opposition of the adversaries of emancipation at the same time with the efforts of its partisans. The Chamber had

* By MM. de Gasparin and Sade. The report of the Duke de Broglie bears date March, 1843. (*Revue coloniale*, 1844, Tom. II. pp. 231, 233.)

the pain of hearing a report against emancipation; the colonial delegates still ardently maintaining that this great act of justice would lead the colonies to ruin and the slaves to barbarism, and the Minister of the Marine speaking of new delays and of the intention of the government to seek in dilatory measures a preparation deemed necessary before adopting the resolutions of the colonial commission.* But humanity was avenged by an admirable reply of M. Agénor de Gasparin; in answer to the pressing questions of M. Ledru-Rollin and M. de Tracy, M. Guizot affirmed anew that it was the steadfast design of the government to abolish slavery; yet, despite the commission, the Chamber voted the reference of the petition to the ministry.†

Nevertheless, the persistence of the legislative power resulted only in determining the government to adopt the one or the other of the bills proposed by the colonial commission; but it at least determined it to propose serious preparatory measures without delay.

In fact, on the 14th of May, 1844, a bill was presented to the Chamber of Peers, designed to amend the statute of April 23, 1833. It is well known that this statute, which organizes the political régime of the colonies, distinguishes between matters which are within the jurisdiction of the law, such as measures relating to civil and political rights (Art. 2), to commerce, etc., and those which may be decided by royal ordinances, colonial councils, or their authorized delegates, such as administrative organization, the censorship of the press, etc. (Art. 3).

The bill proposed to elaborate and define some of the sections indicating the measures of the second category.

Thus, to paragraph 3, framed in this wise: —

* One of the reasons of postponement was perhaps the fearful disaster of which Guadaloupe was the victim on the 8th of February, 1843, the earthquake which, much more violent than that which overthrew Fort Royal (Martinico) in 1839, destroyed 1,222 houses and a great number of lives.

† *Revue coloniale*, 1844, Tom. III. p. 127.

"Ameliorations to be introduced into the conditions of persons not free, which shall be compatible with acquired rights"; —

The bill added, —

"*And in particular on the support and maintenance due the slaves from their masters;*

"*On the system of penal labor;*

"*On the fixing of hours for labor and repose;*

"*On the marriage of persons not free, and their religious and elementary instruction;*

"*On the money acquired by slaves and their right of redemption.*"

To paragraph 7, which reads: —

"On the penal regulations applicable to persons not free, in all cases which do not demand capital punishment"; —

The bill added, —

"*And the penalties applicable to masters in case of their infraction of their obligations towards their slaves.*"

Lastly, it committed to the government, by an amendment to Art. II. § 4, the right of enacting by ordinance on the creation of new justices of the peace and the composition of courts of assizes, charged with applying the new penalties.

We see that this bill prescribed nothing. It gave three things, — to the slaves a promise, to the masters a threat, to the government a power. At first laid aside without discussion, then taken up again on the motion of M. Beugnot, seconded by M. Montalembert,* it was deliberated on by a commission with M. Merilhou for chairman,† and became the subject of an animated debate. If the emancipation were combated by strange arguments, as, for instance, the humiliation of yielding to the example of England, and the aver-

* Session of Feb. 5, 1845.

† Members: Messrs. Laplagne-Barris, Vice-Admiral Bergeret, Duke de Broglie, Rossi, Baron Dupin, Marquis d'Audiffret, Merilhou. The discussion commenced on the 3d of April.

age duration of the life of the slaves, who were declared to live longer than the whites, doubtless as domestic animals live longer than those at liberty, because better cared for, the great cause found a most eloquent defender in M. Montalembert.

"I declare," said he, "that we pure abolitionists wish for immediate measures, while the circumspect abolitionists and the temperate abolitionists wish for nothing at all. We find all the transitionary measures good and acceptable, even when they seem to us insufficient. It is quite different with our rivals, who reject them all without distinction.

"As to the national honor, as to the political influence of England, to which is attributed the design of imposing emancipation upon us, I think that quite the opposite argument may be built on this foundation.

"The humiliation to France will be found in the attitude of England, who will stand before history, before posterity, and say, pointing the finger of contempt towards France, 'Behold the liberal nation which pretended to free the world! Not only have I preceded her in the emancipation of the negroes, but she has not even dared follow me, shunning my mistakes and profiting by my lessons.'"

Under the influence of these generous words, and thanks to the able defenders of the same principle, such as MM. Passy, Beugnot, and de Tascher, the scheme was changed. However great was the embarrassment of incorporating into a law details varying with the climate, — for instance, of fixing the hour when the day's labor should begin and end, without being able to fix the hour when the sun should rise and set in each colony, — the Chamber resolutely determined to go further than the government, and to prescribe thenceforth several measures by law which the bill, contenting itself with pointing out, referred to future regulations. The government had the good sense to enter into the views of the Chamber, and to rally to the support of its propositions.

Thus, not only the concession to the slaves of one free day in a week, and the principle of the reunion of wedded slaves belonging to different masters, were added to the measures indicated in the original bill, but, instead of promises, positive decisions on the duration of labor, the allowance of a piece of ground, the right to personal property, obligatory redemption, followed by the prescription of a quinquennial engagement, the right to instruction and worship, the observance of the Sabbath, the penalties applicable to masters, the number of justices of the peace, and the composition of assize courts, were inscribed in the bill.

The Chamber of Deputies, impressed by the bill of the 19th of April,* persevered in this course. Warmly sustained by MM. de Tocqueville, de Gasparin, and de Carné, and fully explained by the chairman, M. de Lasteyrie, the government commissioner, M. Galos, and the Minister of the Marine, M. de Mackau, the law was adopted by 193 votes against 52, and was promulgated July 18, 1845.

In the course of the discussion, the Chamber had obtained explanations of the government concerning the possession of slaves by the magistrates, and promises that the bill of forced expropriation would be resumed, that the measures adopted would be erelong extended to Senegal, that the last vestiges of the slave-trade in Algeria should disappear, and, lastly, that the slaves of the government, numbering 1,469, should be freed.

This law definitively realized the greater part of the salutary measures which, according to the report of M. de Broglie, were to find place in the preparatory delay of ten years. Several of these measures were already in local usage, but they became laws. The slave could hold property. The slave could obtain his freedom by paying his

* Members of the Commission: MM. Odillon-Barrot, de Tracy, Ternaux-Compans, de Carné, de Golbéry, d'Haussonville, de Las Casas, Delessert; Jules de Lasteyrie, Chairman.

ransom, with or against his master's will; if married, he could rejoin his wife; he was therefore no longer a chattel, but a human being capable of elevating himself to personality, property, and family. Slavery, as M. Passy said, became serfhood, the rights over the person were transformed into rights over labor. Lastly, the state was charged and called upon more and more to intervene; men were weary of leaving the matter to the colonists, who refused everything, and to time, which resolved nothing.

A second bill, presented a few days after, and referred by the Chamber of Deputies to the same commission as the first, proposed a credit appropriated to the introduction of European farm-laborers into the colonies. Passed, not without opposition, in both Chambers, after two remarkable reports by MM. d'Haussonville and de Gabriac, the appropriation was happily increased to 400,000 francs, designed to encourage and perfect redemption, especially in case of the redemption of a husband without his wife, a son without his father, an ill-treated slave, etc. The sum total of the appropriation was 930,000 francs, thus apportioned: —

	Francs.
For the introduction into the colonies of European artisans and farm-laborers	120,000
For the formation, by means of free and paid labor, of agricultural establishments, serving as workshops and schools	360,000
For the valuation of the personal property and real estate of Guiana *	50,000
To aid in the redemption of slaves, by the judgment of the administration, and in conformity with royal ordinances, to be decreed	400,000
Total	930,000

These two statutes, which bear date the 18th and 19th of July, 1845, appeared in the *Moniteur* on the same day,

* This was necessarily renounced.

with a third statute, bearing date the 19th of July, and appropriating extraordinary sums for the support of the naval station on the coast of Africa.*

These statutes were real progress. Nevertheless, the great word was not yet spoken; they mitigated slavery, they did not abolish it.

"The result of the acquirement of property by slaves, and their redemption," said M. de Broglie, "will be good, moral, an amelioration, as it were, of the system of slavery; but, as a means of emancipation, it is almost illusory. For two hundred years this system has existed in the Spanish colonies, without producing there even an appreciable effect. . . . . . Ask yourselves what would be the result in France, if you should put a day-laborer without property in this position of being unable to acquire a privilege except at the price of from two to three thousand francs? He would never acquire it. The number of slaves who succeed in purchasing themselves from their own savings will not probably amount to one hundred in ten years, to one hundred and fifty in twenty years. . . . . I think the law good, as a law which will some day ameliorate the condition of the blacks, and render them worthy of liberty. But I do not wish any one to draw from this law the conclusion that all is done, and that now you have emancipated the slaves as far as you can, or wish to do; for in reality, as to emancipation, you have done nothing. . . . . If no more were ever done, slavery would be perpetual."

Haste was made at least to accomplish what had been voted. The government might have waited before promulgating the laws for the drawing up of the executory ordinances; it deserves credit for having promulgated them without delay, after having sent detailed instructions to the colonial governors on the 30th of July, with a full report of the debates of the Chambers. These were

* *Moniteur*, Aug. 3, 1845, No. 215, p. 2219.

promptly followed by the ordinances of the 23d and 26th of October, the one concerning the manner of fixing the price of ransom when it could not be amicably arranged; the other on the employment of the appropriation allowed to aid in redemption. At length, March 31, 1846, the minister was able to affirm, in a report to the king, that the statute of July 18, 1845, had been put into execution; that labor was regulated according to its enactments; that the power of the slaves to acquire property, obligatory redemption, the new penalties, and the new composition of the Courts of Assizes, were now in full vigor; that a few European laborers (twenty-eight only) had already emigrated; that agricultural establishments had been made the subject of instructions, August 29; that the clergy and the schools were about to be increased; and that the ordinances on discipline, maintenance, religious instruction, marriage, lands, justices of the peace, and workshops, were all ready. He added, that these measures had occasioned some agitation in the colonies, but without serious disturbance. Moreover, he declared that accounts were expected concerning slavery in the East Indies, where it no longer existed; in Senegal, where it was practised only by the Africans; and in Algeria, where the slave-markets had ceased, and where but few slaves remained. He promised, lastly, that the emancipation of the slaves of the domain, demanded by the Chambers, should begin in 1846, and be accomplished during five years.*

The parliamentary authorities did not suffer a demand for appropriations to pass without urging forward the government. Interrogated concerning the delay of the ordinances, and again on the emancipation of the slaves of the crown (May 14 and 15, 1846), the government accepted an appropriation for 1847 of 95,000 francs, proposed for

* 126 urban laborers were freed in 1846 (Ordinance of July 21), — 63 in Guiana, 37 in Bourbon, 22 in Guadaloupe, and 4 in Martinico.

1846 by M. d'Haussonville, in order to indemnify the colonies for this emancipation, as was just.

In fact, the ordinance of August 17, 1825, Art. 3, had transferred to the colonies the estates of the crown *in full ownership*, excepting the military works, but including *the negroes and movables* attached to this property.

The illegality of this disposal was recognized, it being impossible to alienate the property of the state by a simple ordinance; thence it was only necessary to indemnify the colonies for the enjoyment of them of which they were deprived, and to buy out the interest of the third parties to whom these estates and slaves in part were farmed.

Resumed in 1847 by its persevering author, the proposition was discussed anew, and resolved by the vote of an appropriation of 142,145 francs, despite the technical objections and sinister and ridiculous predictions on the effect which would be produced by the example set by the king in emancipating those who were still called *the king's slaves*.

"If sugar-works in the neighborhood of the estates of the crown were offered me," wrote a colonist, "on condition that I should suffer my wife and children to reside there after the crown slaves were liberated, I would refuse, sure that poison would expiate my possession."

Three ordinances were rendered during 1846, the first on the 18th of May, concerning the religious and elementary instruction of the slaves; the second on the 4th of June, concerning the disciplinary régime; and the third on the 5th of June, concerning food, maintenance, and medical care.

In a second report, March 21, 1847,* the Minister was able to declare that the execution of the two statutes of 1845 was everywhere complete, everywhere satisfactory. It lacked, however, several ordinances, especially on the

* *Revue coloniale*, Tom. II. p. 925.

marriage of slaves and the preservation of the property of minors.

A few months previous, an ordinance, dated December 9, 1846, opened to the Minister of the Marine a credit extraordinary of 461,000 francs, and, May 7, 1847, the government declared before the Chamber of Deputies that the hitherto secret object of this credit was the liberation of the slaves in our new possession of Mayotte. 2,733 individuals of all ages and sexes were thus ransomed on condition of remaining bound to labor for five years to the state.

On the 19th of May, 1847, the bill concerning hypothecation and the forced expropriation system in Martinico, Guadaloupe, and Guiana, a plan solicited by the commission of 1840 and already presented in 1842, was submitted anew to the Chamber of Peers. On the 22d of May,* the Chamber of Deputies received another bill, designed, — 1st, to compose the courts of assizes, in cases taking cognizance of crimes committed on or by slaves, of at least four councillors and at most two auditors, instead of four councillors and three auditors ; 2d, to exact that the verdict of guilt should be rendered by a majority of four votes at least, instead of five out of seven. The rumor of several scandalous acquittals rendered this modification of Article 111 of the statute of 1845 very urgent. There were, in 1845, 61 metropolitan magistrates, 61 magistrates natives of the colonies, 14 slaveholders; there was in 1847 very nearly the same proportion.†

This bill, which was reported by MM. d'Haussonville and Foy, and adopted by 230 votes out of 234 in the Chamber of Deputies, became a law, August 9, 1847. The bill concerning expropriation was destined still to remain without result.

* These two bills were proposed by M. Guizot during his brief passage to the Ministry of the Marine.

† Report of M. d'Haussonville.

At the same time that the government pursued the work of legislation, on the sustained provocation of the parliamentary authorities, with the no less devoted co-operation of its superior agents, excited by the zeal of a new Minister, the Duke de Montebello, it developed administratively the consequences of the anterior acts. It published the good results of the system of patronage, encouraged emancipation, ameliorated the system of colonial customs and the sugar legislation,* gave its attention to the happy efforts to let the public lands for a portion of their produce, thought of recruiting labor by others than European workingmen, continued to free the crown slaves,† and, striving to multiply the priests, the brothers de Ploërmel, the number of chapels and schools, negotiating with the Trappists for the establishment of agricultural colleges, it sincerely entreated of Christianity to guide the blacks to make a good use of liberty after bringing the whites to adopt its principle.

The Christian sense of right wrought without relaxation upon public opinion. A grave discussion in the two Chambers was again called forth, in March and April, 1847, by a petition signed by 3 bishops, 19 vicars-general, 858 priests, 86 pastors of the Reformed Church, 7 members of the Institute, 151 elective councillors, 213 magistrates or advocates, and more than 9,000 freeholders, merchants, and workmen.

At the same time, the journalists and publicists‡ brought to the movement the tribute of their indefatigable efforts, which the Academy of Moral Sciences called forth by its prizes and rewards.

* Statutes of 1845.

† In 1847, 218.

‡ *Situation des esclaves dans les colonies françaises*, by M. Rouvellat de Cussac, formerly colonial magistrate; *L'Esclavage coloniale*, by M. Carnot, deputy; *Histoire de l'Esclavage pendant les deux dernières années*, by M. Schœlcher, 1847; *Lettres sur l'Esclavage*, by the Abbé Dugoujon; *L'Esclavage du point de vue théologique*, by the Abbé de l'Estang; *L'Esclavage dans les colonies*, by M. Wallon.

A noble spectacle was this continual action of the Christian conscience of all parties and creeds on public opinion, of public opinion on the Chambers, of the Chambers on the ruling power, of the ruling power on the colonies, by the double ascendency of law and government.

The statute of 1845, and the ordinances which followed it, had been no better received in the colonies than the statutes of 1833, the bills of 1839, and the questions of 1840.

The Colonial Council of Martinico declared the bill, before its adoption, *"odious to the colonists, fatal to the colonies, a new step towards the abyss into which it was sought to precipitate them."* (December 16, 1844.)

The Colonial Council of Guadaloupe called the statute *"a measure which shakes the colonial edifice to its foundation,"* and declared that, *"if it were free, it would again reject the right of slaves to acquire property, and obligatory redemption."* (October 24, 1845).

This is what the colonies thought of the bill, which may be reduced — to what? — to *diminishing* the number of lashes which a slave may receive, to securing to him the right of *owning what belongs to him*, and the power of *buying himself with what he earns.**

It was impossible, however, that so vast a tide of public opinion should not end by shaking opposition, and it must have indeed been very powerful to move the Colonial Councils. Towards the close of 1847, in fact, they voted ad-

* Schœlcher, 1847, Tom. I. p. 114. This impassioned, but well-informed writer cites prodigious instances of the intolerance of the colonists. At Martinico, November 18, 1845, fifty copies of the speech delivered by Count de Beugnot, before the Chamber of Peers, were seized as dangerous. On October 2, 1843, the electors having chosen two colored men to the Municipal Council of Fort Royal, *all the members* except two presented their resignation. In 1845, one of these colored men was made member of the Colonial Council. The Governor thought that he could only invite him to dine *in private*. He refused. In 1846, at the opening of a new session, the Governor invited this time all the members. Out of twenty-seven, twenty-four refused to sit at the same table with their colleague.

dresses to the king, to ask a representation of the colonies in the Chamber, and to propose systems of immigration, association, and central manufactures, in view of the social transformation to which these Councils had always refused to consent, and in which they had so long refused to believe.

After thirty-three years of representative monarchy, things stood in this wise at the beginning of 1848.

The colonies resisted liberty, but they doubted it no longer. They opposed while preparing for it; they still contested the principle in order to flee the consequences, and to render the indemnification more certain and more ample. Opposition multiplied, the systematic non-application of the regulations and laws daily created new arguments against the delusion of those who persisted in expecting liberty from the lessons of time and the good-will of the masters, and contested the opportunity. "To wait is wise," said M. de Broglie, appositely cited by M. de Montalembert, (discussion of the statute of 1845,) "on condition we wait for something; but to wait for the sake of waiting, to wait through pure carelessness or pure irresolution, for lack of possessing enough good sense and enough courage to set to work, is the worst of all resolves and the most certain of all dangers."

In France, in Europe, the victory was complete in the public mind. The public authorities were agreed, the opposition favorable, the press unanimous, public opinion and conscience had but one voice. The cause was so far gained that men were weary of hearing of it, weary of sustaining it, they had become fastidious in evidence. Why, then, hesitate so long to take the last step, to strike the last blow?

This slowness, according as it is styled prudence or indecision, is at once the virtue or the defect, the advantage or the objection, of free governments. By dint of weighing all interests, of listening to all reasons, they succeed marvellously in paving the way for the solution of questions, and end with difficulty in resolving them. Too many motives hinder determination, as too much light hinders sight.

It is for the government to triumph over the ordinary indecision of regular assemblies ; if it partakes it, everything stops short ; the moment comes when it is no longer questions, but parties, with which we have to deal.

In this question, the assemblies determined energetically, the government hesitated.

If slavery had been abolished on the morrow of the report of M. de Broglie, how many evils would have been avoided !

The government of July was cruelly punished for its long delay, since it had the trouble of paving the way for emancipation without the honor of proclaiming it. So rarely here on earth does progress flow peacefully from reason ! Humanity is like poets who compose only in delirium.

Slavery in the French colonies was not abolished until the morrow of the sudden revolution of February, 1848.

CHAPTER III.

EMANCIPATION BY THE REPUBLIC OF 1848.

On the 4th of March, 1848, the provisional government of the French Republic rendered the following decree: —

THE FRENCH REPUBLIC.

LIBERTY, EQUALITY, FRATERNITY.

In the name of the French People.

The Provisional Government of the Republic, considering that no French territory can longer hold slaves,

Decrees: —

A commission is instituted by the provisional Minister of the Marine and Colonies, to prepare with the least possible delay an act of immediate emancipation in all the colonies of the Republic.

The Minister of the Marine will provide for the execution of the present decree.

(*Signed:*)	DUPONT (de l'Eure),	GARNIER-PAGÈS,
	ARAGO,	MARIE,
	LAMARTINE,	MARRAST,
	LOUIS BLANC,	FLOCON,
	AD. CRÉMIEUX,	ALBERT,
	LEDRU-ROLLIN,	

Members of the Provisional Government.

Paris, March 4, 1848.

On the 3d of March, the commission was composed, by a decree of M. Arago, as follows: —

MM. V. Schœlcher, Assistant Secretary of State of the Colonies.
Mestro, Director of the Colonies.
Perrinon, Major of Naval Artillery.
Gatine, Counsel of the Court of Appeal.
Gaumont, Practical Clockmaker.
H. Wallon and L. Percin, Secretaries, empowered to discuss, without voting.

On the 6th of March, the commission commenced its labors, which it continued with ardor during two months.

Whatever may be the judgment of posterity on the revolution of February, it must justly proclaim the generous impulse which signalized its beginning. Let us rejoice that no moment of the history of our country has been lacking in glory. The blast which overthrow political oaths, slavery, the penalty of death for political offences, the red flag, was assuredly pure and magnanimous.

We recognize, in the labors of the commission named by the decree of the 5th of March, this noble inspiration mingled with the inexperience, the prejudices, the utopian schemes, the rancors, the passions, which so soon corrupted the revolution of February. The President brought to the maintenance of the principle of emancipation the laudable persistency which animates his writings. But more eager to invoke without understanding the revolutionary tradition than the experience of England and the studies of the monarchy, more anxious to disguise the negroes as electors than to make them men, distrusting the religion to which facts forced it to render homage, the commission was often in need of being brought back to the rules of political economy by a mechanic, who combated the minimum and maximum of wages,* while extolling the right to labor ; by the veritable principles of the honorable author of that excellent book, *L'Histoire de l'esclavage dans l'antiquité* ;† and

* M. Gaumont, *procès-verbaux*, pp. 87, 122.

† M. Wallon, who was chosen Speaker.

by the lamented Director of the Colonies,* lastly, who had to struggle at once against foolhardy experience and unskilful obstinacy.

We cannot, in fact, qualify otherwise than by the last word the attitude of the Chambers of Commerce and the colonial delegates, with a few exceptions, before the commission.

The letters of the Chambers of Commerce contained nothing but menaces and complaints.

The city of Nantes announced the immediate cessation of labor in the Isle of Bourbon; "it affirmed that the decree might endanger not only the commercial interests of the mother country and colonies, but even the lives of the planters." †

Curious admissions were mingled with these sombre prognostics. The delegate declared that "the slave-trade had continued in Bourbon till 1830, and that consequently the present generation of negroes, still brutish, were incapable of comprehending the new duties of liberty, wherefore serious disorder was to be feared." Thus the law had not been respected, nor the race ameliorated. How then speak of the humanity of the colonists, the happiness and education of the negroes?

The same dolorous complaints arose from the Chambers of Bordeaux, Marseilles, Lyons, Montpellier, Dunkirk, St. Brieux, Morlaix, etc.

The complaints and terrors of the delegates listened to by the commission were no less excessive. I do not dispute their sincerity. But they could be productive of but little effect, mingled as they were with loud protestations of adhesion to the principle of liberty, and reduced to their true value by the testimony of the colonial functionaries.

The Chamber of Commerce of Toulon alone alleged that

* M. Mestro.

† *Procès-verbaux*, p. 96.

emancipation was *illegal* and *inhuman,* both for the master and the laborer.

The abolitionists of yesterday were heard, declaring in words that they desired emancipation, proving by protests that they secretly detested it; objections, prognostics, demands for indemnity and postponement accumulated; it was granted that liberty was inevitable; it was hoped to render it impossible. To the commission belongs the merit of maintaining the great thought which it was charged with carrying out, despite all these difficulties. It was even disposed to deny, which was not to resolve them. Happily, precise information, true solutions, were furnished by the administration, which here, as elsewhere, wisely rendered so much service, as well as gained so much power, by linking itself by practical tradition to the innumerable governments and ministers given to France by the mobility of its revolutions.*

It was glory enough for the Republic to accomplish what the monarchy had made ready, without pursuing the recent past with unjust ingratitude. It is the custom of heirs of an unexpected fortune to execrate the prudent relatives who have amassed it through a thousand trials. Nevertheless, they do not long preserve it without recourse to the examples of those whom they disdain. Such is too often the conduct of new governments.

The proclamations of Victor Hugues afforded little information to the commission of 1848. Neither did the useful attempts of General Desfourneaux to let the colonial lands to negroes for a portion of their produce, renewed by a projected association at Guadaloupe, present a more applicable solution. In fact, paid only at the end of the year, — held till then in constant distrust, exposed to losses which

* Opinion of M. Mestro, in the name of the Colonial Ministry; of M. Feldmann, in the name of the Ministry of War; and of M. Lavollée, in the name of the Ministry of Commerce.

they did not comprehend, and to frauds which they knew not how to avert, — the negroes regarded this system as disguised servitude.

It was necessary, therefore, to project practical measures and to prepare bills of decrees and orders,* the best of which were precisely analogous to those proposed by the commission of 1840. What the government of July had deemed it prudent to do before emancipation, the government of February was constrained to do after it. We cannot long dispense with common sense, even when we care for it but little.

Twelve bills of decrees and two of orders were thus prepared,† and promulgated simultaneously on the 27th of April.

The first proclaimed emancipation; it was then incorporated into Article 6 of the Constitution.

"The commission has not to discuss the principle; . . . . . it lays it down, it no longer discusses it. The Republic would doubt itself, could it hesitate for an instant to suppress slavery; . . . . . it would be false to its motto if it suffered slavery to pollute longer a single spot of the territory over which its banner waves. Emancipation is decreed; it must be immediate." ‡

Two months were granted from the time of the promulgation of the decree in the colonies, in order to effect the gathering in of the year's harvest. But in the interval, all sales of freemen and all corporal punishment were interdicted. (Art. 1.)

Slaves condemned to punishment for deeds which would have involved no penalty if committed by freemen, were pardoned; persons sentenced to deportation by administrative measures, were recalled. (Art. 31.)

Everything resembling or leading back to slavery under

* P. 185 (session of April 7).

† *Moniteur*, May 2, 3, and 4.

‡ Report of M. Wallon.

disguised forms was strictly proscribed, and the pollution of servitude was effaced both from the soil of France and the persons of Frenchmen. Thus Article 2 suppressed the system of bound labor for a given time, established in Senegal. Article 7 proclaimed anew the ancient principle that the soil of France conferred freedom, and that, by a sort of miracle, the mere contact with French territory gave birth to liberty. Article 8 interdicted to all Frenchmen, under pain of loss of citizenship, the purchase or possession of slaves, even in a foreign country, and accorded a delay of but three years to those rendered slaveholders by inheritance, gift, or marriage.

The governors or commissioners-general of the Republic were charged with carrying out these important measures in all the French possessions, expressly including Algeria, where the original slavery still subsisted, the bill of an ordinance for its abolition, dated June 2, 1847, not having yet been carried into effect,* and Mayotte, Nossi-bé, and St. Mary, where, since emancipation, the freed slaves had remained bound by their five years' engagements, and the native masters still retained the right of emigrating with those of their slaves who chose to follow them.†

No mention was made of the East Indian possessions, the commission being assured that slavery had completely disappeared thence.

Article 5 reserved and referred to the National Assembly the fixing of the indemnity to be accorded to the colonists.

Article 6 laid down the principle of the representation of all the French possessions in the National Assembly, which was decreed on the 27th of April.

An immediate letter of instructions from the provisional government fixed the number of these representatives as follows: —

* P. 21, communication of M. Feldmann.
† P. 5, communication of M. Mestro.

	Population.	Representatives.	Substitutes.
Martinico	126,691	3	2
Guadaloupe . . .	129,778	3	2
Reunion or Bourbon . .	105,663	3	2
Guiana	19,495	1	1
Senegal	18,540	1	1
The East Indian Possessions	183,097	1	1

The time of the elections was to be fixed with the least possible delay by the Commissioners-General, and in the making up of lists and the electoral operations the same rules were to be followed as in the mother country.

The Colonial Councils and delegates were suppressed, and the legislative power was intrusted provisionally to the Commissioners-General of the Republic, by two immediate decrees, prepared by the commission.

Another decree, promulgated May 2, abolished the censorship of journals and writings, conferred on the administrative authority by Articles 44 and 49 of the ordinance of February 9, 1827, abolished at the same time the administrative authorization, suspension, and revocation, and extended the liberty of the press to the colonies.

Such was the political régime. The surplus of the measures concerned the local and financial régimes.

A decree instituted the *right to aid* of aged and infirm persons, orphans, and poor children ; and the foundation of hospitals, infant asylums, infant schools, and professional schools, but made them depend on very problematical resources ; to wit, the assessment of the freed slaves for the support of their aged and infirm fellow-laborers (Arts. 1 and 2), and the product of the fines decreed by the justices of the peace and cantonal juries (Art. 4).

In a subsequent decree, the primary, gratuitous, and obligatory instruction of children of both sexes was imposed on each commune, a school of arts and trades promised to each colony, as well as a high school for girls to Martinico and a lyceum to Guadaloupe (Arts. 10 and 11). An order for the foundation of this lyceum at St. Christopher's was prepared by the commission.

The *cantonal juries* in question in the decree on the right to aid, were the subject of another decree. Composed of six members, three chosen from among the property holders and manufacturers, and three from among the working classes, drawn by lot, by the justice of the peace, from the electoral list of the communes of the canton, two being renewed each month, these juries, presided over in public sessions by the justices of the peace, were charged in each canton with conciliating or judging beyond appeal all differences under 300 francs that might arise between masters and workmen, and with punishing disorders in the workshops, and coalitions. The same decree (Art. 6) abrogated Article 1781 of the Civil Code in the colonies, declaring that masters should be believed on affirmation in disputes with those in their service.

The *right to labor* and the organization of national works on the estates of the domain, or lands to be purchased by the state, were the subject of another projected decree and order.

A decree, likewise followed by an order concerning regulations, was destined to suppress vagrancy and mendicity by means of *penal works* and a corps of field overseers.

The government prescribed by two decrees the establishment of *savings banks* in the colonies, and the annual celebration of *festivals of labor*, with the distribution of prizes to laborers designated for their good conduct by the municipal councils, mayors, and justices of the peace.

The Commissioners-General were charged with apportioning anew the poll-tax, which the tax-payer was authorized to pay by three days' labor, and to establish or raise taxes on spirits and the rate of licenses to venders.

Property in the colonies was overburdened with enormous debts ; creditors were the true property-holders.

From 1827, it had been repeatedly projected to introduce forced expropriation. But the inconvenience of disorganizing labor by the mutation or division of estates, and the difficulty of finding bidders or capital in the colonies, had caused the postponement of the measure, the subject of a last bill in 1847, as we have seen. In Bourbon alone, a law had been promulgated on expropriation and the hypothecatory system. In fact, the colonies were very nearly in full enjoyment of the privilege of not paying their debts. The indebtedness on mortgage in Martinico and Guadaloupe was valued at 140,000,000 francs.*

The interest on money, according to official documents, rose from 12 to 16, and sometimes from 24 to 30 per cent. It was important that a *bona fide* liquidation should accompany emancipation, and that the soil as well as men should be made free, in order that, the estates being liberated, the indemnity might go to relieve labor, and not to pay debts, and that interest might be reduced to a less exorbitant rate. In this end, the tenth decree extended to the colonies the expropriation law and the mortgage system (Civil Code, Liv. iii. tit. 18, 19), with modifications.

An order of the commission of the executive power, designed to raise credit by another efficacious means, determined the establishment of banks at St. Pierre, Pointe-à-Pître, St. Denis, Cayenne, and lastly at St. Louis in Senegal (Art. 3). These were to be founded by joint-stock associations (Art. 2), controlled by a director appointed by the government and a council of nine administrators and three censors elected by the stockholders (Art. 8), and for the first time, by the Ministers of the Marine and the Finances (Art. 10). The capital was fixed at 10,000,000 francs (Art. 5), (3,000,000 for each island and 1,000,000 for Guiana,) divided into shares of 500 francs, of which the state subscribed one half (Art. 9). They were authorized to emit

* Testimony of M. Lavollée, *procès-verbaux*, p. 108.

notes of from 5 to 1,000 francs, and to loan at a rate not exceeding eight per cent (Art. 11), with the charge to possess always a reserve fund of specie equal to at least one third their indebtedness (Art. 7). They were to commence operations on the subscription of one half the capital (Art. 15).

In the last place the commission prepared a bill of tariff on sugars and coffees.* It was proposed to lessen the duty on native sugar 5 francs, but to reduce the duty on colonial sugar 15 francs, and the duty on coffee 31 francs. It was calculated that the difference would suffice to reanimate labor in the colonies, and to maintain the traffic of the ports with the mother country with profit to the shipping. Native sugar was held cheaply enough, and one of the members of the commission exclaimed, "*The beet-root is dead.*" It was hoped, by the diminution of price, to bring back an increase of consumption which would compensate for the losses of the treasury, valued, should it remain stationary, at 17,000,000 francs on sugars, and 5,000,000 on coffees.

Another special commission, composed of members of the administration, under the presidency of the general of the naval artillery, de Coisy, had paved the way for the extension to the colonies of the laws on the recruital of the navy, maritime registry, and the national guard. This was the subject of a decree, May 3, 1848. The measure was regarded as an efficacious means for rendering the blending of the races more complete, the education and discipline of the blacks more prompt, the internal tranquillity more solid

The same day, the *Moniteur* recorded the decrees of April 27 and May 2 and 3, 1848, the order of the Minister for the organization of disciplinary workshops, and the instructions in forty-three articles concerning elections. The Commissioners-General, whom we shall follow into each of our colonies, set out to bear thither at once, and unexpectedly, seventeen decrees, emancipation, and the Republic.

* According to a clear and complete statement, presented by M. Lavollée.

But the news of the Revolution of 1848 had preceded them, and, as we are about to see, by a strange caprice of events, if the Chamber and the monarchy had not the honor of voting the emancipation which they had prepared, in return, the honor of proclaiming it was almost everywhere borne off from the agents of the Republic by the functionaries of the monarchy.

CHAPTER IV.

RESULTS OF EMANCIPATION IN THE FRENCH COLONIES.

There was not a single colonist, there was not a single partisan of slavery, who had not announced, with a deep-rooted conviction, that emancipation would produce three results : —

The cessation of labor and the utter ruin of the colonies;

The return of the blacks through idleness to barbarism ;

Pillage and murder.

The Colonial Councils replied by these sombre prognostics to the wise and deliberate preparations of the government of July.* The writers of the colonies wrongfully pretended to rest these predictions on the results of English emancipation,† the example of St. Domingo, and the memories of the Revolution. The commerce of the ports echoed these anxieties, and even at the moment when emancipation was already decided upon, threats were seen to succeed opposition. "The seaports will not fit out ships for Bourbon, and thus the colony will be given up to famine,"‡ said the memorial addressed by the city of Nantes to the provisional government.

These sinister prophets ill divined the future ; they no more truly recounted the past.

M. de Broglie had fully demonstrated that production in the English colonies had diminished scarcely one fourth during the first years of liberty, — a diminution explica-

* Report of M. de Broglie, p. 16.

† *Le Travail libre et le Travail esclave*, by M. Jollivet, Deputy, 1845.

‡ *Procès-verbaux* of the Commission of 1848, p. 93.

ble by many causes and compensated for by the rise in prices.*

"It is a very great historical error," repeated M. de Tracy in 1849,† "to attribute the revolution of St. Domingo to the negroes; it was made by the mulattoes, and they made it to enter into possession of the political rights accorded them by the decree of 1791, which the whites had refused to carry into execution." It was in 1791, 1792, and 1793 that blood flowed in St. Domingo; it was not till 1794 that the Convention abolished slavery.

It was no more just to invoke the memories of the Revolution, which commenced by reducing the duties on colonial sugars to 4 fr. 25 c. per 100 kilogrammes, and increasing from 10 to 14 francs the extra charge on foreign sugars,‡ and ended by exempting colonial sugar from all duty (statute of Sept. 11, 1793). We have briefly recounted the events of this epoch. We are surprised to find, in the *Notices Officielles* published in 1840 by the Ministry of the Marine, the following affirmation: "The Convention speedily proclaimed the freedom of the negroes. Civil war broke out in the colony of Martinico, commerce was interrupted, culture was abandoned, and considerable emigrations took place." §

We do not precisely know at what date to place these direful events, for the Convention abolished slavery on the 4th of February, 1794, while the English attacked the island on the 3d of the same month, and entered it on the 22d of March, so that the decree of the Convention never reached it.

This style of writing the history of the past is calculated to throw doubt on the aptitude of the colonists to foresee that of the future.

* Report, p. 25 and following.

† Colonial Commission, *procès-verbaux*, p. 29.

‡ Statutes of March 15 and 29, 1791. Report of M. Béhic to the Council of State, June 24, 1850, p. 13.

§ *Notice sur la Martinique*, Chap. I. p. 33. The same document informs us that Louisiana was ceded in 1762!

Nevertheless, the most avowed partisans of emancipation would assuredly have shared their fears, had they foreseen that their design would be accomplished by violence, by a democratic revolution, and that on the morrow those would be disguised as citizens whom they had only with infinite precautions dared transform into men.

Despite these predictions, despite these circumstances, liberty, as we shall demonstrate, has not ruined the colonies, it has not brought back the negroes to barbarism, it has not given birth to pillage and let loose vengeance.

To systematize an inquiry so complicated, we will group the results into three great divisions, — *material*, *economical*, and *moral*.

We will first examine what have been the results in the *material* point of view, and begin by recounting the first events which followed the arrival in the colonies of the laws and men of the Republic of 1848.

CHAPTER V.

THE REVOLUTION OF 1848 IN THE COLONIES.*

§ 1. Martinico.

When the news of the abolition of slavery reached Martinico, the colony was not in a condition of thriving prosperity. The competition of indigenous sugar, and the consequences of the bad harvests of 1846 and 1847 in France, had reduced Martinico to the necessity of asking loans and assistance from the mother country. Security was no more stable than prosperity ; the means for defence had been suffered to fall into a very bad condition. Doubtless, this negligence testified strongly enough to the peaceful spirit of 75,000 slaves scattered among 40,000 freemen. Nevertheless, since emancipation in the neighboring English colonies, terror had exceeded danger ; for, in watching over the seacoasts to prevent escapes, the colonies expended not less than 240,000 francs a year.

Despite these circumstances, the news of emancipation at first caused no disturbance, — a generous impulse, on the contrary, drew men nearer each other, and the Municipal Council and Chamber of Commerce of St. Pierre requested the dissolution of the provisional government,† that they might reorganize in a manner to admit colored men with whites. A few years earlier, the majority of the Colonial Council, it will be remembered, had given in their resigna-

* All the facts related in this chapter are taken from official correspondence, imparted by the Colonial Ministry. It will be comprehended that a feeling of delicacy causes us to avoid, as much as possible, the use of proper names.

† General Rostoland, who had replaced Rear-Admiral Mathieu.

tion to avoid sitting with a colored man. Both whites and negroes signed a petition that M. Bissette, a well-known abolitionist, should be added to the government commissioners.

The elections passed off peaceably, under the happy influence of this spirit of mutual concession.* The Revolution of 1848 enjoyed there, as at Paris, a honeymoon of a few days' duration.

But it would have been a miracle if labor and peace had been able to continue during these days of unquiet waiting, when a whole populace, uncertain of its fate, hastened every morning to the town or the sea-shore to receive a liberty, an indemnity, an authority, which was announced, but which did not come.

On the 21st of April, a rising was suppressed at St. Pierre and the neighboring communes of Précheur and Case-Pilote, occasioned by the ridicule cast on the burlesque attire of the negroes, who had gone about beating an effigy, during the Holy Week, which they called *whipping Judas.* A few malicious blacks took advantage of the incident to oppress and stir up the well-disposed negroes. This first trouble was not serious, and proved how great was the number of good negroes; nevertheless, it consummated the falling off of commerce and labor. Besides idleness and discouragement, the spirit of disorder had full play. On the 22d and 23d of May, more serious disturbances broke out, on the occasion of setting at liberty a negro still retained in prison; a number of plantations were attacked, and, one of the planters having fired at the assailants, bloodshed ensued, the incendiary torch was lighted, and all the measures taken at St. Pierre and Fort de France† did not exempt the authorities from accepting the responsibility of the only measure

* M. Pory-Papy, attorney, an influential colored man, was appointed assistant at Pointe-à-Pître.

† *Fort-de-France* was the new name of Fort Royal; Fort *Bourbon* was also named anew Fort *Desaix.*

capable of appeasing the public mind, the immediate abolition of slavery, which they proclaimed in fact on the 23d of May, by the wish of the local authorities.

On landing, June 3, the Commissioner-General, M. Perrinon, had not, therefore, to abolish slavery. The new commissioner found the people well disposed ; a volunteer militia and police organized themselves, and a large number of the negroes entreated by petition the return of their former masters, who had emigrated through fear of disorder. The government was looked to for what it did not bring. The journals of the colony were filled with eighteen decrees, but no measures were taken to raise credit. The postponement of maturities, loans, and discount offices were demanded ; above all, indemnity was loudly called for. We learn only that the Columbo arrived, bringing large chests full of electoral registers, preparatory to balloting. Socialistic and communistic speeches, quarrels, and polemics envenomed and agitated the unhappy island, more tossed by the political tempests of the mother country than by the storms of the ocean. As at Paris, more than at Paris, a people, enslaved but yesterday, was master for four months of the lives of a small and defenceless population. But such were the relations of the majority of the two classes, let it be said to the honor of both, that, after all, the colony had less to suffer from their rancor than from the imprudent acts of some few of the agents destined to maintain peace ; playing upon the word, we may say that, in more than one point, the agents made disorder of order.

From the 26th of July, the *Moniteur* was able to announce a resumption in some degree of labor. The Commissioner-General appointed rural commissioners to visit the plantations and explain to the planters their new rights and interests ; he himself made a general tour, and authenticated some happy attempts at partnership between the masters and the former slaves ; partnerships in which generally one third of the gross products, sometimes more, was given for the share of the labor. He remarked especially a number of plantations, like that of Perrinelle, where beloved and intelligent masters retained the laborers, paying them wages which varied from 50 c. to 1 fr., 1 fr. 25 c., 1 fr. 50 c. Above all, he heard everywhere the unanimous and earnest prayer for an indemnity, and a reduction of the duty on sugars.

Assuredly the colony did not count electoral agitation among the means of bringing back prosperity; this was not spared it. The elections were scarcely legal, for instructions bearing date March 8, had left to the Assembly the right of regulating the mode in which these elections should take place. By a second letter of instructions, April 27, the provisional government, contradicting the first, had settled this mode; but the Assembly, meeting on the 4th of May, had listened to a report from its colonial committee which tended to exclude the new freedmen from the ballot-box, and before the conflict was ended, while the debates in the Assembly were known to the colonies, the Commissioner-General had summoned all citizens, without distinction, to the elections to be held on the 9th, 10th, and 11th of August.* Moreover, more than one colored man was admitted illegally, and more than one white man illegally excluded, especially in the garrison and gendarmery. It was proved that a pressure, too easily exercised on those who neither knew how to read nor write, nor scarcely to think, had not been lacking. The *Journal Officiel* of Martinico had published odious menaces, drawn up, it is said, by the Procureur of the Republic himself, and signed, among others, by his brother-in-law and the brother-in-law of the Commissioner-General. One of the candidates elected, M. Bissette, thought it incumbent upon him to tender his resignation. Nevertheless, as, of 25,000 electors, 20,000 had voted,

* See the Report of M. Charamaule, *Moniteur*, 1848, p. 2878.

and as, of the 20,000 voters, 19,000 had returned the candidates elected, and as the disturbances and irregular proceedings were far from equalling those which had convulsed so many of the cities of France a few months before, the Constituent Assembly refused to order an inquiry, and sanctioned the election.

Six weeks after the elections (Sept. 28, 1848), the appointment of Rear-Admiral Bruat put an end to all these storms. During the month of November, he announced the resumption of labor, estimated the future harvest at two thirds the usual product, and demanded the reduction of taxes and indemnity.

A few months after, a commission, charged by the governor with examining into the state of labor, summed up as follows the facts gathered in twelve out of twenty-three communes, from one hundred and sixty-four plantations, situated under the most varied conditions, and employing more than six thousand laborers.

"It is found by the Commission, as the constant result of all its sittings, that culture on a large scale, already so much injured by the transient legislation of 1845 and 1846, was completely abandoned, with very few exceptions, during the first two months following emancipation, but it is also found that, since this epoch, labor has been gradually resumed and maintained in all parts of the colony."

This testimony bears date May 29, 1849,* that is, precisely a year subsequent, almost day for day, to the mournful days which had witnessed murder and incendiarism.

A month afterwards, June 9, the elections passed off without serious disturbance, and sent to the Legislative Assembly two partisans of order, one of whom, the Honorable M. Pécoul, had been a large slaveholder. Their election was confirmed without difficulty, July 23, 1849.

* The report, which is dated May 29, 1849, was inserted in the *Revue coloniale*, June, p. 247, and in the *Moniteur*, Oct. 14.

Admiral Bruat was appointed Governor-General of the Antilles on the 12th of March. The statute regulating colonial indemnity was passed on the 4th of April. These dates mark the beginning of an era of return, slow and painful, but regular and increasing, towards order and progress.

During this stormy year of transition, what then was responsible for the public calamities in Martinico ? Was it emancipation ? Was it the Revolution ?

In *March*, news arrived of the events of February. The first moment of astonishment was marked by no disorder.

In *May*, the absence of all authority, the annihilation of labor, the excitement arising most of all from the mother country and the free colored men, engendered a few days of lamentable disorder, yet circumscribed and speedily suppressed. Proclaimed May 23, emancipation appeased the disturbance, very far from causing it.

The arrival of the Commissioner-General, his tours of inspection and good words sufficed to bring back and consolidate order in *June* and *July*. But instead of restoring the laborers to the fields, they were sent in *August* to the ballot-box, so that the first months of this painful half-year were passed in waiting and the last in voting, while agitation was the only remedy brought by the government for anxiety and ruin.

But from *September*, with a new power, confidence revived, and in *October* and *November* its first effects were proved, although no measure had been taken by the mother country to secure an indemnity.

Four months after, an investigation ascertained that labor was everywhere resumed. In *June*, the partisans of order triumphed in the new elections.

Let not liberty be accused, then, of the early misfortunes in Martinico ; it was but one difficulty more, less great than might have been expected, added to all the embarrassments which the mother country suffered herself and imposed on her colonies.

It is to the Revolution of February that emancipation is due, but it is not to emancipation that we are to attribute all the consequences of the Revolution of February.

§ 2. Guadaloupe.

Appointed Governor after numerous voyages and labors devoted to the study of the results of emancipation in the English colonies, Captain Layrle of the Marine was destined to attach his name to the proclamation of this great measure in Guadaloupe, where, April 25, he had abolished whipping and other corporal punishment.

Informed of the disorders which afflicted Martinico on the 22d and 23d of May, 1848, on the 27th of the same month, at seven o'clock in the morning, he assembled the Privy Council and resolutely proposed to proclaim emancipation without delay. The Municipal Council of Pointe-à-Pître expressed the same wish. Liberty was proclaimed, and the following decree was everywhere to be read: —

"Liberty, Equality, Fraternity.

"We, Governor of Guadaloupe and its dependencies;

"In view of the decree of the Provisional Government, bearing date March 4, which proclaims that *no French territory can longer hold slaves;*

"In view of the delay caused by circumstances in the application of this principle to Guadaloupe;

"Considering that, through the good spirit of which it has given proof, the slave population has shown itself worthy of the benefit of liberty;

"Considering that everything announces that it will continue to merit it by persevering in its habits of order and labor, and in the accomplishment of all the duties of citizen, confiding in its intelligence and patriotism;

"In view of Article 11 of the statute of April 24, 1833;

"By the unanimous advice of the Privy Council;

"Have ordered and do order:—

"Art. I. SLAVERY IS ABOLISHED.

"Art. II. The indemnity lawfully due to the owners of slaves is placed under the safeguard of the national honor, and recommended to the justice of the National Assembly.

"Art. III. The military commandant and heads of the administration are charged with the execution of the present order.

"St. Christopher, May 27, 1848." *

A solemn mass was celebrated by the Apostolic Prefect, and after addresses by the Governor and prelate, and the blessing of a tree of liberty, the excited and joyous crowd dispersed without disturbance to the sound of shouts of *Long live the Republic! Long live the Governor! Long live Religion!*

The night, which came on a few hours after, was not, perhaps, exempt from fear, but its shadows fell on affranchised souls and tranquillized consciences; it fell on a day which was perhaps to human beings the fairest one of life.

When M. Gatine, appointed Commissioner-General by the decree of April 27, arrived at Guadaloupe, May 15, 1848, order had not been disturbed for a single instant. All his reports attest that it was equally tranquil afterwards. The institution of cantonal juries and the establishment of penal labor sufficed to appease the difficulties arising most especially from the obstinacy of the negroes in keeping the cabins belonging to their former masters, and which they considered as their own.

Doubtless, labor suffered at the beginning. It must not be forgotten that three causes united in its disorganization.

* *Signed:* Layrle, Chaumont, Guillet, Jules Billecoq, Bayle-Mouillard, Bonnet, A. Lignières, A. Mollenthiel, Laugier, L. Richard de Chicourt.

The consequences of the bad harvests of 1846 and 1847 had forced the colonies to supply themselves with grain from the United States, for which they had been obliged to pay a high price in specie, and from which a crisis had resulted. The stupor caused by the revolution was a second most sufficient reason by itself alone for putting a stop to business. Lastly, the sudden liberation of the slaves complicated a position which it had not alone produced.

They were naturally seen to abandon the large plantations, especially those where they had been worst treated, and to divide into two classes, — the idle, who thought themselves called to the liberty of doing nothing, and the industrious, some of whom sought employment in the towns, while others asked permission to settle on a portion of the uncultivated public lands. Even among those who consented to work on the plantations, a great lack of regularity was remarked, — a change of mind, position, and plans was naturally the first fancy of beings always subjected to the same labor, on the same field, and under the same authority.

The energetic colonists, who speedily made the best of the new state of affairs, suffered less than those who were discouraged, than those who had been accustomed to act through the medium of expensive overseers, often harsh and detested, or than those who, burdened with debts, were forced to liquidate them at the most critical moment.

But it is very certain that disorder was not born at Guadaloupe with emancipation, but only through the consequences of revolution. Thus a great part of the loss of time by the former slaves came from their subjection to numerous formalities, not only in registering themselves in the civil state and obtaining the emancipation papers, to which they attached a rightful importance, but also in exercising political rights. They were not disturbed by their recognition as men; they were agitated by their improvisation into citizens.

Here, again, the first elections passed, if not peaceably, at least without incendiarism and vengeance.*

In two communes (Désirade and Anse-Bertrand) a terrible hurricane detained the voters at home; in two others (Grand-Bourg and Vieux-Fort), the tumult entirely put a stop to the voting. But in the majority of the communes, they were sufficiently regular to permit the Assembly to confirm the result without discussion (Oct. 21, 1848).

Martinico suffered in 1848; in 1849 and 1850, Guadaloupe was destined to have its turn.

The Commissioner-General was replaced at the close of 1848 by a new Governor, who, himself replaced in the beginning of 1849, returned at the end of the year. Appeased by some painful examples of severity in the mother country, disorder attempted to emigrate to the colonies. Culpable incitements, arising from Paris, urged on the slaves to conquer for themselves an absolute independence, as at St. Domingo. Names served as rallying-points. An improvised press multiplied appeals and instigations. The clubs were open to orators who a few months before knew nothing of schools, and were subject to the lash. It was under this régime, with these seeds of tumult, that the colony was to proceed the same year to general elections, municipal elections, the installation of new municipalities, and the judgment of grave and hotly contested suits. So much fire could not be thrown upon so much powder with impunity.

At the moment of the elections, in June, 1849, M. Bissette, made deputy by acclamation at Martinico, where the ballot-box, opened fifteen days before, had produced results in favor of order which the vanquished party wished to avenge in Guadaloupe, —M. Bissette came to Guadaloupe with the intent of employing his great popularity in favor of order. Accused of having sold himself to the whites, and of wish-

* Report of Aug. 10, 1848.

ing to return the negroes to slavery, he was assailed at Santa Rosa, and nearly assassinated. At Mary-Galante, the arrest of an agitator caused new disorders, which it was necessary to repress by force.

The elections ended amidst so many menaces and criminal intrigues, that 10,897 voters abstained from voting, and the Legislative Assembly was obliged to pronounce the elections void (Oct. 17, 1849).

The journals envenomed these deplorable struggles during the course of the suits in which the crimes of June resulted. There were forty condemnations and twenty-six acquittals (April 18, 1850). The disturbance that accompanied these suits, with four successive incendiary fires, obliged the Governor, three weeks after, to declare the city and the arrondissement of Pointe-à-Pître under martial law. Approved by the Governor-General, and afterwards by the President of the Republic and the Assembly, this measure was even extended to the entire island by a statute of urgency, July 11, 1850.*

The firmness of the courts and government consummated the discouragement or punishment of the authors of these disorders: it was ascertained that they were the work of political passions; that the negroes had labored with the whites to extinguish the fires; that the most peaceable elections had been in the country; that if the negroes had not voted, the whites, opposed to the free mulattoes, would have suffered much more; in a word, that peace had been troubled, not by emancipation, although it had served as the pretext, but by the clubs, the press, the demagogues and anarchical elections, that is to say, by the same causes, the same passions, perhaps the same men, as at Paris.

Prosperity did not return as speedily as tranquillity. The amount of importations, fallen from 41,759,712 francs in

* *Moniteur*, 1850, pp. 2253, 2294, 2334, 2370, 2376.

1847 to 11,980,480 francs in 1848, had already risen to 22,724,413 francs in 1849.*

From the last quarter of 1849, the regular payment of the indemnity had reanimated confidence and labor, and despite fruitless endeavors, unsuccessful attempts, at partnerships between the colonists and laborers, there was reason to hope for a revival, when the fires and disturbances of 1850 renewed the alarm, and, the commercial buoyancy decreasing from one quarter to another,† the year 1850 was marked by an extremely low figure.

Importation, ...	12,741,735 fr.
Exportation, ...	8,155,932
	20,897,667 fr.

Guadaloupe, which was slower to suffer than Martinico, was also slower to rise. Emancipation had been there a day of rejoicing; the elections brought days of mourning, and politics remain responsible for tears and blood which had not been caused by freedom.

§ 3. The Isle of Bourbon, or Reunion.

Numerous reasons united to give rise to the fear that emancipation would be the signal for a more painful crisis on the Isle of Bourbon than anywhere else; on the contrary, it was milder.

On an island situated four thousand leagues from the mother country, without support in the midst of foreign nations, with feeble local resources, lately tried by hurricanes, and by disease among the sugar-cane, which had become its principal culture, was crowded a population of 37,000 whites, 66,000 slaves, and 7,695 bound laborers of

* *Revue coloniale*, 1850, p. 130; 1851, p. 175.

†

2d quarter,	importations	4,035,217 fr.
3d "	"	3,755,912
4th "	"	1,915,659

all sorts,— Caffres, East Indians, Madecasses, Malays, and Chinamen. In the number of whites were reckoned the free colored men, almost all opposed to labor, and incapable of filling office or maintaining order. The bound laborers were far inferior to the slaves. The criminal statistics * proved that crimes and offences were committed in the proportion of

1 among 300 slaves,
1 " 60 East Indians,
1 " 13 Chinamen.

These bound laborers weighed no less heavily on the wealth of the island; for to support them, it was already necessary to call on the East Indies for from 20,000 to 25,000 sacks of rice, which was paid for in specie.

The prosperity and security of the island were therefore very imperfect. The means of material defence were far from reassuring; the garrison was tolerably strong, but on bad terms with the militia; the number of guns tolerably large, but all without carriages. Without doubt, the kindness of the whites and the gentleness of the blacks facilitated the relations between them. Happily, during the past few years, the negroes had been evangelized with as much success as zeal by excellent priests, whose personal influence contributed powerfully to the union of classes. But the uncertainty left hovering in the public mind by schemes of emancipation, endangered these good relations. The government showed itself neither clear nor decided upon emancipation, nor yet upon indemnity; the slaves were as uneasy as the colonists, and among the latter there were many who, wearied with this long hesitation, wished, and even asked, that, whatever might be the decision, it should be speedily made. There comes a moment when the prisoner has but one wish, — to be judged; to endure the sentence is nothing to the torture of awaiting it.

* Collected by Attorney-General Barbaroux.

This agitation of the public mind, envenomed by malevolent journals, appeared for a moment on the point of breaking out openly. On the king's birthday, May 1, 1848, the prudent and firm Governor of Bourbon, Captain Graeb of the Marine, thought it incumbent on him to postpone the usual review, in order to avoid an occasion of disturbance. He was ignorant, however, that, two months before, the king whose birthday they were celebrating had taken the road to exile. The first rumors of the sudden change in the French government reached Bourbon at the end of May. After calming the public mind by a prudent proclamation, the Governor, receiving official information, on the 9th of June, proclaimed the Republic.

The three months that followed were painful. Letters coming from France threw uncalled for doubts on the question of indemnity. Nothing less was talked of than of separating from France, as in 1794, and resisting, even by force, the Commissioner-General on his arrival. Clubs and journals were established. A general assembly of one hundred and twenty delegates from the communes, a sort of regular central club, was formed by election at the end of July; and when the news of the decrees of April 27 arrived at Bourbon, this assembly declared them rendered by incompetent authority, and drew up a plan to be submitted to the mother country, which, without opposing the emancipation of the slaves, demanded, — 1st, the postponement of the measure, in order to give time to gather in the harvests, and organize schools, hospitals, and penal labor; 2d, the preliminary re-establishment of the Colonial Assembly; 3d, the formation of a National Guard and Municipal Councils before emancipation; 4th, indemnity. The same unanimity appeared in the public square at St. Pierre, where in August, an imprudent speech having exasperated the negroes, five thousand inhabitants assembled on the instant to watch over the maintenance of order.

To guard against the diminution of labor, the Governor resolved to abrogate the order given March 6, 1839, to prohibit the future immigration of Indians, but he did not consider himself obliged to promulgate prematurely the abolition of slavery, though authorized to do so by a despatch dated May 7; and when his successor arrived, (October 13), the colony was at peace, and labor was scarcely anywhere interrupted.

The Commissioner-General, M. Sarda-Garriga, published the decrees of emancipation, October 18, in a solemn audience of the court. He had the good sense to close the clubs, to surround himself with enlightened counsels, and to prescribe, by a provident order, that, before the 20th of December, the end of the delay accorded by the decrees, every slave should hire himself to labor for two years on a sugar plantation, or for one year as a domestic, under penalty of being regarded and punished as a vagrant.

Thanks to these measures, followed by an order to establish penal works,* with the approbation of the planters, and under the control of the former Governor and principal functionaries, the transition was easier than had been hoped. The proclamation of the final liberation of the slaves, December 20,† was a day of rejoicing. The commissioner and commandant of the naval station both affirmed, at the end of the month, that the year would end without disorder, almost without loss.

The elections which followed created little agitation, since few attended them. Of 36,000 registered names, there were but 5,200 voters.

The best proof of the speedy return of tranquillity, and even of labor, despite the real losses and days of anxiety,

* Order of December 23, 1848, maintained in force by the order of September 18, 1852, as well as another order of May 24, 1849, which constituted a special syndic in each commune to watch over and regulate the interests of the hired laborers.

† *Moniteur*, April 6, 1849.

are found in the statistics of productions. Idleness, the first form of the independence of poor devils to whom the right of doing nothing was the natural synonyme of freedom, since servitude had been the duty of doing too much, the lack of capital, the uneasiness born of twofold political and social transformation, weighed upon production so as to make the most important, that of sugar, fall from 24,000,000 kilogrammes, in 1847, to 21,700,000 kilogrammes, in 1848; but in 1849, the first year of freedom, the amount had already increased to 23,660,000 kilogrammes; and in 1850, had it not been for the terrible hurricane of the 1st of March, the consequences of which were severe enough to call from the mother country an aid of 100,000 francs, it would have equalled the amount of 1847, of which it only fell short 500,000 kilogrammes, and which it exceeded in 1851, when the production amounted to 26,000,000 kilogrammes.

These results, due certainly, as was indicated at the beginning by the Commissioner-General,* to the good spirit of both classes, should be also attributed to the facility of procuring labor possessed by the colony. More than twenty thousand East Indians and some hundred Africans were introduced during the first years; an addition unfavorable to good order, morals, and even to wealth,—since the Coolies kept their wages to carry back to their own country, instead of settling in the colony like the negroes,—but most valuable in making up for the desertion of the large plantations.

As in 1794, so in 1848, did the Isle of Bourbon find means of passing through the evil days better than any of the rest of our colonies; an unheard-of success, if we reflect on the great number of blacks assembled on their native soil with the few whites far distant from their country, and if we recall the sinister predictions which scarcely

* Address of December 20, 1848.

a year before announced violence and ruin. We shall have the pleasure of seeing these prophecies contradicted in detail on every point.

§ 4. Guiana.

At Guiana, emancipation might easily have caused general disorganization. An immense territory, covered in part with thick forests, offered to the negroes the temptation of an easy flight and an impenetrable refuge, and, according to their tastes, the choice between a vagrant life and squatting on lands. Great numbers of negroes, who had already thus regained their independence, incited them by their example. With few exceptions, the planters were not rich in this colony, always languishing, although it had cost the mother country over 50,000,000 francs* from 1817 to 1848. The negroes could not, therefore, be restrained by interest any more than by fear, for there were 14,000 slaves to 6,000 whites.† The garrison had been diminished since 1814. The Governor, Captain Pariset of the Marine, vainly asked that it should be filled up, and also that the clergy should be increased. "For ten priests," wrote he, "are worth more to good order than two companies of infantry."

In this little disarmed and suffering community fell the news of the Revolution of 1848, brought in the beginning of May by an American schooner. A wise and firm proclamation from the Governor enjoined patience. The colportage of an address to the government produced a little agi-

* Exact sum:	Expenses of the Colony, . . .	49,386,000 fr.
	Flotilla, ...	3,300,000
		51,686,000 fr.

† Statistics of the census of 1844: — Freemen, 5,902: 25 officials, 726 soldiers (of whom 116 were Africans), 21 gendarmes, 21 Sisters of St. Joseph, 8 lepers. Slaves, 18,988; of whom 10,935 belonged to white, and 3,068 to colored owners, and 525 to the domain, and 117 were lepers.

tation at the end of the month. Notwithstanding, when M. Pariset, whom the Provisional Government had the wisdom to maintain in office, proclaimed, on the 10th of June, that all slaves would be free on the 10th of August, this important measure occasioned no disturbance, although August was precisely the beginning of the harvest, and though nothing was said to the colonists about indemnity. At the end of July, the events in Martinico were known, but this did not seriously affect tranquillity, neither did a protest from the quarter of Approuague, subscribed by several functionaries, nor the opening of clubs and the manœuvres of dangerous mulattoes.

If order did not suffer, it was impossible that it should have been the same with labor. One intelligent and resolute planter * emancipated his slaves directly, without awaiting the expiration of the two months' delay, and agreed with them for immediate wages. But, in general, inconstancy, the love of small estates, the novelty of independence, and the incitement of the republican reunions, estranged the negroes from labor. The letting of the colonial lands for a part of their produce was vainly essayed; the blacks distrusted any system which did not secure them the fruits of their labor day by day. The cantonal juries did not succeed. A commission appointed by the Governor for the regulation of tasks had more success. But in result (and we must in truth be astonished that so many causes united produced no more injury) the harvest of 1848 produced but one half the harvest of 1847. It is true that prices rose from 17 to 24 francs per 50 kilogrammes. The price of annotta increased still more, rising from 80 c. to 2 fr. 50 c. per kilogramme; so that the 215,000 kilogrammes produced in 1849 brought more than the 521,000 produced in 1846. Despite this rise in prices, the enormous decrease in natural products, and consequently in the

* M. Roumy.

value of property, was calculated to dismay the colonists. Never had Guiana been, never could it be, an important sugar colony. The clayey and marshy lands of the sugar plantations give a fine cane, but inferior sugar. Coffee, nearly abandoned in the Antilles, might prosper there, as well as cocoa, spices, and oil-bearing seeds. But how produce them without hands, without money, and without courage. If a great number of blacks returned to Indian life by installing themselves on bits of ground in the uplands, they were not led there merely by an instinct of vagrant independence. Averse to working the plantations on shares, or to hiring the colonial lands for a part of their produce, the tardy results of which inspired them with a natural distrust, they wished to labor only for wages, and their former masters had not capital wherewith to pay them. Now, in the economical position in which this unhappy colony found itself placed, without wages there was no labor; without labor, no revenues; without revenues, no purchases, no importations, no ships in the harbor; and from day to day the fear of a veritable famine, thoroughly abandoned lands, sterile works, ruined machinery, and countermanded shipments, produced such discouragement in the public mind, that leading men were seen proposing to cede Guiana to the United States.

There was no need of elections to complete this uneasiness; the agitation might be increased by want, and this occasion for the negroes to know and compute their strength was by no means reassuring. They passed off, however, without disturbance, and added another proof to the demonstration, furnished by these long months of crisis, of the gentleness of these people, who lacked labor much more than labor lacked them.

Affairs must be very flourishing in France for Guiana to be prosperous; the slightest embarrassment of the few houses that carry on the traffic with this distant country extinguishes all its activity. Even though the revolution of February had not carried emancipation there, it would indubitably have caused its ruin; and here again, it is not the abolition of slavery, but the abolition of commerce, which should be justly accused of an injury which could only be remedied by directing capital thither. Convicts were sent there instead. Since the decree of December 8, 1851, Guiana has completely changed character, and, instead of a commercial, become a penal colony.

CHAPTER VI.

LAWS.

WHILE these events were passing in the colonies, and to remedy the sufferings which the transitory and violent state of affairs — created, not by emancipation, but by revolution, less by the decrees than the agents of the Provisional Government — had drawn upon our possessions, the Minister of the Marine and Colonies, Admiral Romain-Desfossés, proposed to the President of the Republic, November 22, 1849, the appointment of a new colonial commission, the presidency of which, by a choice as just as intelligent, was confided to the Duc de Broglie. This was composed of MM. H. Passy, de Tracy, and Isambert, ancient and devoted friends of emancipation and the colonies. Vice-Admiral Cecil and Vice-Admiral Lainé represented in it the navy; MM. de Laussat, de Lancastel, Fournier, Hubert-Delisle, Sully-Brunet, Demoly, Ancel, and Barbaroux, the ports and colonies; and M. Le Pelletier Saint-Remy was secretary.

The statement presented by the Colonial Director, M. Mestro, called to sustain under a more regular régime the same principles which he had so firmly sustained before the commission of 1848, did not exaggerate the sufferings of the colonies.

"The planters," said one of the members,* "need laws for their protection; the negroes, yielding to a very explicable impulse, at the first moment almost simultaneously

* M. de Laussat, *Procès-verbaux*, pp. 6, 18.

discarded labor. But they have returned by degrees to the culture of the soil; . . . . . they are at work. Let property be protected, let labor be made active, and colonial society will settle down on a solid basis. . . . . . A second example will not, perhaps, be found in the world of this simultaneous concession of civil and political rights to a population which had been deprived of them traditionally by slavery. There is reason to be astonished that such daring should not have involved more disasters. We have not dared do the same thing in Africa, although the Arabs are far superior in civilization to the negroes."

Another member* added: "It may be maintained that the planters have neither been the losers by the emancipation of the negroes, nor by universal suffrage; without them, they would have found themselves face to face with the mulattoes, who are much more hostile to them. In the colonies, as in France, the best elections have been in the rural districts."

Notwithstanding, if material order, despite local excesses, was not profoundly disturbed, legal order appeared wholly insufficient, and it was above all to the establishment of this that the commission had to give their attention.

From its first steps are found the delays of the old parliamentary spirit, with its honorable scruples and interminable objections. Before everything, the commission investigated its own competency. Article 109 of the Constitution declared that the colonies were ruled by particular laws, until a special law placed them under the régime of the Constitution itself. It was very clear that the colonial territory was completely French, that all the inhabitants were free and equal, and that no particular law could derogate from these two primordial principles, but that, concerning all besides, special regulations might be introduced into

* M. de Tracy, *Ibid.* p. 29.

the colonial régime. Now five points appeared to the Commission to demand, before all, an urgent examination: —

The régime of the press,
The legislative and organic régime,
The judicial organization,
The repression of vagrancy,
The immigration of new laborers.

In other words, government, repression, and labor. The Provisional Government had, indeed, seriously compromised these three highest interests of every regular community. The elections to the Assembly were made, and for a long period. There was no thought of taking from the colonies the right of representation. Completely assimilated to the natives by the ordinance of 1642, the colonists, on the opening of the States-General in 1787, had attributed to themselves the right to send deputies; they were received in 1789, and thenceforth in all the great assemblies of the Revolution. The Empire had taken away their franchises, as well as those of France. If the Restoration and the Charter of 1830 had not restored them, they at least had endowed the colonies with local legislatures, and the celebrated Commission of 1840 had proposed to restore them the right of representation which 1848 returned to them so abruptly and so amply. They had not made a bad use of it; but could it be admitted without fear that universal suffrage should be exercised for the municipal and general councils, and that the negroes, fresh from the lash, should be admitted to the ballot-box without transition?

Could it be tolerated, above all, that, in the midst of a community exposed to civil war, an unbridled press should be let loose, sustained by the lowest journalists, and held in little restraint by ignorant, prejudiced, or trembling juries? Was it possible to perpetuate the decree of May 2, 1848, which, fully assimilating the colonies to the mother country, had abolished the system of censorship and preliminary authorization maintained in the Antilles by the ordinance of February, 1847, in Bourbon by that of August 21, 1825, in Guiana by that of August 27, 1828, and had thus hurled the freedom of the press on small communities where it was either an illusion or a peril;—an illusion, where there were scarcely any readers, writers, or printers, so that a monopoly was established by the impossibility of competition; a danger, on account of the antagonism of religions, colors, opinions, and feuds? Could the offences committed by the press be left to jurors or *assessors*, when the decree of May 2 declared eligible as assessors all citizens eligible to the National Assembly,—that is, in the terms of the decree of March 5, 1848, all individuals, even those *not knowing how to read and write French?* *

The Commission voted the promulgation in the colonies of the repressive laws of August 11, 1848, and July 27, 1849; it exacted a security of from 5,000 to 10,000 francs, according as the journal were weekly or daily, payable in specie; it interdicted the introduction into the colonies of writings and periodicals condemned or seized in the mother country, and prescribed the preliminary deposition of writings relative to the colonies; it authorized the provisional suspension, by the Governors, of a prosecuted journal, and its suspension for six months at most, or interdiction by the Court of Misdemeanor; it established special penalties for the provocation or re-establishment of slavery, for the incitement of hatred between the former classes, and for public insult to the Governor; it remitted the cognizance of offences and crimes of the press to the Court of Appeal of each colony, composed of the president and the six most ancient magistrates, judging without the assistance of the jury, and on direct citation, without the medium of the chamber of indictment.

* Report of M. Isambert to the Commission, p. 50.

This plan, submitted to the Assembly, became a law, May 7, 1850.

The Assembly deemed it best to leave to the Court of Misdemeanor the cognizance of the offences of the press, and to suspend the institution of the Court of Magistracy, just mentioned, until the complete organization of courts of justice in the colonies.

This important organization occupied no less than twenty-five sittings of the Commission. Dating back to 1827, the ancient régime differed from the régime of the mother country in four principal points : —

1. The removability of the judicial magistracy. In a country where the firmness of justice is the sole bulwark of peace, removable, the magistracy is not respected ; immovable, it might, by taking sides, paralyze all repression. It was decided, as a mean term, that the judges' seal might be changed, but not revoked, except by the advice of a standing commission of two Counsellors of State and three Counsellors of the Court of Cassation, appointed by their respective bodies for five years.

2. Tribunals of the first instance, composed of a single judge.

3. The absence of the first degree of jurisdiction in cases of misdemeanor.

4. Criminal judgments by assessors joined with judges.

The colonial courts were assimilated on all these points to the courts of the mother country, except in the institution of the jury, which it was not dared establish.

Another chapter, devoted to labor and immigration, will recount the labors of the Commission concerning this delicate subject.

But before these labors were finished, before the deliberated bills were transformed into laws, the change of the government and the abrupt ending of the powers of the Assembly interrupted the sittings of the Commission.

Thus twice, in 1840 and 1850, the same men had the chagrin of seeing revolutions thwart their efforts and ravish from their name the honor of being united to useful reforms ; yet their pains were not without results. Not only was a moral effect produced, for during the sittings of the Commission the colonies regained confidence, knowing their interests in intelligent, liberal, and firm hands ; but, furthermore, the Commission of 1849, like that of 1850, in some sort brought together and prepared the materials of the colonial legislature ; its plans have already been of service, and when it is wished to complete the work, it will always be necessary to have recourse to them.

The law of May 7, 1850, has been abrogated by a decree of February 20, 1852, which has placed the press again within the discretionary powers of the Governors, conformably to the ordinances of the Revolution ; but the necessity of certain guaranties, especially concerning cases of libel, has led to the re-establishment, by another decree of April 30, 1852, of the competence instituted by the law of May 7.

As to the twenty-seven decrees and orders of 1848, they were not long-lived.

The *ninth*, on savings banks ; the *tenth*, on a new apportionment of taxation ; the *seventeenth*, on marine recruital and registration ; the *second*, on charities ; and the *third*, on schools,—have never been executed, or else have been replaced by measures adopted by the Governors.

The *fourth*, relative to *cantonal juries*, was abrogated by Article 11 of the decree of February 13, 1852, on bound labor, which also replaced the *seventh* decree, on vagrancy, and the *eighth*, which instituted a system of penal labor.

The *fifth* and *sixth*, on *national works*, have been nullified by the energetic measure which licensed them in France.

The *eleventh*, which established a festival of labor, several times solemnized, has fallen into desuetude.

The *twelfth*, which suppressed the colonial and general councils and the functions of delegates, useless since the Constitution had admitted the colonies to the national representation, was abrogated by the Constitution of 1852, which no longer admits them, as well as by the *Instruction* for elections, rendered in execution of the decree of March 5, 1848.

The *thirteenth* decree, on forced expropriation, is still in vigor, but is limited to giving effect to the bill under discussion by the Chamber of Peers at the time of the Revolution of February.

The *fifteenth*, on the powers of the Commissioners-General, ended with their mission.

The *sixteenth*, on the press, was replaced by the statute of May 7, 1850.

There remains, therefore, of the legislative edifice of 1848, but a single, yet indestructible stone, — the immortal decree * which forever abolishes slavery, a civil law which is only the final promulgation of the natural law.

* It again appeared necessary to abrogate, in part, Article 8 of this decree, thus conceived: —

" In future, *even in foreign countries*, it is interdicted all Frenchmen to hold, buy, or sell slaves, or to participate, directly or indirectly, in any traffic or profit of this kind. Any infraction of these prohibitions will involve the loss of *the quality of French citizen*.

"Nevertheless, Frenchmen subject to these prohibitions at the moment of the promulgation of the present decree shall have a *delay of three years* in which to conform to them. Those who shall become possessors of slaves in foreign countries by *inheritance*, *gift*, or *marriage*, shall, *under the same penalty*, emancipate or alienate them *in the same length of time*, dating from the day when their possession shall have commenced."

The English law (George IV., June 24, 1834) subjects Englishmen who are *voluntarily* holders of slaves to a fine of £100 per slave, with seizure, but tolerates *involuntary* possession. (Art. 67.)

More logical and more moral, the French law declared that it would no longer recognize a Frenchman in a slaveholder. The penalty of *denationalization* has been maintained against the buyer or seller of slaves.

But, taking into consideration the embarrassing position of Frenchmen, numbering, it is said, about 20,000, settled in a slave country, and often subjected by the decree to the alternative of impracticable emancipation, a loss without

This solemn declaration has been repeated by the Senatus Consultum, May 3, 1854, an act which is the constitution of the colonies, and the framing of which was confided to the Senate by Article 27 of the Constitution of 1852.

By the terms of this Senatus Consultum, the Senate and the Emperor, in a Council of State, share the legislative power of the colonies. The latter send to France three salaried delegates, who compose, with four members appointed by the government, a committee,* presided over by the Minister of the Marine, and purely consultative. General Councils assist the Governors in the establishment of taxes and the use of revenues, and have power to emit suffrages, like the General Councils of our departments.

The Governors exercise ordinary and extraordinary powers, under the direct authority of the Minister of the Marine. There is no longer a Colonial Council. There are no longer deputies. There is no longer a military commandant.

In short, the colonies are ruled on the one hand by the great ordinances of the Restoration, and on the other by the Senatus Consultum of 1854.† The same administration as before 1830, and a more concentrated power than afterwards, — such is the result of these political revolutions.

indemnity, and the forfeiture of the title of Frenchmen, the Legislative Assembly accorded ten years for emancipation.

This delay was on the point of expiring, when another statute, May, 1858, definitively excepted from the application of the decree of 1848, French slave-owners whose possession had been anterior to this decree, or had resulted from inheritance, donation, or marriage.

Thus a Frenchman may hold slaves in a foreign country, but can neither buy nor sell them, — a singular arrangement, as impracticable as Art. 8 of the decree of 1848, but much less moral. The absolute principle hampered the practice, neither more nor less, and did more honor to the French law.

* Decree of July 29, 1854.

† Other laws have been especially designed to extend to the colonies the civil state, the Code of Commerce, the civil legislature, and the civil and criminal procedure of the mother country. (Statutes of Dec. 6 and 7, 1850, decrees of Jan. 22, 1852, Jan. 15, 1853, etc.)

As to the social revolution which set free the slaves, what exceptional or new laws has it exacted? None! Of the preparatory laws of the Monarchy of July, the seventeen decrees of the Republic of February, the measures prepared by the Commission of 1840, the plans elaborated by the Commission of 1849, nothing remains.

We may be permitted to deplore the unfruitfulness of so much pains; from the special stand-point I occupy, I cannot complain of it.

For it had been thought that the so-much-dreaded act of the abolition of slavery could not be accomplished without a complete alteration of the laws, — without being preceded, accompanied, and followed by infinite precautions, combinations, and guaranties, prepared with consummate art and multiplied cares; events have taken it upon themselves to annul or to crush all legislative measures, and things have happened, through a thousand vicissitudes, in a manner to prove that a single and only law was necessary, — the law thus couched: *Slavery is abolished.*

CHAPTER VII.

MILITARY FORCE.

Respect for the laws is a sentiment belonging to civilized communities; the fear of force is the only curb of imperfectly developed nations. We readily conceive, therefore, that the government would not have sent laws to the newly freed men which they would not have understood, but suppose that it sent them gendarmes instead. Emancipation has not exacted exceptional laws, but perhaps it has exacted the use of exceptional force, perhaps security is only the fragile result of continued intimidation.

In the report of 1840, to which it is necessary constantly to revert, M. de Broglie inquires what force would be demanded for the maintenance of order in each colony when emancipation should be proclaimed, after a slow preparation; he had no doubt that this great event would necessitate the increase of the garrisons. What would he have demanded, then, could he have foreseen that it would be the immediate result of a revolution?

Let us compare the effective force of the garrisons in 1840 with that which figures in the budget of 1861.*

At Martinico, there were, in 1840, 3,026 men, viz.: —

Troops of the line	2,512
Gendarmes	148
Workmen	366
Total	3,026

* These figures do not include the garrisons of ports, the sanitary service, and the militia.

The Commission demanded: * —

500 gendarmes,
500 mountain chasseurs.

In 1860, the garrison was only 1,384 men,† viz.: —

8 companies of infantry, 115 men each, and their staff	964
Mounted gendarmes	142
Gendarmes on foot	24
2 companies of artillery	204
Workmen	50
Total	1,384

At Guadaloupe, there were, in 1840, 2,912 men, viz.: —

1 regiment of infantry	2,512
1 company of gendarmery	148
2 companies, artillery and workmen	252
Total	2,912

The Commission ‡ demanded a foot company of gendarmes, and a third company of artillery.

The budget of 1861 § establishes the effective force at 1,384 men, as at Martinico, viz.: —

Line	964
Gendarmes	166
Artillery and workmen	254
Total	1,384

To which are added 150 native troops.

At Guiana, there were, in 1840, 985 men, viz.: —

1 battalion of infantry and one black company	868
½ company of artillery and workmen	67
½ company of gendarmery	50
Total	985

The Commission of 1840 found this garrison, recently augmented, sufficient.

* P. 78. † Budget, p. 106. ‡ Report, p. 76. § Budget, p. 111.

In 1860, the garrison, including that of the penitentiary, which holds 4,000 convicts, was 1,121 men, viz.: —

Infantry and negroes	868
Artillery	76
Gendarmes	177
Total	1,121

At Bourbon, the garrison, in 1840, was 1,719 men, viz.: —

12 companies of infantry	1,412
1½ companies of artillery	156
½ company of workmen	51
1 company of mounted gendarmes	100
Total	1,719

The Commission was also satisfied with this garrison, doubled in the preceding two years.

In 1860, it was composed only of 691 men, viz.: —

4 companies of infantry	480
1 company of artillery	71
1 detachment of workmen	34
Gendarmes	106
Total	691

M. de Broglie, in estimating at 3,326,000 francs the first expense necessary to this augmentation of the armed force, adds these significant words * : —

"This sum does not constitute an expense suited to emancipation; it is necessary to augment the armed force in any hypothesis; the maintenance of slavery will henceforth exact at least as many precautions as the establishment of freedom."

He was right. 8,642 soldiers were not sufficient to guard 249,408 slaves, dispersed among 120,472 masters or freedmen. 4,791 soldiers hold in peace 400,000 freemen.

* Report, p. 79.

CHAPTER VIII.

COURTS OF JUSTICE.

If the law be not exceptional, if the force be not augmented, perhaps repression has been exorbitant, and we shall find in the severity of the tribunals the explanation of the peace.

The organization of the courts of justice, which inspired so much distrust in the friends of liberty before 1848,* and so much uneasiness in the friends of order after 1848, has been modified only by the decrees of August 9 and 16, 1854.

The justices of the peace, whose increase was foreseen and solicited by the Commission of 1840, in view of the numerous difficulties of detail which emancipation would excite and bring before their conciliating and prompt authority, — the justices of the peace have been scarcely increased in number.

There were at Martinico 4 justices of the peace for 26 communes ;† the Commission demanded 26 ; ‡ in the budget of 1861, 8 are found.

At Guadaloupe, 6 justices of the peace for 24 communes, in 1840 ; the Commission proposed 24 ; there are 10.

At Guiana, 3 for 14 communes ; the Commission demanded 14 ; there are 7.§

At Bourbon, 6 for 14 communes ; the Commission demanded 14 ; there are 8.

* See Schoelcher, 1847, Tom. II. p. 146.

† See the *procès-verbaux* of the Commission of 1849, Part II. Report of M. Isambert, p. 292, and Discussions.

‡ Report, pp. 84, 85.

§ Budget, p. 64.

Have these 33 tribunals of peace, the 16 tribunals of first instance, and the 4 Courts of Appeals been more busy in condemning since 1848 than before it?

This is somewhat difficult to ascertain, as the Marine Department published in 1845 and 1846 the report of the administration of colonial justice for the years 1837, 1838, and 1839; in 1855 it published the reports for 1850, 1851, and 1852; but the blank from 1839 to 1849 has not been filled up, and since 1852 no report has been published.

Nevertheless, the comparison between the years 1837–1839 and 1850–1852 is not without interest; perhaps even the parallel between the years nearer and more distant from emancipation would be less instructive. In fact, 1846 and 1847 were signalized by suits in which the partiality of the magistrates towards the masters was signalized as scandalous, even in the Chambers. "I am ashamed to say," exclaimed M. Jules de Lasteyrie, in the meeting of May 7, 1847, "that there is no wish to suppress crime in the colonies."*

M. Ternaux-Compans added: "The Minister spends his life in hoping and regretting. He always hopes that some one will execute his orders, then comes to tell us that he regrets that they have not been executed."

"We are assured," said M. Dupin a few days before, "that care will be taken that it shall be different, if such facts happen again. Are none but second offences punished, then, in the colonies? The report declares that justice is incomplete in the colonies. Where there is not complete justice, there is no justice." The Court of Cassation admitted thirteen appeals at once against thirty decisions of the Colonial Courts, on questions of emancipation, April 27, 1847. The Chamber of Deputies refused the appropriation demanded to increase the *personnel* of the public Ministry, May 7, 1847. M. Guizot, Minister of the Marine *pro*

* Report on the Administration of Colonial Justice, 1855, p 6.

tem., presented a bill of reform in the composition of the Colonial Courts of Assizes, May 21, 1847.

It will be understood, therefore, that we do not wish to take as a standard of comparison years wherein justice deserved such reproaches.

On the other hand, 1848 and 1849 were probably too much or too little repressive ; — too much, where the courts were disorganized or intimidated ; too little, where they were forced to intimidate in turn, by making examples or by giving place to councils of war.

There are, in short, good reasons, therefore, for being contented with the published documents, and comparing regular years, like 1837 – 1839, with the years 1850 – 1853, which may be regarded as the beginning of the normal existence of the new society.

We will endeavor to answer these two questions : —

1. Is colonial society afflicted by more crimes and misdemeanors since the abolition of slavery than before it ?

2. Is colonial society dishonored by more crimes and misdemeanors than French society ?

I. It must be remembered, that before 1848 the misdemeanors of the slaves were rarely carried before the courts ; each plantation had its penal law, its judge, and its executioners. One thing was lacking in these tribunals, judging with closed doors, — the defence. Ordinances intervened to mitigate the application of the lash and other corporal punishments, but did not suppress them. The lash was the last article in that odious series of self-evident axioms which was, as it were, the second *credo* of all slaveholders, even the best, — sugar is necessary to man, the slave to sugar, the lash to the slave.

We must expect, therefore, to see an enormous increase in the number of crimes carried before the courts, and of which they were not before cognizant.

Distrust, fears, and rancors must also, during the first

years, have inevitably increased this number, especially that of complaints, official reports, and denunciations, which must be carefully distinguished from the number of condemnations.

In fact, the number of complaints in 1837 – 1839 was 8,099.

We have the statistics for 1845 – 1847 ; in these years of feeble repression, it was 12,000.

In 1850 – 1852 it amounted to 14,777.

The number of indictments likewise rose from 1 in 249 inhabitants to 1 in 186.

But, of 14,000 cases, more than half, about 7,000, were classed by the parquets as not giving rise to prosecutions, either because the facts were not serious enough or not sufficiently proved, because they constituted neither crime nor offence, or because the criminals remained unknown.*

Of less than 4,000 cases brought in the three years before the Chambers of Indictment, there were nearly 800 decisions of non-jurisdiction, or about 20 per cent ; a high figure, yet inferior to that of 1837 – 1839, which had been 40 per cent.

1682 cases were referred to the Court of Misdemeanors ; 1427 only were brought before the Court of Assizes, which thus received exactly one tenth of the complaints and denunciations.

Among the crimes prosecuted are found fraudulent bankruptcies, forgeries, embezzlement of the public funds, counterfeiting of money, corruption of officials, numerous rapes and attempted violations, — crimes which evidently are not all imputable to the former slaves, — and armed assaults, rebellion, etc., which were the result of political troubles.

But what is characteristic is the proportion of the number of crimes against the person, compared with that of crimes against property.

In 1837 – 1839, 47 per cent of the indictments were for

* Report, pp. 22, 23.

crimes *against the person*; in 1850 – 1852, there were but 21 per cent. In the first period, on the contrary, but 53 per cent of the indictments were for crimes *against property*, which rose to 79 per cent in the second; and almost all of these crimes were thefts. Thus there was less hatred, less revenge, after than during slavery, — a great result, — while there were more thefts, at least more prosecutions for theft; for every one knows how frequent were larcenies under the system of slavery, but the lash took satisfaction for them. Theft is not a result of emancipation; it is a habit acquired in slavery. When one has nothing of his own, he must necessarily take that which is another's. One only respects property when he has the enjoyment or hope of it. The privation of freedom makes murderers; the privation of property makes thieves.

"The increase in the number of indictments of all kinds," says the Minister in his report, "arises from the fact that a host of misdeeds which, before the abolition of slavery, found, for the most part, disciplinary and purely arbitrary repression within the plantations, have since come before the Courts of Assizes. . . . . . Almost all of these are thefts committed by the former slaves. . . . . . This frequency of theft needs to be repressed; yet the penal legislation should be mitigated,* for it is due to justice and humanity not to apply too severe penalties to deeds which lose their gravity by reason of the backward state of morality of the social class to which the delinquents belong." †

Another grievance against slavery, — not only had it encouraged theft, but it had not moralized the slave. Despite so many fine promises and wise regulations, instruction went on diminishing from day to day. In 1837 – 1839, 75 per cent of the accused could not read; in 1850 – 1852, 90 per cent.

* This took place at Guiana, by a decree, Aug. 16, 1854.

† Report, p. 26.

Of 2,000 accused, about one fourth were acquitted, and, of the 1,500 found guilty, more than 1,000 were sentenced only to penalties for misdemeanor.

The number of cases carried before the Courts of Misdemeanor, police courts, and justices of the peace, increased in a larger proportion than that of cases brought before the Court of Assizes. "This increase," says the Minister,* "arises, as with crimes, from the twofold circumstance, that, on one hand, the measure of emancipation was in the beginning the occasion of excesses appearing in the form of vagrancy or misdemeanors, to those to whom it was applied, and, on the other, the cognizance of these deeds, which, before emancipation, belonged to the disciplinary power of the plantation, has since been necessarily brought within the ordinary penal jurisdiction."

It must be added, that the statute on vagrancy, and the local laws on *livrets*,† disciplinary works, etc., have given rise to a host of special misdemeanors, unknown during the period of 1837 – 1839.

In short, since 1852, the reports of the criminal courts establish, that, if the number of prosecutions has increased, it is rather on account of the suppression of the lash than of the increase of crimes and misdemeanors ; there is more theft, but the courts are less surprised at it than at the ignorance in which the masters had left their slaves ; there is less murder, and freedom has disarmed vengeance.

The first effervescence of emancipation turned many heads, but they are now calmed again ; there is not one second offence in a hundred among crimes, not even one in a hundred among misdemeanors.‡

* Report, p. 24.

† Small books, carried by the workmen, containing an ordinary passport, with the date of entering and leaving the places where they work, and subject to the inspection of the police.

‡ Report, p. 34.

In the nomenclature of crimes and misdemeanors, there is not a single coalition to raise wages.

In the nomenclature of commercial cases, there are one, two, or three bankruptcies a year in each colony.

I repeat that the statistics since 1852 have not been published. Statements are contained in the reports or opening addresses of the Procureurs-General. These documents comprise useful information, but such as we must despair of presenting in a methodical manner; they are not drawn up in a uniform style, neither do they all embrace the same periods. Moreover, since 1854, the law has extended the competence of courts of the first instance and justices of the peace. From this result changes in figures which do not correspond to changes in facts.

It was at this time, too, that immigration commenced in the Antilles. Now all admit that the presence of immigrants has increased crimes, especially murders, in a deplorable manner.

However this may be, I read in the reports of the Isle of Bourbon, that the gendarmery effected 1,868 arrests in 1854, 1,782 only in 1859; and of this number official reports point out: —

In 1854,	579 vagrants;	635	in 1856.
"	290 without *livrets;*	124	"
"	5 refusing to labor;	34	"

These figures, which are nearly the same, are not, assuredly, excessive.

At Guadaloupe, I read in the reports of 1853–1856, that the number of complaints diminished until 1854, then increased, then diminished anew; that crimes against property increased; that crimes against the person diminished; that the number of civil and commercial suits increased, — a progress which attests the resumption of activity. At Martinico, the same facts are more methodically presented.

Justices' Courts.		Courts of the First Instance.		Number of Complaints.	
Years.	Cases.	Civil Suits.	Commercial Suits.	Court of Assizes.	Tribunals.
1852	1486	999	267	755	1206
1853	1692	780	467	653	1046
1854	2294	895	473	529	1169
1855	3446	736	503	241	1470
1856	2771	687	419	203	1442
1857	2227	559	464	188	1424

Years.	Crimes sentenced by the Court of Assizes.	
	Against the Person.	Against Property.
1852	31	87
1853	21	87
1854	29	89
1855	30	88
1856	21	75
1857	27	69

Always the same result, — diminution till 1854 ; then, in consequence of a more lively impulse given to prosecutions, a change of cognizances, and the presence of immigrants, increase till 1854, attaining its maximum in 1855, then diminution.

Always an enormous excess of crime against property over crime against the person, always an enormous proportion of illiterate criminals, — nine tenths at Guadaloupe, four fifths at Martinico, and among women, the whole.

II. If now, making use only of the figures published officially in 1855, we compare them with the figures of the last *General Statistics of Criminality in France for* 1856, we ascertain that theft is not a misdemeanor reserved to the colonies. In France, from 1826 to 1850, the number of *qualified* thefts, thanks to the indulgence of the magistrates, diminished, but that of *simple* thefts *tripled.* Theft grows with the progress of wealth and covetousness, and decreases with the progress of morality and instruction. The crimes against the person brought before the Court of Assizes in France increased 31 per cent, while the population increased only 12 per cent; the crimes against property diminished 16 per cent, — inversely to the colonies. Arsons and attempts at violation increased more than in the colonies. There was 1 prisoner held for misdemeanor in 171 inhabitants; in the colonies, only 1 in 186.

But in the colonies, 90 per cent of the accused were illiterate; in France, 55 per cent only.

In short, if emancipation has increased the number of misdemeanors and crimes, it is rather in appearance than in reality, and because the regular course of justice has taken the place of repression; but even the number revealed by the statistics goes on decreasing or remains nearly stationary; it is proportionally inferior to that of misdemeanors and crimes in France, and colonial society, on the morrow of an unheard-of transformation, which has set at liberty propensities, revenges, and cupidities, sleeps more tranquilly than the civilized population of the mother country.

The crimes still committed are individual faults; slavery was a social crime. The latter, at least, exists no longer.

It is difficult to dispute what passes in the streets in broad daylight. It will therefore be willingly admitted, I hope, that freedom is not responsible for the disorders of 1848 and 1849, and that since this time it has exacted, for the maintenance of tranquillity in the colonies, no exceptional law, no extraordinary force, no abnormal repression.

Yes, reply the colonists, we are not massacred, but we are ruined. The negroes do not pillage us, but they do not work. We have been able to save ourselves only by *indemnity*, a large *reduction* of duty on sugars, coffees, &c., and a costly *immigration*, and, despite these measures, our ancient prosperity has forever vanished; we are afflicted by continual crises; we lack capital, labor, and credit.

We will take up each one of these points: —

1. Indemnity;
2. Production and commerce;
3. The question of sugars;
4. Labor and immigration.

CHAPTER IX.

INDEMNITY.

To hear the colonists who demanded indemnity, they were expropriated; they should have been paid, not only the value of their property, but a sum for the damage caused the property of the soil by this dispossession of implements. If these pretensions had been listened to, it would have been necessary to repurchase the colonies in full.

But the slave is not property, and it is precisely for this that he is freed; emancipation is not the deprivation of the right of property, it is the negation of it.

If we carried out these principles to their extent, it is to the slave that indemnity would be due, as he has been deprived violently of the fruit of his labor. The slave-trade having been abolished by law in 1848, it would only have been necessary to institute a strict search into the origin of all the slaves held in 1848,* to declare a great number of the masters in the very act of criminal possession.

This pretended property does not rest on the principles of veritable property; neither has it the essential characteristics thereof. The right of property is absolute, perpetual, indefinite, incommutable; the possession of slaves implies duties, conditions, variations, no guaranty of duration.†

In fine, veritable property is founded on natural right. The work of the law, slavery may be destroyed by the law. The government of Denmark, when it proclaimed emancipa-

* This proposition was made in the Commission of 1848. *Procès-verbaux*, p. 65.

† Report of M. de Broglie, pp. 263 – 265.

tion, set out from the principle that every state has a right to modify the conditions which it imposes on commerce, arts, and manufactures, and even the conditions of property, when they are not in harmony with morality and the general good.* Without going so far as to apply this doctrine to the right of property, since it is anterior and superior to the law, it is just to extend it to exceptional kinds of property, which are the work of the law, as charges and offices, monopolies resulting from a tariff, — in fine, as slavery, a strange fiction which the state has created, an exorbitant favor which the state has conceded.† This fiction, this favor, it has the power to destroy, since it has made them ; it has the right, since it has the duty.

The right to indemnity, therefore, is in no wise of the same order as the right to freedom ; the second is claimed by nature, the first is sustained only by considerations of equity.

If slavery be not a *legitimate* fact, it is at least a *legal* fact. The law has known, authorized, encouraged it. The possessor is such in good faith, his error has been caused by the error of the legislator, and this double error has endured two hundred years. The commerce of the mother country encouraged this baleful institution because it profited by it. Subsequently, the treasury favored indigenous sugar, because it profited by it also. France had thus been an accomplice in different ways, both in the faults of the colonies and in their ruin. It was equitable that it should indemnify them.

Furthermore, this was useful, and before all useful to the interests of the slaves. Freedom would be misery to them, if on the morrow the ruined colonists could not pay them their wages. Indemnity is a subsidy to free labor, it is an advance of wages.

* Despatch of the French Minister at Copenhagen, Aug. 27, 1847, cited in the *procès-verbaux* of the Commission of 1848, p. 136.

† Report of M. de Broglie, p. 273.

From this stand-point, which is the true one, it was important that the indemnity should be both prompt and large; it obtained neither promptness nor generosity.

Article 5 of the decree of April 27, 1848, left to the National Assembly the care of regulating the quota of the indemnity.

All the colonists heard by the Commission of 1848 had demanded a delay before emancipation, in order to be able to gather in the crops and to take precautionary measures, and no delay before indemnity, in order that wages might serve as the immediate attraction to free labor, and that aid might be secured to children and the infirm.* They reminded the Commission that it had been possible to maintain labor in the English colonies because indemnity had preceded emancipation.† They added, that the negro would distrust his freedom, so long as his former master were not indemnified, and that he would thus be impelled to go far from the plantations.

The Commission presided over by M. de Broglie‡ proposed a delay of ten years, during which the interest of the indemnity would be received by the consignment fund for the benefit of the colonists, but not by themselves individually, their rights being only certain and liquidated at the moment of emancipation.

The Commission of 1848 dared not impose on the Republic a burden before which the Monarchy had recoiled. Emancipation, therefore, came to the colonies without indemnity. This suffices to exonerate emancipation from all the calamities of the first moments; labor was disorganized, not only on account of the absence of servitude, but on account of the absence of wages; not only because the hands of the former slave were free, but because the hands of the former master were empty.

* Opinion of M Froidefonds, p. 31.

† Opinion of M. Pécoul, p. 24.

‡ Report, p. 279.

The indemnity was accorded, but more than a year afterwards, by the statute of April 30, 1849.

If the indemnity was not prompt, was it at least large? By no means.

The commission of 1840 * had calculated the indemnity according to the market value of the negroes, and this value according to the average rate of sale in each colony during a period of ten years, chosen during prosperity, in an epoch when emancipation was not talked of (1825–1834). This labor gave as its result: —

At Guadaloupe, an average of 1,102 francs 43 centimes per head for slaves of all sexes and ages;

At Martinico, 1,200 francs;

At Guiana, 1,361 francs 99 centimes;

At Bourbon, 1,600 francs.

The Commission fixed on the general average of 1,200 francs,† which, multiplied by 250,000, the number of slaves, produced a sum total of 300,000,000 francs, to be distributed, half, or 150,000,000, in money, and half in a guaranty of labor for ten years.

Before the Provisional Government, M. Crémieux and M. de Lamartine demanded 150,000,000 francs. The most enlightened among the colonists asked 7,500,000 in three per cents.‡ But the government proposed only 90,000,000. It was calculated that, the wages of the freedmen being 75 centimes, and representing double the amount that the slave would cost, the half of 75, or 37½ centimes, was the difference between the price of free and of servile labor; — this figure, 37½ centimes, was multiplied by the number of able-bodied slaves, computed at 198,000; and this figure, multiplied in turn by the number of working days, 250, for five years, produced a total of 91,575,000 francs, or, in round

* Report, p. 275.

† In England, 1,400 francs; but this did not include children under six years of age, who were declared free without indemnity.

‡ Opinion of M. Reiset, Commission of 1848. *Procès-verbaux*, p. 71.

numbers, 90,000,000. The Commission, taking 1,085 francs as the average value, and reducing the number of slaves 20 per cent, arrived at 214,000,000; but, considering that a relative indemnity only was in question, it reduced the proposed sum to 120,000,000. This it proposed to divide into 80,000,000 capital, and 2,000,000 a year, payable in ten years.* The government obstinately refused to add any new indebtedness to the finances. This mode prevailed, notwithstanding, and by the terms of the law passed April 30, 1849,† the indemnity was fixed as follows:—

1. 6,000,000 francs in five per cent government stocks.

2. A sum of 6,000,000 francs payable in cash thirty days after the decree.

The apportionment among the colonies was based on the figure of the slave population, viz.: ‡—

	Number of Slaves.	Indemnity. fr.	c.
Martinico	74,447	1,507,885	80
Guadaloupe	87,087	1,947,164	85
Guiana	12,525	372,571	88
Bourbon	60,651	2,055,200	25
Senegal { 9,800 slaves, 550 bound laborers }	10,350	105,503	41
Nossi-bé, St. Mary	3,500	11,673	81
	248,560	6,000,000	00

The very incomplete statute of 1849 did not determine, as had been done by the statutes on the indemnity of the emigrants and colonists of St. Domingo, whether the indemnity should be considered as *real estate* or *personal property*, and reserved to mortgage creditors, or distributed between the latter and the ordinary creditors; a vexatious omission, which occasioned innumerable suits, and caused a great part of the indemnity to pass, not into the hands of the newly hired laborers, the true end to be attained,

* 20 per cent was deducted for children and old people.

† Report of M Crémieux, Sept. 30, 1848.

‡ Report of M. Crémieux, Jan. 15, 1849.

but to the seaports of the mother country, where the colonists owed an enormous commercial debt. The same statute omitted to regulate the sub-apportionment in each colony, the mode of payment, and the proofs to be exacted, and a new statute was necessary, November 15, 1849, followed by a decree on the 24th of the same month, to fix all these important points.*

A special commission instituted in each colony pronounced on claims, without excluding recourse to the Privy Council, and the certificates delivered were, except in case of attachments, transformed, through the agency established by the colonial ministry, into government stocks. The work proceeded very regularly, and is now terminated, save as to a few indemnities in litigation. The government bonds date from 1852. We cannot help remembering that by the conditions of the report of M. de Broglie, the payment of the indemnity was to commence in 1843 and to be ended in 1853, at which date slavery was to cease. The opposition of the colonies has resulted, therefore, only in causing them to receive a speedier emancipation, and a longer deferred, but above all smaller indemnity.

The colonists, in short, received only about 500 francs per slave. This indemnity was really insufficient. The calculation made by the government would have been a better basis, if it had been possible exactly to estimate the difference in price between free labor and slave labor. But what did slave labor cost? What would free labor cost? Nothing was known about it; the formula was ingenious, the elements of the calculation were purely hypothetical.

The Commission of 1840 estimated the market value at 1,200 francs, that of 1848 at 1,085 francs. The first, by a subtlety difficult to understand or explain, made a reduction of one half, giving half in money and half in labor; — a

* Report of M. Béhic to the Council of State; Report of M. Fourtanier to the Legislative Assembly, Nov. 10, 1849.

strange and contradictory system ; for the Commission declared that the indemnity was not a true repurchase, yet notwithstanding attributed to the state, for each fraction paid, a right over the person and labor of the slave ; the state denied the right of property, became co-proprietor, and forced payment for its right.

The second Commission, the procedure of which is still less comprehensible, changed the market value after having established it, and, by a purely arbitrary reduction, instead of 1,085 francs, estimated it at 500 francs. It would have been better to be logical, and, since it was proved that the former slaves, still more than their masters, had need that a large indemnity should be paid, — since there was an opportunity, at the same time, to revive the colonies, so crushed by the rivalry of indigenous sugar, — not to haggle about this indemnity. We spend 500,000,000 for a war that slays 50,000 men, we dared not spend 2,000,000 or 3,000,000 to free 250,000 men, and to save the colonies at once from shame and ruin.

Did this meagre indemnity serve, at least in great part, to pay the expenses of free labor ?

By the terms of Article 7 of the statute of April 30, 1849, one eighth was deducted from the indemnity of all the colonists of Guadaloupe, Martinico, and Bourbon, except those who had received less than 1,000 francs, to serve for the establishment of loan and discount offices.

This deduction was truly in conformity to the spirit of the law, which considered the indemnity as a subsidy to labor. Some even proposed to leave it as a common loan fund for the colonists, without apportioning it among them.*

But what became of the rest of the indemnity ? The major part passed into the hands of creditors of all kinds, and not into those of the laborers.

We may say, therefore, that the indemnity was not

* *Procès-verbaux* of the Commission of 1848.

prompt enough, not large enough, and that it failed in its end. Doubtless it served to liquidate property, and consequently to revive credit; but it assuaged the past, it did not pave the way for the future.

Prompter, it would have averted in part the crisis of labor; larger, it would have permitted a less distressing liquidation; reserved to the mortgage creditors alone, it would have directly fed agriculture.

In this point, as in many others, we come again to the same conclusion: —

If emancipation has been followed by some evils, let not the blame be cast on it, but on the unskilfulness, the slowness, or the insufficiency of the measures which might have averted these evils.

Let it not be said that the colonies have been unable to reanimate labor, despite indemnity; for the indemnity has served creditors more than laborers, debts more than wages.

This is the proper place to devote a few words to the influence of the emancipation of the slaves upon the budget of the state.

The emancipation of the slaves had one grave objection in the eyes of the financiers of the ancient Chambers, — it would cost dear. The Duc de Broglie had, so to say, made the estimate.

Indemnity to the proprietors for 249,508 slaves, at 1,200 fr. each,*	300,000,000 fr.
First expenses,†	8,000,000

* Report, p. 276.

† *Ibid.* p. 129.

Armed force	3,326,000 fr.
Tribunals	*Memorial*
Prisons	1,620,000
Educational institutions	1,740,000
Charitable, etc.	678,000
Religious worship	*Memorial*
	7,364,000

Annual expense *	2,718,500

They recoiled before so costly a good deed.

Now the indemnity has cost the treasury but 126,000,000, and a part of this has served to form the capital of the colonial banks.

There have been no first expenses. The annual expenses, far from increasing, have diminished.

If we compare, in fact, the accounts of 1846 and 1847 with those of 1848 and 1849, we establish the following figures.

General service and common expenses of the colonies of Guadaloupe, Martinico, Bourbon, and Guiana : —

1846	5,097,429 fr.
1847	6,167,309
1848	5,679,578
1849	5,289,466

As to the local service, the difference is still more sensible : —

1847	6,167,309 fr.
1848	5,679,568 †

If we compare, article by article, the accounts of 1846 with those of 1850, we shall see that there are a few more police agents in the towns after than before emancipation, and, strangely enough, a few less in the country ; that the expenses of the courts have increased, but that the expenses of jail-fees and flight have diminished ; that religious worship costs somewhat more ; that subsidies to parishes

* *Ibid.* p. 130.

Armed force	1,829,000 fr.
Tribunals	269,500
Prisons	34,000
Education	488,000
Charity	80,000
Religious worship	18,000
	2,718,500 fr.

† Accounts of 1848, p. 59.

and hospitals have somewhat increased ; that the expenses for the recovery of taxes are still the same, and that, in fine, the total expense has diminished.

It is difficult to establish comparisons with the accounts of subsequent years, as, since the Senatus Consultum of May 3, 1854, the decree of July 31, 1855, and that of September 29, 1855, the financial system of the colonies has been modified. The new legislation abandons to the colonies all the imposts which may be collected by them, and leaves them the full disposal of their revenues,* but also the burden of expenses in which the state has not a direct interest.

Notwithstanding the state continues to pay for the army, the government, the courts, and religious worship, it contributes only by a subsidy to public instruction.†

Now, adding together the services retained in the state budget,‡ we find that these civil and military services of the four colonies cost, in 1846, 10,289,136 francs, and, in 1858, but 9,521,244 francs.

In short, apart from the indemnity, emancipation has

* The accountability has been at the same time decentralized. (See the instructions of April 15, 1856.)

†	1846.	1848.
Religious worship	358,082	687,973
Courts of justice	982,606	938,976
Schools	505,160	200,000

‡ 1846.	Martinico.	Guadaloupe.	Guiana.	Bourbon.
Military service, Personnel	1,650,235	1,576,271	572,691	1,023,067
" " Material	545,077	464,098	81,734	382,726
Civil service	1.512,853	1,602,705	586,201	1,291,578
Total	3,708,165	3,643,074	1,240,626	2,697,371
1858.				
Civil and military service	2,212,836	2,413,597	1,512,233	1,548,008
Material	499,365	655,813	307,462	371,930
Total	2,712,201	3,069,410	1,819,695	1,919,938

General total, 1846	10,289,136
" " 1858	9,521,244
Less difference	767,892

passed over the budget of the state* without leaving a trace on it.

* As to the colonial budgets, mark the result, in the three principal ones, of the decree of 1855, as regarded the budget of 1856.*

Martinico had	2,038,600 fr.
It had to pay	2,078,803
It lost	40,203 fr.
Guadaloupe had	1,723,300 fr.
It had to pay	1,865,928
It lost	142,628 fr.
Bourbon had	2,240,900 fr.
It had to pay	1,959,020
It gained	281,880 fr.
The state lost	99,049 fr.

* This information is due to the able chief of accounts in the collection of the colonies, M. Eguyer.

CHAPTER X.

PRODUCTION AND COMMERCE.—WAGES AND PROPERTY.

THE colonies have been ruined by emancipation.

It seems as if we had only to pass sentence on this point, on which the declared partisans of the abolition of slavery and its enemies are agreed.

"Public tranquillity in the colonies leaves nothing to be desired," wrote the reporter of the sugar law, M. Beugnot, in 1851, "but the conditions of production are completely changed."* The reporter of the sugar law in 1860, M. Ancel, likewise affirms, ten years after, "the profound trouble which the suppression of slave labor, violently proclaimed, had brought to add to an already calamitous situation."†

Are we to rely on these affirmations, passed in some sort into commonplaces, and be content with repeating by way of consolation, that, whatever may have been the losses experienced by men enriched by slavery, freedom is a blessing worthy such a price, a reparation deserving such a penance?

No. It becomes us to penetrate into details, and to ascertain scrupulously the exact extent and different causes of the loss of which the colonies complain. Most real and most serious, nevertheless it has been neither so grave, nor so absolute, nor so long, as is commonly asserted. Above all, it has other causes, of longer standing, and more profound than the abolition of slavery.

But how assure ourselves of this?

* P. 63. † P. 17.

When I read the colonial journals, when I consult the writings of the colonists, when I consult the memorials, petitions, and bills, I hear nothing but complaints and mourning. Besides, I lose myself in infinite details, in contestable calculations, in contradictory opinions. To what end can this difficult path conduct me? To a picture of the existing situation of the colonies, — their agricultural, financial, and commercial situation. This picture will never be either complete or like; we may make a resemblance in the portrait of a man, never in that of a whole community. But, moreover, such a picture would not be important to the special end which I propose, which is exclusively to demonstrate that the emancipation of the slaves has not ruined the colonies. Now, for this, it suffices to prove, first, that they are not ruined; in the second place, that the evils from which they suffer are from other causes than emancipation.

To what documents can we definitely refer?

Propounding the same questions in regard to the English colonies, M. de Broglie* said well: —

"In an event of this immensity, what is true in this place is not in that; what is true at one time is no longer so in another; there is room for facts of all sorts, all opinions may draw thousands of examples from it in their favor, according to the bias of the thoughts of the observer; what strikes this one, that one fails to see, and *vice versa*. All design to be impartial, each one is prejudiced at heart...... There is a shorter and surer means, — to place one's self on an entirely neutral ground, where the basis of calculation shall be as it were disinterested, the figures having been neither prepared nor grouped in any determined end.

"In England, as in France, the mother country is the chief market of the colonies; it is to this market that almost all of the products of colonial labor drift; it is to this

* P. 19.

market that the colonists go to provide themselves with all the articles of their consumption. Before coming in or going out, the commodities pass through the custom-house, and are inscribed on its registers day by day with a view to true fiscal accountability. The figures extracted from these statements are witnesses indifferent to any consequences that may be drawn from them, and on which no one can read a lecture before interrogating them."

We will follow this method, and summon these witnesses.

This interrogation is long, dry, and inevitably confused. For these witnesses scarcely agree between themselves. The figures of the *tables of the customs*, those of the *tables of the population, culture, commerce, and navigation of the colonies*, those of the *quarterly statements* and *comparative résumés*, and those of the *statistics of France*, or other special works, are not precisely the same. From this results a veritable embarrassment, which it does not depend on us to surmount, and which can be diminished at least by drawing always from the same source. This will be by preference the series of documents contained in the collection of the *Revue coloniale.*

We will begin with a bird's-eye view, and descend afterwards to details. We will first compare the *total fluctuation* of imports and exports *united*, before and after 1848, in each colony, then the *exports* taken separately.

After *values*, we will examine *quantities*, especially the quantities of *sugar made* or *exported* by each colony. Herein lies the true thermometer of the progress or decline of production.

We will close by some statistics concerning wages, the price of lands, and net costs.

I. In the first place, what has been the general range of colonial fluctuation before and since 1848 ?

If we confine ourselves to comparing the aggregate of the imports and exports of the colonies in 1847 with the aggregate in 1848, the digression appears enormous.

	1847.	1848.
Martinico	41,165,012 fr.	23,366,287 fr.
Guadaloupe . . .	41,759,713	20,854,020
Guiana	4,501,747	3,396,720
Bourbon	28,267,698	19,676,882
Total . . .	115,694,170 fr.	67,293,909 fr.
	67,293,909	
Diminution . .	48,400,261 fr.	

This is a diminution of nearly one half, or 41 per cent; still more, if we calculate only the production of sugar, fallen from an average of 80,000,000 to 90,000,000 kilogrammes* (1838 – 1847) to 63,000,000 in 1848, 57,000,000 in 1849, and 40,000,000 in 1850, or 50 per cent.

But several things must be remarked: —

1. The year 1847 was an exceptional one, exceeding the preceding year by more than 5,000,000 francs. Compared with 1856, the fall of the aggregate of 1848 stands: —

Martinico	37,789,353 fr.
Guadaloupe	34,627,632
Guiana	4,619,861
Bourbon	33,472,393
Total	110,509,239 fr.
1848	67,293,809
	43,215,430 fr.

or only 40 per cent.

2. Was it emancipation, or the Revolution, that caused this considerable loss?

In fact, we have seen that it was not freedom that disturbed order, which it was the sole means of restoring; it was the ballot-box that caused labor to be deserted, armed parties, and stained the soil with blood.

Besides, the result produced in the colonies was produced at the same moment, by the same cause, in the mother country. While the production of colonial sugar fell from 80,000,000 to 40,000,000 kilog., the production of a similar

* Kilogramme = 2.2055 lbs. avoirdupois, or nearly 2¼ lbs.

commodity, beet-root sugar, fell from 60,000,000 kilog. in 1847 to 56,000,000 in 1848, and to 44,000,000 in 1849; 27 per cent, or nearly one third.

The total loss of the external commerce of France at the same epoch is estimated at no less than 600,000,000 fr., or one fourth.*

In Paris alone, it was computed that the Revolution of February caused a decline of from 53 to 75, and even 83 per cent, according to the occupation, amount of business, and quantity of labor.†

Lastly, in studying closely the tables of customs, we see that the imports into the colonies from *foreign countries* had diminished less, in 1848 and 1849, than the imports from *France*, if they had not even increased. At Guadaloupe, there was increase; at Guiana, a diminution of 18 per cent only, while the entrance duties from France fell 25 per cent; at Bourbon, 12 per cent only, against 33 per cent.‡ Thus the crisis of the mother country weighed, before all, on the colonies; in the earliest days of emancipation, they ceased less to buy than the mother country to sell.

* General Commerce.

1847	2,613,500,000 fr.
1848	2,014,900,000

Special Commerce.

1847	1,867,000,000 fr.
1848	1,390,600,000

(Decennial table published by the Administration of Customs in 1848.)

But these figures, rising again from 1850, exceed, dating from 1852, all that precede them; and this magnificent commerce, carried from 1,300,000 to 2,000,000,000 from 1827 to 1847, reached 5,000,000,000 in 1857, having thus increased nearly 60 per cent in thirty years.

† *Statistique de l'industrie parisienne*, published in 1851, pp. 41, 42.

The sum of exports from the custom-house at Paris, which

was, in 1847	168,572,187 fr.
had fallen in 1848 to	149,288,979
Or about one eighth	19,283,208 fr.

‡ Comparative abstracts inserted in the *Revue coloniale*, 1851, pp. 20, 100, 153, 161.

3. If the quantities produced have decreased, the prices have risen so as to diminish the loss of the colonists. In the decennial period 1837 – 1847, the average price of colonial sugar at the entrepôt of Havana was 68 fr. 50 c., duties not included ; the price had risen in 1850 to 87 fr. 50 c. ; or 19 francs increase, that is, 22 per cent.* If the loss of the colonists was, therefore, in these first years, 40 per cent in quantity, it was really but 18 per cent in value, or less than one fifth, while, in respect to the English colonies, it reached one fourth.

4. It is true that the loss did not stop, as regarded colonial sugar, at 1850 ; whilst, as regarded indigenous sugar, the rise of prices raised the production, this year, to 64,000,000 kilogrammes, and also permitted the introduction of large lots of foreign sugar, despite the extra charge of 22 francs.† The presence and progress of these two rivals weighed upon the production of the colonies in proportion as the consequences of the Revolution became effaced. An insignificant reduction was accorded only in 1852. The political crisis finished, the commercial crisis, born indeed before 1848, commenced anew. Let us not forget this, and confound these two crises with the crisis of freedom.

Be it as it may, let us also remark that 1848, 1849, and 1850 were not only years in which politics overthrew labor, but, furthermore, that the meagre harvests of this year were still in part the product of servile labor ; it is in 1851 and 1852 only that we can judge of the results due to free labor. Now, from 1852, before the reduction, the amount of the aggregate of commerce (imports and exports) at

* Report of M. Beugnot, 1851, p. 55. *Document fourni au Conseil géneral de l'agriculture*, 1850, *Annexé*, No. 8.

Price current at Havre, 1839 . . . 115 to 120 fr. per 100 kilog.
1849 . . 130 " 135 " "

† 1849 . . . . 27,941,622 kilog.
1850 . . . . 43,723,405 "

Bourbon exceeded that of 1847; at Martinico, and even at Guiana, that of 1846; Guadaloupe alone had not yet regained its footing.* Here are the comparative results of the five years that preceded emancipation, and the five years that followed it:—

QUINQUENNIAL AVERAGE.

	1843-1847.	1848-1852.
Martinico	39,226,503 fr.	36,676,505 fr.
Guadaloupe	39,226,912	28,461,649
Guiana	4,081,799	4,427,460
Bourbon	33,074,648	34,708,672
	115,609,862 fr.	104,274,286 fr.
Difference	11,335,576 fr.	

If we go further, if we compare the period 1843-1847 with the period 1853-1857, then the advantage is entirely on the side of freedom.

QUINQUENNNIAL AVERAGE (1853-1857).

Martinico	51,546,959 fr
Guadaloupe	39,904,671
Guiana	7,954,376
Bourbon	72,324,705
Total	171,730,711 fr.
Average (1843-1847)	115,609,862
Increase	56,120,849 fr.

Thus, five years after emancipation, the diminution is only 11,000,000 fr., resting almost entirely on a single colony, Guadaloupe; ten years after, the increase is 56,000,000; in the four colonies, the figure is exceeded, at Martinico by more than a third, at Bourbon, more than double.†

II. We will now distinguish the *imports* from the *exports*,

* See Tables A and B, Appendix.

† We also join (Table C, Appendix) the tables of the French custom-house, where the figures are still more significant. At Bourbon they rose from 23,711,051 fr., in 1848, to 99,584,180 fr., in 1857. (*Revue coloniale*, 1858, p. 898.)

instead of presenting united the figures which express them.

We observe that nearly all the increase bears upon the *imports*, while the figure of the *exports* remains almost constantly, on one hand, below the figures anterior to emancipation, on the other, below the figure of the imports ; in other words, the colonies produce less than they formerly produced, and receive more than they produce, — a double loss.

It is just, moreover, to distinguish some colonies from others, for the variation does not follow the same course in all. Now the general table of customs (pp. 58 – 60) proves that the decennial average 1837 – 1846 of *exports* is above the decennial average 1847 – 1856, viz. : —

	1837 – 1846.	1847 – 1856.
Martinico	15,158,394 fr.	14,027,763 fr.
Guadaloupe . . .	18,575,225	12,685,654
Guiana	1,830,606	861,370

It is only at Bourbon that the average rises from 18,712,281 francs to 21,577,330 francs.

The answer to these objections is this : —

There is one country in which the total commercial movement has increased, but in which the amount of exports has so far diminished that it may be said to cease to figure among the colonies which provision the mother country ; namely, Guiana. Is this to say that it is destroyed ? No ; it has changed character. Already very unproductive, abandoning or resuming the culture of the cane, according to the rise or fall of the price of sugar, and producing more anotta than sugar, it has become a penal colony, consuming, with the exception of its woods, nearly all that it produces, especially cattle, the export of which, moreover, has been several times forbidden ; but, after all, employing nearly as many laborers and transacting as much business as before the day when, by reason of the statute of May 30, 1854, it received 4,000 convicts, then 5,000 (1858), 6,000 (1859), and 7,000 (1860).*

As to Bourbon, it is not denied that all the figures anterior not only to 1836 – 1847, but also to 1826 – 1837, are largely exceeded.

As to Martinico and Guadaloupe, it is forgotten that the decay was anterior to 1848, for the decennial average of exports 1836 – 1847 was already below the average 1826 - 1837, viz. : —

Martinico	1826 – 1837	16,015,171 fr.
"	1836 – 1847 . . .	15,158,394
Guadaloupe	1826 – 1837	20,451,685
"	1836 – 1847	18,575,225

It is not just, besides, to take as a whole the average 1847 – 1856, which comprises the disastrous years 1848, 1849, 1850, and 1851. What should be done is to ascertain, by the figures of the last years of this period, at what epoch the years that preceded emancipation and those that followed it were again on a level. Now this level was attained at Bourbon after five years, then doubled after eight years, and tripled after ten years ; at Martinico, attained after seven years, then exceeded by one third after nine years ; at Guadaloupe, attained after ten years, though since diminished.

EXPORTS.†

	1847.	1848.	1849.	1850.	1851.
Bourbon	12,620,602	9,107,507	13,939,032	28,881,893	38,423,669

	1847.	1848.	1854.	1857.
Martinico	18,323,921	9,212,554	18,636,070	24,830,093

	1847.	1848.	1857.
Guadaloupe	20,420,522	8,873,539	23,319,277

	1847.	1857.
* Imports	2,878,628	6,420,789
	1,622,919	961,272
	4,501,547	7,382,061

† All the figures given by the Table of Customs are much higher. (Appendix, Table C.)

Thus, therefore, it is not true that the figure of *exports* has remained inferior, since emancipation, to what it was before.

But it is remarked, with reason, that it remains constantly inferior to that of *imports*. It is thence concluded that, the *balance* being to the detriment of the colonies, they are on the way to ruin.

There are two answers to make; the one general, the other special.

1. "The *balance of trade* is, for small countries as for large ones, only a document for consultation. Its data are too incomplete, the values which it establishes have too much uncertainty, to permit them to be brought in proof of the poverty or wealth of communities." *

These observations of an experienced colonist are perfectly just, and it is long since science has relied on the theory, once so popular, of the *balance of trade*. It is useful information, it is not an infallible argument. It founds affirmations in fact upon variable values, it says nothing of the origin, nature, or end of expenses and receipts; it takes account of what comes in and what goes out, not of what is consumed on the spot, not of what is a source of power without appearing in figures. A country which exports largely seems very wealthy. It is not so; it turns everything into money in order to pay debts. We have a very tangible proof of this assertion in the examination of the total commerce of France after 1848.

While the imports fell to 1,343,000,000 fr. in 1847, and to 862,000,000 in 1848, and did not rise again until 1852 above the figure of 1847, the *exports* did not fall until 1848, and rose again from 1849, without stopping, above the figure of 1847; the equilibrium between the imports and exports was not attained until 1856. What does this mean? Was France richer in 1849 than in 1847? By no means; she bought lit-

* *La Question commerciale à la Guadeloupe*, by Count de Chazelles.

tle and sold all she could, — exhausted all her supplies, and did not replace them.

On the contrary, a country that imports more than it exports seems poor; it is not so if it import machinery, manures, and laborers that increase its capital, or if it have wealth enough to consume largely; a rich man brings more into his house than he sends out from it. Reasoning founded on the balance of trade must therefore be fragile. More just, though subject to numerous exceptions, is the universally accepted formula, *Products are exchanged only for products.* If a man buys, it is because he can pay; if he pays, it is because he has produced.

2. But we forget before all the special position of the colonies.

The continual excess of imports over exports is the normal condition among small communities, which only produce certain special commodities, and receive all the rest from abroad, and whence fortunes, once made, almost always emigrate. This is so true, that when, in 1857, the exports in Martinico exceeded the imports, it was necessary to go back to 1828 to encounter the same phenomenon.*

The same cause is the principal explanation of the *monetary crises,* so frequent and so distressing in the colonies, and of which there has been especial complaint during the past few years.

Well-informed writers see the origin of the last monetary crisis, some in the establishment of *banks,* very useful in reducing the rate of interest and making loans to agriculture, but which they accuse of having replaced specie in local circulation by paper, which cannot be exported, and which comes at length to be no longer redeemable; others in the measures taken to exclude foreign coin, — Spanish doubloons and piasters, American dollars and eagles.† But

* *Revue coloniale,* 1858, p. 682.

† See the writings of MM. de Chazelles, Lepelletier de Saint-Remy, de Cri-

the real cause is that exchanges in kind, rather than sales, are made between the colonies and the mother country; the importation exceeding the exportation, the colonists have to pay a balance in cash. Not producing food for their population in sufficient quantity, they pay again a balance to foreign countries. "The money sent from France to the Antilles in payment for sugar," said M. Reiset * to the Commission of 1848, "goes only to benefit Porto Rico and America, whence our colonists obtain cattle, beasts of burden, wood for building, etc., etc., without being able to pay in sugar." Add, that fortunes, once made in the colonies, emigrate with their possessors, who are eager to go to enjoy them in France. Remember, too, the amount of debts to the seaports, the habit of speculating on 'Change,—here are many causes, in addition to the necessity of paying cash for wages, to explain the frequency of monetary crises. It may be said that they are almost the normal condition in the excess of imports over exports.

But is this excess a proof of impoverishment? Yes, if debts be incurred. How are we to ascertain if this be the case? By the rate of interest. Now, it is well known that the rate of interest is much lower to-day than before emancipation. Once more, what is imported is paid for, and to pay it is necessary to have, and to have it is necessary to produce or to have produced. Is not the capital of the colonies in other hands than those of the exporters? Are not the imports destined in part for others than they, and the exportable articles employed in part for something else than exportation?

This is true, in fact.

If large estates have suffered, small freeholds have in-

senoy, and Basiège, 1859, 1860. See also *l'Avenir de la Gaudeloupe*, Nov. 29, 1859, and the articles of MM. Courcelle Seneuil and Jules Duval in the *Journal des Économistes*.

* *Procès-verbaux*, p. 18.

creased. If the labors of the fields have been deserted, the arts and manufactures of the towns have been filled up; the class which made large profits has diminished, the class which made none has made small ones, importation has gone on faster than exportation, because consumption has increased, because the comfort of the former slaves has increased.

These explanations seem to me to demonstrate sufficiently that the excess of imports over exports is not a proof of poverty, but rather a proof of the increase of local consumption, and consequently of comfort.

But although, despite well-founded arguments, I admit this excess, in default of sufficient information, from inductions rather than certainty, it is at least incontestable: —

1. That this balance was already the normal condition of the colonies before emancipation;

2. That the value of exports has increased since this epoch; that it amounted to less than 53,000,000 francs in 1847, and that it exceeded 82,000,000 in 1857.

III. It is admitted, beside, that "the exports verified by the customs, not in their *values* but in their *quantities*, are susceptible of no dispute."*

Let us leave *values*, therefore, and consult *quantities*, and since it is claimed that the loss has weighed above all on the principal colonial product, sugar, let us indicate the quantities of sugar.

The comparative tables of the quantities of sugar brought to France by the colonies present the following results: —

Quinquennial average, 1843-1847 † .	80,570,800 kil.
" " 1848-1853 . .	58,946,830

A diminution of more than one fourth.

* *Ibid.*, M. de Chazelles.

† Comprising exceptional years, as 1845, 102,000,000 kil.; 1847, 99,000,000 kil.; while none of the years from 1825 to 1844 had reached beyond a maximum of 89,000,000, realized only twice in twenty years.

But 1853 reaches already	65,682,080 kil.
1854 rises to	82,211,428
1855	90,747,276
1856	93,531,027
1857	84,961,781
1858	116,245,177
1859	112,701,138 *

So that from 1854 the average amount of production anterior to 1848 is exceeded, even in sugar.

It is true that the progress was accomplished more or less slowly in each colony, as is proved both by the *Tables of Commerce* published by the Ministry of the Marine and Colonies, and the *Official Table of Customs*, published by the Minister of Finance. But, after ten years, the very high figures of 1847 were exceeded in the Antilles as well as in Bourbon, viz. : —

SUGAR MANUFACTURED.†

Bourbon.		Martinico.		Guadaloupe.	
1847	24,063,689 kil.	1847	29,318,175 kil.	1847	38,007,807 kil.
1857	64,649,170	1856	30,344,650	1854	38,180,200

RAW SUGAR IMPORTED INTO FRANCE.‡

	Bourbon.	Martinico.	Guadaloupe.
1847	17,359,825 kil	19,247,079 kil.	24,225,756 kil.
1848	15,279,875	11,838,865	12,191,904
1849	12,978,406	11,034,983	11,515,545
1850	13,180,666	8,545,310	7,808,5[illegible]4
1851	13,491,119	11,829,555	10,148,075
1852	19,807,142	14,717,577	10,645,556
1853	19,000,326	12,419,440	8,884,377
1854	25,036,845	14,624,649	13,254,673
1855	34,224,912	11,117,530	12,690,933
1856	32,946,224	15,981,976	13,003,032
1857	51,006,067	23,679,905	18,390,842
1858	57,522,342	27,334,585	28,675,144

* *Revue coloniale*, April and October, 1860.

† *Revue coloniale*, Dec., 1860, p. 943.

‡ Decennial Table of Customs, 1846, 1847, pp. 58 – 68. Annual Table, 1857, 1858.

What matters it, say the planters, that our lands produce as much, if their market value be lowered, if the net income be lessened by the increase of wages and the diminution of selling prices.

It is very difficult to obtain precise documents on these points.

In the Antilles transactions are not numerous enough to make a well-established price-current concerning land, which varies in price according to situation. Before 1848, little was sold, and debts were incurred without fear of dispossession. The price of a plantation depended more on the value of its negroes and its annual yield, than on that of the land itself; of which every one had always more than he cultivated. The negroes not being able to hold property, there were in each colony 70,000 or 80,000 less buyers or sellers. How compare such diverse elements?

Is it possible to take as certain the figures enunciated in the two official publications of the Colonial Ministry, the two *Notices* printed in 1840 and 1848, and relating, the first to 1835, a year of great prosperity, the second to 1855, only seven years after the Revolution and emancipation? In 1835, the capital involved in the colonies was estimated at 796,403,641 francs; but deducting the value of the slaves, estimated at 274,304,150 francs, or about 1500 francs per head, there remained 522,099,591 francs for the capital of lands, plantations, goods, and cattle.

Now the Notice of 1858 estimates the same capital in 1855 at 374,173,405 francs. This would be a difference of 147,926,186 francs, or about one fourth.

This difference would bear entirely on Guadaloupe, Guiana, and Martinico, for at Bourbon the capital involved is estimated above what it was worth, including the slaves, before emancipation.

But is it possible to admit the figures given by the *Notices officielles?* Do they not refute themselves? For they inform us that the number of plantations has increased. The number of head of cattle is sensibly the same. The number of laborers has diminished very little, whatever may be asserted.* The interest on money, it is not denied, has fallen. The banks are flourishing, the loans on the crops have brought great relief to property.† The stock of implements has been improved, and consequently the capital involved has largely increased. The establishment of *central mills* has increased profits by lessening expenses. Lastly, and above all, property is consolidated. Always suspicious and of fragile tenure while the abolition of slavery weighed on it as a menace, and loaded with debts, property has been liquidated by indemnity, regulated by expropriation, rehabilitated by emancipation. Surer and more honorable, it must offer more attraction to capital.

If we consult the position of the plantations of the

	1835. — Slaves.	Laborers. — 1855.
* Martinico	56,556	48,970
Guadaloupe	55,416	51,660
Guiana	13,727	7,291
Bourbon	56,059	71,094
	181,758	179,015

† At Guadaloupe, the Bank, with a capital of 3,000,000 fr., has seen its operations increase, from 7,176,347 fr. in 1853 - 1854 to 21,962,212 fr. in 1858 - 1859. The advances on crops, at 4 per cent, have reached 2,861,897 fr. The net profit is 14 per cent. (Report of July 28, 1859.)

At Martinico, the Bank, in 1858 - 1859, has discounted to the value of 27,000,000 fr.; advanced on crops, 1,602,512 fr., instead of 154,000 fr.; and distributed a dividend of 8.81 per cent. (Report of July 19, 1859).

At Guiana, with a capital of 300,000 fr., the Bank has discounted on 1,832,622 fr. of effects; it has made no advances on crops, "because the large proprietors have not needed credit, and the others do not offer sufficient guaranties." It has realized a net profit of 16.27 per cent. (Report of July 24, 1859.)

At Bourbon, the Bank, with a capital of 3,000,000 fr., has loaned from 1853 - 1854, 12,354,612 fr.; and its operations, rising to 19,896,118 fr. in 1854 - 1855, remained the same in 1858-1859. The loans on crops have reached 1,945,694 fr., and tended to exceed 2,500,000 fr. The dividend has been 9.57 per cent. (Report of July 20, 1859.)

I am indebted for this information to the kindness of M. Lepelletier de Saint-Remy, central agent of the colonial banks.

crown, we find that they let higher than before 1848, some of them for double.*

If we follow the sales in the colonial journals, we see that for some years the selling prices have notably increased.†

If, moreover, the capital represented by agricultural property were greater, the mortgage and commercial debts were greater in a proportion exceeding the plus value acquired, rendered illusory from the impossibility of its realization.‡

It is not, therefore, rash to affirm, that the position of property, and its selling or locative value, have improved since emancipation, not only in Bourbon but also in the West Indies.

Have wages greatly increased?

This has been the case in the greater part of the English colonies, and the result seemed inevitable. Nevertheless, emancipation in our French colonies has been remarkably effected. Now, as M. Mestro truly said in 1848, negro labor is, above all, a question of remuneration, and the latter itself is only a question of credit. §

We will continue to except Bourbon, where the rise of wages has necessarily followed the enormous increase of production.¶

In the Antilles the cost of a slave was computed in 1842 at from 50 to 60 centimes per day, for food (whether he received the ordinary allowance, or took Saturday instead),

* Report of the Director of the Interior of Martinico.

† M. Lepelletier de Saint-Remy, in the *Colonies françaises*, 1859, cites a plantation at Guadaloupe, valued at 29,000 fr. in 1854, at 131,000 fr. in 1858.

‡ M. de Chazelles, p. 157, note.

§ Commission of 1848, p. 94.

¶ At Bourbon, where immigration is effected without the financial intervention of the government, the transfers of immigrant contracts, which were negotiated in the beginning at the rate of 300 fr., have reached 800 and 1,000 fr. Thus the power of free labor multiplying by itself, the planter finds himself rich enough to pay, for a hire of five years, a much higher sum than he received from the state for the ownership of a slave. (Lepelletier de Saint-Remy, p. 43.)

clothing, medical care, and the expense of supporting the women, children, and infirm, without including lodging.*

According to another calculation made in 1847, after the adoption of laws for ameliorating the condition of slaves, they cost annually about 400 francs per head.† Regarding these two calculations as extremes, we may adopt a mean of from 200 to 250 francs.

The average wages of farm laborers is, at Martinico, 1 fr. 25 c.; at Guadaloupe, 1 fr., without including the cabin and garden.‡ But there are only about 250 working days, 300 at most,§ while the slave costs the same every day of the year. Moreover, the burden of the children and infirm falls no longer on the proprietor. Now their number is estimated at more than one fourth of the population of a plantation. Between 250 or 300 fr. with these burdens, and 300 or 375 without such incumbrance, we see that the difference is not enormous.

The immigrant costs 12 fr. 50 c. per month, besides board, or from 60 to 80 centimes per day.

In short, the free laborer at the Antilles costs very nearly the same as did the slave laborer.

In consideration of adding to his floating capital the sum necessary to the increase of wages, the planter has the advantage of a more ready credit, and a higher sale price, thanks to the reduction of taxes and the increase of consumption.

In fact, the average actual net cost at the entrepôt‖ of 100 kilog. of sugar was: —

From 1840 to 1844	64 fr.	25 c.
" 1845 " 1849	59	73

It has risen: —

* Computations joined to the report of M. de Broglie, pp. 238, 239.

† Article of M. Jarnier, *Revue coloniale*, 1847, Tom. XII. p. 151.

‡ Lepelletier de Saint-Remy, 1859, p. 41.

§ Broglie, p. 239.

‖ See Table No. 3.

From 1849 to 1854	69 fr.	10 c.
" 1854 " 1859	77	58

In short, whatever road we take, we always come to the same result.

In the four slave colonies, the *aggregate of commerce,* imports and exports united, has risen above the figures anterior to 1848.

The sum of *exports,* and consequently production, is higher than before 1848, except in Guiana, which is transformed into a penal colony. The increase is inconsiderable at Guadaloupe, important at Martinico, extraordinary at Bourbon.

The *quantity* of sugar, the principal, almost exclusive product of the colonies, long below the average which preceded 1848, has attained, and since surpassed it.

Credit is easier, wages are but little higher, the sale-price has risen, even before the reduction effected by the law of 1860.

In 1847, the French colonies employed 2,022 vessels of every kind and destination in a total transportation of 115,694,170 francs.

In 1857, the colonies employed 2,488 vessels in a total transportation of 166,057,692 francs.

In 1859, the colonies employed 3,342 vessels gauged at 593,929 tons, and manned by 37,487 men, in a total transportation of 172,355,614 francs.*

Let us cease to repeat, therefore, that the colonies no longer labor, that they no longer produce, since the abolition of slavery.

* *Revue coloniale,* July, 1860, p. 135.

	1847.	1857.	1859.
Martinico	673 vessels	711	1,180
Guadaloupe	847	956	1,218
Guiana	113	98	215
Bourbon	389	723	729
	2,022	2,488	3,342

Is this to say that their condition is prosperous, and that, imaginary invalids, they complain without reason?

By no means. The condition of colonial property is still far from enviable.

But this chapter already establishes, and we shall continue to prove from our special stand-point, that this condition is not the result alone of the abolition of slavery, and that this great measure has not exaggerated wages, has not for a long time diminished production; that property is more substantial and less involved, production as abundant, the condition of commerce more flourishing.

Why are the culture of the cane and the manufacture of sugar still stagnant? At Guadaloupe, especially, the figures, after surpassing those of 1847, do not stand firm. Is this the fault of the abolition of slavery? This sugar question, so complicated and so much debated, merits a separate examination, which will be the object of the following chapter.

CHAPTER XI.

THE QUESTION OF SUGARS

The history of a lump of sugar is a whole lesson of political economy, of politics, and also of morality.

To man, sugar is not even a need, it is only a pleasure. But since man, by his industry, has extracted this product first from the cane where the Creator has deposited it in such great abundance, and next from the beet-root, he can no longer dispense with it. The production and traffic of sugar have become the origin of an incredible amount of labor and an infinite diversity of interests. I will endeavor to recall their nomenclature :* —

1. The interest of France to possess colonies ; — an interest of power, since they serve in time of war as a refuge to her flag, in time of peace as a fulcrum to her influence ; — an interest of wealth, since the impost on colonial products is one of the most productive resources of the public treasury, the amount of this tax attaining 99,000,000 francs in 1858.

2. The interest of the colonies to enjoy by privilege the commerce of France, and to furnish the mother country with a product which is their principal wealth ; for sugar represents 68,000,000 in the 72,000,000 francs' worth which they export ; it employs 250,000 out of 375,000 inhabitants,

* Consult the reports, statements, and speeches of MM. de Saint-Cricq, Humann, Gauthier de Rumilly, d'Argout, Chégaray, Bugeaud, Charles Dupin, Dumon, Rossi, Benoist d'Azy, Beugnot, Béhic, Dumas, Buffet, Ancel, Kolb-Bernard, Lavollée, etc.

and occupies 168,300 out of 374,351 acres of cultivated land.*

3. The interest of the merchant shipping, the nursery of the navy. Coal is the principal transport of the English shipping ; cotton, of the American shipping ; wood, of the Swedish shipping ; sugar, of our own. Our sugar colonies employ eight hundred of our finest vessels, and about eleven hundred sailors, the *élite* of the service.

4. The interest of commerce in the colonies, which export, in the seaports which build, man, fit out, and commission, and in the towns where commerce imports, stores, re-exports, sells, and retails.

5. The interest of a host of secondary arts and manufactures which have sugar for their basis, — refineries, distilleries, confectioneries, the manufacture of liquors, drugs, etc.†

6. The interest of science, which unceasingly perfects the processes of fabrication, invents the means of separating crystallizable from uncrystallizable matter, of heating in vacuum, and of drying by turbines, improves apparatus, increases the quantity extracted,‡ utilizes the residuum, and demonstrates more and more the healthfulness of sugar and coffee by analyses which reveal their elements. §

7. The interest of the immense capital involved in all these operations.

8. The interests of the numerous workmen which it employs. A ship is not launched without having given labor and

* Report of M. Béhic to the Council of State, 1850.

† At Paris alone, the single commune of Villette, annexed to Paris by the statute of June 24, 1859, contained at that time 7 refineries, consuming annually 30,000,000 kilog. of coal; and 100 distilleries, employing 1,000 workmen, and doing a business of 10,000,000 fr. (*Observations du Conseil municipale de la Villette, dans l'enquête de* 1859.

‡ The cane contains from 15 to 20 per cent of sugar; but 5 or 6 per cent is as yet extracted from it. The beet contains 80 per cent water, 10 per cent pulp, and 10 per cent sugar; 5 or 6 per cent is extracted.

§ Works of MM. Dumas, Payen, etc., which establish the chemical analogy of sugar with wine, fecula, and butter.

wages to 600 or 700 workmen, — carpenters, joiners, calkers, blacksmiths, locksmiths, sailmakers, ropemakers, coopers, painters, nailsmiths, tinsmiths. The number of workmen employed directly or indirectly in the service of a lump of sugar is immense, from the negro who plants the cane to the grocer who sells the loaf, from the porter who unloads to the cook who grates it.

9. Lastly, the interest of the consumers,* whose demand is increasing, since France contented herself in 1810 with 4,000,000 kilogrammes, and in 1816 with 24,000,000, while she now consumes more than 120,000,000, constantly demanding a greater quantity, but a lower price, so as to make the use of a healthful product possible among the poorer classes.

This list is the incomplete picture of the effects produced here on earth, because it pleased the Divine Creator to hide in an obscure vegetable, exiled to a torrid corner of the earth; a saccharine juice which pleases our palates. We willingly wander from this little object of human labor to the contemplation of those beautiful laws, so well set forth by masters of moral philosophy and political economy, the freedom of the gifts of God, the creation of all things in view of an enjoyment rendered legitimate by effort, the fruitful division of labor, the close solidarity of all interests from one end of the planet to the other, the fraternity, even commercial, of all members of the family of men, the neces-

* It follows, from a table joined to the Decennial Table of Customs, 1858, p. 47, that sugar has borne an almost incredible part in the progress of public consumption and revenue during the last half-century. If we add the quantity which France has fabricated to that which she has received, and deduct that which she has exported, the exact amount remains of the quantities which she has consumed.

These quantities are		542,317	metrical quintals in	1827
They rose ten years after to		1,128,999	"	1837
"	"	1,280,640	"	1847
"	"	1,651,799	"	1856

The consumption has more than tripled, therefore, during thirty years.

sary union of intellect, capital and labor. Yes ! we should admire without reserve, if so many interests had not reposed for three centuries upon two conditions regarded as indispensable, — slavery and the slave-trade.

Thus, no nation without shipping and commerce, no shipping and commerce without colonies, no colonies without culture, no culture without slaves ; — this is the odious series of reasonings passed into the rank of political axioms, and substituted, during three centuries, for these beautiful, too ideal harmonies.

The slave-trade has been condemned ; have the colonies perished ?

Slavery has been abolished ; have production and commerce been annihilated ? We have demonstrated the contrary.

Is it at least true that the special production of sugar, the most important by far in the colonies, has been subjected, since the abolition of slavery, to ruinous conditions? Is emancipation to be held responsible for this situation ?

Yes, if it did not commence until 1848. No, if it were already critical before 1848. We will examine separately the history of these two periods.

§ 1. The Question of Sugars before Emancipation.

The true knot of the question is, as is well known, the competition of the *beet-root sugar*, which was not thought of in 1820 ; which already produced 10,000,000 kilog. in 1830, approached 30,000,000 kilog. in 1840, and exceeded 60,000,000 kilog. in 1847, precisely the year when the duty on both sugars became equal by law, August 1, 1847, six months before the Revolution of February.

The history of this competition is another very curious lesson in political economy.

It owes its birth in part to the Continental blockade, its

progress to the excessive protection obtained by the colonies, its triumph to their improvidence. "Indigenous sugar is a creation of taxation," said M. Rossi.*

At the time of the blockade, our colonies were lost or ruined, and debarred from selling to the mother country, to friends, to enemies, or to neutrals ; misfortune, as usual, was inventive, and obstacles served progress. It was then that men set to work to extract sugar from the beet-root ; but, despite the ministerial circulars, the instructions of M. Parmentier, and the encouragements amply tempered by licenses of importation, this sugar long remained an experiment of the laboratory rather than a product of manufacture. The processes were imperfect ; the net cost was too high.

While scientific men continued their experiments on indigenous sugar, colonial sugar was subjected to the essays of financiers.

From the statute of May 15, 1791, to and including the decree of November 1, 1810, we count eighteen statutes or decrees which altered or rather tormented the tariff on sugars, carrying the duty on colonial sugars from 0 to 35, 45, and 90 fr. per 100 kilog., and the duty on foreign sugars from 36 fr. 22 c. to 7 fr. 34 c., then to 30, 75, 100, 200, and 400 fr.†

The first movement of the Restoration was to enter upon a liberal path, and an ordinance of Monsieur, dated April 23, 1814, subjected French and foreign sugars to the same duty, a measure demanded by the consumption, which the colonies could not satisfy, but which excited their complaints to such a degree that, on the 17th of December of the same year, a statute fixed at 60 and 95 fr. the duties on raw or clayed sugars of foreign production, maintaining at 40 and 70 fr. the duties on similar French sugars.

* Report to the Chamber of Peers, June 20, 1843.

† Question of the tariff on sugars, General Council of Commerce, session of 1850.

The statute of April 28, 1816, raised to 45 fr. the duties on French sugars, to 75 fr. the duties on foreign sugars imported by French ships, and to 80 fr. those brought under a foreign flag. The extra charge, which was thus 30 fr., was raised to 50 fr. by the statute of July 22, 1822.* In 1826, all privilege was taken away from sugars produced by the French East Indian possessions. A premium on exportation had been accorded to refined sugars, June 7, 1820, and this premium, suppressed to make way for a simple drawback duty in 1822, was also re-established in 1826.

We thus digressed more and more from the starting-point, not ceasing to profess the doctrines of free trade, and not ceasing to practise — while setting forth exceptional necessities, and declaring that they should be provisional — a progressive system of protection, even of privilege.

Doubtless, the colonies, if sick, became convalescent under this régime; they produced in 1816 above 17,000,000 kilog., while France consumed 24,000,000 kilog.; in 1818, 30,000,000 kilog., while the consumption attained 36,000,000 kilog.; thus leaving but 6,000,000 kilog. to be furnished by foreign countries. In 1822, the production, more than tripled in six years, was 52,000,000 kilogrammes.

Doubtless also the Treasury found its account in this progress, no less than the shipping and commerce.

Doubtless, lastly, the consumers saw with pleasure the prices fall from 90 and 93 fr. per 50 kilog. to 74 fr. 50 c. and even to 63 fr. 85 c. in 1822. But the colonists, to whom this rate still left a remunerative price higher by 20 fr. per 50 kilog., complained and obtained new favors (statute of May 17, 1826), which finally expelled foreign sugar, and carried the price to 83 and even 106 francs.

Foreign sugar was vanquished, profits were enormous, the premiums on the exportation of refined sugars paid by

* From April 21, 1818, a reduction of 5 fr. had been accorded on sugar from Bourbon, on account of the distance.

the Treasury, carried from 90 to 110 fr. by the statute of June 7, 1820, were raised from 300,000 fr. to 2,128,000 fr. in 1822 ; replaced by the simple restitution of duties (statute of July 27, 1822), but re-established by the statute of May 17, 1826, they attained 6,300,000 fr. in 1828, and exceeded 19,110,000 fr. in 1832.*

The colonies flattered themselves that they triumphed by these exorbitant privileges ; but one does not triumph over the laws of nature by the laws of society. These privileges had their baleful results to the colonies : —

1. The high prices kept away consumers ;

2. They decided the colonists to plant sugar-cane in lands unfitted to this culture, and to sacrifice the production of commodities which had no rivals in France, and exempted them from the care of seeking less costly and more efficacious processes of manufacture ;

3. They encouraged the producers of indigenous sugar, who in a little time profited more than the colonists by the premiums on exportation.

When the statute of April 26, 1833, returning to the drawback system for the exportation of refined sugars, divided raw sugars into two classes, *white* and *brown*, reduced the tariff on each class, and lowered the extra charge on foreign sugars, it was no longer with the latter that colonial sugar had to contend. The production of indigenous sugar, which in 1828 did not amount to 3,000,000 kilog., was 9,000,000 in 1831, 12,000,000 in 1832, 19,000,000 in 1833, and was destined to reach 50,000,000 in 1836.†

* The impossibility of fixing the exact proportion of the conversion of raw into refined sugar, leaves a margin for enormous profits in re-exportation, and this explains the prodigious increase.

† From 1816 to 1835, the number of acres employed in the culture of the sugar-cane rose, in Martinico, to 13,587
Guadaloupe 17,924
Guiana 2,484
Bourbon 35,336

Too many favors, by raising up rivals, had paved the way for the ruin of the colonies.

The beet-root sugar was taxed in turn, but after fourteen years of freedom ; — it was for the interest of the colonies that it should be subjected to a tax, it was for the interest of the Treasury that this tax should be light, to encourage the growth of the taxable material. The tax was at first 10 fr. per 100 kilog., and was raised, two years after, to 15 fr. (Statute of July 18, 1837.) This insignificant tariff, which was adopted, however, by a majority of but one, did not prevent the manufacturers from throwing 50,000,000 kilog. of sugar into market in 1838 ; the crops having been abundant this same year in the colonies, the fall was excessive, and the embarrassment became such that the Governors of the Antilles and the government took the responsibility, in 1839, the one of authorizing the colonies to sell elsewhere than in France, the other of making a reduction, by ordinance, of 13 fr. 50 c. on colonial sugars.

Indigenous sugar was subjected to a duty of 25 fr. by the statute of July 3, 1840, which fixed at 45 fr. the duty on colonial sugar. This reaction in a different direction struck a death-blow to numerous small mills.

Despite this blow, despite these burdens, such was the progress of indigenous sugar-making,* placed within the reach of science, capital, and markets, that production, at first lessened, resumed its upward movement,† and the

The number of acres devoted to the culture of coffee, cotton, cocoa, and spices diminished to 3,268 in Martinico,
5,506 in Guadaloupe,
404 in Guiana,
7,561 in Bourbon. — *Notice Officielles*, 1840, I pp. 35, 143.

* To produce 3,000,000 kilog. in 1828, the indigenous sugar manufacture employed 6,800 acres, while in 1836 it produced 50,000,000 kilog. with 4,207 acres only, thus producing sixteen times as much with less than half as much land.

† 1840	23,000,000 kilog.
1841	27,000,000
1842	31,000,000

uneasiness of the colonies, shared by the government, was so lively, that, January 10, 1843, a bill proposed the absolute interdiction of the manufacture of beet-root sugar, except in consideration of preliminary indemnity.

An interdiction pronounced at the beginning might, perhaps, have been comprehensible. England, in establishing, at first sight, without circumspection, equality of duties for all sugars, had stifled a manufacture in its cradle, the development of which might endanger her maritime interests, her colonies, and her revenue,* while agriculture had as yet no need of this new product. The same might have been done in France. Labor and capital did not lack employ there, while the new manufacture menaced our colonies, shipping, and exports as much as our importations.

But at the point which things had reached, the position was much more complicated, and both causes had witnessed the growth of the importance of their motives and the number of their advocates. Thus the struggle was terrible.

On one side the colonies and ports, on the other the manufactures and agriculture, ranged their arguments in battle.

The colonies said: —

Either free us from the colonial compact, and let us sell and buy in all places; or else, if you preserve the monopoly of our purchases, guarantee us the monopoly of our sales; there is but one means to do this, absolutely to suppress indigenous sugar. Whatever may be the tax, it will either suppress it indirectly and without indemnity, or it will suffer it to live; iniquitous in the first case, it is insufficient in the second. Equality of taxation does not involve equality of position; now we have not the resources of indigenous sugar, yet we support the burdens of transportation, commission, and waste, to which it is not subject.

The ports added: Threatened with being deprived of

* Rossi, p. 13. This branch of manufacture has nevertheless since assumed great importance.

coasting, by the rapid growth of railways, we lose, by the rivalry of indigenous sugar, the principal homeward freight of our distant navigation. The weakening of our merchant shipping endangers the navy, and reduces more laborers to want than are employed in the culture of the beet-root and the manufacture of indigenous sugar, — a culture and manufacture which are yearly reducing the quantity of wheat produced by French soil.

But the agriculturists replied, that 75,000 acres of beet-root would produce more sugar than France could consume, — and what were 75,000 acres out of our 100,000,000 acres of arable land? This culture of a tap-rooted, weeded plant was excellent to prepare the earth for the production of wheat, and wheat sown after a crop of beets would produce a tenth more than after any other crop.* The alliance of agriculture and the arts and manufactures, the maintenance of the country population, the augmentation of wages, the increase of the yield and market value of lands, the improvement of the food of cattle, the production of manures, were favored by this important innovation. The manufacturers added that the production of 100,000 kilog. of sugar corresponded to the distribution of 43,500 francs' wages; that an enormous sum had been employed in improving processes and apparatus; that, if indigenous sugar were free from certain charges, property in France was subject to much heavier charges than in the colonies; that the produce of these colonies had attained its maximum; that the ports would have no reason to complain if the ships received a less value in a greater bulk. Lastly, and above all, indigenous sugar presented itself as the benefactor of the nation, since it had enriched the Treasury, lowered prices, increased consumption, improved agriculture.

Some devised a sort of mobile scale which was to equalize

* *Analyse de la question des sucres*, by Louis-Napoleon Bonaparte. Fortress of Ham, August, 1842.

conditions, raising or lowering the duties on either sugar, according as their comparative production was greater or smaller. But this sort of financial dynamics, operating blindly in the future, had few partisans.

A glimpse was also had of a simultaneous reduction on both sugars, and the liberty to introduce foreign sugars.* The shipping interest demanded this liberty without renouncing the privilege of the flag. The *refiners* † also demanded it, complaining that the duties paid on 100 kilogrammes of raw sugar were restored on 70 per cent of refined sugar, and pretended that the production was below 60 per cent, while scientific men affirmed that it was over 80 per cent. But the Treasury, greatly embarrassed between these diverse claims, — since indigenous sugar had made it lose more than 200,000,000 francs which it would have collected on colonial sugar, but in turn brought it in nearly 10,000,000 francs yearly, — the Treasury relied little on the uncertain increase which the extension of consumption would bring it in exchange for a certain loss; it was admitted, that, to influence the habits of the peo-

* In January, 1837, a bill, in which M. Duchâtel took the initiative, and which was reported by M. Dumon, proposed a reduction of 20 fr. It was rejected by the Chamber of Deputies.

† For the sake of brevity, we do not begin the history of the struggle until the birth of indigenous sugar. But all know how much it had long been hampered by the trade of *refining*.

Refining on the spot diminishes the quantity of exportable matter, but increases its value, reduces the expense of transportation, and leaves to the producer the profits of the rum and molasses produced by the distillation of the coarser materials arising from the sugar.

But it was to the advantage neither of the refineries nor the harbors of the mother country. Leaguing together, they obtained a prohibition of the establishment of new refineries by the colonies, by a decree of council, Jan. 21, 1684, and a tax on colonial *refined* sugars, which was increased from 8 liv. to 22 liv. 10 sols per quintal; then lastly an absolute prohibition, Nov. 26, 1698, renewed by the statute of Dec. 17, 1814.

In default of refining, the colonies adopted *claying*, a more imperfect process; but the same interest procured the taxation of *clayed* sugars in 1791, and the extra charge imposed by the statute of April 28, 1816, was almost prohibitory.

See *L'Étude sur le système colonial*, by M. de Chazelles, Chap. II. p. 76, etc.

ple, the reduction must be considerable, and this was estimated at one half, or 25,000,000 on 50,000,000 francs. Now it was not to be supposed that the population of a country rich in wine and fruits were about suddenly to prefer coffee to beer, tea to cider, lemonade to wine.

These two systems of a reduction and a mobile scale being set aside, there remained only the systems of equalizing duties and of suppressing indigenous sugar, with an indemnity. The government had strongly proposed the second, the Chambers preferred the first.

The indemnity had the advantage of settling the difficulty forever, by buying out the interest of the sacrificed rival. But, in principle, how comprehend that the state should pay an indemnity for exercising its right? in practice, how assign this indemnity so that it should not fall arbitrarily into the hands of the manufacturers, instead of those of the laborers and freeholders? How kill a hardy, intelligent, and useful business, and sacrifice its interests with those of the consumers to the dissatisfied interests of the colonies?

They preferred, and the statute of July 2, 1843, sanctioned, a system of equality, leaving indigenous sugar but four years to wait for it. From August 1, 1847, the duty was therefore 45 francs per 100 kilogrammes on sugars of the first *type*, *colonial* or *indigenous*, with the exception of a reduction of 7 fr. 50 c., by reason of distance, on those of Bourbon; from 65 to 85 francs on *foreign brown* sugars, according to the production and flag; from 80 to 105 francs on the same *white* sugars.

The next day witnessed the closing of the mills which

* There was an increase of one tenth for superior types. The type is not a model, but a limit. A first type being given, those inferior to it pay the same duty, those superior, pay more. The decree of June 13, 1851, which was not put into effect until the end of 1852, substituted for the system of types, taxation according to saccharine matter and production.

had reopened or had exaggerated their production in view of an indemnity, but the gradual augmentation of duties* did not arrest the progress of indigenous sugar.

We will sum up in a few lines the condition matters had reached in 1847, the eve of emancipation.

Both sugars paid equal duties. The colonial sugar, protected little, then much, then too much, had seen this favor raise up a dangerous rival. This rival, unperceived, disdained, then dreaded, taxed more and more, and threatened with total interdiction, had conquered equality before the Treasury.

But this was the only equality between the two rivals. The same force of impulse did not regulate their progress, — the one made rapid strides, the other nearly stood still.

SUGARS CONSUMED OR REFINED IN FRANCE.†

	Foreign Sugar. Met. quintals.	Colonial Sugar. Met. quintals.	Indigenous Sugar. Met. quintals.	Total. Met. quintals
1827–1836	13,983	708,651	130,500	853,134
1837–1846	80,829	773,079	366,763	1,220,671

Thus, in twenty years the quantity consumed or refined had increased one fourth.

In this sum total, *foreign* sugar represents a quantity *seven* times larger, *indigenous* sugar has *tripled, colonial sugar* has not increased even one seventh.

In 1827	Colonial sugar furnished	593,733 m. q.
	Foreign sugar	9,444
	Indigenous sugar	0

of a total quantity of 603,177 m. q. subjected to duties, or almost the whole consumption.

In 1847, colonial sugar no longer furnished even one half.

* While the collection of the tax on exotic sugar was effected without difficulty, that of the tax on indigenous sugar gave rise to enormous frauds, and to numerous legislative measures. (See the excellent reports of M. Damon, April 29, 1842, and M. Benoist d'Azy, July 16, 1844, April 12 and June 16, 1845.)

† Decennial Table of Customs, 1858, p. 67.

Colonial sugar	878,261
Foreign sugar	96,261
Indigenous sugar	523,703
Total	1,498,225 m. q.

And indigenous sugar absorbs by itself alone almost the whole of the increase attained in consumption.

Meanwhile, the price of sugar, which had been 73 fr. 50 c. per 50 kilog. in 1820, fell to 55 fr. in 1847.*

Diminished to 22,748,204 kilog. in 1840, under the empire of a statute which no longer permitted any to make indigenous sugar, except those who *had a monomania for it,* as exclaimed Marshal Bugeaud, † the indigenous production remounted in 1847 to 60,169,000 kilog. ‡ The beet-root, which did not occupy 50,000 acres before 1840, extended over nearly 75,000 in 1847, and employed more than three hundred mills.

In short, § in 1847 the beet-root had conquered the sugar-cane, — a production which may be infinitely extended, which can lack neither labor nor ground, in an orderly community, within reach of markets, science, and credit, threatened more and more a production which was limited at once by a confined territory, the insufficiency of labor, and the defects of a state of society exposed to inevitable transformation. ||

Thus the condition of commerce and property in the colonies was every year represented to the public authorities of the mother country as in decline, and in peril of death.

* See Table No. 3.

† Report of Count Beugnot, 1851.

‡ In 1836, M. Crespel declared before the Commission of the Chamber of Deputies, that the establishment of a *duty* would result in destroying indigenous manufacture; that it would close all its factories and transport them to foreign countries. (Report of M. Dumon.)

§ Report of M. Dumon, 1848.

|| Exposition of the reasons of M. Guizot in the Chamber of Peers, May 19, 1847.

To form an idea of the condition of colonial property before 1848, read the reports of M. Rossi to the Chamber of Peers, and of M. Dalloz to the Chamber of Deputies, on the bill relative to mortgages and. forced expropriation in the Antilles, and the discussion in the Chamber of Peers.* All the testimony agrees in confirming the estimate given by an official document,† which fixes at one fourth or one third of the territorial value the amount of mortgage debt in the colonies of Martinico and Guadaloupe, or 140,000,000 or 150,000,000 francs on a value of 500,000,000, while the mortgage debt of France did not exceed 23 per cent of its landed capital. It was asserted that the expenses of civil courts in Martinico amounted to 1,700,000 francs per year, nearly the sum of the appropriation inscribed in the budget for the colony. The absence of credit and the scarcity of ready money had raised the rate of interest in the colonies to 12, 16, 24, and 30 per cent. One of their defenders rejected the application of the expropriation law for fear of what he called *putting them up at universal auction;* and in fact, this law, postponed, except at Bourbon, at the time of the promulgation of the Civil Code (1805), deliberated on in 1822 and 1839, proposed in 1840, then withdrawn, presented in 1842, discussed and voted by the Chamber of Peers, reported in the Chamber of Deputies, postponed anew, then again brought up in 1847, was not destined to precede the abolition of slavery. The colonists were to lose at once what an ardent abolitionist ‡ called the privilege of owning men and of not paying their debts. A graver authority, Admiral Roussin, in 1842, had summed up the position in these strong words:

"At Martinico, Guadaloupe, and Guiana, it may be said

* *Moniteur*, 1848, pp. 106, 459, 471, 479, 481, 490.

† Report of M. Lavollée, Inspector of Finances.

‡ M. Gatine, *procès-verbaux de la Commission de* 1848. The word *whitewashing* was commonly used to express liquidation without expropriation.

with certainty, that, save very rare exceptions, private property exists no longer, and is only a word devoid of meaning. Those who own property there have no more credit than those who own none, so general is the opinion that all estates are encumbered with debts above their value. I do not seek here into the cause of this condition, but I affirm the fact." *

The learned defender of the colonies, M. Charles Dupin, sought the cause, but did not deny the condition, and seemed unable to find expressions strong enough to characterize *such excess of want, such immensity of suffering.*†

In 1822, M. Portal verified the same trials. In 1822, the Minister of the Marine addressed a report to the king, containing these words: "The suffering of our colonies is a veritable public calamity." ‡

It is known by what laudable efforts the Restoration and the Monarchy of July combated and diminished these sufferings, but in 1847 they are seen again as poignant as before.

The complaints of the colonies equalled, and even surpassed, their sufferings, and they demanded with one voice, not only equality of taxation, but a large reduction in favor of colonial sugars.

Such was the state of affairs in 1847. It is important to characterize it clearly, so as not to suffer to be imputed to the abolition of slavery the responsibility of the evils which preceded it.

§ 2. The Sugar Question from Emancipation to the Law of May 23, 1860.

After the Revolution, emancipation, and universal suffrage had fallen simultaneously upon "this most suffering, most

* Chamber of Peers, March 8, 1842, *Moniteur*, p. 471.

† *Ibid.* p. 460.

‡ M. de Chazelles, p. 102.

delicate, and most fragile body," as styled by M. Rossi in 1841, immediate indemnity and reduction of duties were loudly demanded. It was justice, it was necessity.

From 1850, government had proposed a bold and radical reform.* The overthrow of the colonies seemed regarded as almost admitted and irremediable. Their production, which had surpassed 102,000,000 kilog. of sugar in 1845, fell to 63,000,000 in 1848, to 57,000,000 in 1849, to 40,000,000 in 1850. Doubtless, the indigenous manufacture had also fallen from 60,000,000 kilog. in 1847, to 56,000,000 in 1848, and to 44,000,000 in 1849, but to rise again, in 1850, to 64,644,994 kilog.

The consumption had followed the same decline, descending from 132,000,000 kilogrammes in 1847 to 98,000,000 in 1848, to return to 116,000,000 in 1849 and 121,000,000 in 1850, checked by a rise of 17 fr. 4 c. per kilogramme. The receipts of the Treasury, from 59,000,000 francs in 1847, were but 46,000,000 in 1858, and 58,000,000 in 1849.

It was clear that the equality of taxes corresponded to extreme inequality of conditions ; it was necessary to change them. To lower the duties on colonial sugars 6 francs ; to increase the consumption by a large reduction, from 45 to 25 francs, but progressively and at stated periods, so as to popularize the use of so salutary a product, while restoring to the Treasury what it abandoned ; to open the door somewhat wider to the introduction of foreign sugars, to the same end, and also to indemnify the shipping for the diminution of colonial transportation, — such was the policy of the bill in which a distinguished Minister, M. Buffet, took the initiative, and of which Count Beugnot was the intelligent, complete, and impartial reporter.

Some went further, and MM. Levasseur and Desjobert proposed to declare the colonial compact broken, and to

* See the two remarkable reports, already cited, of MM. Béhic and Beugnot.

leave to the colonies full internal and external liberty, preserving only the national sovereignty and political bonds. A bold, logical, but premature proposition, it was at least entertained at a moment when the mother country and the colonies were scarcely in a condition to support, after so many shocks, the experience of new economical theories.

The law on sugars, worked over, discussed, at length passed, June 13, 1851, after three deliberations, by 450 votes against 228, appeared in the *Moniteur* on the 26th of June. But it was not to take effect until January 1, 1852.

Before this epoch, the Assembly had ceased to exist, and from March 27, 1852, a decree * returned to the old duty of 45 fr., fixed in 1816 on colonial sugars, and 57 fr. on foreign sugars, according for four years a detax of 7 fr. on colonial sugars. Continued by the law of June 28, 1856, but reduced gradually to 3 fr., this detax was to end June 30, 1861, but has been prolonged by the law of May 23, 1860, till June 30, 1866.†

Boldly resuming the idea of 1851, in the face of a consumption which amounted to 200,000,000 kilog. in 1848, and to 185,000,000 in 1849, and poured into the treasury 99,000,000 fr. net in 1858 and 94,000,000 in 1859, this law ventures on a sudden diminution of four ninths (from 49 to 25 fr.), which will cost the treasury nearly 50,000,000 the first year, counting confidently that the consumption encouraged by the fall of prices will descend to the working classes, and restore to the treasury what it hazards. This confidence is reasonable, since in England the consumption is 15½ kilog. per head, in Switzerland 8 kilog., in Holland 7 kilog., in France 3 kilog. only. At the same time, the colonies will be released from a duty nearly equal to half the value of the product, and will continue to be protected against indigenous sugar, as the latter was formerly against them. Indigenous sugar, pursuing its progress

* *Moniteur*, March 29, p. 809. † Report of M. Ancel.

after having braved duties, will brave, as M. Dumas announced in the discussion of 1851, the foreign sugar that will be introduced more freely. The shipping, still protected, will profit by a double element of transportation. The consumer who paid 11 fr. per kilog. in 1810, and 3 fr. in 1816, will pay less than one franc.*

These reductions of tariff are bold, risking as they do more than 50,000,000 francs of the resources of the Treasury, but intelligent and popular. The example of England encourages them, as we shall see. Financial science approves them, demonstrating more and more, that the reduction of taxes makes cheap markets, when the reduction is notable and sudden enough for its insensible action not to be lost on the way in the adroit profits of middlemen,† and that cheapness makes bulky duties and draws large sums out of small profits. Imprudent, sterile, when accorded to products the use of which cannot be extended, as wine, salt, etc., the reduction of duties is wise and profitable when it suffers commodities to come within the reach of all, which all desire and do not consume. Hygiene also approves it. Politics cannot complain of it, since this measure results from no international engagement. Humanity felicitates it on seeing comfort descend among all ranks.

As to the colonies, the time for receiving great benefit from it had gone by. For twelve, or rather twenty years, they had demanded a large reduction on their commodities. Proposed in 1837, then again in 1850, they have at length obtained it. If they do not profit by it, it is not emancipation that they should blame, but themselves ; for it is found that this reduction came at a moment when emancipation had finished its work, when labor and production had attained or surpassed the figures of 1847. Neither let it be

* We refer to the close of the chapter for the conditions of the law of 1860, concerning coffees, cocoas, and teas.

† The middlemen here are unfortunately very powerful and very numerous.

said that emancipation had done so much harm that it was necessary to make the reduction. The reduction was not obtained for the first time until 1852, when it could no longer repair the early disasters; and was effected the second time after these disasters had been effaced.

All secondary cultures have been sacrificed to the sugar-cane, and this sugar, protected to excess, has been conquered by indigenous sugar, the birth of which grew out of this very protection. Such is the truth. Not freedom, but the beet-root, has caused the present position.

But, lastly, why and how has colonial sugar been conquered by indigenous sugar to such a degree that it is necessary to-day to protect it? It is interesting to press the question more closely, and to elicit, not the only, but the principal cause of this inferiority of long standing.

Two essential lessons, if I mistake not, may be drawn from it; the one interests political economy, the other especially concerns the question of slavery.

Extreme protection, the search after a chimerical equipoise, equality, interdiction, are wellnigh vain formulas. We can neither revive an expiring trade, nor kill a hardy one by a blow of the tariff. Dams do not make a running stream of stagnant water. Barriers do not prevent the river from flowing, should it wear itself a new bed.

Now colonial sugar was the stagnant water, indigenous sugar the running stream. An exaggerated protection has killed the colonies, which sacrificed everything to the culture of the sugar-cane. At the same time it has killed the sugar-cane, by raising it up an unlooked-for rival. Continual changes in the laws have hampered this rival greatly, yet in vain. Neither the treasury, nor the colonies, nor business, has been benefited by these essays.

"In this long table," said M. Benoist d'Azy,* admirably, "in this long table of the successive variations, or rather

* Report of July 16, 1844.

alternations, of opinions and decisions, we see with pro found regret how distressing these continual oscillations must have been to all the trades which are bound up with these great questions, and there is reason to be astonished that the evil is not greater than it is. Who could have been daring enough to invest capital in real estate in far-off colonies, to change all the processes of fabrication, to build ships, to apply his mind to distant trade and navigation, to fix his fortune and children there, or even to attempt with sufficient help, on the national territory, great and expensive enterprises, uniting agriculture and manufactures, in the face of this species of intermittent fever, which every year called in question the existence of those who devoted themselves to such operations? We often seek the cause of the suffering or comparative weakness of some one of our branches of trade; it comes, in great part, from the everlasting inconstancy of our doctrines concerning the protection which is due them.

"Uncertainty in the commercial and industrial government of a country is a hundred times worse than a bad system, for nothing is more opposed to all spirit of enterprise or progress, to all generous and useful effort."

There comes a time when, weary of this long uncertainty, of these barriers which check nothing and these favors which develop nothing, all interests are wellnigh united in demanding of freedom of production that formula which all the financial combinations have been unable to find.*

But there is a lesson more directly applicable to the subject which occupies our attention.

Of the two countries which produce sugar, on which side has Nature placed the advantage?

Evidently on the side of the colonies; the soil is more fruitful, the sun more ardent, the seasons more regular, the

* It was demanded by M. Passy in 1832, and report of M. Béhic, 1830, p. 9, and by M. Humann in 1826. (*Moniteur*, p. 298.)

sugar-cane twice as saccharine and easier worked than the beet-root.

What, then, have the colonies lacked?

Not time, for during two centuries they had the monopoly. Not favor, for, before the first Revolution, the colonies paid only 5 fr. duty per 100 kilogrammes.* After the first abolition, they ceased to pay any tax; † since the Restoration, they have had fifteen years' monopoly and thirteen years' protection. Not labor, for, till 1830, they had the slave-trade, till 1848, slavery. Not wealth, ‡ for they long sold sugar at high prices, not only at 1,100 fr. per 100 kilogrammes during the blockade, an epoch when smugglers profited more by these prices than the colonies, but during the Restoration at 88, 91, 99, and even 116 fr. per 100 kilogrammes; lastly, even after the rivalry of indigenous sugar, very often at a price superior to the net cost, — a price burdened, doubtless, with charges of transportation to which this rival was not subject, but obtained by laborers who demanded no wages, on estates protected against dispossession.

During this long endurance of privilege and prosperity, what prevented the colonists then from improving their processes of manufacture, from securing the immigration of first-rate mechanics and artisans, from extracting a more abundant and less costly yield from the admirable plant placed in their hands by the Creator, — in a word, from doing *beforehand* through interest what they courageously did *afterwards* through necessity?

"With the stationary capital, uselessly lavished on the colonies," said M. Rossi, § "more sugar might have been made than the five continents consume. Two thirds of the

* Letters patent of 1777.

† Statute of 1793.

‡ To hear the former colonists of St. Domingo, there was not one that had not lost from 50,000 to 100,000 livres' income.

§ Report, 1843, p. 49.

sugar of the cane escapes in the operations of a manufacture yet in its infancy."

"Such is the state of agriculture," said M. de Broglie, "that, by the aid of easy reforms, the colonies might, without additional expense, obtain an increase of one third, perhaps even one half, of their present yield. The processes of manufacture are still what they were one hundred and fifty years ago. . . . . . It is astonishing that it is possible to obtain any sugar by working in this manner." *

See, on the contrary, the manufacture of indigenous sugar. By reason of the high prices, this beautiful branch of industry departed from the hands of science, and passed into the mills. The imposition of a tax suppressed ill-begotten works, but stimulated those which were viable; favored, the business grew; fettered, it became transformed, changed apparatus, † changed markets, and such was the progress that 283 mills, in 1848, produced 56,000,000 kilogrammes, while 386 mills, in 1841, produced only 26,000,000 kilogrammes; the same number of acres, sown at the two given periods, produced in the second a yield superior to that of the first; the same quantity, 100 kilogrammes, exacted 14 fr. 80 c. in the first, and 5 fr. only in the second.‡ Lastly, the same product which, in 1837, objected to 5 fr. 50 c. duty per 100 kilogrammes, supported 54 fr. in 1859. §

Who then, once more, prevented the colonists, before this formidable rivalry, from realizing all this progress?

A competent and well-informed witness, in 1847, wrote words from Martinico which may be applied to all the slave colonies, and which are the best reply to this question: —

"Agriculture here is in an almost savage state, and also demands emancipation. With incredible exuberance of

* Report, p. 69.

† Processes of Rousseau, Melsens, Dubrunfaut, etc. Remark, however, that if the substitution of large mills for small ones be a progress in manufacture, it is not a happy change in an agricultural point of view.

‡ Report of M. Béhic, p. 28.

§ See Table D.

labor, scarcely a third of the lands are improved. Productive estates are daily abandoned for new clearings ; the slave toilingly attempts the most barbarous cultivation with impossible implements, and, the processes of manufacture aiding, there is obtained from the soil scarcely one fourth of its product. . . . . . What can matter agricultural amelioration to men whose condition seems destined never to be ameliorated ? And how fail to comprehend the disgust of the colonist at unsuccessful experiments ? The slave detests the soil, the mulatto and the freedman despise it, and the white works it hastily, as one eagerly searches a mine, thinking soon to abandon it." *

In 1843, the illustrious M. Rossi summed up the leading feature of the picture in these words : —

"What the colonist should dread are his own habits." †

The colonist is indolent, the Frenchman is active ; the colonist follows routine, the Frenchman is in quest of progress ; the colonist takes his pleasure and runs in debt, the Frenchman speculates and undertakes new enterprises ; to one, idleness is the sign of wealth, to the other, labor is the condition of it. The first drives slaves, the second employs machinery ; on one side is servile labor, and Creole society, its work ; on the other is free labor, and French society, its offspring.

Let no one repeat, then, that the abolition of slavery has killed the colonies ; so many proofs establish that they had already long been dying of a disease which was no other than slavery.

If ever economists seek a proof of the superiority of free labor over servile labor, of a community that labors over a community that makes others labor, let them study this

* M. Garnier, employed in the Direction of the Interior at Martinico. *Revue coloniale*, p. 138, 1847, Tom. XII.

† See also the excellent pages 18, 19, and 22 of the report of M. Benoist d'Azy

curious history of the struggle between the sugar-cane and beet-root; the demonstration is striking, and is worth the trouble it gives the mind to make its way through these rebutting and confused details.

§ 3. Coffee, Cocoa, Tea.

Emancipation is not to be accused of having diminished the coffee plantations of our colonies; as we have already seen, the exaggeration of the protective duty on sugars has caused the sacrifice of coffee, indigo, and cotton to the planting of the sugar-cane and the large revenue that it promised. "Warnings have not been lacking," said M. Benoist d'Azy, in 1844. "It has often been told the colonies, that it would be more prudent for them to return to the culture of coffee, cotton, and indigo, which find no rivalry on French soil, and which, perhaps, will be better suited to the coming condition of the population. These counsels have not been followed." A most grievous result, especially as it concerns coffee; for it is well known that the culture of this little shrub, transported from Persia or Arabia, at the close of the seventeenth century, to Java, and afterwards to Surinam and the Antilles, exacts less labor, less capital, and a less fertile soil than the culture of the sugar-cane; that, once in full bearing, after three or four years the coffee shrub, if the victim of no insect, lasts fifteen years and more, and bears in abundance the berry which comes to us rid of its outer envelope, keeps, improves with age, and gives us an exquisite, and at the same time healthful drink, if we are to believe chemistry, which affirms that a quart composed of equal parts of milk and coffee represents *five times* as much solid substance and *three times* as much azote substances as the same quantity of soup.*

* *Revuê coloniale*, 1858, article translated from the Tropical Agriculturist, pp 410, 447.

It is also known that the consumption of coffee has assumed an enormous growth. England consumes forty times as much as at the beginning of the century. Brazil, where coffee was not introduced until 1774, now produces 173,000,000 kilogrammes of the 338,000,000 which represent the total production of the globe. The consumption is, in Belgium and Holland, 4 kilog. per head; in the United States, 2 kilog. 445 gr.; in the Zollverein, 1 kilog. 600 gr.; in England, 6 kilog. 40 gr.; and in France, but 750 gr. per head.

Of 35,415,000 kilog. imported in 1847, our colonies furnished us but 1,274,000 kilog., while Brazil sent us 10,123,000 kilog., Hayti, 7,108,000, Cuba and Porto Rico, 5,057,000, etc., etc. The amount fell to 728,000 kilog. in 1848. It rose again to nearly 1,000,000 kilog. in 1857, in the three colonies of Martinico, Guadaloupe, and Bourbon, without including Guiana.*

Coffee has not nor can have an indigenous rival like sugar.† For this reason little attention was paid to it, and the duty which burdened it was not once changed until lately from the tariff at which it was fixed in 1816. At this epoch, coffee was worth 300 fr. the 100 kilog.; to-day, it is worth about 60 fr. The duty nevertheless remained 60 fr. on colonial coffees, 95 fr. on foreign coffees imported by French vessels. Equal to the value of the commodity, it did not stimulate the colonies; higher than that of foreign coffees, it did not hinder their importation; it only threw an obstacle in the way of a greater fall of price, and consequently of an extension of consumption. The law of 1860 has reduced the duty one half, from 60 fr. to 30 fr., and from 95 fr. to 42 fr.; the colonies and foreign countries

* Formerly, St. Domingo alone exported 37,000,000 kilog. of coffee.

† "Chicory cannot be honored with this name, though it is pretended that from 4,000,000 to 5,000,000 kilog. of *chicory coffee* are sold annually, — a mixture of coffee, chicory, burnt roots, pulp of the beet-root, and often earth or clay." Report of M. Beugnot, 1843.

will produce more ; the shipping, which already employs 34,000 tons in the service of foreign coffee, the principal resource, after sugar, of our distant navigation, will see its transportation increase ; the treasury will recuperate its sacrifices (one half our 28,000,000 fr. collected in 1858), if, as is probable, so sudden a fall, decreasing the price of coffee 32 centimes per pound, popularizes this excellent production, already widely diffused by the habits of our soldiers of the Crimea and Italy. This reduction is combined with that of the price of sugar ; both concur in the same end, as 1 kilogramme of coffee consumed causes the consumption of 6 or 7 kilogrammes of sugar.

The same law diminishes one half the duties on cocoa, which formerly amounted to 30 per cent of the value of the commodity.* It also aids in the consumption of sugar, which is mingled with the cocoa in nearly equal parts in the manufacture of chocolate. It gratifies an indisputable desire for consumption, since, despite the high duties, the importation of cocoa into France, which did not exceed 2,008,000 kilog. in 1830, amounted to 4,091,000 kilog. in 1859. It may be hoped that this large reduction will restore this culture to favor in our colonies, where it is now unimportant, having been sacrificed like that of coffee to the production of sugar. Doubtless the West Indian cocoa has not the reputation of that of Martinico or Maracaybo. Doubtless, too, the preparation of a cocoa plantation demands six or eight years ; but after this first labor, it lasts fifty years on the sea-coast and thirty years in the interior, and the owner can walk under the shade of his trees, analogous to our cherry-trees, with no other trouble than that of seeing that they are watered. The culture is very easy,

* By French ships	Colonies	20 fr. per 100 kil.		
" "	Elsewhere	25	"	"
" "	Entrêpots	35	"	"
By foreign ships		40	"	"

since the Mexicans had no difficulty in cultivating the cocoa-tree, abandoned at the moment of the Spanish conquest, the seeds of which they used as money; while the savage tribes of America, according to Humboldt, throw them away, and suck the acid pulp which surrounds them. This culture has, above all, the advantage of requiring little labor, and also of being suited to small families. One man is sufficient to take care of one thousand trees, which yield 1,320 pounds of cocoa in average years.

The colonies reap no direct profit on the duty on teas, reduced by the law of May 23, 1860, from 120 fr. on teas imported from China or Manilla, and 150 fr. on all others, to a uniform rate of 75 fr., with the exception of an extra charge, diminishing according to the production and flag, until 1866. Even though the soil were suited to the culture of the tea-shrub, how could it be disputed with the vast empire of China, which consumes it in so great quantity that, it is said, if the consumption of all the rest of the world were suppressed, the price would not decrease there, and which pays its wretched laborers but five or six pence a day? But the production of colonial sugar will profit by this reduction, for the consumption of this leaf of a sort of small orange-tree, unknown in Europe two hundred years ago, has already become popular to an almost incredible degree. In England, it amounted to 13,601,109 kilog. in 1831, to more than 25,000,000 kilog. in 1859, and brings no less than 140,000,000 fr. into the Treasury. The French show the same slowness in taking from the English their teas, as from the Hollanders their coffee, and from the Spanish their chocolate; we decidedly prefer our wine.* Nevertheless, the importation of tea has risen from 92,500 kilogrammes in 1850 to 283,570 in 1859. It is still an article of luxury, like cocoa, but was not sugar also an article of luxury fifty years ago?

* Annals of the Agricultural Society at Martinico, Tom. II. p. 474, quoted by the *Revue coloniale*, 1853, p. 98.

CHAPTER XII.

LABOR AND IMMIGRATION.

The reduction of the impost on colonial products is not the only remedy necessary for the salvation of the colonies. A large *immigration* is earnestly solicited; there is need of new laborers, it is said, because the old ones will no longer work, because the abolition of slavery has been the abolition of labor.

This question merits the most attentive examination.

We briefly style *immigration* the contract for free laborers or immigrants in divers countries, their transportation to the colonies, and their engagement for a term of years for agricultural labor. This operation is costly and complicated, but before all it raises many scruples.

Can the contract be made, at the starting-point, with precautions sufficient to insure clearly the consent of the contracting party? In offering employment to a numerous population, does it not encourage the petty covetous and ferocious sovereigns of thickly peopled countries to make war, take captives, and resort to inhuman measures in order to procure this advantageous commodity?

Is not the transportation difficult to watch over, difficult to distinguish from that of the slave-traders, to whom it also offers another means of accomplishing their ends in disguise?

If this spring be imprudently opened, will the waters that escape from it be pure? Will not the colonies, if in haste to receive laborers, have erelong to mourn for having introduced on the soil, in the midst of their families, an inferior, ignorant, and heathen population?

Thus, at the departure, during the voyage, and after the arrival, — three perils, — arise three questions, questions of supreme importance, the solution of which makes of the same thing a crime or a benefit, a pollution or a progress, a future of life or of death.

The question of *immigration* thus touches, on the one side, the slave-trade, and, on the other, the question of labor and good order in the colonies. The latter only we shall examine here.

Good or evil, has not immigration become a necessity since the abolition of slavery? Is it not the proof and result of the repugnance manifested by the former slaves to labor? This is daily repeated, and in terms which seem irrefutable, because in appearance nothing is more specious. Why is there need of a multitude of new laborers? Because it is no longer possible to count on the old ones.

Such an affirmation proves great ignorance of the history of our colonies, or rather of all colonies.

I. Immigration is not a result of emancipation, but of slavery.

From all time, the colonies have complained of the lack of labor; a very natural complaint, so long as a portion of these fertile and vast territories remained unworked. We know that in our four principal colonies more than half the soil remains waste.

In Martinico, 163,351 acres out of 244,497.

In Guadaloupe, 217,564 acres out of 346,451.

In Bourbon,* 394,839 acres out of 620,996.

In Guiana, of about 138,650,000 acres, but 14,247 acres are cultivated.

Nevertheless, the colonies have received an enormous in-

* It must be remarked that at Bourbon a large portion of the uncultivated land is not susceptible of cultivation.

crease of laborers. The number of Africans brought thither during two centuries of the slave-trade is computed at several millions. The number of Africans sold in the different slave countries from 1788 to 1848 is estimated at not less than from 100,000 to 150,000 per year. What cities have these men built? What countries have they civilized? What forests, what savannas, have they cleared? Where do they live happy, instructed, Christian, progressing? At least, what descendants, what family, what population, have they formed?

One half of these human beings died on the voyage or during the first year's labor. Moreover, it is proved that the deaths outnumbered the births by reason of the disproportion of the sexes, and that, while freedom and prosperity multiply races, slavery subjects them to a continual and rapid decrease.

It may be added, that, through his obsolete and miserable routine of culture, the colonial agriculturist multiplied his hands in vain.*

Thus the demand for hands in all the colonies has always had three causes, — the disproportion between the territory and population, the diminution of the laboring class under the system of slavery, and the bad system of cultivation engendered by slavery.

Before the abolition of the slave-trade, hands were already lacking; the slave-traders brought but few, to keep up the price.†

After the abolition of the slave-trade, the need of new laborers was naturally more felt; at the same time the com-

* "Why do you leave half your lands fallow?" was asked of the overseer of a plantation. "Because we lack hands." "That is, you lack a harrow, a horse-hoe, a double plough, and a little strength of will to make your slaves use these instruments, which cost 250 fr. in France." For three years the overseer had been writing to the proprietors in France for a harrow. (*Revue coloniale*, 1847, p. 170.)

† *Notices officielles*, 1840, p. 138.

fort of the slaves was somewhat increased, as each master had a little more interest in taking care of an implement difficult to replace.

The colonies of all countries have not ceased for a single day to seek the means of procuring new laborers without having recourse to the slave-trade. On the other hand, excess of population or excess of misery urges the people of certain countries to flee a soil where they have received wretchedness with birth; the spirit of adventure and desire of gain attracts other nations from home. The negroes, captured or hunted like flocks, repair every year to the eastern or western coast of Africa. The Philippine Isles, the Dutch East India Islands, the peninsula of Malacca, Siam, and Cochin China, overflow with Chinamen. They are also found at the remote points of the globe, at the Cape, in Guiana, but in far the greatest numbers in California and Australia. Multitudes of Indian laborers, known by the name of Hill Coolies, descend to the principal towns of the coast to procure occupation there.

It is natural, and doubtless conformable to the mysterious laws of Providence, that a current should be established, when distance does not render it too costly, between these races which are seeking labor and these lands which are awaiting it.

On the 18th of January, 1826, an order of the Governor of Bourbon provided regulations for the introduction of East Indians, and before 1830, 3,012 were already introduced there. In 1843, another order provided for the introduction of 1,000 Chinamen.* In the Isle of Mauritius, neighboring to Bourbon, the Indians were imported for the first time in 1834; and from 1834 to 1839, more than 25,000 were brought thither by private speculation. The immigration was interdicted, then authorized anew, and 46,000 were introduced in 1843. The African immigration, demanded by

* Memorial of M. Challaye. (*Revue coloniale*, 1844, Tom. III. p. 552.)

the English colonies in 1842, and authorized with restrictions in 1843, then more largely in 1847, despatched numerous laborers to Guiana, Jamaica, and Trinidad. A law was proposed by the French government, April 22, 1845, to devote 600,000 fr. to the introduction of European laborers into the West Indies. The statement of the reasons verifies and defines the position which we wish to sketch.

"The advantage which a few of the planters of Guadaloupe and Martinico have already derived from the introduction of European laborers on their plantations, indicates that the first attempts should be made in this direction. Without excluding from the scheme French Guiana and the Isle of Bourbon, we must acknowledge that these two colonies are found in conditions which imperatively demand another mode of immediate assistance. At Guiana, the population is sensibly decreasing, hands are lacking, estates formerly cultivated are left in a state of almost complete ruin. . . . . . At Bourbon, the births no longer keep pace with the deaths, and the progressive movement which has been manifested for a few years in cultivation, daily proves the insufficiency of the working population. But the geographical position of the Isle of Bourbon places it within reach of the labor which it lacks. It has already taken the initiative, in 1828, in procuring hired Indians. . . . . . More recently, again, regulations have been made for the introduction of a thousand Chinamen. These immigrations may be extended. Instructions have been given in this direction."*

Thus, twenty years before the emancipation of the slaves, European, African, Chinese, and Indian immigration had been essayed or solicited by the colonies of all nations; it has not been an invention of emancipation.

II. Is it true that, since this emancipation, it has become absolutely indispensable? Is it true that labor has almost entirely ceased?

* *Revue coloniale*, 1845, p. 436.

One of the best informed and most able writers among those that occupy themselves with colonial questions, M. Jules Duval, wrote, December 1, 1859 * : —

"The great matter of emigration is beginning to be settled. *On condition of taking no account of the former slaves and their descendants,* who, abandoned to themselves, without the paternal solicitude of their former masters, fall back into savage life, the solution seems found."

In a more recent and more profound work,† devoted solely to the Isle of Bourbon, the same writer thus expresses himself: —

"Of about sixty thousand slaves freed in 1848, it is estimated that not more than one fourth are attached to any plantation."

This opinion sums up the most wide-spread assertions. The necessity of two special laws, the decrees of February 13 and March 27, 1852, on the labor police, vagrancy, and immigration, followed by numerous and severe measures by the Governors, is often also alleged as a proof of the difficulty of obtaining regular labor from the former slaves.‡

It is very natural that minute and severe measures should have been needed to prevent the abuse of a wholly new condition; it was at the same epoch that a law was made in France subjecting workmen to the obligation of the *livret.*

It is forgotten that, from all time, the colonial governors had been obliged to impose bounds on vagrancy, in a country where half the lands are unoccupied, as well as rules respecting change of residence and permits of sojourn, on a soil where so many distinct races were landing, embarking, and mingling together pell-mell.

* *Journal des Débats.*

† *La Colonie de la Réunion. Revue des Deux-Mondes,* April 15, 1860, p. 862.

‡ Bourbon: Orders of Oct. 24, 1748, Dec. 23, 1848, May 24 and June 13, 1849, July 7 and Sept. 18, 1852; Circular of Sept. 21, 1852. Guadaloupe: Order in 147 Articles of Dec. 2, 1857. Martinico: Order in 88 Articles of Sept. 10, 1855. This last order, due to Admiral de Gueydon, is admitted to have exercised a most beneficial influence.

It is also forgotten that the decree of February 13, 1852, only gives a stricter definition to vagrancy,* but purely and simply refers the penalty to the penal code (Art. 18), abrogating the special rules of the decree of April 27, 1848.

It is forgotten, lastly, that one of the causes of the aversion of the freed slaves for large estates has been precisely the severity of the measures taken to bring them back to them, — the *livrets*, engagements, etc. To the law that said, "*The laborer is free,*" regulations have added, "*The labor is compulsory.*" It will be admitted that the shade of difference was not easy of comprehension to the newly freed men. Escaped from constraint, they distrusted all that resembled it.

But is it correct that *the labor of the former slaves and their descendants is no longer to be taken into account*, or *that scarcely one fourth remain attached to the plantations?*

If we speak of the first years, this result is true, at least in part.

Here is an impartial witness : —

"In the Isle of Bourbon, the new citizens accomplished scrupulously, and without stirring from their respective glebes, an engagement of free labor which they had been obliged to contract before the promulgation of the new decree. In the West Indies, ... even on the few plantations which were not completely disorganized, there was a marked impulse of change of place and dispersion. It seemed as if the negroes were feeling themselves to be fully convinced that this freedom at length proclaimed was not an illusion. They passed continually from one plantation to another."

Notwithstanding, it must be said that, even in these first

* Art. 16. Vagrants, or unacknowledged persons, are those who, having no means of subsistence and habitually exercising neither trade nor profession, do not give proof of habitual labor by an engagement for a year at least, or by their *livret*.

days of intoxication, there was, properly speaking, no cessation of labor. It was in the midst of harvest in the West Indies, and large quantities of the sugar-cane, already cut, had remained for some days in the mill under process of fermentation. Almost all the planters succeeded in making their hands understand that it was necessary to begin by *putting to mill*, after which they could rejoice with full hearts over the freedom proclaimed." *

The years 1849 and 1850 were much more calamitous than 1848. We have seen that the diminution of labor during these years should be attributed in great part to political excitement; but it is perfectly true that it was also among the first effects of emancipation.

This was natural. What prisoner does not escape when his prison door is broken? What bird does not take flight when his cage is opened? What! we expect of an ignorant, wretched being, less intelligent than a *gamin* of Paris, less virtuous than a Regulus, what none of those who speak or write on these subjects would assuredly have done! We expect of him to make his freedom consist in resuming, under another title purely ideal, the same tool, in the same place, under the same authority, to content himself with changing name without changing condition, and to receive this precious boon, freedom, the object of all his dreams, without endeavoring to make use of it!

Not only was the contrary natural, but it was foreseen. "The culture and preparation of colonial commodities have always been a labor left exclusively to the hands of slaves. For this reason alone, this labor has become in their eyes the very token of slavery. Doubtless, one of the first uses that the negroes will make of their freedom will be to abstract themselves from this kind of labor."† This extract from a report of M. d'Haussonville, and the foresight which

* Lepelletier de Saint-Remy, *Les Colonies depuis l'abolition de l'esclavage.*

† *Moniteur*, May 24, 1845, p. 1478.

it expresses, will be also found in all the reports devoted to colonial questions for fifteen years before emancipation.

Let it not be said, therefore, that it is emancipation that has caused culture to be shunned;—it is the horror of slavery, it is the spectacle of the idleness of the whites. Slavery and labor, sloth and freedom, — these words were synonymous in the colonies, and the phrases, *to work like a negro, beaten like a negro, slothful as a Creole,* had become proverbs. If it is freedom that has made them flee labor, it is slavery that has made them detest it.

There is reason to be surprised, not that the former slaves deserted their labor, but that they returned to it.

Now they have returned to it in great numbers, and, without entering into the details of multitudinous correspondence carried on regarding this between the colonies and the government, here are two incontestable proofs of it.

At Martinico, according to the notices published by the government in 1858,* the number of laborers employed in cultivation is 48,970. The indemnity was accorded for 56,556 slaves, of whom one third at least were infirm persons, women, and children.†

* It is not exactly clear who the notices style *laborers;* whether they are only those who work continuously on the same plantation, or also those who hire by the day here and there, as in France. The statistics of these notices appear inexact; for they indicate a diminution of 30 per cent at Martinico in the number of laborers from 1847 to 1856, and of 13 per cent only for Guadaloupe. Now, Guadaloupe has produced less than Martinico. This is impossible. We will take the figures, however, as they are given us. The abstract is as follows: —

1835 . . 181,758 slaves. 1857 . . 179,015 laborers.

† *Déclarations des délégues des Colonies devant la Commission Parlementaire,* July 10, 1839, *procès-verbaux,* p. 418.

Delegate from Guadaloupe: Scarcely two thirds of the slaves labor effectively.

Delegate from Martinico: My opinion is the same.

Delegate from Guiana: Of two hundred blacks, from sixty to seventy laborers may be counted.

Delegate from Bourbon: Of three hundred slaves, there are about two hundred laborers.

Who, then, form the present contingent of laborers? Immigrants? In ten years, 1848–1857, but 4,578 were introduced into Martinico. The great majority must be, therefore, the former slaves, unless they may be the former masters.

At Guadaloupe,* the number of laborers was 51,660; the indemnity was computed on 55,416 slaves. Now, before 1856, but 1800 immigrants were introduced; the former slaves and their children are not therefore idle.

At Guiana,† 7,291 laborers; indemnity had been accorded for 13,727 slaves; there were 1,312 immigrants, the result is not so good, but far from void.

At Bourbon, the number of hired laborers has been incomparably greater. Since 1852, it has been about 7,000 a year, amounting in 1856 to 50,227, and in 1857 to 53,000;‡ that is, nearly to the number of the former slaves, 56,059. But of these 53,000 hired men, a number have died or returned; as in the 56,000 slaves, at least one third may be counted as women, children, and infirm; there are therefore about 35,000 able-bodied slaves, to which may be added, up to 1856, about 40,000 hired laborers; now at this epoch, the number of workmen indicated by the official notice is 71,094.§

There is another manner of measuring labor, — by the amount of product.

It must not be forgotten that the cultivation of the sugar-cane, from the time of planting to that of maturity, demands from sixteen to eighteen months, and that the immigrants need acclimation. The product of their labor does not commence, therefore, until about two years after their arrival. Now in the Antilles, East Indian immigration commenced at the close of 1854, and African immigration not till 1857; the latter has only been considerable

* *Ibid*, p. 28. † P. 42.

‡ M. Duval, *Revue des Deux-Mondes*, p. 868, 1860. § P. 55.

since 1855 at Bourbon, where that of the East Indians remains stationary, as is proved by the following table, for which I am indebted to the Colonial Direction.

MARTINICO.

	East Indians.	Madeirians.	Africans.	Total.*
June 30, 1854	889	58	....	1,234
Dec. 31, 1854	1,247	60	....	1,594
" 1855	1,563	34	....	2,885
" 1856	2,987	33	....	3,307
" 1857	4,037	..	541	4,578
" 1858	5,279	..	1,248	6,527
" 1859	6,748	..	2,976	10,256

GUADALOUPE.

Numerical Position of Laborers in the Colony.

	East Indians.	Chinamen.	Africans.	Total.†
June 30, 1854	..	..	..	189
December, 1854	314	..	..	495
" 1855	691	..	..	855
January, 1856	1,646	..	..	1,790
December, 1857	2,884	..	69	3,094
" 1858	3,989	..	1,138	5,264
November, 1859	4,155	184	2,995	7,334

BOURBON.

Numerical Position of Foreign Laborers in the Colony.

	East Indians.	Africans.	Total.‡
December, 1854	34,461	6,366	41,287
" 1855	35,201	10,265	45,914
" 1856	36,071	13,701	50,227
" 1857	36,144	16,580	53,175
" 1858	36,251	24,143	60,839
" 1859	36,025	25,636	62,104

It is only since 1857 and 1858, therefore, that the pres-

* Including a few hundred Europeans and laborers from the English colonies, and 500 Chinamen, arrived in 1859.

† Including a few Europeans.

‡ Including a few Chinamen.

ence of the immigrants has had power to exert an appreciable influence on the value of the products. Now we have seen that the product of the years subsequent to slavery, after five inferior years, rose, during the following quinquennial period, above the product of the years anterior to slavery. Let us refer again to the statistics.

AGGREGATE OF COMMERCE.

	1843-1847.	1852-1857.
Martinico	39,226,503 fr.	51,646,959 fr.
Guadaloupe	39,228,912	39,904,671
Guiana	4,081,799	7,954,376
Bourbon	33,074,648	72,324,705

To be still more precise, we will compare only the statistics of exportations ten years distant.

	1847.	1857.
Martinico	18,323,921 h.	24,830,093 h.
Guadaloupe	20,420,522	23,319,277
Guiana	1,622,919	961,272
Bourbon	12,620,602	33,130,125

Except at Guiana, where immigration is also almost void, the product has been everywhere higher. Now at Martinico and Guadaloupe, the number of immigrants before this epoch was insignificant; the product was therefore almost wholly the result of the labor of the former slaves. At Bourbon, we will admit the hired men to have doubled the number of laborers; but the product has tripled, — the former slaves count for something in it, therefore, without forgetting machinery.

It is objected, that the number of acres under cultivation has diminished in three colonies.

	1846.	1856.
Martinico	85,257 acres	78,253 acres
Guadaloupe	108,163	58,844
Guiana	21,766	14,161
Bourbon	152,140	227,209

We see that the extent of culture has diminished in the colonies, except at Bourbon ; especially at Guadaloupe and Guiana, where it has fallen off nearly half, although the amount of the products has been increased.

But it is impossible to escape from this dilemma. Since the products of the labor have increased, either the greater part of the slaves have worked, — in which case it is unjust to accuse emancipation of having killed labor ; or else the number of laborers has diminished, — in which case less hands have sufficed for more products, which is the best proof of the superiority of free labor over slave labor.

It must therefore be concluded, that free labor is more productive than slave labor, and that better management of plantations and improved processes of cultivation have been brought about by the spur of necessity. It is evident that the diminution of hands was one of the most important advantages of all others to realize. "It is surprising," wrote an already-cited observer in 1859, "to see hundreds of slaves and droves of mules and oxen employed on a hundred acres, ... and cultivating an estate which in France would be tilled by a few farm servants and half a dozen horses." Let no one complain, therefore, of the diminution of hands, without remembering that they were formerly in superabundance, — with fewer, more is produced.

But it must be admitted, at the same time, that important cultures have been abandoned. Coffee has continued to be neglected, perhaps because the soil is too far exhausted ; but the sugar-cane, to which so much has been sacrificed, has been in more than one place abandoned, as I do not deny.*

Let us directly remark, that this proceeds from three causes, and not from one alone.

* Mark the statistics of 1856, the last year of which they are officially known, as compared with those of 1846. These statistics are extracted from the *Notices sur les colonies*, by M. Ray, and from the *Tableaux de population, de culture, de commerce, et de navigation*, for the year 1856, published in 1860, Nos. 12 - 17.

1. It is not only the negroes that flee the plantations, but also the whites. Labor has been less in demand, but also

	Martinico. 1846.	Martinico. 1856.	Guadaloupe. 1846.	Guadaloupe. 1856.
Number of hectares under cultivation	34,530	31,723	44,813	23,876
Sugar-cane	20,232 h.	18,202	14,189	22,349
Coffee	1,856 h.	625	4,736	2,206
Cotton	159 h.	47	1,139	656
Cocoa	592 h.	423	134	122
Tobacco	19 h.	345	10	311
Provisions	11,672	12,081	16,379	6,360
Plantations	3,256	4,748	3,562	3,963
Workmen	65,228*	43,794	51,522	51,659†
Machines	28	62		
Horses	2,293	2,954	3,861	3,385
Asses	152	205	892	430
Mules	5,483	4,460	9,114	4,485
Cattle	16,661	15,094	23,450	8,075
Sheep	13,578	11,145	27,238	8,427
Goats	1,388	3,644	6,142	8,057
Hogs	3,902	9,249	9,023	9,331‡

* In the report of the table of population (p. 12), it is stated that this number, 65,228, includes the women, children, and infirm, while the effective laborers number 43,794. The same table proves that the number of children under six years old exceeds one third. Without speaking of women, if one third, or 21,742, be subtracted from 65,228, but 43,000 slaves remain; the exact number of 1846.

† For Guadaloupe the deduction has been made. Now, the statistics of 1846 and 1856 are precisely the same. This makes it difficult to admit the figure indicated for cultures. How could 23,000 hectares employ as many laborers as 44,000? The error is confirmed by the amount of products. Would the 22,000 hectares planted with cane in 1856 produce, in raw and clayed sugars, syrup, molasses, and tafia, only 31,892,050 fr., and the 11,000 hectares of 1856 have produced 33,912,780 fr.? The prices having generally fallen, this rise could not be attributed to their variation.

‡ In the sequel of the excellent report of M. Jules Duval, in behalf of the special jury of the colonies and Algeria, at the general exhibition of agriculture in 1860 (*Revue coloniale*, Dec., 1860), is found a *résumé* of the statistical documents concerning the colonies, for 1837, 1847, and 1857, which is full of interest. But, although drawn from official sources, it contains (as the author takes care to warn us) more than one hypothesis and more than one inaccuracy; and especially several figures, which it is impossible to reconcile either with each other, with the *Tableaux* of 1856, or with the notices which serve us as a guide. These disagreements are vexatious, but irremediable, on account of the imperfection of the statistics sent by the colonies. See also the *Statistique de la France*, published in 1860, by M. Maurice Block, Tom. II. chap. xx.

less to be had. The moment of the payment of the indemnity was that of a general liquidation.

I read in a despatch of Vice-Admiral Fourichon, Governor of Guiana: —

"The planter who was involved in debt before emancipation, and who in general sacrificed his indemnity to satisfy his creditors, has been constrained, for want of capital to furnish wages, to let his old laborers go. From this results stoppage of manufactories and decrease of works, canals, and dikes."

2. Hands are lacking at Bourbon, which produces more, as at Guiana, which produces less; the same effect must, therefore, ensue from two opposite causes, — the diminution of laborers and the increase of labor.

3. It is not only in the colonies, but everywhere, that, under the sway of an impulse more easy to comprehend than to fetter, the working classes quit the fields for the towns. Hands are lacking in the environs of Paris, as in the environs of Cayenne; the labor of the fields seems forsaken; the amount of labor is the same; labor is not destroyed, it has changed place. The petty urban branches of trade and fishery thus receive numbers of former slaves, disgusted with the rude labor of the fields. It is known that from all time the mulattoes and colored men, both free and freed, have preferred the trades to culture, and their example has naturally influenced the newly freed men. To general reasons — the attraction of higher wages, the love of change, the desire for the unknown, the temptation of a less monotonous life — is joined in the colonies the special reason already given, — the horror of their ancient condition and the fear of falling back into it, or, above all, of seeing their wives do so, which is so great, that the negroes, it is everywhere remarked, hasten to escape from the labor of the soil; then, lastly, the facility of possessing a little freehold and supporting themselves from its profits.

For a double movement is wrought; the one towards populous centres, the other towards unoccupied space. There, alone with his family, the negro lives on little, on a soil fructified by the sun, and measures his labor by his needs, which are almost nothing, and his enjoyments, which are precisely idleness and a roving life. But it is the admirable moral mechanism of freedom, that its duties support and are linked one with another; because he has a family, man wishes property,— to acquire it he devotes himself to labor; if he shuns labor, he is constrained to it by privation; that this labor may be advantageous, he labors for another, and is thus brought back by the desire of his personal advantage to contribute to the common good.

In a report on English Guiana, in 1840, I read that the number of negro freeholders, including the members of their families, was already 15,906 individuals; having constructed on their lands, at their own expense, 3,322 houses. The report adds: "When the peasant of Guiana rises a degree in the social scale, and becomes the proprietor of a little plot of fertile soil, there are few conditions so worthy of envy as his, few countries so happily apportioned. At the sight of this prosperity of the laborers of English Guiana, one is tempted to say of the cultivated part of the colony, as Goldsmith said of Old England and its products, 'Each inch of ground supports its man.'"

I do not assuredly pretend that this picture, drawn six years after emancipation, is the portrait of our colonies. Let us not hasten to believe, however, that emancipation has transformed all slaves into vagrants who have been unwilling to cultivate sugar-cane; a great number do other things, busy themselves in the towns, or raise their support from a bit of ground. I repeat it, labor has changed place rather than been destroyed.

The statistics of the customs transform this hypothesis into a real fact. At Martinico and Guadaloupe, while the amount of sugar imported into France produced on large plantations diminished after 1848, almost all other industrial or agricultural products increased. At Martinico, *rum, cocoa, cassia, hides, wood,* and *divers articles.* At Guadaloupe, *rum, anotta, wood, copper, hides, cotton,* and *divers articles.*

Another thing attests the same fact. Where are the paupers? where the mendicants? Emancipation has impelled one portion of the slaves towards the towns, another towards the unoccupied lands, very few towards the prisons and hospitals; it has made artisans and small freeholders, some vagrants, few beggars, and few criminals.

Large plantations have suffered without causing the entire community to suffer. But as it is possible that the desertion of the cultures, less considerable than is affirmed, may still increase, and that the scarcity of hands may raise wages, how revive the large plantations, how triumph, without raising wages, over so many causes of desertion of the laborers? A common voice answers, By *immigration.*

Yes, immigration is necessary, *provisionally,* to develop production and diminish its expense. It is a means of lowering wages by the competition of labor, and of diminishing the costs of manufacture by manufacturing on a larger scale.

Herein is the true end, the true reason, — to render the labor of the former slaves less costly, to lessen the net cost.

We repeat it, hands are demanded less to replace the former workmen than to stimulate them, to lower wages and to develop cultures; not substitutes, but competitors, are sought.

I admit so evident a necessity; it explains all the demands of the colonists, all the efforts of the French government to obtain new laborers.

III. It is known that the government did not authorize

recruital on the African coast until 1852, and that it regulated minutely all the conditions of immigration by the two decrees of March 13 and 27, 1852.*

A first agreement was made between the Minister of the Marine and two shipping merchants of Granville, in 1854 and 1855. Others less important followed. A more recent treaty was concluded, March 14, 1857, between Admiral Hamelin and the celebrated house of MM. Regis, of Marseilles, which has agents all along the African coast. Here is the literal text of the first articles of this curious agreement: —

Art. 1. M. Regis, Sen., binds himself to introduce into Martinico and Guadaloupe 20,000 hired Africans suited to agriculture.

Art. 2. The introduction shall commence in 1857. The whole number of 20,000 shall have been introduced by January 1, 1863.

Art. 3. The contingent for each colony shall comprise women from twelve to twenty-five years of age, in a proportion which, in the aggregate immigration of each year, shall not be less than one fifth, nor exceed one half.

* The immigrant engages himself in the presence of a government agent, and for five years only. He must be assured of his freedom, and must understand the contract that is proposed him. He is entitled to his homeward expenses, with those of his wife and children, if he wishes to return, or to a premium equal to these expenses if he prefers to re-engage himself.

During the passage everything is regulated, — his bed, his food, the space to which he is entitled, his clothing, his treatment if sick.

A cruising squadron is kept, at great expense, on the coast of Africa, and the commandant watches with extreme solicitude over frauds, infractions, or encroachments through negligence or cupidity in these complicated operations.

At the place of disembarkation, the immigrant is placed under the care of another government agent,* and his wages, premium, and return are guaranteed by this protection. He is vaccinated, cared for, fed, and clothed in the manner provided for by the regulations. Those who fail in their engagements to him are menaced with severe penalties.

To undertake the transportation of immigrants, an authorization is necessary.

* This agent is generally a surgeon of the navy, chosen as best acquainted with the details of salubrity and hygiene.

Art. 4. The immigrants can only embark on the ships of M. Regis in a state of freedom.

This agreement is in full execution. The colonists anticipate the most happy results from it.

But what! is not this a most remarkable fact from the stand-point that we take? It is from the African race that laborers are borrowed, destined to replace other Africans who are accused of caring only for idleness.

Europeans, East Indians, Chinamen, and Africans have been successively tried.

In 1845, as we have seen, the French government desired to encourage *European* immigration. This was a wise and far-seeing measure, for the colonists were lacking most of all in choice artisans, mechanics, overseers, and agricultural managers, to perfect their stock of implements, and direct or train less intelligent workmen. It is often said, that this attempt failed because it is impossible for Europeans to labor under a tropical sun, and a proof is frequently alleged in the lack of success of the former bound whites, who were the first laborers of the colonies. But it is forgotten that these bound men labored nevertheless for 148 years, from 1626 to 1774.* It is, above all, forgotten that, chosen at random by sea-captains, transported without calculating for these Frenchmen, as is done for an Indian, the height of the deck of the vessel, and the quantity of respirable air and drinkable water, treated during the eighteen months or two years of their engagements like true slaves, badly fed, and often without wages, these bound laborers nevertheless became the heads of numerous families who still inhabit the colonies. They were not destined to labor, but to people, and the decree of 1774 checked immigration because the end was attained, because the white population was sufficiently augmented. The bound men ended, therefore, not because they had failed, but be-

* *Revue coloniale*, 1847, p. 217. *Hist. du travail aux colonies*, by M. Maurel.

cause they had succeeded. In any case, there is nothing comparable between the two epochs, unless it be the climate, which has remained the same. Now whites have been seen to labor even at Guiana; there are many at Porto Rico; the railroad from Kingston to Spanish Town, in Jamaica, was constructed by whites, in 1845, without a single one having died in the task.* Doubtless the whites have more difficulty than the blacks in becoming acclimated; but after all, if French or European immigration tends little towards the colonies, it is less because Frenchmen cannot live there, than because they like better to live in France. It is known that, for various reasons, the French is the least emigrating of nations.† Moreover, they are accustomed to wages and food which renders their employment very costly. But the introduction of good European workmen into the colonies should not be renounced, even at great expense; there is greater need of heads there than hands.

The races accustomed to emigration and adapted to labor under a tropical sun are, in Asia, the Chinamen and the East Indians; in Africa, the negroes of both coasts, and the inhabitants of Madeira, the Azores, and Madagascar.

The East Indian is sober, more intelligent than the black, but less robust. Ill treated in his own country, he emigrates willingly, but with the intention of returning.

The immigration of East Indian laborers, known under the name of Coolies, was easy to England, since she found them in her own possessions. More than 150,000 have been hired and transported to her colonies.

France has naturally been tempted to imitate her example. A first convoy was organized in 1852 by the *Louis*

* *Revue coloniale*, 1845, pp. 7, 216.

† Of 400,000 persons that annually quit Europe, England counts more than 240,000; Germany, 100,000; France, from 17,000 to 18,000. (Report of M. Hubert-Delisle to the Senate on the law of immigration, July 10, 1860.)

Napoleon, with infinite precautions for the health, liberty, and family reunion of the engaged Coolies. Several convoys followed, with satisfactory success, and 12,000 East Indians were thus despatched to our colonies, principally to Bourbon. The East Indians sailed from our stations of Pondicherry and Karikal; but the territory of these wrecks of our former power is exceedingly circumscribed, and nearly all the Coolies came from the interior, and were natives of the vast Britannic possessions.

Now, what has England resolved? She has constantly refused legally to sanction this immigration; and our recruiting agents have been more than once, even at the time of the Crimean war, seized, fined, and imprisoned. She demands that we shall renounce Africans, and refuses us East Indians. For several years, things have stood in this wise. It needed the skilful energy of the delegate from Bourbon, M. Imhaus, to obtain of the English government, in 1860, a treaty insuring to this colony 6,000 Coolies.

China does not give us what was refused us in the East Indies. More remote from our possessions, — closed, despite constantly violated treaties, to all relations with Europe, — it offers us but insufficient resources. England had counted greatly on Chinamen; * and in 1851 Mr. George Barclay wrote to Earl Grey, "We shall find laborers in China more capable of enduring the climate than the Madeirians, more energetic than the East Indians, and more tractable than the Kroomans" (free Africans from the Kroo coast).

Another agent, Mr. White, wrote, at the same epoch, from Macao: —

"The Chinese population in the south is superabundant. Its means of existence are not in proportion to its daily increase; a superhuman effort is needed for it to procure the prime necessaries of life. In spite of the regulations,

* Parliamentary papers. Reports to the Committee of Emigration, 1851.

which strictly prohibit emigration, the Chinamen desire to quit their country, and are ready to go wherever there is a chance of earning their livelihood. Thousands go from Singapore yearly, and spread over the neighboring islands. There are several hundred thousand in Java. They swarm at Manilla. They are found in masses in Australia and California."

The climate of the south of China is, moreover, the same as that of the Antilles. Sugar-mills and well-cultivated sugar-cane plantations are to be seen near Amoy. At Singapore and Penang, under the same latitude as that of Guiana, the Chinamen have cleared forests, planted spices, etc.

Moreover, they are generally robust and laborious. Despite these advantages, while the Chinamen become easily acclimated at Cuba, accept in Peru the repugnant labor of loading guano, and finish the Panama Railroad under the tropical sun, it appears that they have not wholly succeeded in the English colonies, unless it may be in Guiana and Trinidad, nor in the French possessions, either because the length of the voyage has rendered the price high and the mortality fearful,* or because the obligation to recruit only at open ports has created too many difficulties,† or, lastly, because the danger of mutinies on shipboard, which were very frequent, has compelled the ship-owners to raise the price of freight very high, or to refuse their vessels.

Abuses besides have been numerous; they were the origin of serious disturbances at Amoy, and the English papers contain abominable details of the illicit embarkation of young girls under the Portuguese flag, and of cruelties of which Chinamen transported under the English flag to the Chincha Islands were the victims, to the point of committing suicide to escape their fate.‡

* 24 ships took on board 7,356 Chinamen for Peru, and landed but 4,754.

† The glorious treaty signed at Pekin, Oct. 25, 1860, removes these difficulties; emigration and engagements are free.

‡ Correspondence of Lord Clarendon and Sir John Bowring, 1854.

But the principal obstacle to the immigration of the Chinamen, as the East Indians, rose from the ruling cause in every question of race, — the cause on which religion alone can act, — morals. The East Indian after arriving in the colony, restrained by his prejudices of caste, will not marry; he founds no stock, and as it is impossible to bring as many women as men, a revolting immorality ensues.* The Chinamen have not the same scruples, and numerous half-breed Chinese are seen at Borneo and the Philippine Islands. But, in our colonies, few are disposed to marry Chinamen, and the condition of women in China renders their emigration impossible. The English correspondence is full of curious information on this head, perfectly in conformity with the accounts of our missionaries. The Chinese pride themselves on having ancestry, and consequently on leaving children; but the female ancestry is naught in their eyes; the infanticide of female infants is very common, the sale of young girls for prostitution has nothing shocking; women are bought, and marriage is only a bargain, — a great number of them are slaves. There is no other means, according to the testimony of Mr. White, of procuring them for the colonies than to buy them. But we comprehend that Sir John Bowring energetically opposed this traffic; we also comprehend the immorality induced by the immigration of Chinamen without family, and heartily applaud the language of Sir George Bonham: "If no means are found of obtaining an immigration of women, that of men should directly cease, — morality, and the duties which it imposes on us, command it"; † and the words of the Duke of Newcastle, writing to the colonial governors: "If the proportions of

* The filthiness of the East Indians is no less repulsive. I read in an interesting report of M. Leclerc, a surgeon delegated by the government to accompany 429 emigrants who left Pondicherry, Aug. 2, 1859, for Guadaloupe, on the *Siam* (*Revue coloniale*, March, 1860): "The itch is a very common affection, and one very difficult to destroy among the Indians, who regard it as a useful eruption, necessary to the health."

the two sexes cannot be re-established, an end must be put to immigration, however lamentable may be the necessity."* This immorality of the Chinamen and Indians, and these inveterate usages, one power alone could conquer. But these are the races of all others most difficult to convert to Christianity. At Bourbon, a special chapel for the Indians, adorned in the style of their country, has been erected by the care of the bishop ; and two Jesuit missionaries and a curé devote themselves to the laborious task of instructing more than 30,000 Indians. But their apostleship extends only to a very small number, and ends with the duration of their stay. The greater number live heathen and like heathen.

In Africa, the islands of Madeira and the Azores furnished, in 1847 and 1848, 15,000 persons to the English, and a few hundreds to our colonies ; but this evidently is not a sufficient source.

Bourbon might have recourse to the Malgaches, inhabiting the coast of the large island of Madagascar ; they are born free, and regarded as hardy and intelligent ; but the tribe of Hovas holds them under their yoke, and as long as this oppression lasts, their engagement will be always impossible or precarious.

The vast African continent lay yonder, fronting by its east coast our American possessions ; by its west, the Isle of Bourbon and our settlements in the Comoros. Moreover, the negro was already familiar to our colonists, more submissive than the Indian, more moral than the Chinaman, more open to religious influences than either, more easily established and mingled with the population.

This race has been, and is still, universally preferred.

Is it not curious, from our present stand-point, to see the colonies return by preference to the African race ?

At the close of a memorial written in 1844, on the advan-

* Correspondence of the English Government, 1854, pp. 22 - 25.

tages of Chinese and East Indian immigration,* I read these words : —

"We shall witness, perhaps, the elucidation of the fact that the providential march of events has in store for the human race.

"The black population, driven and crowded back on all sides by other families placed a degree higher in the development of the human species, will disappear from the countries subject to the sovereignty of the whites."

The contrary is realized. These higher families bow less willingly to toil, and open themselves less readily to Christianity, than this always despised race ; and after having carefully sought how to replace the freed negroes, we have been forced to conclude that it must be by other freed negroes.

Does not this immigration, which seems the remedy for all the evils of the colonies, menace them with serious evils, which will endure longer than the transient services they can render ?

The evils induced by immigration were pointed out at first, and have been realized ever since the day that it was accomplished. It is baleful to the freedmen, the colonies, the colonists, and the hired laborers.

Immigration weighs on the wages of the freedmen, and, designed to supply the place of those who do not labor, it comes in competition with those who do labor ; far from encouraging labor among them, it consummates its discouragement.

It imposes on the colonists expenses† which would be

* M. de Challaye, ex-consul in China, *Revue coloniale*, 1844, pp. 3, 557.

† *L'Avenir*, Guadaloupe, Dec. 2, 1859, states that the colony had already received 5,773 East Indians, 188 Madeirians, and 3,205 Africans, — in all, 9,166 immigrants, since 1854; but that, the immigration fund failing, it became necessary to replenish it, in part, from the engaged laborers, and in part by a poll-tax. Is it not iniquitous to lay this tax on those to whom it is designed to raise up competitors?

better employed in improving their stock of tools and paying the freedmen higher wages; it accustoms them to remain in the old routine of bad management.

In his report on the administration of Jamaica, in 1845, the Governor, Lord Elgin, declared that he had but indifferent confidence in the effect of the introduction of immigrants, viewing it, says he, "as a means of not admitting the improvements dictated by experience, and also of lowering the price of labor by the creation of a factitious competition."*

The Governor of Bourbon, M. Darricau, exclaimed in 1858, with laudable frankness: "They ask me everywhere for hands, and everywhere I see nothing but abuse of hands. They remember very well that they have a rival in indigenous sugar when the regulation of the differential duties is in question; they think little of it when the question is to regulate the industrial economy of the sugar production."†

Baleful to the freedmen, an evil counsellor to the colonists, immigration creates above all a permanent danger to the social and moral state of the colonies. On thinking of these nooks of the globe, where crowd and mingle together masses of negroes, Indians, Chinamen, and Malays, with a handful of whites, one shudders for the race, threatened by deplorable mixtures, and for morality and good order, afflicted by this invasion of a heathenism which Christianity has not time to break through. By the admission of all,‡ this new population is shamefully immoral; to its presence the magistrates attribute the progress of criminality, and how should it be otherwise? Of 25,458 East Indians introduced into Mauritius by private speculation,

* *Revue coloniale*, 1847, No. 11, p. 323.

† *Journal des Débats*, Sept. 18, 1859.

‡ At no epoch, not even in the worst times of slavery, has the country had to mourn heinous crimes so numerous and so various, as since the East Indian immigration. (Jules Duval, Bourbon, *Rev. des Deux-Mondes*, April 15, 1860, p. 868.)

from 1834 to 1839, there were 500 women; of 46,000 introduced in 1843, 6,000 women. No priests of their tongue, no chiefs, no schools, no examples among these laborers, the lowest of their country, which the priests are attempting with infinite pains to evangelize. Mauritius has already received more than 107,000 East Indians, a number superior to that of the entire population; Bourbon more than 50,000. If these men return, their costly transportation ruins the finances;* their wages, which they carry with them, swallow up capital; their fleeting stay introduces no progress, — agricultural and moral instruction must constantly begin again for the new-comers, as the art of war for conscripts; if they remain, they end by being the stronger, and can rule over everything after having corrupted everything, unless mortality, enormous both during the passage † and after the arrival, should serve as remedy.

This last danger threatens neither the freedmen, nor the colonists, nor the colonies, but the immigrants themselves. They are exposed to many more dangers in Africa and the East Indies, if it be true that the temptation of the certain hire of human merchandise resuscitates the slave-trade, slave-hunts, and the crimping of East Indians.

Considering here exclusively the colonial interest and the question of the emancipation of slaves, we come, in brief, to these conclusions: —

It is not true that the desire of introducing new laborers into the colonies was born on the morrow or in consequence of the abolition of slavery; it was conceived, expressed, and realized long before.

It is not true that emancipation has wholly suppressed labor, and rendered this immigration absolutely necessary.

* In 1845, the immigration of Mauritius had cost the colony 9,500,000 fr., and the government, 8,116,300 fr. The colony still owed the mother country 7,119,350 fr., and was forced to expend 1,250,000 fr. annually for new immigration. *Revue coloniale*, 1846, p. 511.

† *Revue coloniale*, 1844, p. 57.

Labor has fallen off as much on account of the general position of affairs, and the special position of colonial estates, as on that of the first impulse which impelled the freedmen to flee agricultural labor, which was to them the sign of servitude, and the plantations, which had been its scene.

It is not true that this falling off of labor endured much longer than in the mother country, nor that it increases more and more ; for the statistics of labor and production prove that the greater part of the former slaves take part in the labor.

But it is true that labor has changed place, that the trades, small freeholds, and, lastly, vagrancy, have taken many hands from the large plantations, and that the freedmen distrust the *livret*, engagements, and measures which remind them of their past.

It is true that wages are somewhat higher ; that a greater increase is to be feared ; that the price of products, particularly of sugar, which rose at first, has since fallen ; that the demand of consumption has greatly increased ; that the colonies are in need of new hands, at some points, to save the cultures ; at others, to develop them ; at all, to diminish the net cost by competition. This need still continues, and justifies the measures taken to facilitate immigration.

But it is demonstrated that this expedient, difficult, costly, and equivocal, is dangerous to the future of colonial society, and, if not strictly limited to the proportion necessary to re-establish the equilibrium between the population and capital, will make inhabited Babels, gatherings of all races and all creeds, of Paganism and Christianity, of Caffres and Chinamen, Hindoos and Malgaches, — vast factories where workmen and master will be eager only to make the most of each other and flee. I cannot suppose that a hundred years from hence the number of Chinamen and Indians will have centupled in our colonies, without believing at the same time that the number of Europeans will have diminished in proportion. Fancy a St. Domingo peopled by Coolies!

It is also demonstrated, that the best immigrants are Africans.

If the Africans are the race of all others easiest assimilated to our manners and faith, if it is to this robust and vigorous race that we always return after so many trials, why then go afar to seek Africans more brutish and ignorant than the former slaves? Because there is obtained of the new-comers engagements, a *livret*, forced services, — in a word, what may be called provisional slavery. Would it not be better to attempt with the freedmen, and above all with their children, who have not the same reasons for distrust, measures calculated to attract and retain them, through greater sacrifices and better treatment? It is said that the freed negro is prejudiced to believe that freedom is the right to idleness. Is not this also the prejudice, the conviction, of the former masters? Apart from intelligent exceptions, what have they done to diminish in practice the distance which the law has just effaced between the classes?

It is certain that more anxiety has been shown to replace the former slaves than to retain them. Functionaries have been appointed to protect and watch over immigrants, who make minute reports on the mode of life, food, labor, and well-being of these new-comers; it is surprising that no analogous patronage has been organized for the freedmen. Yet there has from all time been a firm conviction that the Creole negro is superior to the African negro.*

"The 24,000,000 francs," says M. Duval, very truly, "which Bourbon has expended in eight years to bring Coolies from India, if applied in premiums to labor, and in the elevation of wages, would certainly have not been

* See especially the declarations of the colonial delegates before the Commission of 1839, p. 109.

sterile. . . . . . It would be well also to modify local customs, if there remain in them any vestige wounding to the pride of men who, without fully appreciating the conditions of liberty, know very well how to escape from slavery; though it should cost a sacrifice of money or self-love, the immense advantage of constituting a homogeneous community, and retaining the amount of wages in the country, would be worth some trouble."

There is another means of replacing labor; namely, to improve the economy and stock of the colonial cultures and manufactures, to copy the processes of the makers of indigenous sugar, and to diminish general expenses by the establishment of central factories. The central sugar-mill is to the sugar-plantation what the central grist-mill is to the wheat-field, — one mill serves for a hundred farmers; until very lately, each planter had his own mill. The improvement of sugar-works has made the fortune of Bourbon. Guadaloupe and Martinico possess central sugar-works, the result of which is admirable; according to the latest statements,* the yield of the cane has been increased from 5 to 13 per cent, and it is hoped to obtain still more. The planters who make no sugar, but sell their cane, are no longer in debt; the tenants of the sugar-works pay large rents, and make fine profits. At the same time, the machinery and mechanism imported figures more largely every year in the tables of customs.† At the exhibition of 1860, the Bourbon sugars were as fine as the refined sugars; its coffees, vanillas, tobaccos, and nutmegs, the coffees of Guadaloupe and the cottons of Désirade, the cocoas, rums, and tafias of Martinico, proved that great and small cultures were progressing, ‡ and medals accorded to the

* *Revue algérienne et coloniale*, Sept., 1860, p. 350.

† At Martinico, in 1856, of 542 plantations, only 62 possessed steam-mills; while at Bourbon, 113 out of 118 were moved by steam. Bourbon imported 530 000 fr. worth of machinery; Martinico, 40,000 fr.; Guadaloupe, 50,000 fr.

‡ M. Jules Duval, *Journal des Débats*, July 6, 1860.

former slaves demonstrated that many among them only needed freedom to equal their masters.

To attract the former laborers, while furnishing a fresh supply of new ones, to return to the old cultures, to adopt new processes, and (as we are about to see) to enlarge the market, — such should be the future of the colonies.

To summon an inferior population without circumspection, to sacrifice products which have no competitors in France obstinately to sugar, to persist in abortive attempts to resuscitate an accursed past, to fall back into old habits, to seek in a disguised slave-trade, followed by a provisional servitude, the better organization of labor, — this would be a path full of shame, deception, and peril.

To the honor of the colonists, it is just to say, that most among them do not hesitate between the two paths. "The emancipation of the slaves," says an enlightened witness, "which dealt the colonies for a moment so rude a blow, must be to them in the future a source of fruitful and salutary results, by forcing the planters to shake off the apathy into which they had fallen, by the facility of production and its trifling net cost." *

* *Étude sur la situation économique des Antilles françaises*, by J. de Crisenoy, 1860, p. 43.

CHAPTER XIII.

THE COLONIAL COMPACT.*

THE colonies have received an indemnity, the average production has increased, the impost on colonial products is reduced, the body of laborers is augmented. Is this all? Is this enough?

The colonies go further, and loudly demand the *rupture of the colonial compact.* Formerly they solicited a growing protection, forced labor, reserved flag, protective tariff, privileged sale. To-day labor is free, and the colonists claim, as a logical sequence, the freedom of the products of labor. This is an entire revolution, the indirect and unlooked-for result of the abolition of slavery, and merits our attention for a moment. We shall only sum up some excellent writings, especially the "Studies" of a highly respected colonist, M. de Chazelles.

The meaning of the colonial compact is well known.

The colonies were at first undivided tracts conceded to companies. The representatives of these companies subdivided a portion of the soil among themselves. This appropriation continued, either through grants or under the form of sale, after the reunion of the colonies to the domain of the state. Receiving everything from the state, it was just that the colonies should bring back everything to the state. In proportion as the planters began to support themselves,

* *Étude sur le système colonial*, by Count de Chazelles, Guillaumin, 1860. — *Le Libre Échange colonial,* by Lepelletier de Saint-Remy, *Journal des Économistes*, June, 1860. — Baudrillart, *Journal des Débats*, Aug. 3, 1860. — Count Caffarelli, *Rapport au Corps législatif*, June 30, 1860, etc.

the state had less burdens, with less rights. But the state, as well as the colonies, found it to their advantage to remain united by the bonds of a reciprocal monopoly; — to the state, the monopolies of transportation and supplying the colonies with *European* products; to the colonies, the monopoly of supplying the mother country with *colonial* commodities. The shipping owed its prosperity to this assured transportation, the most important part of which to it, as to the colonies, was the slave-trade. The *outward voyage* was thus as certain as the *return voyage;* the commerce of the ports and that of the colonies was limited to a simple and easily regulated operation; the obligations were mutual, the interests common; and in a time when intercourse between nation and nation, between province and province, was checked by severe prohibitions, each country attached the greatest importance to opening thus, by the foundation of distant colonies, vast outlets for its ships and exchange.

Spain, Portugal, and France entered successively upon the same course.

Other nations, like Holland, intelligently placed their shipping at the service of others; and the Dutch vessels, thanks to the moderation of their rates of freight, had obtained the greater part of the transportation of the English colonies, when, December 1, 1651, a first bill intervened, followed by the celebrated *Navigation Act* of 1660, entitled, *An Act to declare by whom Merchandise may be imported,* by the terms of which it was interdicted the English colonies to carry their products to foreign countries, to receive from foreign countries any product, or to make use of foreign means of transportation.

France adopted the same system; and from the edict of December, 1674, which revoked the charter of the West India Company, and reunited to the domain of the crown the *lands, islands,* and *countries of America,* to the regulation of August 30, 1784,— the last act rendered on colonial customs by the old monarchy, — the whole commercial legislation of the trans-oceanic settlements constituted, by the absolute exclusion of foreign commerce and flags, the system of reciprocal exchange between the colonies and mother country which is still called the *colonial compact.**

This is not a compact, a contract, a treaty, properly speaking, since the mother country alone makes the law; but for the very reason that it acts alone in a question in which it is interested, it is bound to be more equitable; and this reciprocity has always been regarded as a sort of pledged word, which holds more firmly than all writings.

This system made the prosperity of our colonies. In the midst of the eighteenth century, the provisioning of Europe passed almost entirely to French commerce. When, under the empire of a hackneyed prejudice, men accuse the French of not possessing the genius of colonization, they forget that, masters of St. Domingo, Martinico, Guadaloupe, Bourbon, the Isle of France, Guiana, and Louisiana, even after the loss of Canada (1765), the aggregate of their commerce surpassed that of all the European states, including England. In 1787 this aggregate represented 600,000,000 fr., while that of Great Britain did not exceed 450,000,000 fr. The merchant marine was flourishing, and was protected by a powerful military marine.

A quarter of a century after, there was no longer either Dutch or Spanish marine, the marine of the United States was only merchant, the marine of Russia was in its infancy, the Ottoman marine did not venture beyond the Sea of Marmora, France had lost her marine and nearly all her colonies. England had become the sovereign of the seas.†

It may be thought that, the smaller the colonial possessions, the greater was their need of protection from the mother country, by the aid of the system which had caused

* *Étude sur le système colonial*, by M. de Chazelles, p 9.

† M. de Chazelles, pp 23 - 37.

their prosperity ; but circumstances were changed, and the colonial compact had had its day.

It was good so long as it was respected.* But the system daily became onerous, impracticable, and unjust. It becomes onerous to the colonies, if they produce more than the mother country can consume,† or if they find better conditions under which to buy or sell elsewhere, — onerous to the mother country if it can itself produce the commodities brought it by the colonies, or can buy them cheaper of foreign countries, ‡ — unjust, if conditions change, if, to benefit the Treasury, a constantly increasing impost is laid on colonial products, or if the shipping exacts a higher and higher freight, § — impracticable, lastly, if circumstances prevent the colonies from selling to the mother country, or the mother country to the colonies.

Circumstances and interests are modified daily, — the interests of shipping, of consumption, and of humanity. When confined to colonial commerce, the merchant shipping is apt to fall into routine, and to neglect the spirit of enterprise, sure of an easy and perpetual outward and homeward freight. If China, Australia, and California call it to a wider diffusion, it neglects the colonies.‖ The series of monopolies which the product passes through before reaching the consumer, raises the price to its detriment. Either the colonies become too large markets to feed the mother country, or they de-

* Before the Revolution the duty on colonial sugars was, in 1777, 5 fr.; in 1791, 4 fr. 28 c. per 100 kilog.; it did not even compensate for the expenses of the state in the colonies.

† M. de Chazelles affirms that there was a time when it was the custom to set fire to the surplus crops.

‡ The net cost of sugar per quintal is from 24 to 25 fr. in the Antilles; 17 fr. in Cuba. (*Journal des Économistes*, June, 1860, p. 435, art. of M. Lepelletier de Saint-Remy.)

§ From 1831 to 1848 freight from the Antilles did not once reach 100 fr. per ton; from 1854 to 1860 it has been but once below this figure (1857), and usually higher. (*Ibid.*, p. 432.)

‖ A circular of the Minister of the Colonies (1860), urges the ports to send ships to Guadaloupe, the roadsteads of which are empty. (*Ibid.*, p. 433.)

mand, if small, too great sacrifices for a slender result. It thence follows, that they are now attacked, now sustained, by public opinion and political science ; on no subject is infatuation sooner followed by discouragement. Around the colonies form new communities, rich, powerful, and active, with power to enrich them if free, or to crush them if dependent. Wars arise that transfer them from one nation to another, and from prosperity to ruin.

By degrees, the colonial compact has thus been rent by a thousand changes, all realized without exception.

England, at first logical, prohibited within her own bounds the culture of tobacco (1652), then that of the beet-root ; but the too rigorous application of the Navigation Act cost it the United States, and we see it, in 1845, abolish this act, and accept the doctrine of universal commercial freedom.

Holland makes French ports of her little colonies in the Caribbean Sea, like the Danish and Swedish islands. Spain has accorded, since 1805, the commercial franchise to Cuba and Porto Rico.

France has been drawn, step by step, into the same path. After the loss of Canada, which furnished the Antilles with timber, it became necessary to suffer them to procure it from the United States. The regulation of August 30, 1784, permitted this importation, with some others. Revolution, war, and conquest disturbed all laws during twenty years. On the return of order, it was really necessary to accord favors to the distracted colonies. The list of foreign products admitted to entry increased by degrees, and foreign flags appeared habitually by the side of the French colors. The mother country itself passed through years of famine or dearth, which prevented it from supplying its colonies with corn and flour, especially the most distant, — Bourbon. So many events, so many exceptions, authorized sometimes, in cases of urgency, by the governors, sometimes by ordinances and statutes ! * Foreign wheat, prohibited until 1826, then admitted in consideration of a duty of 21 fr. 50 c. per barrel, falling by degrees to 2 fr. per quintal (25 c. for maize) in 1853, for one year, then two, then seven, is now admitted with this duty of 2 fr. by the provisions of the statute of 1860, which for the first time has admitted foreign *grain* at the same duty, and lowered the tax on rice from 4 fr. to 25 c. per quintal. A statute of the same month reduces the premium on cod imported into the colonies by foreign fisheries from 7 fr. to 3 fr. per 100 kilogrammes.†

We have read the history of indigenous sugar, and that of the impost on colonial sugar, and on foreign sugar, which, free to enter France by paying only 3 francs per 100 kilogrammes by the provisions of the statute of May 23, 1860, is released even from this extra charge by the decree of January 13, 1861.

Lastly, we are not ignorant that the obligation to supply themselves from France imposes on the colonies the burden of paying the agents of improvements in the manufacture of sugar, twice as much for machinery, four times as much for bone-black, and six times as much for coal, as is paid them in the mother country.‡ It does not occur to us, that the price current of articles of great consumption in the Antilles is, by the effect of the same system, maintained about one third higher than the prices of the same articles in the neighboring English and Spanish colonies.§

All the clauses of the colonial compact are therefore at once effaced. The colonies demand its abolition by this irrefragable reasoning, — We are deprived of the advantages of the compact, deliver us from the burdens.

* Ordinances of Jan. 5, 1826, Nov. 9, 1832, Dec. 8, 1839, Dec. 2, 1846; Statute of April 29, 1845; Decree of Sept. 30, 1853. See the remarkable report of Count Caffarelli to the Legislative Corps, June 30, 1860.

† Report of M. Ancel, July 6, 1860.

‡ Chazelles, p. 265.

§ *Journal des Économistes*, June, 1860; *Libre échange colonial*, by M. Lepelletier de Saint-Remy, p. 484.

Already the General Councils of Guadaloupe, Martinico, and Bourbon have uttered this prayer, to which the new economical system of France gives more opportuneness and force.

The statute which lowers the tariff on corn and rice imported into the colonies fixed June 30, 1866, as its limit, with the thought that the question of colonial free trade would from this time be resolved.* "For," says the report, "*we consider the solution of urgent importance.*"

This disquieted the ports, and a report read a few days after gave assurance that "the government does not intend to give to the laws presented a more extended scope than they express ; the colonial compact is not in question, but simpler measures suited to facilitate the alimentation of the colonies." †

In fact, the shipping interest — an interest of prime importance — alone can check it. For the colonies cannot attract foreign capital and dispose of their products to foreign countries without making use of foreign shipping. It does not enter into the object of the present study to take sides on so grave a question.‡

But we can affirm without temerity, what so many politicians have long foreseen, that the colonial compact is drawing near its end, and that time will speedily complete the transformation of the consequences which still survive the principle.

We can also affirm that the colonies, less protected, will

* Report of M. Caffarelli. † Report of M. Ancel, 17.

‡ It may be observed, that for seven years past the importation of foreign flour into the colonies has been nearly free; yet they have not ceased to supply themselves, by preference, from France, because the quality is superior and the relations better established. Even Mayotte, where commerce is free, trades only with France. On the other hand, the franchise, and a protective duty of 40 fr. per ton, have not sufficed to insure a supply of rice to the Antilles by French vessels. It is probable, therefore, that, habits being stronger than laws, the change of tariff will have no influence on the movement of navigation between France and its colonies.

aspire to be less governed, and that political freedom will quickly follow the establishment of commercial freedom.

"The Antilles are no longer either the gardens or the fiefs of Europe," exclaimed General Foy in 1822.* "We must renounce this youthful illusion. Nature has placed them on the shores of America. With America is their future. It is as entrepôts of commerce, as great markets placed between the two hemispheres, that they will henceforth figure on the world's stage."

If the enlargement of the colonial market correspond to a large growth of production, a new future, full of magnificent promise, opens before the colonies.†

Would it have been possible for them to pretend to it without the abolition of slavery?

This great act has consummated the destruction of the colonial compact. The maintenance of slavery was one of the privileges secured by the mother country to the colonies, and, as it were, the corner-stone of the structure. Furthermore, emancipation has killed routine, and wrested colonial society from its stupor by a violent but salutary awakening. The affranchisement of labor will thus have contributed to the franchise of the product, and, like France, which uprises from fearful concussions with constantly increasing energy, the colonies, her offspring, will succeed in drawing more power and wealth from freedom than were ever given them by protection.

* Cited by M. de Chazelles, p. 102.

† Bourbon, which before 1848 had never exceeded 30,000,000 kilog. of sugar, now exceeds 61,000,000. At Guadaloupe, with central works, the production may be doubled. The same is true of Martinico. The colonies might furnish 200,000,000 kilog. of freight. St. Domingo gives but 115. (Lepelletier de Saint-Remy, *loc. cit.*, p. 441.)

CHAPTER XIV.

POPULATION, FAMILY, SOCIAL CONDITION.

I. We need not question whether there is a law that presides over the propagation of the human species among the Mahometans, Chinese, Indians, or those heathen races which occupy two thirds of the surface of the habitable globe. There is no regular law, but precepts in which selfishness has more share than morality, — polygamy, corruption, voluptuousness, infanticide, — crimes without name, maladies without number. These horrors teach us to take literally the text, "The Devil is the prince of this world." We no longer doubt it when we see in reality evil keeping the gates of life, — debauchery drawing man from nothingness, crime, or contagion, to fling him back again into death.

In the bosom of Christianity, communities are perpetuated by a few pure and simple laws, which corruption disturbs, yet does not succeed in overruling. Regular families compose the community; they find their source in legitimate marriages, alliances recognized by the laws, blessed by religion, formed by the free consent and perpetual vow of a single man and a single woman. The proportionate number of men and women favors monogomy. The habitual excess of births over deaths progressively increases the population, and such is the regularity introduced into a series of facts, ruled notwithstanding by the most mysterious laws, that it has been possible, without greatly erring, while making allowance for inevitable perturbations, to fix, in figures sufficiently exact to form the basis of financial calculations, the laws of increase of the human family, and the common rules of births and deaths.

To draw moral information from these figures, we usually consult the number which expresses the equal proportion of men and women, that which indicates the statistics of legitimate marriages and births, and that which verifies the excess of births over deaths; the first proves that the population is moral, the second that it is honorable, the third that it is growing.

One of the effects of slavery, in whatever place it exists, is to cause perturbation in these laws, thus at once attacking the regularity, morality, and vitality of nations.

Wherever slavery reigns, there is no proportion between the number of men and that of women.

Mark what was the population of the slave colonies, December 31, 1847.

MARTINICO.

White population	Men,	4,451	9,542
	Women,	5,091	
Mulatto population	Men,	17,071	38,729
	Women,	21,658	
Slave population	Men,	34,432	72,859
	Women,	38,427	
Total			121,130

GUADALOUPE.

White and mulatto population	Men,	18,955	41,357
	Women,	22,402	
Slave population	Men,	41,915	87,752
	Women,	45,837	
Total			129,109

GUIANA.

White population	Men,	692	1,264
	Women,	572	
Mulatto population	Men,	2,211	5,168
	Women,	2,957	
Slave population	Men,	6,645	12,943
	Women,	6,298	
Total			19,375

BOURBON.

White population	Men,	16,182	31,818
	Women,	15,636	
Mulatto population	Men,	5,544	11,211
	Women,	5,667	
Slave population	Men,	37,136	60,260
	Women,	23,124	
Total			103,289

GENERAL TOTAL.

White and free mulatto population	139,089
Slave population	233,814
General total	372,903

In all the colonies, among the white and the mulatto population, the number of women is nearly equal to that of men, in general a little exceeding it. Among the slave population, the latter is in the ascendency, two thirds at Bourbon, one thirtieth at Guiana. This is explained by the slave-trade, which imported more men than women. In the Antilles, on the contrary, the women outnumber the men. Is it because the labor in the sun kills the men, while the women work generally within doors? Is it because proximity to the African coast has perpetuated the slave-trade at Bourbon, while, since the suppression of this traffic, the proportion of the sexes has regained at the Antilles a more normal equilibrium? Be this as it may, it is demonstrated that slavery destroys in the slave race the proportion which exists in the two free races.

Which race, among the three, progresses with greatest rapidity? Unfortunately, the statistical tables, since 1848, have ceased to make any distinction. But let us compare the years anterior to emancipation, taking a single colony, Martinico, to avoid complication: * —

* *Notice officielle*, 1840, p. 33.

	Whites.	Mulattoes.	Slaves.	Total.
Jan. 1, 1790	10,635	5,235	83,414	99,284
" 1836	9,000	29,000	78,076	116,076
" 1845	9,139	36,626	76,117	121,882
" 1848	9,542	38,729	72,859	121,130

The white population has remained almost stationary foi sixty years.

The mulatto population has increased prodigiously.

The slave population has continually diminished.

It is true that two causes co-operate in the variations of the last two classes; not only the fluctuation of births and deaths, but also that of emancipations, which causes a transfer from the third to the second. The number of these is known; from 1836 to 1848, 8,538 slaves were freed in Martinico.* Now the mulatto population, despite the deaths,† which we do not take into account, has increased 9,726, or 1,188 individuals more than the number freed, while the white population has not increased 400. The mulatto population, therefore, is the only one that has progressed.

But how has it grown, — through marriage?

The answer is in the colonial proverb: "The white is God's child, the black is the Devil's child, the mulatto is nobody's child." It is also in the well-known repugnance of the whites to any alliance with the blacks. It is lastly in the statistics of the civil state.

From 1838 to 1847, there were 6,175 marriages among the free population, and 1,754 marriages among the slave population, that is, only one third as many marriages in the population twice as large as the other. Again, we have chosen a period signalized by prodigious efforts to initiate the negroes into the family relation. The official table which contains these results informs us that in Bourbon, till 1840, trouble was not even taken to authenticate regularly the number of marriages among the slaves.

* Table of 1847, published in 1850, p. 33, No. 13.

† About 5 per cent a year, Table No. 11.

"It is a system of universal promiscuousness and concubinage," said M. de Broglie.* "The child has no faher, the father no family. . . . . The negresses are in general abandoned by the men who have rendered them mothers; the children are always abandoned by their fathers, and sometimes by their mothers."

At least, do the births furnish a notable increase to the population, and a greater number of laborers to agriculture? †

Among 139,089 *free* inhabitants, the average number of births from 1838 to 1847 was 4,076 per year, or 1 in 33.

Among 233,814 *slaves*, there were 5,994 births only, or 1 in 39.

Is the influence of comfort and good care seen to prolong the duration of the life of the slaves, rid, it is said, of all anxieties?

At the same epoch, the births among the freemen amounted to 4,076, the deaths to 3,797. There were *less* deaths than births.

On the contrary, the births among the slaves amounted to 5,994, the deaths to 7,443. There were *more* deaths than births.

Thus, in short, the only part of the population which increased in the colonies before emancipation was the mixed breed; it increased by illegitimacy. Among the slaves were few marriages, few births, and many deaths.

Are we to attribute these results to the law? Not at all; the law, especially towards the last, encouraged marriage by every means, and forbade the sale of husband and wife separately. To the masters? Not at all; they favored marriages, and married slaves were the objects of their predilection.

* Report, p. 151, etc.

† Official tables of population, 1847, p. 28, No. 10.

M. de Tocqueville gives us, in his beautiful language, the true reason.*

"There exists a profound and natural antipathy between the institution of marriage and that of slavery. A man does not marry when he is disabled through his condition from ever exercising conjugal authority; when his children must be born his equals, and irrevocably destined to the same miseries as their father; when, having no power over their fate, he can know neither the duties, nor rights, nor hopes, nor cares which accompany paternity. It is easy to see that almost all that induces the freeman to consent to a legitimate union is lacking to the slave *through the sole fact of slavery*. The particular measures of which the legislator or master may make use to stimulate him to do what he prevents him from desiring, will therefore be always futile."

II. Have these melancholy facts been modified since the abolition of slavery?

It could not be demanded of emancipation to exercise any influence on the proportion between the sexes; the figures remain in this respect as they were. The immigration of laborers has even resulted in increasing the number of men, without bringing in an equal number of women.

The tables of population having, since 1848, confounded all classes, it is impossible to ascertain whether the difference pointed out between the number of births and deaths among the whites and that among the blacks has subsisted. Notwithstanding, if we rely on a general, and consequently approximative, comparison between the total aggregates of the colonial population in 1836, 1846, and 1856, *without including the number of immigrants*, we ascertain that this population, which diminished during the first period, increased, on the contrary, during the second.

* Report on the proposition of M. de Tracy, *Procès-verbaux* of the Chamber of Deputies, Session of 1840, p. 39. See also the report of M. de Broglie, p. 135.

1836	376,296
1846	374,548
1856	387,821 *

At Martinico, the excess of births over deaths rose in

1848	447
1849	135
1850	1,051

At Guadaloupe, the excess of deaths was in

1848	259
1849	196

The excess of births was in

1850	513

Thus, from the very beginning, in these two colonies, the law of population resumes its regular course,—slavery depopulated, freedom populates the land.

The same tables make no distinction between legitimate and illegitimate births. These last must still be numerous, since the repugnance between the two classes is the same, and since the number of celibates continues to prevail over that of married persons.

But marriages, legitimations, and acknowledgments have increased in a most startling proportion.

In ten years, from 1838 to 1847, there were 1,754 slave marriages, or about 250 a year, of which 29 were in Martinico, 61 in Guadaloupe, 24 in Guiana, and 135 in Bourbon. With that of marriages between free persons—6,175—the total amount was 7,929. In nine years, from 1848 to 1856, there were 38,468 marriages; the first years saw from 1,000 to 3,000 marriages contracted between freed persons in the colonies, instead of 50 or 60 between the slaves.† The average is naturally less since this first flood. It is still, if we compare 1846 with 1856, at Martinico,

* Notices of 1840, Official Tables for 1846 and 1850.

† *Revue coloniale*, 1852, p. 284.

637, instead of 46; at Guadaloupe, 907, instead of 101; at Guiana, 138, instead of 17; at Bourbon, 627, instead of 225.

At the same time, according to another document, which verifies the results accomplished from May, 1848, to August, 1855, in the three principal colonies only,* the number of legitimations during these six years has attained nearly 20,000, that of acknowledgments nearly 30,000.

40,000 marriages, 20,000 legitimated children, 30,000 acknowledged children, — such is the glorious gift offered, in less than ten years, to colonial society by emancipation. We may close our chapter with statistics like these, and this is its conclusion. On the same day, at the same hour, the colonies witnessed the birth of two divine things, — liberty and the family!

III. We will add a few more words on the happiness of these families made free.

It may seem superfluous to ask whether they are happier. Moreover, a dangerous confusion arises, which should be avoided. Freedom and happiness are two different things. They even appear to exclude each other; for freedom is struggle: is not happiness repose? This confusion is habitual in the colonies. It was said of the slaves, "They are happier than if they were free." It is said of the freedmen, "They were happier when they were slaves." Once more, the question is not of felicity, but independence; not of the belly, but the soul; not of a being that eats and sleeps, but a being that thinks, wills, and loves.

It is in vain to draw the most seductive pictures of what is called the patriarchal life of the plantations; the true picture of the colonies is sketched in a few bold strokes in a letter from Bailly de Suffren to Madame d'Alais, written from Fort Royal, February 8, 1779.†

"The country is most beautiful, — nature, always ani-

* *Revue coloniale*, 1856, p. 310.

† Letters published by M. Ortolan, *Moniteur*, Nov. 2, 1859.

mate, keeps the trees and plants in continual vegetation. Almost all have flowers and fruit at the same time. All that is necessary to the nourishment of man comes of itself. Foreign productions alone are forced by industrious avarice to yield, such as sugar and coffee, which exact great labor. The inhabitants may be considered as divided into two classes, — hard masters, and slaves brutalized by slavery."

What was true in 1779 was true in 1839, was true in 1848. The masters were not willingly hard; but was not labor imposed without remuneration, under the most severe penalties, a hard condition? They did not wish to brutalize their slaves, but it was for their interest that they should pass as brutish and incapable of freedom; and is not servitude brutalizing of itself? It impels to theft, for the slave lives in the midst of luxury without possessing anything; to idleness, for labor, always painful to man, becomes hateful to him as soon as he is forced to it; to falsehood, through fear of punishment; to drunkenness, because it produces the momentary forgetfulness of sufferings; to debauchery, because, in a climate which stimulates the passions, to say nothing of the masters who excite them, it is the only enjoyment which demands neither money, which the slave has not, nor the permission which it is necessary to solicit for marriage.

A comparison strikes me forcibly. There is a horror of the Black Code, which ruled the colonies from 1685 to the statutes of the Restoration. It is affirmed that its rigors fell into disuse. I believe it, but the same is true of its beneficent provisions. When the ordinances of 1833, 1839, and 1846, and the statutes of 1845, were prepared with so much care, it was regarded as a great good to re-enforce several of the humane and Christian articles of the Black Code;* its framers dared not go as far even as this stigma-

* Or the ordinance of Oct. 15, 1786, cited by the statute of July 18, 1845, Art. 2.

tized law, for example, to punish the master who debauched his slave. Thus, despite the law, despite good intentions, slavery had inevitably produced disorders and evils which it was sought to prevent in 1685, and which were still to be cured in 1845, two centuries after.

Freedom does not destroy in a moment the vices engendered by three centuries of concubinage, humiliation, and oppression; but these vices are no longer a sort of necessity of position.

Is not this great happiness?

But perhaps the slaves do not avail themselves of it; perhaps they return to a vagrant, idle, depraved, savage life? Do they seek to instruct themselves? Are they seen at church, or in prison? We have viewed the state of criminality, we will see the progress of religion and instruction.

Is it necessary to take the word *happiness* absolutely in its lowest sense? Is it believed that the *comfort* of the freedmen is less than was that of the slaves?

We are not always to take model plantations as standards of comparison. Let us not forget that wealthy proprietors were a first exception, virtuous proprietors a second exception, proprietors living on and managing their estates a third exception. The bulk of the slaves were divided into small groups of ten, twenty, or fifty at most,* let to others or laboring on the plantations of proprietors too poor to establish hospitals, and to feed or clothe their slaves properly.

If a statute (statute of July 18, 1845, Art. 1), an ordinance (ordinance of June 5, 1846), a circular from the Ministry (June 13, 1846), and orders from the Governors (Oc-

* At Martinico there are 335 small sugar plantations to 60 large ones; at Guadaloupe the number of small estates is still greater; at Bourbon there were in 1838,

196	owners	of from	50	to	500	slaves.
1,150	"	"	10	"	50	"
4,063	"	"	1	"	10	"
5,409						

(Broglie, p. 242.)

tober, 1848), were needed to prescribe that the master should give his slave six pounds of tapioca flour and three and a half pounds of codfish and salt meat a week (Art. 1), and two shirts, a pair of trousers, a jacket, and a hat every six months (Art. 7), it was apparently because the common allowance of food and clothing remained almost everywhere below these modest proportions.

One day in the week was generally accorded them instead of their food; and such was the superiority of free over servile labor, let us say in passing, together with the fertility of the soil, that the day's earnings sufficed to support the slave a week.

This still suffices, it is said, and is precisely the reason why the freedman does not work. Few wants, little labor. He satisfies his needs, then reposes. To this I have nothing to say, except that he does like the immense majority of mankind. After all, the want is the motive and measure of the labor.

But in the state of freedom the wants increase daily, and to satisfy them comes increase of labor. This is what happens to the negro who has a taste for comfort, luxury, even for dress; he labors to enjoy, and at the same time to pay for these. Meanwhile, the freedman participates in the collective burdens; he pays imposts and town dues, and to pay, to spend, it is necessary to labor.

Is material proof demanded?

It results from several documents.

We might compare the land-taxes, but the statistics are not at our disposal.

Two elements remain: —

The tables of population and culture include the number of cattle in the colonies. It is remarked that the number of mules, asses, and horses has decreased, because they have been economized or have been replaced by machinery, while that of hogs and goats has increased; now the hog and goat are the fortune of the small freeholder, on the lowest round of the ladder.

Another item of information is more significant, — the amount and nature of the importations, from which may be deduced the influence of emancipation on the consumption of the products of the mother country.

In 1848 and 1849, the commodities that advanced in the midst of the general decline were *wines* and *tobaccos*, *wheat-flour*, *lard* and *salt meats*, *soaps* and *oils*, *cotton cloths*, *umbrellas*, *watches*, *hats*, and *shoes*. The former slave wishes to drink and smoke, to eat better, to wash better, to dress better, to imitate the gentleman who carries an umbrella, not to go always with bare head and feet. He takes a particular pride in torturing his feet in shoes, which may be ridiculous, but is easily understood, if we remember that letters-patent, of 1723, revived — would one believe it? — by an ordinance of May 18, 1819, forbade the slave to wear coverings for the foot.

It cannot be denied that this change in the manners of the newly affranchised individuals influences production, and the movement of commerce. On one hand, much labor is done outside of agriculture, the products of which figure only in official statistics, and do not go to swell the column of exports; on the other, many small resources which did not formerly exist create a demand for imports. As we have already said, labor has rather been transformed than diminished. The wealth is not destroyed, it is only differently divided. Whatever may be said in dispute of the arguments to be drawn from the two statistical statements of imports and exports which we have previously cited, the first proves that these idle people produce largely,* the second proves that these poor people consume largely.†

* But the increase of wines in the four colonies bears only upon 1849; the amount fell again, and has since remained below that of 1847, even at Bourbon. (See General Table of Customs, pp. 58, 59.)

† *Revue coloniale*, 1851, p. 195.

But perhaps, while satisfying their appetites, the slaves return to the nomadic, idle, savage life? Do they seek to be instructed? Are they seen at church, in school, or in prison? We have witnessed the condition of criminality. Let us examine the progress of religion and instruction.

CHAPTER XV.

RELIGION, INSTRUCTION.

"Therein is the safety of our colonies." — BROGLIE, p. 125.
"Christianity is a religion of freemen." — DE TOCQUEVILLE, p. 41.

§ 1. BEFORE THE ABOLITION OF SLAVERY.

I THINK I can affirm that no one in the colonies was happier at the emancipation of the slaves, after the slaves themselves, than the priests worthy the name. Among them, the great majority were opposed to slavery. It fettered the ministry, and degraded the conduct of those even whose conscience it did not wound.

If I were asked what is most beautiful on earth, I should answer, Christianity! If I were asked what appears to me most odious among Christian nations, I should answer, Slavery!

But I should directly add: Slavery is impossible with Christianity.

Nevertheless, it is again and again repeated that slavery was introduced into the French colonies by the monarchy and the clergy.

Montesquieu, who combats slavery with so much force and spirit, has written, after Father Labat: * —

"Louis XIII. troubled himself extremely about the law which rendered the negroes of his colonies slaves; but when it had been fully gotten into his head that this was the surest way to convert them, he consented to it."

This error in so great a writer is incomprehensible. The

* *Esprit des lois*, Liv. XV. Chap. IV. p. 182. Father Labat, *Nouveaux Voyages aux îles de l'Amerique*, Tom. II. p. 114, 1772.

first legislative act that emanated from the mother country concerning the slave-trade is dated November 11, 1673, thirty years after the death of Louis XIII.*

It is also commonly repeated that the Dominican Las Casas gave the fatal counsel to introduce negroes into the Antilles *to relieve the natives.* A single historian, Herrera, long subsequent to Las Casas, has accredited this calumny. In the discussions which he was forced to sustain against the slavery of the Indians with Quevedo, Bishop of Darien, or with the confessor and historian of Charles V., Sepulveda, this opinion is found neither on his lips nor on those of his adversaries. He wrote his eloquent protests in 1514. Negroes were already sold at Seville in 1403, at Lisbon in 1442; there were slaves at St. Domingo in 1500; Charles V. accorded the privilege of the slave-trade to the Flemings in 1511.†

It is not, therefore, a Christian king, it is not a monk, whom we are to accuse of having originated slavery.

Who then, in fine, introduced slavery into the colonies?

This point of history is very obscure; it is never known who has sown tares in a field, and no one boasts of having been the originator of evil. Nevertheless, it is possible to seize in ancient documents — and particularly in the collection of printed acts and manuscript notes made by M. Moreau de Saint Méry, and bequeathed to the Archives of the Colonies,‡ and in the archives of the Community of the Holy Spirit, so long charged with the religious service of the colonies § — some indices which will set us on the track of the true origin of slavery in the colonies.

* Lacour, *Histoire de la Guadeloupe*, Tom. I. Chap. IX. p. 104.

† *Ibid.*, p. 102. — Moehler, translated by the Abbé de la Treiche. — *Œuvres ae Johannes Genesius Sepulveda*, 4 vols. in fol. A fine copy is in existence in the valuable library of M. Cousin. — Robertson's History of America, Book III.

‡ I am indebted for the knowledge to the kindness of the present keeper of the archives, the worthy and intelligent successor of Moreau, M. Pierre Margry.

§ These archives have been opened to me with a liberality for which I cannot show myself too grateful, by the Rev. Père Schwindenhammer, Superior, and Père Levavasseur.

These documents prove that the clergy had no share in it.

We scarcely ever go farther back than the edict of 1685, known under the name of the Black Code, issued in the same year with another deplorable law, the revocation of the edict of Nantes. This edict, with which the son of Colbert, the Marquis de Seignelay, and King Louis XIV are so justly reproached, came to correct the abuses of slavery, while unhappily sanctioning some few of them; it resembles rather the laws of 1845, which reformed slavery, than the law of 1802, which re-established it. It is necessary to refer to prior documents.

The act of *Association of the Lords of the American Islands* (1626) is a contract by which M. d'Énambuc and his associates engage to form a capital of 45,000 livres, and to freight three ships to colonize the *islands of St. Christopher, Barbadoes, and others, at the entrance of Peru, from the* 11*th to the* 18*th degree of latitude, in order to instruct the inhabitants of the said islands in the Catholic, Apostolic, and Roman religion, as well as to traffic there.*

When the Cardinal de Richelieu, created Grand Master of Navigation in 1626, secured the authorization of this first company in the same year, the letters-patent declared that the first end of the enterprise was to *plant the Christian faith to the glory of God and the honor of the king,* and was authorized on condition *of carrying priests and of cultivating and working in all sorts of mines and metals,* in consideration of a duty of one tenth to the state. The question was not of slaves, but of European laborers.

The new contract of February 12, 1635, which extended the privilege of the company from the 10th to the 30th degree, contained analogous measures. Conversion remained the principal end (Art. II.). The company was to settle 4,000 persons in twenty years (Art. III.). All of these were to be Frenchmen and Catholics (Art. IV.). But here are two very significant articles : — "Art. XI. The descendants of the colonists and the *converted savages* shall be reputed native-born Frenchmen, *capable of all charges, honors, successions, and donations.*" "Art. XIII. Artisans shall, after six years, be reputed master-workmen, and eligible to open shops in any of the cities of France, even at Paris, after ten years."

It appears that the conditions were at first fulfilled, since an edict of March, 1642, confirms the company, and declares that it has introduced 7,000 colonists, instead of 4,000, *with a good number of monks.*

It is known that Pope Alexander VI., by a bull of May, 1493, addressed to the kings of Castile, forbade any other than Spaniards to approach the American islands, under pain of excommunication.*

On the demand of Cardinal de Richelieu, Pope Urban VIII. raised these censures, and, July 12, 1635, gave power to four Dominican monks to repair thither,† under the protection of the king of France, — a power which was confirmed a number of times to the same order, then shared with several others. Father Du Tertre, from whom we borrow these details, made part of the second expedition of Spanish missionaries. Before this permission, before the settlement of Frenchmen, Dominican monks had already

* Father Du Tertre, *Histoire générale*, 1st ed., 1654, p. 30, gives a portion of the text of this curious bull: "Quibuscumque personis, cujuscumque dignitatis, etiam imperialis et regalis status, gradus, ordinis, vel conditionis, sub excommunicationis latæ sententiæ pœna, quam eo ipso, si contra fecerint, incurrant, districtius inhibemus, ne ad insulas et terras firmas inventas, et inveniendas, detectas et detegendas, versus occidentem et meridem, fabricando et construendo lineam, a polo artici ad polum antarticum, sive terræ firmæ et insulæ inventæ et inveniendæ sint versus Indiam, aut aliam quamcunque partem, quæ linea distet a qualibet insularum quæ vulgariter nuncupantur *de los Azores y Capo Verd*, centum leucis versus occidentem et meridem, ut præfertur, pro mercibus habendis, vel quavis alia de causa accedere præsumant, absque vestra ac hæredum et successorum vestrorum licencia speciali."

† Fathers Pélican, Griffon, Nicolas, and the excellent Father Raymond, who devoted himself to protecting and evangelizing the Caribs. Du Tertre, p. 29.

attempted to evangelize the Antilles, and had met their death.* The islands had martyrs before having colonists.

On the 16th of August, 1661, the privilege of the Company of the Islands was revoked. It had degenerated; instead of working the lands, it sold them; instead of civilizing the savages, it exterminated them, despite the remonstrances of the missionaries. It was necessary to reconstitute another, — *the West India Company.*

The edict of May 28 – July 31, 1664, which approves it, and accords (Art. XVI.) a premium of 30 livres per ton to the colonies and 40 livres per ton imported, continues to make the interest of religion its first care (Art. I.), and, in assuring to the associates seignorial rights (Art. XXIII.), repeats that artisans and *converted savages shall be reputed native-born and French citizens.* Thus, very far from organizing servile labor in view of compulsory conversion, all these edicts proclaim ennoblement by labor, and provide for the employ of no other workmen than the colonists and the natives.

But there is not a single spot on earth inhabited by men where slavery does not appear as a universal fact. The savages had slaves through their wars with each other; even, if Du Tertre is to be believed, those Caribs whom he pictures as so *gentle,* so *simple,* so *little vicious,* so *sociable,*† although *drunken, polygamous,* and *anthropophagous,* after having killed their enemies,‡ reduced their women to servitude, then married them, and, if they had male children, killed and ate them.§ The mountains were inhabited by fugitive slaves. As soon as the colony began to be productive, the same historian relates that it attracted *Frenchmen to dwell there and merchants to sell slaves, which are, as it were, the two bases of a colony.*¶

The inhabitants had reduced the savages to servitude;

* Six in 1603 and six in 1604. Du Tertre, *ibid.*

† P. 397. ‡ P. 449. § P. 403. ¶ P. 26.

they bought negroes; they treated the hired whites like slaves; there were thus three kinds of slavery.

But we have seen that the royal edicts anticipated and permitted nothing of the sort. The missionaries opposed the extermination of the Caribs with all their might. "The first obstacle to the conversion of the savages," said Du Tertre, "is the abhorrence which they have conceived for the name of Christian, on account of the extreme cruelties practised by the Christians on them and their fathers." *

As to the negroes, the same monk well expresses the opinion of his coadjutors, by stigmatizing *the shameful traffic which the inhabitants of the Indies* † *make of their fellow-beings*, and the manner in which they treat these *poor wretches, neither more nor less than we treat horses in France, ... beating them on the naked flesh, neither more nor less than the Turks, ... and saying, that to beat a negro is to feed him. . . . . .* ‡ He then exclaims, in touching language: "I must at last ingenuously confess, and with all humility adore, the profound and inconceivable mysteries of God, for I know not what this unhappy nation has done, that God has attached to it a particular and hereditary malediction, not only the blackness and ugliness of the body, but slavery and servitude." §

Avaricious and cruel passions were stronger than these charitable sentiments, which themselves were not without mixture and alteration.

The negro slaves multiplied in little time. The Dutch expelled from Brazil brought 1,200 to Guadaloupe in 1635. These unfortunates were sufficiently numerous to necessitate an ordinance of the Governor of Martinico, July 13, 1648, prescribing the cultivation of food *for the slaves.* On June 19, 1664, M. de Tracy, Lieutenant-General of the American Islands, made a regulation to prevent masters from hindering hired men and *negro slaves* from going to

* P. 460. † P. 473. ‡ Pp. 475, 481. § P. 480.

mass, under penalty of a fine of 120 pounds of tobacco, or, in case of a second offence, of seeing them *sold,* to be *placed in more Christian hands,* and to forbid their debauching them, under penalty of from twenty to fifty blows, and the branding of a *fleur-de-lis* on the shoulder.

We also see, by an ignoble order of March 2, 1665, the Council of Martinico negotiate with a certain negro, Francisco, to hunt fugitive slaves, *with his band,* in consideration of 1,000 pounds of tobacco and his freedom, and the same Council (October 4, 1667) punish the receiving of *negroes, indigo, sugar, cocoa, ginger, wearing apparel, utensils, furniture, and other merchandise,* by corporal punishment, and a fine of 4,000 pounds of sugar, then (July 17, 1679) invent atrocious penalties against fugitive slaves, such as slitting the nose, cutting the legs, etc.

Thus, by an infallible and rapid logic, cupidity and idleness had engendered oppression and barbarism. It was then that the edict of March, 1685, or the Black Code, intervened, designed, says the preamble, *to maintain the discipline of the Church, and to regulate what concerns the condition and quality of slaves.*

This edict did wrong in not abolishing slavery, but it did not create, and was designed to alleviate it. It left subsisting odious penalties, — whipping, slitting of ears, branding of lilies on the shoulder, hamstringing, death, — penalties which justly shock us, as well as the penalties inflicted by more ancient edicts, such as piercing through the tongue of blasphemers with a hot iron, slitting the tongue, slitting the lips in case of a second offence (edicts of December 5, 1487, and July 10, 1493), and whipping till blood was drawn for offences of the chase (edict of March, 1515). But the Black Code gives to the slaves baptism (Art. 2), marriage (Art. 8), religious worship (Art. 3), Sunday (Art. 4), burial in consecrated ground (Art. 14), emancipation (Art. 55), and recognizes to the freed slaves the same rights as to freemen (Art. 59). It prescribes the employment of Christian commanders, punishes debauchery, permits slaves to be appointed guardians, etc. This act is a shame, and nevertheless a progress. After a century and a half, men would be scarcely more advanced, milder, but no more just; they would still attempt to prevent evil from being evil, but again without succeeding. Several articles of this Code and of the letters patent of December, 1723, would be still in force, and a commentator of 1844, in relating the provision by which a master who should debauch his slave was punished by a fine of 300 livres, would content himself by saying, "This article is not carried into effect." *

Whatever may be the consequences, the examination of the origin of slavery proves that neither the monarchy nor the clergy are responsible for its establishment in the colonies. It is to the monarchy, and in part to religion, that France owes the colonies. It is not to the government and the clergy that the colonies owe servitude. They are guilty of having tolerated, then shamefully practised it.† This is enough, and too much. It is not true that they introduced it. What called it? — the cupidity of the first colonists. What introduced it? — the slave-trade. Who organized the slave-trade? — the seaports and the mother country. Innocent of slavery, the government of the mon-

* *Code de Bourbon*, by Delabarre-Nanteuil, 1844.

† Minutes of the meetings of the Company of the Islands, held on the first Friday of every month, at the house of M. Daligre. Meeting of May 5, 1645: —

"The monks of St. Domingo, residing on the island of Guadaloupe, demand twelve negroes for the service of their houses. The Company requested Sieur Houel, governor of the said island, to give four of the first negroes who should come to the island to the said monks, who are entreated carefully to instruct in the faith the negroes and savages upon the said island.

"And respecting the proposition of the said monks to be empowered to have a lot of the negroes exposed to sale on their arrival in the said island, by paying the same price as others, the said Sieur Houel shall be written to to give liberty to the said monks to purchase the said negroes like other private individuals." (Colonial Archives.)

archy was, as we shall see, directly guilty of having authorized and encouraged the slave-trade in the interest of the commerce of the ports, and it succeeded in coloring this abomination by religious pretexts; but the responsibility of the Church is here again out of the question.

The same Pope Urban VIII., who gave to the Antilles, in 1635, missionaries of the order most hostile to slavery, protested in 1639 against the Portuguese, the great organizers of slavery and the slave-trade, and a century after, in 1741, Benedict XIV. called the attention of Brazil to the same principles, which another century later, 1839, Gregory XVI. repeated to Europe and the world.

Thus, thank God! the clergy have not propagated slavery, but whatever motives may justify their conduct, it is a lamentable misfortune that they did not reprove it more severely, and that they ended by disgracefully accepting it for their own use.

Religion has been the victim of this fault, which the clergy have grievously expiated, for slavery has corrupted the priesthood, and, even where it has not corrupted it, has *fettered its preaching, perverted its position, and degraded its ministry.*

"Christianity is a religion of freemen," said M. de Tocqueville, admirably. . . . . . "How succeed in elevating and purifying the wishes of him who does not feel the responsibility of his own act? How give the idea of moral dignity to him who is nothing in his own eyes? Do what we may, it will always be difficult to enlighten and spiritualize the religion of a slave, whose life is filled with coarse and incessant toil, and who is naturally and invincibly plunged into ignorance by the very fact of his condition. . . . . . If we look with care, we shall be convinced that the negro is entirely indifferent to religious truths, or else that he makes of Christianity an ardent and gross superstition." *

* Report of 1839, p. 41.

But, besides the moral incompatibility, slavery opposes material obstacles to religious preaching.

When and how shall religious instruction be given? If the priest asks of the master an hour devoted to labor, will he obtain it? If he asks of the slave an hour devoted to rest, will he, can he, obtain a hearing? What will he say, moreover? Distrusted by the master if he awakens an instinct of freedom, — distrusted, detested by the slave if he makes himself the sanctifier of slavery, — the priest is reduced to hold in turn one half of the Gospel in slavery, and to preach a lame justice and virtues not exacted by Heaven. Facts confirm these predictions. I draw at random from the documents around me, and read in the official proceedings of the commission appointed in 1838 * to examine the proposition of M. de Passy, these answers of the witnsses interrogated: —

"Parish priests have been expelled on complaint of the masters, under the pretext that they inculcated ideas of freedom on the negro population, and the Catholic prefects have been obliged to recommend to their priests to abstain from all allusion to the subject of liberty."

"Moreover," said the Batonnier of the barristers of Fort Royal (Martinico), "the negroes have regarded the priests as charged with a mission to deceive them, and exclusively to defend the interests of the masters. It is, perhaps, to this that we are to attribute their present incredulity."

So false a position was not of a nature to inspire many vocations. The clergy of the colonies, therefore, was always insufficient; consequently, imperfectly recruited and thus mingled with corrupt elements, the refuse of the dioceses of Europe, it became the disgrace of colonial communities.

This calamity was averted as soon as an appeal was made to associations, the subjects of which, prepared by a special

* Library of M. de Broglie.

education, easily replaced, and received in their old age, were moreover subject to more efficacious authority than that of apostolic prefects over priests from every corner of France. The great labors of the Jesuits, the Dominicans, the Carmelites, the Capuchins, the brothers of Saint Jean-de-Dieu,* and lastly, the members of the Congregation of the Holy Spirit at Guiana, Martinico, and Guadaloupe, are not forgotten.

Not only did these monks form a pure and efficacious clergy for the colonies, but they managed their plantations in a manner to make them models. A good example which, for my part, I dare call a scandal, so repugnant is it to me to accept the idea of a model, virtuous, and lucrative slavery practised by priestly sugar and coffee planters.

In so false a position and despite aggravated obstacles, sometimes by the reactions of the revolutions of the mother country, at others by difficulties with the local governments, such is the beneficent power of Christianity, and such the zeal of the greater part of its ministers, that, notwithstanding, much religious good has been done at all times in the colonies from the day of their foundation.

The Gospel rendered the masters milder, the slaves happier. Of all races, the negro is perhaps the most eager for religion, and the Catholic worship, exclusively recognized

* Commission of 1839, *Procès-verbaux* of the Chamber of Deputies, session of 1840, p. 108:—

Delegate from Martinico: "On the plantations of the monks, the number of families was greater, and the arrangement of labor more perfect; and this has continued. The good effect produced by these monastic orders makes itself felt wherever their useful influence is exercised."

Delegate from Guadaloupe: "I have precisely the same testimony to render."

Delegate from Guiana: "There were considerable plantations in Guiana belonging to monks. These plantations were well administered. The monks had even civilized the Indians, who are more difficult to civilize than the negroes."

Delegate from Bourbon: "There never were any monastic orders in the Isle of Bourbon [the delegate is here in error], but the colonial workshop where religious instruction was most common ranked highest of all others in morals, and labor there was active and regular."

by the edict of 1685, and since remaining that of the majority of the inhabitants, has incomparable attraction for them. Despite some little distrust, how could it be otherwise? Religion not only gives hope to wretched souls, abandoned, if they do not look for a better world, to the spirit of rebellion, the desire of flight, the dejection of sadness, or the stupefaction of a carelessness maintained by depravation; it gives, through baptism, godfathers and godmothers to beings without family; it elevates their freed conscience to the serene heights of moral liberty; it transforms their misfortune into a merit.* They have, in the priests, defenders, confidants, and friends; at the altar, they receive equality before God; a family is given them in His name; festivals occur to break their monotonous existence; — the church was the place of refuge of the slaves, it was the only spot in the world where they were really free or momentarily happy.

It is not useless to show, by an extremely brief history of religion† in each of the slave colonies, what were its calamities, its labors, and its progress, unto the moment of the abolition of slavery.

I. Guiana.

Before the Revolution, the mission of Guiana was intrusted to the Jesuits. They had but a single parish in Cayenne when visited by Father Labat in 1694; nevertheless, their labors had not been sterile. The missionaries had a great and salutary influence over the negroes, who were most de-

* A merit often heroic! Negroes, worn out, aged, sure of being punished on the morrow, were seen to walk a league at night, three times a week, to go to catechism.

† This history is the summary of published writings, such as *La Mission de Cayenne*, by Father de Montezon; *Lettres sur l'esclavage*, by M. Dugoujon, Apostolic Prefect of Guadaloupe; *L'Esclavage aux colonies*, by M. Castelli, Apostolic Prefect of Martinico; the *Annales de la Propagation de la foi;* and, lastly, MS. memorials and unpublished letters addressed to the Department of the Marine and to the Community of the Holy Spirit.

voted and docile to those whom they styled the *Monpères*. It is still remembered in the colonies, that, under the government of M. d'Orvilliers, a considerable number of negroes having gathered together on a mountain and in the forests, the planters and all the troops marched against them, but without success. A general rising of those who had remained tranquil was feared, when a Jesuit, Father Poque, went alone into the midst of the fugitives, brought them back, and effected a reconciliation. These zealous priests did not neglect the Indian tribes, in general gentle, laborious, distrustful because they had been deceived, but who had been* and could still, by better treatment, be civilized and made useful. Three special missions were organized for these tribes in 1782 by Father Jean-Xavier-Padilla.

"The Indians descend the rivers," says a missionary,† "they brave the waves in their frail periaguas, and present their children for baptism. . . . . . It is touching to see the proud Indian, his neck adorned with a collar of tiger's or alligator's teeth, with bow and arrows in one hand, and tomahawk in the other, witness the baptism of his child with the greatest respect, ... then, after the ceremony, joyful, and blessing the father, place his infant in the little periagua and dart again upon the waves."

The priests of the Holy Spirit, dispatched after the expulsion of the Jesuits (1773), under the ministry of M. de Sartines (1776), to the number of twenty, with an apostolic prefect, continued their good work with success. Thanks to this influence, the relations of the two classes were exceptional in this colony,‡ and so harmonious that the first outbreak of the Revolution passed without disturb-

* *Aperçu de la situation des peuplades indiennes à la Guyane française*, by M Devilly. *Revue coloniale*, July, 1850, p. 45.

† *Mission de Sinnamary*, by M. Hardy.

‡ *Observations sur l'état de la colonie de Cayenne*, by M. Terrasson, planter (MS. of the Seminary of the Holy Spirit).

ance. But erelong, labor being checked by the causes indicated elsewhere, the negroes dispersed through the forests. The priests, having courageously refused to take the oath, were arrested, and condemned to deportation. Thirty-two were in fact deported from Guiana, while other French priests were, on the contrary, deported to Guiana, and came thither to die of fever and want, and to find a humble, to-day venerated tomb. The churches were fired. The re-establishment of slavery, in 1802, finished what emancipation, by violence, had begun. "A great part of the blacks," says a colonist,* "take refuge in the forests, especially those who have lost all principle of religion, and become true negro Jacobins. When they have provisions and see themselves in sufficient numbers, they attempt incursions on our settlements, maltreat and assassinate the proprietors, carry off the faithful slaves, and, not content with abandoning themselves to plunder, make use of poison, a fearful weapon in their hands."

During this time, the deported priests were dispersed by Providence to serve, revive, or second, after a thousand trials, arrests, and shipwrecks, religion on other points, some at Guadaloupe, others at Martinico, one at St. Christopher, another at St. Croix.

Of all the priests deported, one alone, M. Legrand, returned to Guiana, but not until 1809, where he exercised his ministry with the title of Apostolic Prefect, even under the Portuguese occupation. He wrote, at the close of 1816, to the Duke de Luxembourg, Ambassador of France to Portugal: † "I am the only French priest at Cayenne. I do what I can in the town, but the country is almost abandoned. Besides, my age and infirmities give me reason to believe that the end of my career is not far distant. Entreat the government to send us co-workers." He had the

* MS. of the Seminary of the Holy Spirit.

† Archives of the Seminary of the Holy Spirit.

joy of witnessing the arrival of three priests, in November, 1817, then died in January, 1818. Deplorable administrative dissensions retarded the effects of the mission, without rendering them wholly fruitless, — thanks to the impregnable zeal of M. Guillier, the successor of M. Legrand, — until the beneficent administration of M. Jubelin, who, happily for the colony, governed six years (1829 – 1835).

The brothers and sisters were re-established, the churches rebuilt, the parishes increased, and, when the revolution of 1848 broke out, it had been preceded by an evangelization which, although incomplete, contributed, nevertheless, powerfully to the maintenance of the public peace.

II. Martinico.

We find again at Martinico the same founders of the mission, — the Jesuits, — and, by a touching coincidence, the same restorers of religion as at French Guiana. The Jesuits arrived there at the beginning of the French occupation (1649). In 1694 Father Labat found there with them the Dominicans and Capuchins, who remained alone after 1773, with an apostolic prefect for each order. The brothers hospitallers of Saint Jean-de-Dieu had established there the admirable plantation of Saint Jacques. The religious condition was tolerably satisfactory at the moment of the Revolution, followed so speedily by English occupation. A few priests remained during the duration of this occupation. We find M. Legrand there in 1807, deported from Guiana, to which he was soon to return. Several years passed with a disorganized clergy, under superiors whose delegation was contestable, until the moment when the venerable head of the Community of the Holy Spirit, M. Bertout, — who may be called the spiritual father of the colonies, for he raised up the priesthood in all of them, — sent two priests in 1819, and obtained the appointment, by an ordinance of December 31, 1821, of two apostolic prefects, one for Martinico and the other for Guadaloupe. The first, M. Carraud, did immense good there, which would have been still greater had it not been for the inadequateness in every respect of nearly all the colonial clergy, and the administrative difficulties which, at the time of the Revolution of 1830, caused a long and distressing interim. From 1834 to 1848, the prefecture was confided to a priest well known for his abolition sentiments, — M. Castelli. They were not the only, but the principal * cause of the obstacles which, after having fettered his ministry, determined his removal. He had the pleasure of being restored to his functions at the moment when the slaves were about to be freed. Despite these trials and faults, good was done. Religion had long since effected in many parishes the habits of prayer, instruction, and moralization which the law came to enjoin ; and, if the preparation for the abolition of slavery was not further advanced at Martinico, it was not the majority of the clergy of the colony that were to blame for it.

III. Guadaloupe.

With the first colonists, MM. Duplessis and l'Olive, four Dominicans landed in 1635. The story of the efforts of one of them, Father Raymond, to protect the unfortunate Caribs, has been preserved to us in a very curious manuscript,† and in the history of Father Du Tertre, another Dominican sent shortly after. When the island was sold to M. de Boisseret and M. Houel, the latter, after a difficulty with the Dominicans, invited thither the barefoot Carmelites of Touraine (1664). Father Labat also found Jesuits and Capuchins there thirty years after. The great lepers' hospital of Désirade was established in 1728. All the statements authorize the belief, that, at the end of the eighteenth century, the

* Letter from a missionary, 1841: "What completes his destruction is his abolition opinions, which he has not sufficiently concealed."

† Purchased by the author at the sale of the Erdeven collection.

religious and moral condition of the colony had made as much progress as its material prosperity. After the Revolution, religion had to pass through continual trials ; — proscribed and overthrown at first, then represented by an incapable or even scandalous clergy ; at length intrusted for long years to the direction of a respectable apostolic prefect, whose charity was admirable during the yellow-fever of 1838, and at the moment of the terrible earthquake of 1843, but timid, and instructing his clergy to repair to the plantations only when they were summoned there. As he said himself in his correspondence, "The religious instruction of the slave class does not make great progress. . . . . . The colonists of an important part of the colony seem to have given each other the cue to receive neither the visits of priests nor of magistrates." There was less indifference or opposition at some points. It seemed, above all, as if the great trials which overwhelmed the colonies opened souls to better resolutions, encouraged towards the last by instructions and laws from the mother country. The patient zeal of the clergy, directed by a new superior, obtained, in fact, the most satisfactory results, but the ill-will of the masters remained the same, with some noble exceptions, until the Revolution of 1848. It was the destiny of Guadaloupe to arrive at moral progress more tardily than the other colonies, and more tardily also, by an equitable coincidence, at material progress.

IV. Bourbon.

The Isle of Bourbon was more fortunate. When, a century after its discovery by the Portuguese Mascarenhas, it was colonized by the French, the Gospel was carried thither by Capuchin monks ; one of whom, Father Hyacinth, after the compulsory departure of the Governor, in 1675, governed the island for three years. The religious worship was intrusted to the Lazarists from 1736, and when, during the Revolution, the colony administered itself, the goods of the Lazarists were confiscated, but worship was not abolished. Nevertheless, it may be said that religion expired. The divorce law disorganized the families of the whites ; if it had not the same effect upon the blacks, it was because marriage was unknown to them. The missionaries of the Holy Spirit found on their arrival, in 1818, three cures vacant out of eleven, no instruction, and no piety ; progress was very slow, the chief obstacle being the opposition of the greater part of the masters, an opposition to which they were condemned by falsity of position rather than hardness of heart.

I read still in the correspondence of this epoch the same state of affairs. A few colonists were exceptions, and are models ; to them, and above all to their wives, the slaves were a family ; to others, they were cattle. When the slave had labored enough to pay for what he was worth, he might die for aught they cared. Between these two extremes, it pleased many masters to choose among the Christian virtues, to detach from the Gospel the pages on patience while blotting out those on equality, and to walk abroad accompanied by two men, the one bearing a crucifix to preach submission, the other a lash to enforce it. They were willing to accept the instruction which develops the faculties, provided it did not elevate the sentiments. They were willing to give an hour to the school, provided it were not taken from the work.

Is it necessary to add, that the superior authority did little for a long time to change a state of affairs which seemed in some sort admitted and without remedy ?

The faults, the vices of a fraction of the clergy were responsible at Bourbon, as elsewhere, for a part of this deplorable sterility. Instead of converting others, more than one priest suffered himself to become corrupted ; above all, more than one suffered himself to become discouraged. To preach chastity in such a climate, fraternity under such a system; to talk of disinterestedness to men burning to make a fortune, and of divine goodness to wretches bowed down by force to toil; to please two parties which detested each other, to be suspicious to none; to inculcate the subtle truths of the Gospel on young creoles, bachelors of the colleges of Paris, and young Africans reared on the coast of Zanguebar, mingled with Pariahs from India and China, — ah! this was, it will be granted, an ungrateful mission!

It demanded Christian heroes, — they were found at Bourbon. The Abbé Monnet, who arrived in the island in 1840, resolved to devote himself exclusively to the moralization of the blacks; he obtained the co-operation of some of his *confrères*, and his success won a signal notice in the report of the Duke de Broglie, who thus sums up the testimony of the Apostolic Prefect of Bourbon, heard by the Colonial Commission, April 29, 1842.*

"Instruction has truly taken a new impulse at St. Denis and the surrounding localities. The Abbé Monnet has displayed admirable zeal and rare intelligence. There are to-day not less than 10,000 blacks catechised by his curés. . . . . . He has found powerful auxiliaries in a few pious negroes, who have become sufficiently advanced in religious instruction to teach the Catechism and repeat the lessons on the plantations. For three years past the number of first communions has been considerable, even among adults. . . . . . The masters take the initiative most honorably in this respect. . . . . . A great impulse has been given to marriages. . . . . . More than 400 have been contracted in two years among the black population."

The movement which rejoiced some masters filled others with consternation. We know that M. Monnet, as is said in a correspondence, "like a true priest of Jesus Christ, desired nothing so much as to see the day of liberty and

* Report, p. 153.

spiritual regeneration dawn at length upon the unhappy negroes." On his return to Bourbon in 1847, after a short sojourn in France, the opposition of the colonists was such that the Governor ordered him directly to set out again for home. He died on his way to evangelize Madagascar.

Happily, his work was not abandoned. God raised up, no longer a few men, but a whole community, for its continuance and extension.

A few years subsequent to 1830, there were found in the Seminary Saint-Sulpice, at Paris, a Creole from Bourbon, a Creole from Mauritius, and a Creole from St. Domingo.* They confided to each other their idea of devoting themselves to the evangelization of the negroes. This was the origin of the *Community of the Sacred Heart of Mary.* "The general end of our society," wrote one of the three founders with sublime simplicity, in an unpublished document, "is to care for the poorest and most forsaken people of the Church of God. The negroes being found at this moment in this position, more than any other people, we have offered ourselves to evangelize them."

Having become a priest, the first of these men was sent to Bourbon, the second to Mauritius, and the third died in sight of St. Domingo. They had taken for their superior a holy man, Father Libermann, a converted Jew, who prepared the foundation of the community destined, in the idea of its institutors, to evangelize the negroes in Hayti and the Antilles, as well as in the two Guianas, Senegambia, and the rest of Africa.

We cannot read without emotion the memorial addressed by Father Libermann to the congregation of the Propaganda, on the general condition of the black population in the world.

"Within reach of Europe," says he, "millions of men are wallowing in ignorance and wretchedness, yet no one

* MM. Levavasseur, Laval, and Tisserant.

thinks of rescuing them. Nevertheless, these men, as well as others, are created in the image of God. . . . . .

"In the very country where a merciful Providence seems to have conducted them to free their souls, by subjecting their bodies to a toilsome servitude, — in these countries, where they should find the riches and consolations of grace, their souls are perishing of want in the midst of abundance, and there is no one to aid them."

The labors of the missionaries at Bourbon were an invaluable preparation for emancipation, and the principal cause of the union and peace which reigned when it was declared.

In short, the statesmen who labored in France for this great work were not mistaken when they summoned religion to their aid; * the colonists who opposed it were not mistaken when they distrusted it. Religion is not freedom, but it is the mother of freedom.

But the history of religion in the four slave colonies of France, until emancipation, ends in this conclusion : —

1. All the effort, all the credit, all the encouragement, did not succeed in drawing a sufficient number of laborers to the ungrateful mission of carrying the Gospel into the bosom of servitude.

Before the ordinance of September 6, 1839, there were in our four colonies but 82 priests, scarcely 1 to 4,500 inhabitants on a considerable surface.† After the ordinance of May 18, 1846, there were only 127, or 1 for about 3,000 inhabitants. It was hoped that the lists would be filled in 1847.‡

2. Christianity, which brings duty and hope to all conditions, has power to alleviate and moralize even slavery;

* Ordinances of 1839 and 1846.

† Report of the Duke de Broglie, p. 122.

‡ 6th Supplement to the Report of the Minister of the Marine to the King, March, 1847.

the black population has a soul peculiarly open to its teachings, which bear fruit when the master is exceptionally good, the apostle exceptionally holy. But in general, the slave, the master, and the priest are depraved by servitude. Religion itself seems perverted and corrupted. Its progress is impossible before emancipation, infallible after.

§ 2. After the Abolition of Slavery.

In all the colonies, liberty was proclaimed before the altar. The negroes received it as a sacrament, in one of those rare, sublime, and joyous hours in which justice triumphs here on earth. God was taken to witness the reconciliation of men.

"Some young negroes of the town," writes the Apostolic Prefect of Guiana,* "came to entreat me to say mass that grace might be given them not to abuse their freedom."

"God be praised!" exclaims the Apostolic Prefect of Martinico,† "we have here now but a free people, a people of brethren, whom we are all called on to console, to enlighten, and to direct. . . . . . The harvest is great; let us enlarge our hearts!"

"The colonial missions are becoming admirable and worthy of envy," writes the Apostolic Prefect of Guadaloupe.‡ And in a report to the Minister of the Marine, he declares that "the negroes repair with eagerness to religious instructions, marriages are multiplied, and so many scholars flock to the schools that it is necessary to triple the number."

At Bourbon, where the missionaries wrote already before 1848, "We are the mediators of the two popula-

* Unpublished letter of 1848.

† Pastoral letter of August 15, 1848.

‡ Circular of June 17, 1848; Report of Aug. 22, 1848.

tions; . . . . . they feel the need of our presence, and we profit by it to do good,"—only a handful of negroes were seen to go tumultuously to cast chains into the sea; all remained patient and confiding; they had waited ten years for their freedom, they waited two months longer for the Commissioner-General who brought the decree, then another two months without trouble or disorder for the proclamation of this decree, which took place in the temples of God; they entered into liberty as it were by a second baptism.

"It would doubtless have been better," wrote Father Libermann, in 1850, "if the slaves had been well prepared; but as they never would have been sufficiently so, on account of the opposition of their masters, this sudden emancipation may be regarded as a gift from God." *

But, far from being finished, the moralizing work of religion was beginning. Not only was it necessary for it to pass through days of revolution and ruin, to transfuse into manners the fraternity which had just been inscribed in the law, and to struggle against ardent rancors and guilty incitements; but before all it was fitting to reform the clergy itself, inefficient, too scanty, and imperfectly organized. For a long time the colonies had demanded bishops. The apostolic prefects were invested with simple administrative supremacy. They had neither the external dignity, nor the real authority of bishops, nor the independence which results to them from immovability. The Colonial Commission of 1840,† while demanding bishops, had hesitated before this condition, through a love of excessive centralization. Placed face to face with an all-powerful Governor, a dependent bishop would have been without influence, and this dependence was precisely what lowered the character of the prefects.

* Unpublished memorial, Archives of the Seminary of the Holy Spirit.

† Meeting of Feb. 22, 1843.

The Community of the Holy Spirit, charged with maintaining the supply of the colonial clergy, had rendered the greatest services. Its missionaries were already evangelizing Canada and Acadia at the moment of the expulsion of the Jesuits (1773). Guiana was then confided to it (1776), next, Senegal (1779), recovered, thanks to two of its missionaries, and the islands of St. Pierre and Miquelon. Founded in 1703, suppressed in 1793, re-established in 1805 by Napoleon, who suppressed it anew in 1809, re-established in 1816, installed at the expense of the state in 1820, and endowed with a subsidy, which the July government suppressed in 1830, then restored in 1839, the Community of the Holy Spirit had made the greatest effort to augment the number and quality of the colonial priests. When the ordinance of September 6, 1839, placed an annual appropriation at the disposal of the government for the increase of the clergy and churches, the community could support, —

At Martinico,	44	priests, serving	28	parishes;
" Guadaloupe,	46	" "	32	"
" Bourbon,	30	" "	14	"
" Guiana,	10	" "	14	quarters; —

to say nothing of fifteen priests at Senegal, St. Pierre, the East Indies, and Madagascar. This was one priest for some 2,000 or 3,000 inhabitants.

But the clergy continued to have for superiors only prefects and vice-prefects. The Superior of the Community of the Sacred Heart of Mary, united by the Pope to that of the Holy Spirit, — Father Libermann, — as wise as disinterested, took immediate measures, although unfavorable to the influence of his community, that bishops should be finally given to the colonies. His prayers were granted by the decrees of June 22 and July 12, 1850.

Under the inspiration of a minister to whom the Church and society owe so much, — M. de Falloux, — men ceased thus to haggle for the true conditions of religious power.

Three bishoprics were created by the decrees of June 22 and July 12, 1850, at Basse-Terre (Guadaloupe), Port Royal (Martinico), and St. Denis (Bourbon).* The National Assembly repeatedly † declared itself in favor of their institution, and, by statutes of November 6 and December 16, 1850, ‡ provided for the expenses of their installation. The Holy See approved and hastened to sanction this important measure, which was definitively regulated by a decree of February 3, 1851. Guiana alone remained under the ancient régime.

At this time, the effective force of the colonial clergy was raised,

At Martinico,	to	80	priests.
" Guadaloupe,	"	85	"
" Bourbon,	"	65	"
Total, . .		230.	

The bishops of the colonies were attached to the diocese of Bordeaux, as belonging to the mother country, and consequently called to the councils of that province, held, the one at Rochelle in 1853, the other at Périgueux in 1856. The acts of these councils subjected the colonial dioceses to the rules established by the preceding council, held at Bordeaux in 1850, and which had expressed wishes for their erection. The first movement of the fathers of the Rochelle Council was to bless God for the foundation of the colonial bishoprics and the emancipation of the slaves. The terms in which this was done deserve to be cited : —

"Before all, we render thanksgivings to God the Father for the mercies which, disposing everything with gentleness, have happily ended, through his providence, an affair so necessary to the salvation of souls, and likewise to the sovereign

* The bishops appointed were M. Lacarrière, for Guadaloupe; M. Leherpeur, for Martinico; M. Desprez, for Bourbon.

† May 4, July 29, 1850.

‡ On the report of M Dariste, *Moniteur*, 1850, p. 3601.

pontiff, Pius IX., who, acceding to the religious prayers of the Prince-President of the Republic, and changing simple apostolic prefectures into veritable and perpetual bishoprics, as he has done for England and Holland, despite the resistance and anger of heretics and politicians, thus refutes, by the most evident facts, the pretended discoveries, calumniously spread, of a change of bishops into papal vicars." *

As to emancipation, this admirable declaration, approved by the Holy See, should also be retained : —

"Numerous constitutions of the Roman pontiffs, dating back several centuries, attest how much the holy mother, the Catholic Church, has always deplored the hard slavery in which a multitude of men were retained *to the loss of their souls*, and by what efforts she has unceasingly labored to remedy so great an evil. Now, thanks to God, whose providence does not err in its designs, a new order of things has broke forth, and we rejoice in the Lord for the capital benefit accorded to so many men, who, though of a different color, are our brothers in Adam, and appear to wish to use the liberty so long desired to acquire the liberty of the children of God.

"But alas! *the harvest is plenteous, but the laborers are few!* (Matt. ix. 37.)"

The bishops did not reach their dioceses until the close of 1851, nearly three years after the abolition of slavery. Here, again, what should have taken place before was not done till afterwards, and long enough afterwards for the good and harm of emancipation, abandoned to itself, to be already effected and judged.

But the religious good has begun, and continues more and more to prevail.

The clergy could not be suddenly augmented; it has, nevertheless, been increased.

* Decreta concilii provinciæ Burdigalensis, Rupellæ celebrati, anno Domini 1853, Cap. V. p. 48.

† *Ibid.*, Cap. VI. p. 50.

The official list is still : —

80 for Martinico ;

85 for Guadaloupe ;

74 for Bourbon.

But, besides this list, there are parochial chapels, curacies, and almonries unrecognized. One priest is computed for about 2,500 inhabitants ; now it will be remembered that, before 1848, there was but one for 3,000 ; before 1839, but one for 4,500. The present number is, moreover, far from sufficient. In France, there is one priest for 700 inhabitants, and the distances are much less, no diocese having 60 leagues, as at Bourbon, 65, as at Martinico, or 85, as at Guadaloupe.

The number of churches is considerably increased. Several have been built by the negroes. But the parishes are still too large and the churches too scarce.

The moral good wrought has been immense. This has been judged, in a preceding chapter, from the number of marriages ; it will also be judged from the progress of schools.

Before the ordinance of June 5, 1840, and the financial encouragement in the budget of 1839, the report of the Duke de Broglie * stated that the elementary and moral instruction of slave-children in our colonies was deplorably neglected, and, so to say, null. There was not one child in twenty-five that could even follow the Catechism. The impulse given in 1840 by the Apostolic Prefects and the Governors produced some happy results. Nevertheless, the Colonial Commission demanded an expenditure of 1,740,000 francs for the foundation of indispensable schools. In the English colonies, during the three first years of *apprenticeship*, the government had appropriated £75,000 to the schools, and such had been the zeal of the missionaries and authorities, that the English colonies possessed 1 school for 600 inhabitants, instructing 1 child in 9, at the same

* Report, p. 92, etc.

time that France counted only 1 school for 1,000 inhabitants, instructing 1 child in 12.

What the Colonial Commission proposed in France in 1840 is not yet everywhere realized.

It demanded, at Martinico, 47 Brothers de Ploërmel, instead of 14; in the budget of 1860, 50 are paid from the local fund; — 54 Sisters of St. Joseph, instead of 6; there are 40.

At Guadaloupe, it considered it necessary to raise the number of brothers from 15 to 54; there are 50; — the number of sisters, from 7 to 54; there are 53.

At Guiana, 23 brothers were proposed instead of 5; there are 14; — 31 sisters, instead of 9; there are 14.

At Bourbon, where the boys' schools are superintended by the Brothers of the Christian Schools, it was wished to increase the number of these and of the girls' schools to 12 each; the number has been increased, but in a less proportion.

We see that a perceptible progress has been accomplished; but it is lamentable that still greater sacrifices have not been made. The programme drawn in 1840 is not yet carried out, twenty years after.

The eagerness of the freed population to profit by teaching has been lively and lasting. A school-fee might be imposed almost without lessening it.*

Primary instruction is progressing; let us not forget that it was null twenty years ago; it is relished, desired, and encouraged, it was rejected, fettered, and distrusted.

The religious good, strictly speaking, is no less. The letters of the bishops are full of the most admirable details of the number of communions, the attendance of the churches, and the progress of works of charity and religious associations.

* The full statistics of the number of pupils, unhappily, have not been collected.

I open a simple collection, entitled, "Religious Almanac of the Isle of Bourbon, for 1860," and mark what I find: —

The island is divided into two districts, — the *Windward* district and the *Leeward* district; the first comprises 21 parishes, and the second 24. The population being about 140,000, without including 40,000 immigrants, there are therefore about 3,000 souls to a parish. There are, moreover, 42 chapels.

In these 45 parishes exist: —

Two ecclesiastical colleges;

Fifteen schools of the Brothers of Christian Schools;

Seventeen infant schools of the Sisters of St. Joseph;

Two military hospitals;

A hospital for the aged;

An insane asylum;

A penitentiary, kept by the Monks of the Holy Spirit;

Two Malgache establishments;

A special parish for the Indians;

Two communities of the Sacred Heart and the Christian Mothers;

Two societies of the Sisters of St. Vincent de Paul;

Three institutions of the Sisters of Charity;

Eight orphan asylums, lepers' hospitals, schools, or other establishments of the Daughters of Mary;

Twenty-three societies of St. Francis Xavier;

Sixteen institutions of Our Lady of Good Succor.

These last societies are associations for mutual aid, the first among working-men, the second among working-women, to assist each other in case of sickness, and to combine with the church. Drunkenness is a cause of exclusion. At St. Denis, the Society of St. Francis Xavier contains more than 1,000 working-men, and exists in almost every parish. The Daughters of Mary are an order founded since 1848; the Sisters are both white and black, and the former slaves have been seen to become the superiors of the daughters of their ancient mistresses. Can the triumph of Christian equality go further?*

I add this sentence, extracted from an unpublished letter from one of the first bishops of the island: "Almost all the freedmen of 1848 are practical Christians. . . . . . It is said that they are idle and in want; I should not need a hundred francs a year to succor all these paupers."

A work of special evangelization has been established for the East Indians and Malgaches; but, ill chosen, maltreated, and without wives, these Indians are the scourge of a diocese, and often the disgrace of humanity. (Périgueux, IV.)

At Martinico, before 1848, there existed only charitable boards. Since this epoch, the Society of Saint Vincent de Paul, the Workingmen's Society of St. Joseph, two workshops, societies of the Sisters of Charity, and missions for the moralization of the blacks, have diffused their benefits. There are 3,000 or 4,000 first communions a year, at least one half among adults and the aged. Morality is progressing; marriages and legitimations, thanks to the diminution of the prejudice of color, continue to be numerous. The progress is no less perceptible in instruction. A large seminary was founded in 1851 at St. Pierre. The same town and Fort-de-France contain a small seminary college. The schools of the Brothers de Ploërmel,† for boys, and of the Sisters of St. Joseph, for girls, together contain from 3,000 to 4,000 pupils; and the document from which this information is borrowed contains this sentence: "It is only

* Some are astonished that priests are not formed from a population which has so much inclination for religion. Ten years have not been sufficient to give enough consistency or enlightenment to the family of the freedman. The chief obstacle is in the prejudice of color. The whites would scarcely respect a black priest, and the blacks themselves would not turn to him.

† This admirable order, which transforms Breton peasants into apostles of the Antilles, Senegal, Guiana, and India, has just lost its venerable founder, the Abbé Jean de la Mennais, whom God destined to do more good than his unfortunate brother made noise.

since 1848 that moral progress has begun to be perceptible. The former state of things by no means favored it." *

The religious movement at Guadaloupe has been no less decided since the same epoch. Schools in every parish, evening classes for adults, the Society of St. Vincent de Paul, the workshops at Basse-Terre, Pointe-à-Pître, and Mary Galante, numerous first communions of adults, — such are the facts signalized by most veracious documents.†

Lastly, the Guiana mission has founded new residences, and the admirable priests who go, braving death, to evangelize convicts, Indians, and negroes, are full of consolation and hope.‡

It is in this manner that, with the forces of a clergy inadequate and not always irreproachable, although greatly improved, the Church struggles on in these distant lands against ignorance, drunkenness, concubinage, idleness, the hostility of classes, — sad results of our nature, aggravated by three centuries of slavery. Compare these colonial dioceses with a diocese in the heart of France, — the French diocese will unite more resources, the colonial diocese will bear more fruits. Compare the hopes conceived since 1848 and the sterility verified before. How is it that so little good was effected in the first period in so many years? how is it that so much was effected in the second in so few years? From the beginning of the chapter, we have indicated the true reply, — no liberty, no religion.

The progress is so much the more satisfactory, inasmuch

* Archives of the Seminary of the Holy Spirit.

† In 1840, an energetic effort raised for the first time to 10,237 the number of freed persons and slaves, both over and under fourteen, attendant upon parochial instructions. In 1860, the number of *adults* knowing the Catechism was, according to the report of the Governor, 23,761.

‡ "I have 18 missionaries at my disposal," wrote the Apostolic Prefect, September 18, 1860, "several of whom have to officiate over 10 or 12 leagues. Three quarters, two of which comprise 20 and 40 leagues, are without pastors. The number should be doubled!" (Archives of the Propagation of the Faith.)

as the means of the bishops are still extremely inadequate, as it cannot be too often repeated.

"The curés almost all lack vicars," said the fathers of the Council of Rochelle,* "and the parishes are for the most part too extended. The heats are overpowering; the acclivities are steep and continual, and as the priest toilingly surmounts them, he sees crowds of freedmen besieging the church doors to marry and to prepare for the first communion, so that one may say of these people, with the prophet: 'The children lack bread, and there is none to give it them.'"

There are not enough priests, nor enough missionaries, nor enough brothers, nor enough sisters, nor enough churches.

Despite this mournful destitution, the colonial dioceses are rapidly progressing Christian communities.

"It is scarcely six years," we read in the acts of the Council of Périgueux,† held in 1856, with the concurrence of the Holy See and the French government, "since three new dioceses were erected in our colonies. It is marvellous what abundant fruits the Church has already gathered from them."

Returning to emancipation, the fathers of the same Council exclaimed: —

"It delights us to recall here the opinion of the Apostle Paul, in whose eyes there were neither Greeks nor Scythians, so that, united in Jesus Christ, the faithful may forget nation, *and be all of one body with Christ and members of his members*." ‡

Will religion work this desirable and difficult harmony? It has God and the future on its side. These words of the Council at least measure the whole distance which separates the system of freedom from that of slavery. For-

* *Archives de la Propagation de la foi*, p. 53.
† P. 51, Cap. I. Tit. 4.
‡ P. 55, Cap. III. Tit. 5.

merly, religion said to the masters, "Be clement!" to the slaves, "Be patient!" It can say at length to both, "Be brethren!"

This word can fall sincerely from the lips of the priests only since the abolition of slavery.

In short, religion did all the good that it could to the colonies before this epoch. The colonies had not yet European colonists when it counted martyrs. When the Caribs were unjustly slaughtered, it defended them. When slaves were introduced, it protected them, instructed them, enjoined their kind treatment, and counselled their freedom. The masters owed to it the tranquillity of the slaves; the slaves owed to it the gentleness of the masters, and by degrees the only joys that could raise their souls above the rigors of their condition. But religion did not penetrate beyond this.

The complete evangelization of this unfortunate race exacted the freedom of the soul, the freedom of preaching, the freedom of marriage. Without the first, there was no responsibility for the moral being; without the second, no enlightenment for the mind; without the third, no good morals. The master held the will captive, refused the time necessary for preaching and the authorization necessary for marriage. Such was, such is, in all places, the narrow part left by servitude to the Gospel.

On the day when the slaves were emancipated, religion, with them, was set at liberty.

CHAPTER XVI.

RESUME.

Before the emancipation of the slaves, every step taken towards this solemn hour was lighted by immense labors, reports, discussions, and inquiries. A father does not follow with more vigilant eye, from day to day, the minute notes which attest the progress of his child, than the public authorities brought care, passionate curiosity, and active perseverance to ascertain the results of the measures obtained of the government.

To-day the work is accomplished, and no one seeks to verify the results of an experiment which was the object of such generous expectation. The most ardent promoters of emancipation are like the architects who go every day to see a house while it is building, and never set foot in it after it is finished. It would, however, be most useful if public opinion would call on the government to prescribe and publish an extended inquiry into the results of the abolition of slavery in our colonies.

The study of an isolated writer can be only an imperfect sketch of this desirable work ; it has no other merit than to group together scattered documents, doubtless incomplete, yet already numerous enough to lead to precise conclusions, which it is fitting to sum up.

It will be thought that it is too soon to judge well of so recent events. Those who, in 1849 or 1850, groaned over the first outbreaks of reconquered freedom, deserve the reproach of being in too great haste. If the always painful consequences of a great social transformation still weighed upon the colonies, one could have a right to say of them, Wait! Is it surprising that ten years of freedom have not effaced the evils accumulated in two centuries of servitude? But if these evils are almost entirely healed, is not such promptness a remarkable fact, and does it not deserve that we should hasten to establish it? It would be too soon to complain, it is not too soon to congratulate ourselves.

Another motive for choosing the present moment is added to the first reason. The statute of May 23, 1860, which effected a large reduction of imposts on colonial commodities; the statutes of July and August, 1860, which, by facilitating the provisioning of the Antilles and Bourbon, conducted to the rupture of the colonial compact, a rupture which is becoming the prayer and watchword of the colonies; the treaties enacted to increase the laboring population, — all these circumstances are to the colonies like the beginning of a new era, and of a transformation which will not be effected without complaints from many in behalf of the treasury and marine of France. The abolition of slavery will be accused, if this great experiment succeeds, of having rendered it necessary, and if it does not succeed, of having rendered it sterile. It was useful to pause at this stage, to fix the first effects of emancipation, and to demonstrate that, before the important laws of 1860, and without their aid, the French colonies had already returned to a state of prosperity exceeding that of the previous period.

It will give rise to astonishment, perhaps, that, in a general work, so large a place should have been accorded to the French colonies. They are so small that the experiment attempted on this narrow theatre seems indecisive. What are two or three hundred thousand slaves, belonging to a few thousand masters? Their affranchisement is a benefit, it is not an argument.

I believe the contrary.

The French colonies merit a place apart; first, because they are French; furthermore, because their example is a doubly shining demonstration, a triumphant condemnation of slavery, an irrefragable justification of emancipation. Never, in fact, will better conditions be encountered to soften, regulate, and in some sort civilize slavery ; never could it be abolished in worse conditions.

Humanity and intelligence were not lacking to the masters ; will and force were not lacking to the government, or the governors, almost always admirably chosen. Statutes, ordinances, despatches, regulations, translating all the fears of the public conscience, seemed to anticipate everything, and to leave no room for abuses. Despite so many cares, the situation of colonial society was really pitiable. Amidst laments, resistance, and threats, combated by passionate accusation, it was difficult to grasp the truth; yet, notwithstanding, an involuntary agreement between the most dissimilar testimony was established on some points. The complaints of the colonists and the pictures of the abolitionists vied with each other in demonstrating that the colonies were ruined. While the sentences of the courts revealed odious excesses, scandalous acquittals arraigned the corruption of the courts. Figures, those impassible tale-bearers, teach that the population grew only by illegitimacy, and that concubinage was universal. In vain the laws had multiplied emancipations ; under the influence of the ordinances of July 12, 1832, April 29, 1836, and June 11, 1839, they had increased ; but their number did not exceed from 1,500 to 2,000 a year, from 300 to 500 only among the agricultural population. The aggregate, from 1830 to 1847, was 50,240, of which more than half were in Martinico ; scarcely 6,000 in seventeen years in Bourbon.* At this rate, it would have

*	
Martinico	25,661
Guadaloupe	16,111
Guiana	2,603
Bourbon	5,865
Total	50,240

Table of Population for 1847, No. 13, p. 33.

required more than a century to finish it, in a manner often immoral and always dangerous; for the false position of these freedmen, who distrusted labor and were forced to chaffer for equality, increased the uneasiness without advancing its solution.*

The permanent conflict of two hostile races, the smothered war of abuses and rancors, the corruption of morals, luxury in the face of abject want, idleness conducting the whites to apathy and routine, compulsory labor leading the blacks to brutishness; no public life, no country; the earth and sky unweariedly lavishing abundance, but the soil, treated also like a slave, wearing out and unceasingly deserted; the absent proprietors represented by hard and covetous agents; wealth endangered, involved, and disgraced; justice suspicious and halting; religion debased and perverted; the laws sometimes inhuman, at others cavilling; the slaveholders themselves the slaves of the law, which penetrated in an intolerable manner into their abode, struck the hours, weighed out all rations, and abolished property without abolishing servitude; — in the midst of such a community lived a number of good, intelligent, sincere masters, victims of a situation which they had not made, which grieved them, yet the end of which they dared not anticipate, much less solicit, so firmly rooted was the belief that the emancipation of the slaves was to the colonies perhaps massacre, certainly ruin.

The sinister prophecies troubled those even whom they did not check, and the most resolute partisans of emancipation, in the government and in the chambers, took infinite precautions, and proceeded slowly, like a man carrying a lighted torch near a barrel of gunpowder.

Events made sport of this resistance and slowness. The colonists wished a preparatory delay, — there was no delay.

* The number of emancipations, says M. de Broglie (Report, p. 132), the most frequent cause of which is a secret to no one, increases from day to day, to the great detriment of public order.

They wished, by the preliminary application of the law on expropriation, to secure a regular liquidation of the enormous colonial debt; — it was sudden and violent.

They wished that the indemnity should be preliminary, — it was not paid until after emancipation; that it should be at least prompt, — it was waited for two years; that it should be large, — 1,200 francs had been rejected, — it scarcely amounted to 500 francs; that it should serve as a subsidy to paid labor, — it was swallowed up by debts.

They wished to found hospitals, schools, and prisons, for which appropriations were voted; — there was no time to increase the former, scarcely to apply the latter.

They wished a wide-spread outpouring of Christianity and instruction, a sort of preparatory training for the dignity of freemen, and demanded a better governed, more numerous, and purer clergy; — the colonial bishoprics were not established until three years after.

They wished to fortify the garrisons and tribunals, and to proclaim freedom in the midst of a fully armed peace; — it was proclaimed in the midst of a revolution let loose.

They wished, by the introduction of free workmen, to conjure down in advance the desertion of the works, and to set an example of labor without constraint; — capital remained unemployed; they had to organize labor in the colonies while essaying socialism in France.

They wished, by a heavy reduction of imposts, to encourage production and indemnify the producers;— the reduction was not obtained until after four years, and did not become complete until after twelve years.

They wished slowly to initiate the freedman into civil life; — the slave, scarcely made man, was made voter, and was endowed, without transition, with the unlimited liberty of the press and universal suffrage.

In a word, the abolition of slavery was contemporaneous with the abolition of order and the abolition of commerce.

In such circumstances, if colonial society had been overthrown, stained with blood, and plunged into ruin, who would have been surprised?

Now, at Martinico, in 1848, at Guadaloupe, in 1849, blood was shed and the incendiary torch was lighted. But the revolution, not emancipation, is responsible for these fleeting disorders. What would have happened without it? This is what we should justly ask. It was invoked with a common voice as the only means of calming the revolution, and of transforming vengeance into gratitude, wrath into gentleness. Where, since the first moments, are the victims which freedom has made? Where are the reprisals which it has let loose? Where are the prisons which it has necessitated? Where are the regiments whose presence it has rendered necessary? At Martinico, at Guadaloupe, the social revolution has done less harm than in thirty departments of France. At Guiana, no disturbance, despite the facility of fleeing and hiding; at Bourbon, not an incendiarism, not an act of vengeance, not a bankruptcy. Everywhere noisy elections, yet everywhere conservative.

Doubtless production has been reduced, but has never been annihilated; labor has been diminished, but has never wholly ceased; property has suffered; that this last blow has consummated the ruin of the proprietors involved in debt, is incontestable; but these sufferings were felt in France and the rest of the world at the same time as in the colonies. They have lasted longer; nevertheless, five years had scarcely elapsed when the aggregate of commerce exceeded, in the four colonies, the amount anterior to 1848; after ten years, the amount of exportation alone was tripled at Bourbon, exceeded at Martinico, attained at Guadaloupe.

Guiana, scarcely a producing colony, transformed into a penal colony, supplied with inhabitants by the deportation of from 4,000 to 6,000 consumers, exported less, without the aggregate of its commerce having ceased increasing.

The facilities for procuring new laborers by immigration do not alone explain the success of Bourbon and the progress of the Antilles ; for at Bourbon the products have increased more than the laborers ; at the Antilles, the former figures had been attained before immigration could have contributed perceptibly thereto.

Doubtless, numerous blacks refuse to labor, flee to the mountains, and regard freedom as the right to do nothing.

Cast the blame of this on the nature of the soil, and the nature of man. In no country of the world does man labor more than is necessary to satisfy his needs, tastes, and desires ; in no country of the world does man labor willingly for others, when he can find it to his advantage to labor for himself.*

Cast the blame of it, above all, on slavery. Whence comes, then, this abhorrence by the former slaves of their former labor? Freedom is the occasion of it, but servitude the cause. A man visited an abandoned plantation, about which the freed slaves were lazily sleeping. "See what freedom has made of labor," said his companions. "See what servitude has made of laborers," was his reply.

But the number of laborers has diminished much less than is affirmed, and, furthermore, labor is rather transformed than diminished. The peasant has become an artisan, or, rather, a freeholder ; he has not always become a vagabond. Dispute as one will arguments drawn from the progress of imports and exports, the lowest figure proves that these pretended paupers consume largely, and that these pretended idlers produce largely.

Now one of two things is true ; either so many laborers are needed for so many products, — in which case the number of laborers has not diminished so largely as is affirmed, — or many less free men, working less hours a day, have produced more than a large number of slaves ; in which

* Broglie, p. 323.

case the superiority of free over servile labor is demonstrated.

This last hypothesis is the true one, in a double point of view.

The labor of the white is no less improved than that of the black. Now this is the gist of the matter. The intellect of the whites, the vigor of the blacks, — these are the first two elements of wealth to the colonies. St. Domingo is an example of a country abandoned to blacks alone; but if it had been abandoned to whites alone, without their former slaves, what could they have done with it? During slavery the indolence of the whites was proverbial; they let themselves be conquered while sleeping.

We say it to the honor of freedom and the colonies. Since emancipation, they have courageously resigned themselves, they have ceased to mourn in order to act. At Bourbon, implements have been changed, and processes of manufacture improved; the income is doubled; they are not afraid to pay for five years' hire of a laborer double what they received as the price of a slave. Those who confidently bought plantations in 1848 have realized immense fortunes; progress has followed wealth, and the last Agricultural Exhibition showed us sugar from Bourbon which did not need refining. At the Antilles, they no longer content themselves with execrating indigenous sugar, they imitate it; they have established central works, they are introducing machinery and manures, attempting drainage, taking out patents, demanding landed credit, availing themselves of agricultural credit, and calling for free trade. In a word, they are departing from hackneyed and ruinous traditions, — the fatal companions of slavery, — and are seeking to realize those first four conditions of all economical progress, — the improvement of processes, the abundance of hands, the facility of credit, and the enlargement of the markets.

The following fact has always struck me : —

The prosperity of the Isle of Bourbon is incontestably far superior to what it was before the abolition of slavery. It is, furthermore, impossible to pretend that this island has received from nature a perpetual advantage over the rest. For, before 1848, Guadaloupe was the most flourishing of our colonies, Martinico next, Bourbon last ; the order is now exactly reversed, — Bourbon comes first, then Martinico, lastly Guadaloupe.

However disagreeable, therefore, may have been the sequel of emancipation, it is not justifiable to affirm that the ruin of the colonies has been the infallible and inevitable consequence of this measure, since this consequence has been averted at Bourbon.

In the second place, since three colonies, under the influence of the same cause, are in wholly different conditions, this cause has not been the only thing that has acted on them.

Either it is joined to other evils, or it has prevented other remedies. It is unjust to say that this cause has done all the harm, since the same cause elsewhere has not done the same harm. Facts fully justify this reasoning.

At Bourbon, the government was more far-sighted ; contracts for labor were effected through its care without delay. The negroes were more religious. The colonists, more numerous, have shown themselves more active and more resolute ; they have counted more upon themselves ; they have reduced the number of sugar-mills, but have increased the machinery. Of 118 mills, 113 are worked by steam-engines (1856). They have brought in laborers, and purchased guano ; with 116 sugar-works, they work more than 100,000 acres.

Martinico, with 544 sugar-works, does not work 50,000 acres ; it has received but 50,000 francs' worth of machinery (1856), while Bourbon has received 530,000 francs' worth. Nevertheless, this colony has uprisen. An energetic governor, Admiral de Gueydon, has given the most intelligent attention to the re-organization of labor. Martinico has surpassed Guadaloupe, to which, formerly, it remained inferior. The latter has, notwithstanding, more laborers, more land, and better conditions. In short, the activity of the whites has repaired at Bourbon, and might have repaired everywhere, the consequences of the freedom of the negroes. The superiority of the manufactures is the cause of the prosperity of this island, much more than the facility of manual labor. It suffices that a country without exceptional conditions prospers with free laborers, to destroy all excuse elsewhere for retaining them in servitude.

No one will accuse me of having forgotten material interests, while I risk astonishing or wearying those who will not see clearly enough the close tie which unites the question of wealth and that of moral progress. It might have been said, — After all, it was not in favor of the colonists that freedom was proclaimed; they profited by slavery, they have suffered by emancipation; it is an expiation sanctioned by justice. There are two or three million kilogrammes less of sugar in the world, which is a misfortune; but three hundred thousand human beings who were enslaved are free. Whatever may be the loss, the gain exceeds it, and there is too much pity in the face of so magnificent a progress.

This reasoning consoles the moralist, but does not persuade the interested. Now, the question is in the hands of the interested. At Cuba, at Richmond, at Porto Rico, at New Orleans, at Surinam, at Madrid, at the Hague, they will not be satisfied with such an argument. To interests we must use the language of interests.

The moralist himself would be wrong to be contented

with moral progress. What it is important for him to demonstrate is, that what is morally bad is not materially good.

Nevertheless, moral progress takes evidently the first rank. Now, in this point of view, the success of emancipation is complete.

The number of marriages, of acknowledgments, of legitimations, has been enormous. In the beginning, these acts may have been a fashion; the slaves hastened to be called *Mr.* or *Mrs.*; the oldest, especially, fell back into former habits; concubinage is far from having disappeared. But, after all, the impulse has lasted; the freeman has resumed his rank in the esteem of the woman, whom formerly the desire of freedom, the need of protection, the love of dress or of comfort, and the satisfactions of vanity, as well as the ascendency of dependence, impelled to concubinage. Children are no longer abandoned. The family is constituted; the love of property consolidates the family; the small freehold extends; the negro pays taxes, learns to understand French institutions, and easily adapts himself to them, enters at Bourbon into mutual-aid societies, and would make deposits in savings banks if such were established.

The schools are full, though instruction is neither compulsory nor gratuitous. Religion is respected, relished, and practised, and, under the authoritative direction of the bishops, has regained its dignity, while extending its beneficent influence.

"Three classes are to be remarked in the slave population," wrote the authorities of Guadaloupe in 1840.* "The first, having an inkling of civilization, is tolerably inclined to labor and economy, and would not be greatly averse to the family spirit. . . . . These are the sedate negroes, married, or living as if they were so; unfortunately, *they are in a small minority.*

"The second is composed of active, vigorous men, but

* Report of M. de Broglie, p. 184.

13 *

without morals or behavior; *these are the most numerous.* If they work, it is only to procure the means of satisfying their passion for women and drink.

"The third is that class of indifferent idlers who devote to sloth and sleep every moment that is not their master's. Without passions as without desires, they would let themselves starve if it were necessary to obtain the means of existence by hard labor."

It may be to-day affirmed, that the class of sedate, married slaves, which was in the minority, has become much more numerous; that the class of drunken and licentious slaves has diminished; and that the idle slaves remain idle, yet do not beg or die of hunger. I do not know whether a more satisfactory picture could be drawn of several of the agricultural regions of France, to say nothing of the manufacturing counties.

Is this to say that the colonies are a paradise? No; but they are much further than they were from resembling a hell.

Is it to say that their situation is without peril, and their prosperity without shadow?

Not at all.

In a moral point of view, the reconciliation of the races is far from being complete. The immigration of new races, without family, without morals, without God, is a serious danger, which would be fatal if this immigration were not essentially provisional and strictly superintended. It would aid the colonists to fall back into their old habits, to discuss the price of Coolies as they did formerly that of negroes, and, under the names of voluntary enrolment and temporary engagement, to practise the slave-trade and slavery, minus the words and appearances. It is already every day increasing immorality and criminality, and paving the way for the degeneration of the race.

In a material point of view, the colonies, like European

communities, have to struggle against the general difficulties born of the present condition of the laboring classes, more capricious, more mobile, more enlightened, and more fastidious than heretofore; since emancipation — the fact is most remarkable — the wages of the laborer have not perceptibly risen in price, but less reliance is evidently to be placed on his labor. They have to struggle, besides, with the special difficulties of their position in the world, — a population too slender for the extent of territory, a territory which produces with incomparable fertility the valuable commodities which are nevertheless produced also, and in constantly increasing quantities, in countries a hundred times larger and a hundred times more populous, and the principal one of which, sugar, has become on the soil of the mother country itself the object of a thriving manufacture.

This was their misfortune forty years ago; it is still the same, — emancipation has no share in it. But, thanks to emancipation, these little communities come to the conflict more upright, stronger, more active, and freed from the anxiety of a constantly threatening crisis, which weighed at once upon positions and consciences.

They can brave, and they solicit, instead of a single market, the free sale of their products on every spot of the globe.

This commercial affranchisement is not the rupture of the tie which binds the colonies to the mother country, even commercially. Habits, existing relations, the avenues of credit and transportation, survive tariffs and regulations. Politically, is it to be feared that our colonies will ever think of separating from France? The fear is chimerical. If they were not French, they would wish to be so. A great nation, a great marine, is necessary to the protection of these little communities, which would not exchange, for the lot of islets lost in the immensity of the seas, the honor and advantage of being styled external provinces of France.

But it is clear that the emancipation of the slaves has loosened one of the knots of the colonial compact; the existence of indigenous sugar, the admission of foreign sugar, the lowering of the import duties, the decree which charges the colonies with all local expenses, break another mesh. The state no longer guarantees to the colonies either the sale of their commodities or the enslavement of their laborers. Freedom of products will be the consequence of freedom of labor.

This inevitable crisis is the accomplishment of what may be styled the law of colonial growth.

The history of the colonies presents three successive phases. In infancy they received everything from the mother country. Stronger, they exchanged everything with her, as a garden yields its fruits to the one who has planted it. Grown with time, they emerge by degrees from these protecting leading-strings, and provide independently for the satisfaction of their needs, and the sale of their products; whether powerful enough to free themselves entirely from the sovereignty of the mother country, like the United States and Brazil, or, weaker, they remain like Cuba, and the English colonies which are left, subject to the sovereignty of a mother country, but only in the political order.

Communities, in the development of their commercial or political destinies, begin thus by monopoly, and rise to liberty. Men have thought to found colonies for the exclusive interest of a nation; this narrow-sighted patriotism is inevitably thwarted by time. If they had sought to labor for the general good of humanity, they would not have been disappointed. The colonies are to great nations what foundations are to large families. The day comes when they cease to depend exclusively on these, but only when they can exist of themselves; humanity profits by them, and leaves them the name of the founders.

Let us rise to higher lessons, while casting a general glance on the long history of slavery and emancipation in the French colonies.

Slavery, in conclusion, is defended in a moral point of view by but a single motive, — *the education of an inferior race.* This motive calmed the scruples of Louis XIII. and the remorse of Louis XVI.; it was on the lips of the adversaries of Wilberforce and Clarkson, and, three centuries before, in the speeches of the antagonists of Las Casas,* it was the sole argument of the colonists of Guadaloupe and Jamaica; it is the habitual answer of the tender-hearted ladies of Havana, it is the pretext in the sermons of the preachers of South Carolina, the thesis amplified by the writers of Baltimore, the summary excuse of the planters of New Orleans.

They do not fail to add, that slavery is a means of converting a heathen race to Christianity.

The slaves, therefore, are scholars and catechumens, the masters are instructors and preachers, the plantations are boarding-schools and little seminaries, slavery is a method of education and conversion.

After three centuries of this system, freedom is talked of. "Take care!" exclaim the masters with one voice; "you are about to thrust ignorant and depraved beings into society!" What! the education and conversion of your scholars is not finished? Either the pupils are incorrigible, or

* It is known that Charles V. presided, in 1513, at Barcelona, over a solemn conference, to listen to Quevedo, Bishop of Darien, and Barthélemy de Las Casas, the illustrious and indefatigable protector of the Indians, in the presence of the Admiral of the Indies, Don Diego Columbus. The Bishop of Darien declared that all the inhabitants of the New World whom he had observed appeared to him a species of men designed for servitude, through the inferiority of their intellect and natural talents, and that it would be impossible to instruct them, or cause them to make any progress towards civilization, unless held under the continual authority of a master. Las Casas rose with indignation at the idea that there was any race of men born for servitude, and attacked this opinion as irreligious, inhuman, and false in practice. — Robertson, History of America, Book III.

the method is bad; it is time to change it and to renounce this pitiful argument. The fears of the masters give the lie to their promises.

By the grace of God, servitude is decidedly not a means of civilizing or converting any member of the human family. The true doctors of the faith know this well. To one of the sovereigns who had suffered himself to be touched by this hope of conversion, John, king of Portugal, mark what Pope Benedict XIV. wrote, December 20, 1741: —

"Men who call themselves Christians so far forget the sentiment of charity diffused in our hearts by the Holy Spirit as to reduce to servitude the unhappy Indians, the people of the eastern and western coasts of Brazil, and other regions. . . . . . Much more, they sell them, they despoil them of their goods, and the inhumanity which they display against them is the chief cause which turns them away from embracing the faith of Christ, by making them look on it only with horror."

A century before, in 1637, one of the first missionaries and the first historian of the colonies, Du Tertre, pointed out the same cause as the principal obstacle to the promulgation of the Gospel.

Two centuries after, in 1853, the first Council held in France, after the emancipation of our colonies, the Council of Rochelle, pronounced these noble words: "The Catholic Church has always mourned the harsh servitude imposed on innumerable human beings, *to the great detriment of their souls, — in animarum suarum perniciem.*" *

How is it that the partisans and adversaries of slavery invoke, on both sides, the support of the Christian religion? The benefactor of men in servitude, it alone teaches how to endure so great an evil; the moderator of men restored to freedom, it alone teaches not to abuse so great a good. Religion, after having taught the master kindness and the slave

* *Acta Concilii Rupellensis*, Cap. VI. I. p. 51.

patience, inspires both with the desire of affranchisement; and it is to it again that we turn to arrange the transition to freedom, and to temper its consequences. Religion is not liberty, but the mother and first instructress of liberty.

How is the slave raised to the rank of freeman? By three degrees, — religion, family, and property. How does the freeman descend to the level of the slave? By losing property, family, and religion. What does Socialism make of men, therefore, by ravishing from them these essential goods? Slaves.

Slavery would never have disappeared from the French colonies without a very strong central power; we see this clearly from the United States; it is one of the cases in which the initiative cannot come from the individual interest, since it is this interest itself which it is in question to subdue. But the central power would have done nothing if public opinion had not been free and greatly excited; we see this clearly from the reign of Louis XV. or of Napoleon. We see it also from Spain. A concentrated power works out great designs, on condition that they are counselled by a free public opinion. Power has the virtues, but also the faults of experience, from which come incredulity, tardiness, and an easy resignation to what are called *necessary evils.* Public opinion is the conscience; it experiences remorse, it looks to the ideal, and is generous, even in chimeras. If slavery had not caused the remorse of public opinion, emancipation would not have become the design of power; the latter pronounced emancipation, the former desired it.

What is the best mode of emancipation?

The experience of the French colonies answers us, — immediate and simultaneous emancipation.

By waiting, we obtain nothing; by venturing, we risk nothing. For two centuries the colonies waited for the hour to strike, and it never came. Twice freedom was hurled upon them with revolution; twice revolution did much harm, freedom very little. The negro race is so gentle, that under the yoke it makes no resistance ; free from the yoke, it commits no abuses. Liberty has not the virtue of restoring to it the faculties denied it by the Creator ; alone, deprived, as at St. Domingo, of the intellect of the whites, it will return to a slothful life, and give birth to a very inferior state of society. But, after all, under this climate, which enervates the whites, after essaying all the races one after another to replace the negro race, we are forced to return again to the latter ; we find none more vigorous or submissive, more capable of devotion, more accessible to Christianity, more happy to escape its native degradation. This race of men, like all the human species, is divided into two classes, the diligent and the idle ; freedom has nothing to do with the second, while it draws from the labor of the first a better yield than servitude.

Slavery was so little founded on nature, that, created by brute force, it was maintained only by legal force, that is to say, by the constraint of an infinite number of laws and regulations. To pave the way for the transition to liberty, a no less number were framed ; eighteen decrees were promulgated for the guidance of freedom in its infancy. Now all laws against the dangers of servitude have been impotent, all measures against the perils of freedom have been useless. Doubtless, the ancient kings, who were Christian, humane, and sincere, said to themselves in permitting slavery, "Let us take the greatest precautions that the evil may do good." In abolishing it, the reformers said, in their turn, with equal good faith, "Let us take care that the good does no evil." Twofold error! Evil engenders evil ; good does nothing but good.

But we do not pass from evil to good without expiation, and we do not make expiation without suffering. The history of the abolition of slavery in the French colonies is an almost scientific proof of these great laws of morality.

BOOK SECOND.

ENGLISH COLONIES.

CHAPTER I.

SLAVERY IN ENGLAND AND ITS COLONIES UNTIL THE EMANCIPATION BILL OF AUGUST 28, 1833.

THE history of slavery is connected with the history of England by five memorable dates.

What Africa is to-day, England was in former times. What the English think to-day of the Africans, the Romans thought in former times of the English.

Cæsar tells us that the Britons sacrificed human victims,* Diodorus Siculus affirms that they ate human flesh,† Cicero writes, that the only booty to be brought back from this barbarous land was brutalized slaves,‡ Strabo relates that these slaves were sold like cattle, and often offered in the markets of Rome.§

The historian Lingard, in recounting this testimony, adds: "The savages of Africa sell to the Europeans negroes taken in war or the chase; more barbarous, the conquerors of Britain sold without scruple their fellow-countrymen, and even their own children."

To what does Great Britain owe the disappearance of these abominable crimes? To Christianity. To whom is

* *Bell. Gall.*, Lib. VI. Cap. 16.

† Lib. V. Cap. 32.

‡ *Ad. Att.*, Lib. IV. Cap. 16.

§ Buxton, The Slave-Trade, Introduction, p. 14, according to Henry. History of England, Vol. II. p. 225.

she indebted for her conversion to Christianity? To a Pope and to slaves.

In the beginning of the fifth century (403), an Irishman, named Cothraige, made a slave at sixteen among the Gauls, twice delivered and twice enslaved, became St. Patrick, the apostle of Ireland. Half a century after, he smote a petty king of Britain, named Carotic or Caractacus, with anathema, and commanded Christians no longer to eat or drink with a prince guilty of having reduced to slavery the servants of Jesus Christ.*

The venerable Bede† recounts that, in 577, St. Gregory the Great, thirteen years before becoming Pope, was walking in the market of Rome, when he spied among the objects exposed for sale some children with fair skin, fine features, and light, curling hair. He asked from what country they came, and was told that they were from the island of Britain. He then asked of what religion they were, and was informed that they were heathens. "What a pity," exclaimed he, sighing, "to see the prince of darkness rule over so transparent a skin, and so beautiful a brow cover a soul wholly devoid of grace! What is the name of their nation?" "They are Angles, *Angli*." "It is well said, for they resemble angels, *Angeli*; I wish that the angels had such Christians in heaven. What is the name of their province?" "Deira." "Which signifies *de ira eruti*, snatched from the heavenly wrath and called to the mercy of Christ. How is their king called?" "Aella." "Alleluia, — the praises of God must be sung in these regions." Immediately after this ingenious and charitable dialogue, Gregory went to entreat the Pope to

* Ecclesiastical History of Ireland, Vol. I. Chap. IV. 9 Mgr. England, Letter VIII. 141.

† See the original, complete in Appendix. See also the *Moines d' Occident*, by Count de Montalembert.

send missionaries to the Angles, and offered himself to bear to them the Word of God. The pontiff gave him permission, but the people of Rome were unwilling to let him undertake so distant a journey. On becoming Pope, in 580, he followed out his generous project, ransomed the young English slaves, and placed them in a monastery, in order to fit them to become missionaries to their country. Their progress was not rapid enough to satisfy his impatience, and he despatched forty missionaries to Britain, under the guidance of St. Augustine. On reaching Aix, in Provence, the recitals which they heard of the barbarity of the kings of the Heptarchy made them pause. They sent to represent to the Pope the difficulties and probable abortiveness of such a mission among a ferocious people, of whom they did not even know the language. He enjoined them to proceed, and recommended them to the French bishops and the kings Theodoric and Theodebert. A few years after, the island of Britain was converted.*

Servitude did not disappear immediately, but rapidly softened under the breath of the Gospel preached everywhere by ardent missionaries. The conquered became assimilated to the conquerors. Humanity tempered the fierceness of strife. Property became more secure, human life more sacred. The love of fraternity, the proof of equality, the idea of liberty, entered into souls, while the baptismal waters traced their majestic symbol upon every brow. The child and the servant found a hitherto unknown protection in the law.† Marvelous examples dazzled the eyes of the beholders. Bishop Wilfrid received of the king of Sussex the island of Anglesea, with two hundred and fifty slaves; he baptized and freed them. Lanfranc obtained of William the Conqueror the interdiction of the slave-trade. There, as in

* England, Letter IX., On Domestic Slavery. Blakey, Temporal Benefit of Christianity.

† Lingard, Ant. Anglo-Saxon England, *loc. cit.*

the rest of the world, the Church did not rudely break the bond of servitude, but she profited by it; she did not impose on the master a constraint which he would have violated; she did not precipitate the slave into an independence which he would have abused, and from which he would have suffered: she proclaimed the truth; she showed the way; she brought fresh life. Nevertheless, the inflexibility of the Saxon character, foreign invasions, and the disorders which they involved, prolonged the existence of servitude in England two centuries longer than in France, Italy, and Germany.* The sale of slaves to foreign countries was proscribed in 1009 by the Council of Aenham,† convoked by King Ethelred at the entreaty of Archbishops Elfeag of Canterbury and Ulstan of York. The sale of slaves within the dominion was solemnly condemned by the Council of 1102,‡ convoked by Henry I., at the prayer of St. Anselm,§ and held, under his presidency, in that city of London where, seven years after, the Parliament hesitated before the same prohibition.

In a third Council, that of Armagh,‖ held by Henry II.,

* Moehler, *Abolition de l'esclavage par le Christianisme dans les quinze premiers siècles*, translated by the Abbé de la Treiche, Chap. IX. pp. 289, 290, and notes 53, 54.

† *Conc. Achamense*, Lib. I. c. 77: "Sapientes decernunt ut nemo christianum et insontem pretio tradat extra patriam."

‡ *Concil. Lond. Hard.*, Tom. VI. Pars II. p. 1863, Lib. I. Cap. 27: "Ne quis illud nefarium negotium, quo hactenus in Anglia solebant homines sicut bruta animalia venumdari deinceps ullatenus præsumat."

§ Rémusat, *Saint-Anselme*, p. 163.

‖ *Conc. Lond.*, *Girald Cambreus. Hibern. Expug.*, Cap. XXVIII.: "Convocato apud Ardmachiani totius Hiberniæ clero, et super advenarum in insulam adventu tractato diutius et deliberato, tandem communis omnium in hac sententia resedit propter peccata silicet populi sui, eoque præcipue quod Anglos olim, tam a mercatoribus quam a prædonibus et piratis, emere passim et in servitutem redigere consueverant, divinæ censura vindictæ hostis incommodum, ut et ipsi quoque et eadem gente in servitutem vice reciproca jam redigantur. . . . . . Decretum est itaque in prædicto concilio et cum universitatis consensu publico statutum, ut Angli ubique per insulam, servitutis vinculo mancipati, in pristinam revocentur libertatem."

the Irish bishops loudly proclaimed that all the misfortunes of their country were the just punishment of the perpetuated crime of slavery, and freed all the English captives in the island.

Servitude had nearly disappeared from England at the end of the eleventh century, at the epoch of the Norman Conquest.* Five hundred years afterwards, this nation, emancipated from slavery, converted through slaves, arrived at the highest degree of power, did not blush in its turn to reduce men to servitude. On that vast continent of North America, which she received from Providence as a gift as magnificent as unexpected, won to the mother country by those whom she proscribed, England, in the seventeenth century, imposed slavery. In the eighteenth century, she employed her vessels to transport slaves; she made this monopoly the object of her covetousness, and, at the time of the treaty of Utrecht, one of the conditions of the peace of Europe. By an agreement of May 26, 1713, known by the name of the treaty of *Asiento*,† negotiated by John, Archbishop of Bristol, and Lord Strafford, his Britannic Majesty received of his Catholic Majesty the ignoble privilege of transporting to Spanish America 144,000 *head of Indians*, in consideration of 33⅓ piasters a head, and numerous other advantages. Both kings reserved an interest in the affair.

Thus the race which was the first in Europe to suffer slavery, and the last to emerge from it, was the first to impose it on other nations, but the first to rise again from it. It had owed its affranchisement to Christianity, it owed to it its repentance. It is well known that to the heroic perseverance of a handful of Christians reverts all the honor of the abolition of the slave-trade, in 1807, then

* Yanoski, *De l'Abolition de l'esclavage au moyen âge*, Paris, 1860.

† *Tratados*, etc., by Alejander de Cantillon, Madrid (Archives of Foreign Affairs).

of slavery, in 1834. Before studying the results and influence of these measures on the Britannic possessions, we will rapidly sketch the imposing picture of the colonial greatness of the first maritime power in the world.

It is a known fact, that the immense development of the English colonies dates no further back than the last two centuries,—witnesses of the parallel decrease of the colonial greatness of Spain, Holland, and, it must be added, France.

In 1578, Queen Elizabeth authorized Sir Humphrey Gilbert to discover and occupy distant countries peopled by idolaters. In 1584, Sir Walter Raleigh formed a settlement in Virginia. But it is only from the time of James I. and Charles I., before the Civil War, then of Cromwell and Charles II., that we can date the infant, yet erelong vast, impulse of the foundations of England beyond the seas.

In the beginning of the year 1860, two sons of the Queen of England set out, the one to inaugurate a bridge on the St. Lawrence in Canada, the other to lay the corner-stone of a jetty at the Cape of Good Hope, while their father, Prince Albert, offered congratulations, in a public speech, for this incomparable greatness of a nation, mistress at once of the northern boundary of America and the southern point of Africa. The same flag is planted on English ground in the most extended regions of Asia and Oceanica. An Englishman cannot know the territory of his country without unrolling entire the map of the world.

In Asia, the merchants who, under the name of the East India Company, established warehouses at Bantam (1602), at Surat (1612), on the coast of Coromandel (1640), and on the Hooghly (1656), with the assent of the mother country, showed themselves by degrees bellicose and encroaching Warehouses were transformed into fortresses ; possessions swelled into provinces ; soldiers were armed, kings dethroned, peoples subdued or purchased ; Mogul was invaded (1687) ; Bombay, Madras, and Bengal became English presidencies. The company received charters, and its enterprises presented England, in less than seventy-five years, with more than 130,000,000 subjects.

In 1796, Colonel Stuart took Ceylon from the Dutch.

Half a century after (1843), China was forced to cede Hong Kong, and, in 1860, the territory of Coolon. In 1857, Europe suffered the invasion, in the Red Sea, of the island of Perim, occupied, it was said, for the purpose of building a light-house, but rather to lodge there a keeper of the gates erelong to be opened through the Isthmus of Suez.

New conquests brought new annexations in India. This great empire, convulsed by a rebellion which is not yet completely subdued, passed, in 1858, from the hands of the company to the direct government of the state.

By dint of energy or astuteness, by arms or policy, and in different conditions of prosperity or agitation, of faithful or fragile attachment, England possesses, in this part of the world, an aggregate population of 171,000,000 inhabitants, an army of 300,000 men, a revenue of 14,000,000 francs, and a commerce whose transactions exceed 1,000,000,000 francs, and employ nearly 30,000 vessels.*

In Africa, the East India Company took possession (1651) of St. Helena, abandoned by the Dutch, the rocks of which were to be the living tomb of the great captain whose triumphs and reverses would one day destroy, then aggrandize, the colonial power of England.

Gambia, polluted by a traffic in slaves, the profits of which were shared by England and Spain, fell from one

* *Revue coloniale*, 1858, p. 820. *Ibid.*, 1847, No. 17, p. 86. Official Statistics of 1855.

Superficies	1,367,193 sq. miles.
Population	171,859,055
Army	281,910
Revenue	1,406,672,300 fr.
Imports / Exports	1,000,000,000 fr.

Navigation, 26,000 vessels, gauged at from 3,000,000 to 4,000 000 tons.

bankruptcy to another, from the hands of the company, who surrendered it in 1713 to this infamous trade, to the hands of the crown (1821), already placed in possession of the Gold Coast (1772) by a treaty with France, and of Sierra Leone by a treaty with the native princes (1787).

Taken (1797,) restored (1799), then retaken from the Dutch (1805), the colony of the Cape of Good Hope became an important possession, to which the crown, by simple declarations, annexed in 1844 Natal, and in 1847 Caffraria, which received (1848 – 1854) distinct governors.

The fairest of all the African colonies, — the island of Mauritius, — possessed by France, whose name it bore for a century (1710 – 1810), was wrested from us by General Abercrombie, and the treaty of Paris ratified this conquest (1814).

Less important than the colonies of Asia, the African colonies give to England nearly 1,000,000 subjects. About 3,000 vessels serve a commerce which exceeds 160,000,000 francs.

NORTH AMERICA belonged almost entirely to England, before belonging to itself. If it has lost this vast and magnificent domain, England has at least preserved or acquired twenty-five colonies in this part of the world. It owes them to the adventurous audacity of its sons; as the Barbadoes (1605), the three hundred little islands which form the group of the Bermudas (1611), St. Christopher (1623), Nevis (1628), Monserrat (1632); — or to the sagacious grasp of its kings; as Antigua, given by Charles I. to Lord Carlisle; the fifty Virgin Islands (1648), given by Charles II. to Sir William Stapleton; Barbadoes, given to the Coddington family, in consideration of a certain number of turtle (1684); Hudson's Bay, conceded to Prince Rupert and a company of merchants by Charles II. (1668 – 1713); Vancouver's Island, annexed by Queen Victoria (1849); New Brunswick (1783); the Falkland Islands (1833); — or to the more or less loyal conquests over the Spaniards; as the valuable island of Jamaica, one of the four large Antilles (1655); Honduras Bay (1714); Bahama (1783); Trinidad (1797); — or over Holland and France; as Guiana (1803); Nova Scotia (formerly Acadia), and Cape Breton (1714–1758); the ever to be regretted land of Canada (1759); Prince Edward's Island, Dominica, St. Vincent, Granada (1763); Tobago (1794); St. Lucia (1815).

The twenty-five American colonies represent in the official statistics a population of 2,500,000 inhabitants, and a commerce employing 15,000 vessels, and transporting the value of 800,000,000 francs.

Captured and recaptured, several of our colonies returned to their first possessor, but to be soon lost again, and each of the fatal treaties which terminated our great wars — the treaty of Utrecht (1713), the treaty of Aix-la-Chapelle (1748), the treaty of Paris (1763), and lastly, the treaties of 1814 and 1815, — let our colonies fall, as a sort of odd change and balance, into the hands of England; they brought to it, and ravished from us, perhaps for long centuries, the empire of the seas and sceptre of the world.

The nineteenth century was destined to open to England a new part of the world, and to continue the astonishing dissemination of the Saxon race over the surface of the earth.

France discovered Australia, the Hollander Tasman discovered Van Diemen's Land; England occupies, peoples, and possesses these vast regions. From 1788 to 1840, it sent 80,000 convicts to the eastern coast of Australia, and founded Sydney. At the same epoch, it cut off New Zealand from New South Wales, but sent no colonists there until 1814. In 1803, it deported convicts to Tasmania, and founded Hobart Town. Norfolk Island was annexed in 1834; Western Australia had been occupied five years previous (1829), and the town of Perth settled. In 1834 Southern Australia was declared an English colony, and received for its capital the town of Adelaide.

In less than a quarter of a century, on this land vaster than Europe, cities are founded, churches and schools diffuse moral civilization, railroads offer themselves to intercourse, an empire rises like ancient Rome from a den of robbers, and England counts there 700,000 subjects, a budget of 80,000,000 francs, a transportation of 4,000 vessels, a commerce of 400,000,000 francs.

We will mention, to be complete, the colonies of EUROPE, — the islands which guard our coast of La Mancha, Gibraltar, which weighs on Spain and shamefully protects Morocco, Malta, and the Ionian Isles, whose name, language, spirit, and prayers belong to Greece, — all these ports, which are not colonies, all these lands, which are rather the captives of English policy than the offspring of its civilizing genius.

In a speech delivered February 8, 1850, Lord John Russell thus enumerated the colonial acquisitions of England, in chronological order. From 1600 to 1700, Nova Scotia, New Brunswick, Prince Edward's Island, Newfoundland, the Bermudas, Jamaica, Honduras, the Bahamas, Barbadoes, Antigua, Montserrat, St. Christopher, Nevis, the Virgin Islands, Gambia, St. Helena, — *sixteen* colonies. From 1700 to 1793, Canada, St. Vincent, Grenada, Tobago, Dominica, Gibraltar, Sierra Leone, the Gold Coast, New South Wales, — *ten* colonies. From 1793 to 1815, St. Lucia, Guiana, Trinidad, Malta, the Cape, Van Diemen's Land, Mauritius, Ceylon, — *eight* colonies.

If Western and Southern Australia and the Falkland Islands be added, there is, without counting the Indian Empire, and after the loss of the United States, a total of thirty-seven colonies, acquired in two hundred and fifty years. Taking them in geographical order, there are: —

In Asia, three presidencies, embracing eighty-five kingdoms or provinces, with an extent of 1,367,193 square miles, and 171,859,055 inhabitants; with an island and harbor on the territory of China;

In Africa, six continental colonies and two islands;

In America, six continental colonies, 2,480,326 inhabitants, and nineteen islands;

In Australia, three vast continental colonies and two islands.

In the whole, one fourth of the civilized world, peopled by nearly 2,000,000 men, furnishing to the industry of the mother country outlets worth, at the present time, 1,500,000,000 francs, and to its commerce a business exceeding 1,000,000 francs, and corresponding to the navigation on the seas of more than 100,000 vessels of all nations.*

The aggregate expenditures of the English colonies, without including India, are 220,983,000 francs, viz.: —

Local expenses of the chartered colonies	69,705,000 fr.
Local expenses of the colonies of the crown	62,320,000
Expenses of the state or sovereignty †	88,958,000
Total	220,983,000 fr.

The receipts are 117,904,000 francs, viz.: —

For the state	.....
" " chartered colonies	72,423,000 fr.
" " colonies of the crown	45,481,000
Total	117,904,000 fr.

The excess of receipts over expenditures is, therefore, 103,079,000 francs.

In an administrative point of view, the colonies are di-

* Statistical Tables relating to the Colonial and other Possessions of the United Kingdom, 1856. *Revue coloniale*, 1857, p. 85; 1858, p. 833. Colonial Constitutions, by Mr. Mills. See also the Tables of Montgomery, Martin, and Porter, in the sequel of the Report of Jules Lechevalier.

† Military expenditures	75,082,000 fr.
Civil "	12,483,000
Maritime "	[illegible]

(Official Statistics of 1851, 1852. *Revu*

vided into *military and maritime stations, settlements and colonies, and penal settlements.*

In a more special point of view, they are divided into *chartered colonies*, and *colonies of the crown.**

The *chartered* colonies are Antigua, Bahama, Barbadoes, Guiana, the Bermudas, Canada, Dominica, Grenada, Jamaica, Honduras, Montserrat, Nevis, Newfoundland, Nova Scotia, New Brunswick, New Wales, Prince Edward's Island, St. Christopher, St. Vincent, Tobago, the Virgin Islands, and Victoria.

The colonies *of the crown* are the Cape, Ceylon, the Falkland Islands, Gambia, Gibraltar, the Gold Coast, Hong Kong, Labuan, Malta, Mauritius, Natal, New Zealand, St. Helena, St. Lucia, Sierra Leone, Trinidad, Southern and Western Australia, and Van Diemen's Land.

Among these possessions, some were *free colonies*, others

* It is said, It is despotism that is new; liberty is old. This saying applies precisely to the system of the English colonies. A new contradiction of that historical theory which considers liberty as a fruit slowly matured on the vigorous stem of absolute power! When the king of England gave Barbadoes to Lord Carlisle, in 1627, he authorized him, as well as his heirs, to frame such laws as they might deem useful, with the consent, assent, and approbation of the free inhabitants of the said province, or a majority among them. "We wish, moreover," adds the patent, "through a sovereign concession, which shall bind our heirs and successors, that all the inhabitants of the said province, themselves and their children born or to be born, shall enjoy the same liberty as if they had been born in England; so that they may receive, take, keep, purchase, possess, give, sell, and bequeath, according to their good pleasure, and also freely enjoy all liberties, franchises, and privileges enjoyed by our subjects in England, without hinderance, molestation, annoyance, damage, or trouble on our part, and on the part of our heirs and successors."

Who thus insures liberty to Barbadoes? Charles I. Cromwell gave a military government to Jamaica; it received a constitutional government from the hands of Charles II.; and the counsellors of James II. opposed the levying of any subsidy without the consent of the inhabitants or an act of Parliament. The same liberties were assured to Grenada in 1763. (Speech of Lord John Russell, already quoted.) Unfortunate kings! why did they not love liberty in the British Isles as well as in the West Indies?

But, thenceforth, the colonies acquired preserved the Spanish, Dutch, or French institutions by which they were ruled, and were considered as depending directly on the crown.

slave colonies. We will cite, in order to study them by themselves alone, the colonies which held slaves before 1834.

They were nineteen in number: — Antigua, Barbadoes, Montserrat, Nevis, St. Christopher, Tortola, Anguilla, Bahama, and the Bermudas, colonies of English origin;

Dominica, Grenada, St. Lucia, St. Vincent, Tobago, and Mauritius, colonies conquered from France;

Jamaica, Trinidad, and Honduras, conquered from Spain;

Guiana and the Cape of Good Hope, conquered from Holland.

Thirteen* were chartered colonies; six, † colonies of the Crown.

All of these colonies possessed, at the beginning of this century, nearly 800,000 slaves, ‡ owned by less than 150,000 whites, who annually increased the slave population by the horrors of the slave-trade.

As is well known, the slave-trade was attacked and abolished before slavery.

* Antigua, Bahama, Barbadoes, the Bermudas, Dominica, Grenada, Jamaica, Montserrat, Nevis, St. Christopher, St. Vincent, Tobago, and the Virgin Islands.

† Trinidad, the Cape, Guiana, Honduras, Mauritius, and St. Lucia.

‡

Colony	Slaves
Jamaica	311,070
Trinidad	20,757
Tobago	11,589
Grenada	23,640
St. Vincent	22,266
Barbadoes	83,150
St. Lucia	13,291
Dominica	14,175
Antigua	29,121
Nevis	8,815
Montserrat	6,401
St. Christopher	19,780
Tortola	5,135
Bahama	10,086
The Bermudas	4,026
Guiana	82,824
Honduras	1,901
The Cape	35,750
Mauritius	66,613
Total	770,390

Nevertheless, the immortal authors of the abolition of the slave-trade did not for a moment abandon the thought of instigating the abolition of slavery. This was announced by Wilberforce in 1792. But a double motive restrained them.

They hoped that, in default of fresh supplies, slavery would become extinct, as a brook dries up when its source is cut off. They thought that it was wise to arrive at liberty step by step, by gradual ameliorations, and "that this celestial plant could only spring up on a soil fitted to receive it.*

Such was for twenty years the dominant opinion; no project prevailed against it, and so great was still the ascendency of these ideas, that, when Buxton, in his own name and that of Wilberforce, formally proposed *abolition* in Parliament, May 15, 1823, he dared only speak of gradual abolition, and Mr. Canning, adhering in behalf of the government to this proposition, amended it by a celebrated formula, in which the word freedom is not pronounced, and the word abolition is replaced by the promise of *decisive and effectual measures to ameliorate the condition of the slave population.*† It was on the 15th of May, 1823, that the proposition of Mr. Buxton was adopted; it was on the 15th of May, 1833, that Lord Stanley, ten years after to a day, introduced into Parliament the Act of Emancipation.

In the interval, great efforts and a curious experience took place.

On the 9th of July, 1823, Lord Bathurst, Secretary of State of the Colonies, addressed a circular to the Governors, commanding them to submit definite *ameliorations* to the legislatures, a sort of preparatory programme of the measures adapted to bring about freedom, of which the following is a summary: —

* Wilberforce, session of April 2, 1792.

† Abstract of the Abolition of Slavery in the Colonies, Royal Printing House-1840, Tom. I. p. 4.

1. Before all, to strengthen and diffuse religion, — "the source of all true amelioration"; the government should make free those whom religion has made men. They should contribute to the support of a more numerous clergy as soon as the legislature should have rendered the action of this clergy possible by the abolition of Sunday markets, and the concession to the slave of another day instead of Sunday, in which to cultivate their own fields.

2. To accord to slaves the right to *testify in court*, to see in their word conscientiousness and reason, as soon as religion should have taught these regenerated beings to respect the name of God. To admit no slave to testify except those provided with a certificate of piety from the ecclesiastic of his plantation or parish ; in case of doubt, the presumption to be in favor of freedom.

3. To encourage *marriages*, especially among slaves of the same plantation, as soon as religion should have revealed to the slaves the dignity and duty of father, mother, and spouse ; to establish the Christian family, the true basis of society, the corner-stone of civilization and crowning work of Christianity.

4. To encourage *emancipation ;* to abolish the taxes by which it was fettered ; to take measures that infants and the infirm should not be abandoned, under pretext of emancipating them ; that the act, once registered, should not be lost; that the capacity of transacting business should not be denied the slave ; and lastly, that the rights of *thirds* established on his person should be *purged*, and should not indefinitely hold his liberty in suspense and his security in peril.

5. Without absolutely forbidding the sale of slaves in payment of their masters' debts, (for the greater part of the slaves mortgaged and substituted belonged less to the masters than to their creditors,) not to sell the slaves in general without the land ; to accord sequestration rather than sale ; to sell everything, slaves, implements, and planta-

tions, as far as possible without division; to prohibit the sale of the husband without the wife, or the mother without the children under fourteen; and to appoint commissioners or protectors for husbands, wives, and children *reputed* such, in consideration of the custom of non-marriage among the slaves, to watch over these provisions.

6. To lessen punishment, to exempt women from the lash, to abolish the use of the whip as a stimulus to field labor, to punish no offence until the next day, and then in the presence of the one by whom the punishment was ordered, and of a free person to keep a register of the cause, the time, and the degree of the punishment, and to inflict penalties on masters who abused it.

7. To secure to the slaves the enjoyment of such property as it was eligible for them to possess; to this end, to establish *savings banks*, and permit the depositor to declare to whom the deposit should revert after himself.

Curious provisions, still timid, but wise and well fitted to demonstrate, on the one hand, how freedom proceeds from religion, and is based on right; on the other, how all abuses are born inevitably of slavery. The statesman who wrote this page of philosophy, as well as policy, seems a physician treating at once of the diseases and remedies of human nature, — deep-seated diseases, simple remedies, and without equivalent.

Not a colony had anticipated these counsels; not a colony accepted them pacifically or fully. The chartered colonies declared the intervention of government unconstitutional; the colonies of the crown offered resistance. The hopes of the slaves were raised as far as the resistance of the masters; there were insurrections, incendiarisms, and capital executions, especially at Guiana (1823) and Jamaica (1824).

After seven years, eight * colonies had adopted none of

* Honduras, Mauritius, Antigua, the Bermudas, Montserrat, Nevis, St. Christopher, and the Virgin Islands.

the reforms prescribed. The twelve others had absolutely refused the measures relative to religious instruction and the amelioration of justice; three* only had abolished the Sunday markets. All the chartered colonies refused the appointment of protectors, the concession of one day in the week to the slaves, the savings banks, the restrictions on sales, and the modification of punishment. Except at Trinidad and St. Lucia, no important amelioration was accepted, and those which were adopted remained wellnigh without effect.

It was really necessary that the government should exact what it must despair of otherwise obtaining. This duty was fulfilled. The government commenced by setting the example. A circular from Lord Goodrich, March 12, 1831, informed the colonies that all the slaves of the crown domains were free.

Eight months after, the king, by an Order in Council dated November 2, 1831, prescribed and elaborated all the measures enunciated in the circular of 1823.

Officers, under the name of *protectors* or *assistant protectors* of slaves, were instituted in all the colonies (Arts. 1 – 26), paid by the crown, and invested with extended authority; they were to be in no wise interested in slave property.

Sunday markets were declared illegal (Arts. 27 – 31), and labor on Sunday was punished (Arts. 31 – 35). It was no longer permitted to use the whip on the plantations to stimulate the slaves like horses, to whip a woman, or to give a man more than fifteen lashes on the spot without witnesses, or on unhealed wounds; and punishments were to be recorded (Arts. 36 – 53).

Marriage between slaves was permitted and regulated (Arts. 54 – 59). The slave was declared eligible to be

* The Cape, Barbadoes, and Tobago. Published Statement of the Secretary of the Navy.

cited in court, and to hold all property, except boats, instruments of flight, arms and ammunition, instruments of insurrection, or other slaves, through shameful forgetfulness of his own hopes (Arts. 60 - 62).

Courts of petition were instituted for slaves, — a special, summary, inexpensive, and decisive mode of justice (Art. 63).

The separation of families by sale or bequest was prohibited (Arts. 66 - 69). Emancipation was rendered easy, and exempted from taxation, and its renunciation made impossible (Arts. 70, 71). The slaves were empowered to ransom themselves (Arts. 74 - 85). The legal presumption in favor of freedom was sanctioned (Art. 86), and the testimony of slaves admitted in law (Art. 87). Minute provisions regulated the food, maintenance, clothing, lodging, bedding, medical attendance, and religious liberty due slaves from masters, and the duration of labor due masters from slaves (Arts. 88 - 104). Severe penalties (Arts. 105 - 110) served as sanctions to these prescriptions, placed under the guard of the protectors and judges (Arts. 105 - 116), bound in their turn to make frequent reports to the Governors, who were not to order the payment of their salaries until after having received their reports (Art. 118), and who were, moreover, themselves bound to the crown by the obligation to submit their ordinances to its approbation (Art. 119), and bore a responsibility equal to their authority.

The order of 1831 aroused the most violent opposition. In all the colonies the masters protested against this violation of their property.

They were right indeed!

The law prescribed to the colonist at what hour his property should rise and go to rest; what it should receive a week, — that with twenty-one pints of flour, or fifty-six bananas, seven herring or shad, it should have a hat of bark, straw, or leaves, a cloth jacket, two shirts, two pairs of trousers, or two Osnabruck skirts; that it should also have a woollen blanket, two pairs of shoes, a knife or scissors, razors, a stove, and an iron pot (Order, Art. 97). The law added, that the colonist could no longer sell this property at his will, or lash it at his caprice, or hinder it from marrying or emancipating itself. It was clear that this property was no longer a chattel, nor even an animal, but a person, a human being, a soul. What an outrage on property!

Yes, if the master had a right, the law was abusive; but if the master's right were no right, the law was just, it failed to be logical; it was necessary to proclaim liberty, this was done.

The policy of the government led to it, the opposition of the colonists compelled it.

A committee of inquiry, appointed by the House of Commons, to investigate the means for attaining the abolition of slavery, made a report, August 11, 1832, which called for the most urgent attention of legislation. The government, placed between the excited hopes of the slaves, and the obstinate resistance of the colonies, resolved to proclaim a general emancipation, with the double condition of an indemnity and an apprenticeship. Lord Stanhope, the Secretary of State for the Colonies, introduced this memorable measure, May 14, 1833.

On the 20th of May it announced this determination to the colonial governments by a despatch containing these words: —

"The government regrets taking the initiative in this measure. But it has been forced to yield in this respect to the declared wish of public opinion, after having lost all hope of seeing itself anticipated and seconded by colonial legislation. The security of the colonies, moreover, permits no longer hesitation."

The act was passed June 12, 1833, by the House of Commons, and June 25 by the House of Lords, and was promulgated, with the sanction of the crown, August 28, 1833.

This noble law, which delivered a great nation from the opprobrium of a crime, and 800,000 men from the weight of servitude, is composed of sixty-six articles.

Article 3 declares all slaves instantly free who shall be transported upon English soil.

Articles 1 and 2 transform, from August 1, 1834, all slaves inhabiting the soil of the colonies into apprenticed laborers, bound to labor for the benefit of their former masters.

The apprenticeship was to last: —

1. For *rural apprentices attached to the soil,* that is, habitually employed on the plantations of their masters, until August 1, 1840. (Arts. 4 and 5.)

2. For *rural apprentices not attached to the soil,* that is, habitually employed on plantations not belonging to their masters, until the same date. (Arts. 4 and 5.)

3. For other than *rural* apprenticed laborers, until August 1, 1838 (Art. 6); these delays were prolonged four months for the Cape of Good Hope, and six months for the Isle of Mauritius. (Art. 65.)

The apprentice might be liberated before the expiration of these dates (Art. 7), or might redeem himself (Art. 8). But emancipation did not release the master from his duties towards the aged and infirm. The law also protected children, by charging the justices of the peace to prepare for them special contracts of apprenticeship. (Art. 13.)

In this still incomplete state of freedom, the apprentice was placed under the guardianship of special justices of the peace (Arts. 14, 15, 18, 19). It was forbidden to separate families (Art. 10), to defraud liberty by transporting the apprentice from the colony to which he belonged (Art.

9), and to degrade the dignity of manhood in him by the punishment of the lash (Art. 17). The observation of Sunday, the grant of the necessaries of life, or of a spot of ground on which to raise them, was secured to the former slave (Arts. 21, 11). The classification of apprentices, the forms and conditions of redemption, the regulations necessary to public tranquillity, the suppression of vagrancy, the allowance of lodging, clothing, food, and medical care, the appointment of the hours of labor and repose, in a word, all the measures fitted to secure the execution of the law and contracts, were intrusted to the local legislatures or authorities (Arts. 16, 23).

To facilitate these measures, the plan of an Order in Council, rendered October 19, 1833, and divided into twelve chapters, was addressed to the colonies, a sort of *regulation of public administration* was proposed as a model.

These authorities remained free to exclude from the rank of citizens those who had just been admitted to the rank of men; they could exempt them from certain military services, or declare them ineligible to the enjoyment of certain political franchises (Art. 22). The law secured to the former masters, at once as a compensation for the services of which they were about to be deprived and a subsidy to labor, an indemnity of £20,000,000, to be apportioned by committees of arbiters, appointed by the crown, among the nineteen slave colonies, islands, and lands depending thereon, according to the number of slaves enumerated in conformity with the terms of Statute 59 George III., and to the average sale price computed during the eight years preceding 1834 (Arts. 24 – 60).*

The Indies, Ceylon, and St. Helena were excepted from

* Number of slaves freed	770,390
Average value from 1822 to 1830	£56 8s.
Average rate of indemnity per head	£25 15s.
Total amount of indemnity . . .	£19,950,066 0s.

the application of the law, which, on the contrary, was declared applicable at the colony of Honduras as soon as the registration of the slaves should have been accomplished there (Art. 62).

Such was the celebrated law which devoted £20,000,000 to the ransom of 800,000 men.

There was reason to fear that too much prudence had rendered it imprudent. It loosened knots without untying them. It inflamed all passions and contented none. The right of the master was recognized and broken; more extended duties and narrow limits were imposed on its enjoyment; interested in order, he was almost as much so in the disorder that would ensue to justify his sombre predictions and make liberty distrusted. The slave received the name of liberty without its use, — a postponement very short to him who enjoys, very long to him who suffers, rendered uncertain this hope, which a reaction easily to be feared might yet retard or suddenly destroy, — he saw the shore without touching it. A perilous transition, which exposed the colonies to disorder, property to ruin, liberty to a costly and bloody check!

The wisdom and firmness of the Governors, the influence of religion on the negroes, and the intelligent resignation of the masters, secured, on the contrary, a marvellous success.

"Wherever the planters wish the thing to succeed, it is successful," wrote the Governor of Jamaica, September 19, 1835. To this Governor, the Marquis of Sligo, his predecessor, Lord Mulgrave, and his successor, Sir Lionel Smith, reverts the honor of having directed so difficult a work in this beautiful colony, which represents by itself alone one half of the revenues of the British colonies, and contained nearly half the slaves possessed by English hands; 35,000 whites being found face to face with 322,421 slaves on a territory of 750 square leagues.

At Antigua and its dependencies — Montserrat, Barbadoes, St. Christopher, Nevis, Anguilla, the Virgin Islands, and Dominica — the clergy and missionaries, consulted by the Governor, Sir Evan Murray MacGregor, declared that the moral and religious instruction of the slaves was sufficiently advanced to entitle them to an immediate liberation, which was pronounced June 4, 1833, by the counsel of the Assembly.*

At Guiana, despite the extent of territory and the neighborhood of more than 10,000 refugees in the interior, order reigned, labor was maintained, production increased, schools multiplied, a few disturbances were repressed without shedding blood, thanks to the zeal, firmness, and kindness of the Governor, Sir J. Carmichael Smyth, whose death, occurring March 4, 1838, was mourned as a public calamity.

At Mauritius, where the act of 1833 was not carried into effect until 1835, the consequences were somewhat more distressing, but the facility of procuring Indians sustained production. The government refused to authorize the importation of hired laborers from the coast of Africa and Madagascar, for fear of reviving the slave-trade, but encouraged the measures taken by the Governor, Sir William Nicolay, to attract the Coolies thither; and, at the close of 1837, the island already contained 8,690 immigrants.

We breathe freely, and thank God, when, after having gone through the immense collection of despatches, circulars, orders, and decisions of the crown, which put into execution, with as much effect as intelligence, the act of 1833, we open a despatch of Lord Glenelg, dated November 6, 1838,† which, nearly five years after the beginning of the apprenticeship, thus sums up its effects: —

"Hitherto, the results of the great experiment of the abolition of slavery have justified the most ardent hopes

* Abstract IV. Part III. p. 258.

† Abstract I. Part I. p. 63; and Part II. entire.

of the authors and advocates of this measure. On examining attentively the abuses which have grown out of its execution, it seems to me that they should be attributed, in great part, to the ancient colonial system. No one who had reflected on human nature and the history of slavery could have expected such a reform to be wrought without inconveniences. I esteem myself happy, therefore, in being able to affirm, that, in this short lapse of time, a progress has been effected in the social condition which will add to the happiness of humanity, and of which history has never offered a greater example. The distinguishing feature above all of this progress is, that it has been accomplished without the smallest disturbance, without the slightest commotion, without the overthrow of any social institution, or the least weakening of sovereign authority. On the contrary, greater respect has surrounded laws which offered a more equal protection to the rights of all classes of society. With the feeling of growing security, the value of property has increased to such a degree that there is reason to hope that the final crisis which is now so near will be effected without the disturbance of good order."

Lord Glenelg proceeded to indicate to the Governors the inquiries and precautions by which they should pave the way for the moment of definitive emancipation, — a moment which he awaited with visible anxiety.

In fact, by an apparent contradiction which will only surprise a superficial mind, the nearer the *dénouement* approached, the more formidable it seemed, despite the admirable tranquillity which had followed the act of 1833.

This act had divided the slaves into three classes, and fixed distinctive dates for the liberation of the first two and the third; a difference based on slight motives, and leaving room for practical difficulties and numerous frauds. It had abandoned numberless details to local regulations; now life is made up of details, through which it is materially happy or unhappy, and under the shelter of which abuses, ill-will, dissimilation, and rancors take refuge. Either the regulations were incomplete, or the masters failed in their observance, or such failures were not repressed, so that the slaves were in many places maltreated or mutinous. In proportion as the moment of freedom approached, some broke loose prematurely from their duties, others aspired prematurely to their rights. Patience long delayed is easier than patience whose end is approaching; it is at the last moment that one grows weary of waiting.

M. de Tocqueville says that the very prosperity of the reign of Louis XVI. hastened the Revolution.*

"It is said that the French found their position the more insupportable, the better it became. . . . . It often happens that a people which has endured the most oppressive laws without complaint, and as if it did not feel them, throws them off violently the instant the burden is lightened, ... and experience teaches that the most dangerous moment to a bad government is usually that in which it begins to amend. The evil which one suffers patiently, as inevitable, seems insupportable as soon as he conceives the idea of escaping it. All that is then taken from abuses seems to uncover what remains, and render the feeling of it more poignant; the evil has become less, it is true, but the sensibility is keener."

The colonies then presented this spectacle.

On the other hand, public opinion in the mother country availed itself sometimes of the abuses, at others of the good effects of the apprenticeship, to demand that it should be abridged, and that freedom should be proclaimed definitively and without distinction, from August 1, 1838. Innumerable petitions uttered this prayer; one, addressed to the queen, was signed by 600,000 names. From the halls

* *L'Ancien Régime et la Révolution*, Chap. XVI. p. 269.

of meetings, public opinion crossed the threshold of Parliament, and petitions became motions.

In the Upper House, on the 20th of February, 1838, Lord Brougham proposed the final suppression of slavery on the ensuing 1st of August.

Analogous motions were made in the House of Commons, by Sir G. Strickland, Mr. James Steward, and Sir Eardley Wilmot. In 1836, Mr. Buxton had obtained the appointment of a committee of inquiry.* Important discussions followed the report, and the most radical motions. "It would be easier to turn back the Thames in its course," exclaimed O'Connell, "than to keep the negroes in slavery against the unanimous wish of the English people." The cabinet of Lord Melbourne, supported in its hesitation by Lord Wellington, Sir Robert Peel, and Mr. Gladstone, sustained the system of apprenticeship because it had succeeded, and because it constituted a sort of pledge to the colonists. It preferred, moreover, to leave to the local legislatures the merit and popularity of emancipation. But, admitting the abuses and insufficiency of the act of 1833, it proposed a modifying act, which regulated all which that of 1833 had omitted or abandoned, abrogated the measures injudiciously taken by the colonial powers, and interposed the will of Parliament and the crown with greater authority in all the relations between masters and apprentices. This act was dated April 11, 1838.

Upon its promulgation, the colonial legislatures and government councils hesitated no longer to declare in favor of immediate emancipation, already accepted at Antigua.

It was proclaimed at Jamaica, Trinidad, Dominica, Barbadoes, St. Lucia, and Guiana, in June, July, and August, 1838; and at Mauritius, March 11, 1839.†

* Composed of Messrs. Buxton, Sir George Grey, O'Connell, Gladstone, Baines, Sir Stratford Canning, Labouchère, Andrew, Johnston, Thornly, Patrick Stewart, Charles Lushington, Oswald, Sir James Graham, Lord Sandon, and Lord Henrick. See Report of August 13, 1836. Abstract III. p. 3.

† Abstract of the Abolition, etc., II. p. 16.

The act of August 28, 1833, which promised freedom after an *apprenticeship* destined to last until 1840, was therefore anticipated; prudence itself counselled that patience should not be so far prolonged.

The partisans of a gradual preparation for emancipation may draw an argument from the manner in which the period of apprenticeship transpired. In fact, from the statements which fill the preceding pages, and the despatch of Lord Glenelg, which we have cited, it results : —

1. That the transition of the negroes from slavery to freedom was effected without commotion ;

2. That, from 1834 to 1838, the crimes and misdemeanors, null or very nearly so with respect to the person, continually diminished with respect to property ;

3. That production, less on certain points, equal or superior on certain others, was maintained in general during the four years of apprenticeship.

But the end of the apprenticeship was abrupt, and those who have no fears of an immediate solution of the question of slavery may in their turn draw an argument from this unexpected cessation ; for it has been followed by a no less satisfactory success, as we are about to see.

It is difficult, and would be useless, to enter into the detailed history of each of the nineteen slave colonies of England. Documents are superabundant. From 1834 to 1840 only, the English government published fifteen folio volumes containing 7,256 pages. Under the impulse of the Commission presided over by M. de Broglie, the French government, from 1840 to 1843, followed this great experiment with praiseworthy attention, and published reports, translations, and official documents of the highest interest.*

* See Abstract of the Abolition of Slavery in the English Colonies, published by order of Admiral Duperré, 5 vols., 1841, and especially in the 4th and 5th volumes; the Reports of Procureur-General Bernard and Captain Layrle on Jamaica (1834 - 1842), Barbadoes (1834 - 1841), St. Lucia, St. Vincent, Granada, and St. Christopher (1838 - 1840), Antigua (1836 - 1841); of MM. Aubert, Ar-

We cannot sufficiently thank these two governments for having given so much importance to this genesis of the elevation to liberty of a part of the human family.

To guide ourselves without being lost in this forest of documents, but one means will avail; namely, to open boldly two or three broad roads, and to plant at the entrance, as so many guide-boards, the two or three principal questions which overlook the whole history, then to go on our way gathering up all the facts, the aggregate of which will be the answer to the questions propounded.

What has been the influence of emancipation on the condition of the former slaves?

What has been the influence of emancipation on the production, labor, and prosperity of the colonies?

All the documents may be classed, with a few subdivisions, under these two capital heads.

So long a study would be wearisome, if it had not a vast compensation in store. It is with the affranchisement of a slave as with the education of a child; nothing is more monotonous in detail, but when we see that all these petty cares have made a man, we feel no regret for the fatigue which they have caused. I do not complain of the pains which have led me to irrefragable conclusions, raised, in spite of interested denials or objections drawn from partial observations, to the height of historic truths. They repose at once on the testimony of the most eminent and diverse English statesmen, and on the authority of figures, impassive witnesses which can no more be accused of sentimentality than of imposture.

mand, and Arnous on Trinidad (1839, 1840); Vidal de Lingendes and Guillet on Guiana (1838, 1839); and Dejean de la Batie on the Island of Mauritius (1838 - 1840). See the extended Report, in two volumes, fol., of M. Jules Lechevallier to the Duke de Broglie. Consult, above all, the documents so usefully inserted in the *Revue coloniale*, 33 vols., from 1842 to 1860.

CHAPTER II.

INFLUENCE OF EMANCIPATION ON THE FREED CLASSES.

At the end of 1838, after five years' experience, Lord Glenelg, Secretary of State of the Colonies, recounted the happy transition from servitude to *apprenticeship.* The same facts were verified by the committee charged with directing the inquiry of 1836, and which counted among its members Mr. Buxton, Mr. O'Connell, Sir James Graham. M. Labouchère, and Sir George Grey.

After three more years, Lord Stanley, Secretary of State of the Colonies, characterizes in the following terms, March 22, 1842, the transition from apprenticeship to full liberty.*

"Upon the whole, the result of the great experiment of emancipation, attempted upon the collective population of the West Indies, *has surpassed the most lively hopes of even the warmest friends of colonial prosperity ;* not only has the material prosperity of each of the islands greatly increased, but, what is still better, there has been progress in industrious habits, improvement in the social and religious system, and development, among individuals, of those qualities of the heart and mind which are more necessary to happiness than the material objects of life. . . . . . The negroes are happy and satisfied, they give themselves to labor, they have ameliorated their manner of living and increased their comfort, and, while crimes have diminished, moral habits have become better. The number of marriages has increased and, under the influence of the ministers of religion, instruction has been diffused. Such are the results of

* Report of M. Lechevallier, Part II. Chap. XIV. § 3, p. 929.

emancipation ; *its success has been complete, as to the principal end of the measure.*"

The salient facts which appear, from all inquiries, are these : complete tranquillity ; no vengeance, no tumult, no incendiarism, no civil war ; a prodigious number of marriages ; schools and churches filled to overflowing ; lastly, a growing love of property.

This last feature is worthy of remark.

"The number of negroes become freeholders through their industry and economy amounted, in the whole island of Jamaica, to 2,114, in 1838 ; two years afterwards, in 1840, they numbered 7,340.* . . . . . At Guiana, from 150 to 200 negroes associate together to buy estates worth 150,000, 250,000, and even 400,000 francs. Considerable villages † have been formed, composed of pretty cottages, with a good church, and occupied by numerous inhabitants, industrious and well clad." ‡

Lord Stanley completed these testimonials concerning the happiness and progress of the freedmen by another proof drawn from the value of the exportations of England to the colonies.

During the last six years of slavery it was . .	69,575,000 fr.
During the apprenticeship (1835 – 1838) it amounted to	89,450,000
In the first year of freedom it attained . .	100,061,575
The second year	87,318,350

On all these points the French testimony accords completely with the English reports.

* The lots generally comprise two or three acres, and sometimes do not exceed a few fathoms. *Revue coloniale*, 1843, p. 27. *Ibid.*, p. 830.

† On the 1st of January, 1843, the negroes had built, in the county of Berbice alone, 1,184 houses since emancipation, and had brought under cultivation nearly 7,000 acres of land purchased by them. *Revue coloniale*, p. 30.

‡ In the other colonies, — in Trinidad, for instance, — a host of negroes settled illegally as *squatters* on the crown lands, and a proclamation of the Governor was needed to prohibit this. *Ibid.*, p. 634.

Captain Layrle of the Navy wrote from Jamaica: * —

"The negroes have not abandoned cultivation, this is a fact; now if by labor is understood that which refers to the planter, that which, under the preceding system, profited a handful of whites who monopolized it, less labor is done, it is true; but if the labor of the negroes on their own lands be brought into the computation (for it is notorious that purchases to the value of 2,500,000 francs have been made during the past three years by the freedmen), it is found that the diminution of labor is not as considerable as it first appeared; only labor has taken another direction."

To the declarations of Lord Stanley is added the report of the Committee of Inquiry, the appointment of which his speech was designed to call forth. The first conclusion of this report, July 25, 1842, is as follows: † —

"The religious, moral, and material amelioration of the negroes is incontestable.

"The seven years (1842 – 1848) which followed these beginnings witnessed the continuance of the same progress, but with characteristic phases.

"At Jamaica, to which it is necessary to give special attention, because it was the most important of the slave colonies of England, and because the differences which arose between the local legislature and the mother country rendered the work of emancipation more difficult there than everywhere else, — at Jamaica, the number of free villages settled by the freed negroes before 1843, on an extent of at least 10,000 acres, was estimated at from 150 to 200.‡ About 10,000 heads of families had constructed more than 3,000 cabins, and expended in four years, for the purchase

* Publications of the Marine, Vol. V. p. 21, and Broglie, p. 42.

† Report of M. Lechevallier, Part II. p. 992.

‡ Past and Present Condition of Jamaica, by James Philippo, Baptist Missionary in this colony for twenty years. 1843. *Revue coloniale*, 1844, II. p. 489.

of lands and erection of houses, more than 4,000,000 francs. About 14,800 marriages of freed persons were celebrated annually, or 1 in 29 individuals. The negroes had imposed great sacrifices on themselves for the foundation of a considerable number of chapels and schools. Concubinage and drunkenness had become exceptional, and a journal of Kingston could announce, at the beginning of 1843, that the prison had not received a single inmate for five days, a fact which had never occurred before since the settlement of the town. Lord Elgin, in 1844, continues to signalize the progress of the population in morality, the improvements brought about in the construction and interior arrangement of the cabins, and the abandonment of superstitious practices.*

In a report addressed to the political court of Guiana by the special magistrates of the different districts, in 1843, we read that the number of negro freeholders was 15,906, and that they had constructed more than 3,000 houses.† A law was necessary to prescribe the immediate sale of lands occupied without sufficient titles.

The freedmen had been accused of having kindled the incendiary fires which, in 1844, filled Guiana with consternation; an inquiry demonstrated that they had, on the contrary, contributed with all their might to extinguish them. The same was true of the burning of Bridgetown, in Barbadoes.‡

In June, 1844, a negro insurrection broke out in Dominica, but only in a very limited part of the island. The negroes had mistaken the taking of the census for a return to slavery. The insurrection was prompted by a few malefactors, and, it is alleged, a few negroes escaped from the French colonies. After three days order was

* *Revue coloniale*, 1844, III. p. 192; 1845, V. p. 181.

† *Ibid.*, IV. p. 265; 1845, V. p. 431.

‡ *Ibid.*, 1845, VI. p. 122.

re-established, and a capital execution served as an example.*

In 1844 a portion of the freedmen had returned to the plantations, and the documents of this year inform us that at Jamaica the proportion of land under cultivation was nearly the same as in the time of slavery, and that wages had fallen again to 1*s.* 6*d.* per day of nine hours. A speech of the secretary of the government at Guiana contains this saying: "In no other part of the world are laborers better, wages lower (from 1 fr. 25 c. to 2 fr. 5 c.), and provisions cheaper, than in English Guiana."

In the other colonies, such as St. Lucia, Barbadoes, Trinidad, St. Vincent, and Antigua, in 1844, as before this epoch, results no less satisfactory are described. At Trinidad especially the planters did not waste their time in vain recriminations, or enter into coalitions to reduce wages or increase the rent of the cabins and gardens; they directly created competition by immigration, and wages at 2 fr. 60 c., and even 5 fr. 20 c. in the time of harvest, fell quickly to 2 fr. 50 c. and 3 fr. 10 c. It is well known that at Antigua the production speedily exceeded that of the years of servile labor.

In general, the progress of civilization was in a direct ratio to that of religious instruction. The zeal which the Baptist, Moravian, Wesleyan, and Anglican missionaries displayed to lead the negroes to freedom, then to virtue, is worthy of admiration. And where religion was not encouraged, at Mauritius, where the English government supported but eight, then ten clergymen for 80,000 souls, because the population was Catholic, religion and morality were seen to flourish among the freedmen, evangelized by heroic priests like the founder of the mission, M. Laval;

* *Revue coloniale*, 1844, III. pp. 420, 552.

† *Ibid.*, 1845, VII. pp. 80, 90.

but outside this salutary influence, the greater part of the negroes were devoted, through ignorance, to every vice, above all to drunkenness.*

When, in 1846, the government presented to the Houses a summary of the reports of all the Governors,† a uniform picture was presented of the excellent effects of freedom on the conduct of the freed negroes at Jamaica,‡ St. Lucia, Montserrat, the Virgin Islands, Nevis, and St. Christopher.

The chief share in these results was due to these Governors and to the government itself. I take pleasure in citing the admirable words of Lord Grey. Scarcely arrived at power, he charged the Committee of Public Instruction in the Colonies to examine the question of the moral and industrial education of the freed negroes, and by a circular of January 27, 1847, § warmly recommended *education,* in order that emancipation might be, he said, "the beginning of an era of enlightened liberty, resting on a more solid basis than human laws, and inaugurating the progress of Christian virtues and public felicity," and also *instruction,* "which makes the laborer intelligent and sedate, creates new needs, increases the action of the body and mind, and is the best means of bringing labor into connection with the wants of the planter."

These sentiments, these efforts, were not the exclusive appanage of the Whig party ; the ministers were changed, without the devotion to this great work experiencing the least change. Never was more persevering ardor consecrated to the service of a juster cause. Success encouraged these noble actions by surpassing all hopes ; and when, February 7, 1848, Lord Bentinck, shortly before his death,

* *Annales de la propagation de la foi,* Letter of March, 1845

† *Revue coloniale,* 1846, X. p. 425.

‡ See specially for Jamaica in 1845 and 1846, the Reports of Lord Elgin, *Revue coloniale,* 1847, p. 316; and 1847, XII. p. 231.

§ *Revue coloniale,* 1847, XII. p. 124.

demanded of the House of Commons the appointment of a committee* to investigate the condition of the colonies, Lord John Russell, on opening the discussion, June 16, on the conclusions of the report of the committee, was able to sum up the history of the results of emancipation at this epoch in these words: —

"The object of the act of 1834 was to give liberty to 800,000 persons, and to secure the independence, prosperity, and happiness of those who were slaves. No one denies, I think, that this has been accomplished. I believe that there is nowhere a happier class of laborers than in the West Indies. This satisfactory condition is the consequence of the act of 1834."

Let us interrogate the history of the ten years following, and we encounter the same facts verified by the most severe or the most indulgent testimony.

At Guiana, a magnificent province of 60,000 square miles, — traversed by the beautiful river Essequibo, 21 miles broad at the mouth, — and inhabited by more than 120,000 souls, a colonist, who is, moreover, very much of a pessimist, writes: † —

"The portion of the native population which, in other countries, constitutes the laboring class, is estimated at 70,000 souls. They present the singular spectacle, which can be contemplated in no other part of the world, of people scarcely emerged from slavery, yet already possessing property in houses and lands for which they have paid more than a million pounds sterling."

A French commission, charged, in 1853, by the government of Martinico, with visiting the two islands of Barbadoes and Trinidad, writes: ‡ —

* *Revue coloniale*, 1848-1849, p. 6.

† *La Guyane anglaise après quinze ans de liberté*, by a Proprietor, *Revue coloniale*, 1854, XII. pp. 132, 223.

‡ Report of MM. Northumb-Percin and Hayot, *Revue coloniale*, 1854, XI. p. 253.

"The aspect of Barbadoes is dazzling in an agricultural and manufacturing point of view ; the entire island is one vast field of sugar-canes standing evenly one after the other, planted at an average distance of six square feet. Not a weed sullies these beautiful and regular plantations The sugar-works are extensive and neat, and all the arrangements for manufacture are exquisite. . . . . . The population of the island is immense, amounting to 136,000 souls on 167 square miles, on a soil which does not and cannot belong to it.. . . . . .

"Trinidad has endured harder trials, from which she has emerged, as we shall see, by replacing her 20,000 freed negroes in part by Indians ; but the happiness and tranquillity of its freedmen are the same."

Behold the picture which a colonist of Jamaica drew, at the same epoch, of the state of the colored community, which almost entirely composes the population of this island, occupied, on a surface of 6,400 square miles, by 369,000 blacks and only 16,000 whites : * —

"It may be supposed that the whites have the pre-eminence there. . . . . . But, apart from that pre-eminence which results from wealth and intelligence in every community, the whites have no privilege over their fellow-citizens. . . . . . The colored man holds a position in no wise inferior, and we find no reason to complain that he is on the same footing with ourselves. . . . . . Our bar is not crowded, but colored lawyers hold the first places there. Colored physicians practise in concurrence with the whites. . . . . . These are facts which it is important to establish, for all this progress has been accomplished since the abolition of slavery in the island. We have proved by experience that the colored man can raise himself to the first rank of civil society, and hold his place there as well as any European by origin."

* *Revue coloniale*, 1851, VII. p. 459.

If we consult the reports on education, religion, and criminality, in the different colonies, we verify everywhere the progress of the family through marriage and property, the zeal in attending and even founding churches and schools, the perfect tranquillity enjoyed by person and property from the earliest date. Doubtless these sentiments and these efforts are not universal; over a great number of human beings depraved at once by their nature and by slavery, idleness has resumed its rights, debauchery and drunkenness have not lost their dominion. "Great indulgence is needed," wrote a colonist,* "towards those who have experienced in their life both the weight of the chains of slavery, and the boundless joys of freedom; their memories are not sufficiently effaced, their sentiments not sufficiently changed, for them not to continue to seek the enjoyment of idleness after a long day of labor; but it will be the fault of the colonists if the children of these men are suffered to grow to become a reproach and danger to the country, as has already been the case with too great a number."

But, in conclusion, five years, ten years, twenty years after the abolition of slavery, we have the right to repeat: —

Liberty has not led 800,000 men to barbarism. Their moral, intellectual, and religious amelioration is incontestable; the earth has several thousand more freeholders, humanity counts several hundred thousand men elevated a degree in the scale of being. A great action has been accomplished by a great people.

* *Revue coloniale*, 1854, XII. p. 226.

CHAPTER III.

INFLUENCE OF EMANCIPATION ON THE COLONIES.

To have set men at liberty is not all; it is necessary to place them in society. Now, the former slaves have eagerly acquired property; they have in great numbers desired and they relish family life; but have they continued to labor, or have they broken off all connection with their old masters, and withdrawn far from cities and inhabited places?

It is affirmed that this has been so; and the necessity of renewing the agricultural force of the colonies by a large immigration, as well as the disastrous diminution of their production, are given as proofs of the assertion.

It is fitting to reply separately to these two exaggerated affirmations.

§ 1. Labor and Immigration.

The economical condition of colonial society is very different from that of European society.

In Europe, the territory is occupied by a considerable, sometimes superabundant population. The first labor of this population is to cultivate the soil which yields them a support. When hands are scarce, and wages increase under the influence of a large demand for labor, either the competition of laborers intervenes to maintain a reasonable rate, or it is decided to reduce production in proportion, without going to a distance to seek foreign labor at great expense.

In the colonies, vast territories are occupied by an insufficient population, whose principal production is commodities for exportation, instead of food destined for the support of the inhabitants. It is necessary, therefore, to obtain everything from without, and consequently impossible to reduce the production without being exposed to famine. Besides, if the scarcity of hands increases the price of labor, there is not a neighboring population at hand to reduce it by competition; whence it follows, that the more the price of labor increases, the more the quantity of labor diminishes; if the price of the product be protected by monopoly, the producer does not fear to pay high, but he sells high, and the consumption suffers or is checked; if the monopoly be destroyed, it being impossible to reduce the price of labor, the commodity is produced at a loss, and the producer is ruined. But it is much worse when labor is wholly lacking. Now, the colonies always live under this menace. How fix the laborer in one place? By wages? He can supply his own needs by laboring for himself on a land and under a sky which labor for him. By property? The parcelling out of lands is unfavorable to large production; sugar especially, the true wealth of the colonies, can only be produced on a large scale. It seems as if we were reduced to a single means, slavery, which holds the laborer by force to his work.

This serious difficulty explains the obstinacy of the colonists in maintaining so disgraceful an institution. They always believed that they had to sacrifice fatally either their conscience or their wealth, and conscience was worsted in the struggle; but, at the same time, this economical position gives the true reason of one of the incontestable consequences of emancipation in the English colonies, as everywhere else, — namely, the desertion of a part of the plantations, and consequently the decline of production, and the ruin of some proprietors.

It is said that freedom has urged the negroes to idleness;

this is not correct. The idle have become vagabonds; but the diligent have become freeholders and artisans. Labor has been transformed, not destroyed; that has happened which happens in every place where a scanty population has before it an extended and fertile territory, attracting it by the temptation of property, and towns, offering it a more varied, more agreeable, and more lucrative existence.

Herein is the great difficulty of the emancipation of the Russian serfs; the lands will cease to be cultivated if the cultivators change place, and it is quite natural that they should change place if they find elsewhere what every man seeks, — greater happiness. Let it not be said, therefore, that freedom has killed labor; it has produced what it was naturally destined to produce in the economical condition of colonial society; and this is so true, that, on asking in which of the English colonies the labor of the former slaves has most diminished, and in which it has least changed, it is found that there has been serious perturbation at Guiana, where the proportion of the population to the territory is smallest, and none at all at Barbadoes, where the proportion of the population to the territory is greatest.

We must also take into account the natural wish of every man to flee the place where he has suffered, and fully to secure himself by flight from being brought back to it; what released prisoner chooses lodgings within two paces of his prison? This repugnance is the more keen as the freedman has suffered more and is less intelligent. Wherever the slave had been well treated, wherever freedom had been preceded by a solid intellectual and religious education, the transition was easy, as at Antigua, Trinidad, and St. Lucia.* Wherever the treatment had been harsher, as in so many places that might be named, wherever education had been neglected, as at Tobago and Mauritius,

* *Revue coloniale*, 1843, pp. 26, 38.

the desertion was almost universal and continuous. Was this the fault of liberty? No, it was the fault of slavery.

In conditions so formidable and so easy to foresee, it was due at least to take some precautions in advance. The intermediate state of *apprenticeship* was designed to smooth transition, but it ended abruptly, and neither the local powers nor the government took any effective measures against vagrancy.

"It is generally admitted," wrote Lord Grey in 1853,* "that the measure of the abolition of slavery voted in 1833 was unhappily very defective, inasmuch as it contained no adequate prescription to oblige the negroes to labor at the time when the means of direct constraint to which they had been subjected as slaves were about to be withdrawn from the masters."

It did not occur to the legislators, as at the Isle of Bourbon, to propose to the negroes engagements for a term of years. A few years later, the same Lord Grey ingeniously advised the colonies to force the inhabitants to labor by taxation, a means of creating resources to the colonies, and rendering living so expensive that it would be impossible to escape labor; but these taxes were not at first established. Furthermore, instead of retaining or recalling the slaves by kind treatment, and concerting together to effect this end, some brutally haggled with them for the cabin and garden which attached them to the plantations; others consented to exorbitant wages, which exaggerated the pretensions of the laborers and the prices demanded of the consumer. This took place especially at Jamaica, where so many years were wasted in unreasonable struggles.

It may be said, that in all places labor was wellnigh abandoned to itself, and that the freed slaves of yesterday were placed face to face with the condition of laboring for others without being forced to it either by con-

† *Revue coloniale*, 1854, p. 256.

straint or necessity. In truth, if anything can be surprising in the midst of these facts and errors, it is, not that labor has diminished, but, on the contrary, that it has not wholly disappeared. Now as we see, in the first years of freedom, the production of some colonies, instead of diminishing, has increased; in others, it is true, it has been reduced one half; in all, on the average, it has decreased only one fourth; in none has it been entirely interrupted.

Be it as it may with respect to these causes and effects, it is evident that the colonies feel after freedom more than before what is at all times their great necessity, — the need of increasing the population by a large immigration of new laborers, in order to bring back wages to a reasonable rate and production to a high standard. On all sides, the colonists demand of the government to authorize and favor this immigration.

This wish and the preceding considerations are precisely the conclusions of the Report of the Committee of Inquiry appointed in 1842, as we have said, on the motion of Lord Stanley, and which so loudly proclaimed the religious, moral, and material progress of the freed classes; the committee added: —

"1. .

"2. Labor has ceased, because the negroes have applied themselves to work more profitable to them than field labor, and because, for the most part, they have been able, especially in the large colonies, to procure lands with facility, live at their ease, and enrich themselves without being obliged besides to give to the planters three or four days of seven hours' labor in each week. The low price of lands, the consequence of a fertility which yields beyond the needs of the population, the ill-will of the proprietors, and the severity of the laws which regulate the relations between the laborers and their employers, — these are the principal causes of the difficulties experienced.

"3. The scarcity of hands and the high price of wages have ruined many large estates, especially at Jamaica, Guiana, and Trinidad, and diminished the export products.

"4. It is expedient to make more equitable arrangements with the laborers, to revise the laws, and, under the surveillance of responsible public officers, to encourage the immigration of a new population."

But how effect this immigration? Both before and since emancipation, it had already been undertaken by private enterprise, but on a somewhat small scale; Indians, Chinamen, Madeirians, and lastly a few free or *liberated* Africans,* had been brought to the various colonies, and this immigration had been regulated by numerous acts of the government and local legislatures.† But the colonies by addresses, and the ports by petitions, unceasingly demanded that it should be more freely authorized and more largely encouraged. Here begun in the mother country, in public opinion and the authorities, a lively struggle between the practical needs of the colonies, the honorable scruples of the abolitionists, and the political spirit of the government.

Lord Stanley had demanded the appointment of a second committee to examine into the state of the English settlements on the coast of Africa and the possibility of an immigration of laborers from this coast to the West Indies; this committee asked that these settlements, instead of being administered by English merchants, should be replaced under the government of the crown. These merchants in fact, if they did not carry on the slave-trade, at least facili-

* England derived great advantage from *liberated* Africans; that is, from the slaves seized by her cruisers on slave-ships, who were declared free, but held to an engagement towards their liberator. A doubtfully legitimate procedure, it will be granted, of a subtle and contestable philanthropy!

† See the acts on the Abstract of Abolition, published by the Secretary of the Navy, III. p. 491, especially the despatch of the Secretary of the Colonies, Lord John Russell, to the Governor of Sierra Leone, March 20, 1841 (*Ibid.*, p. 506), and the Order in Council of September 7, 1838, which exacts that contracts shall not be closed until after the arrival in the colony.

tated it by selling to the slave-traders the cargoes which the latter afterwards exchanged for slaves. The committee did not doubt the immense advantage which a sojourn in the West Indies would assure to the Africans; civilized and Christianized, they would carry back to their country the benefit of new enlightenment, if they returned; if they remained in the colonies, they would lower the price of labor by their competition, — a most important result, for on the day when free labor should be cheaper than servile labor, the latter would receive its death-blow. But the committee believed this supply possible only from among *free* Africans, of which it was estimated there were 40,000 or 50,000 in Sierra Leone, a few hundreds in Gambia and the other English settlements on the Gold Coast, and some thousands among the tribes without slaves, as the inhabitants of the Kroo Coast.*

The committee no more than Lord Stanley admitted that *immigrants could be redeemed*, an operation which too closely resembled the slave-trade not to lead to the same abuses.

In 1842, the planters of Guiana had wished to purchase slaves on the Gold Coast, who were to be immediately emancipated and taken to Demerara as free laborers. The Governor communicated this plan to Lord Stanley, who consulted the judicial counsel of the crown, and received the following curious reply :† —

"The purchase of slaves on the Gold Coast, even for the purpose of emancipating them immediately and transporting them with their full consent to Guiana, would be illegal; the parties engaged in this transaction would be guilty of having infringed Statute 5 George IV., ch. 113, and liable to the penalties pertaining thereto.

"The purchasers of slaves are declared guilty by Art.

* Report of M. Lechevallier, II. 983.

† *Revue coloniale*, 1843, p. 151.

10 of this statute, and sentenced to fourteen years' deportation.

"In our opinion, the terms of this statute clearly include the case of the purchase of slaves, *even in the end of their emancipation.* It probably wished at the same time to discourage the traffic in slaves and favor the civilization of Africa; but it is evident that, if the purchase of slaves is an evil, in the sense that it induces those who sell them to procure them in order that they may be redeemed, the detriment is the same whether the ransomed slaves receive freedom or not."

The committee arrived at similar conclusions. The result of these counsels was the despatch dated February 6, 1843, by which immigration of free or slave Africans was permitted only from three places, where the surveillance of slaves was possible, Sierra Leone, Bonavista, and Loando. Immigration by means of redemption remained absolutely prohibited.

The immigration of Indians had not been interdicted, and England had in her own possessions an enormous population of men accustomed to tropical labors, an incomparable resource for those of her colonies who were not prevented by distance from profiting by it.

Since 1815, the convicts of Calcutta had been transported to Mauritius, and the inhabitants of this colony had adopted the habit of availing themselves of these Indians, which they preferred to making the efforts or sacrifices necessary to utilize the freed negroes, less civilized, as we have seen, at Mauritius than anywhere else. In 1837, 20,000 Indians had been already introduced.* Whether the Governor-General of India was terrified at this emigration, which raised the price of labor and of rice in India,† or whether the government of the mother country was ter-

* Documents of the Secretary of the Navy, II. 252; V. 473.

† *Revue coloniale*, 1843, p. 461

rified at the idea of the future which such competition was preparing for the freedman, East Indian immigration was prohibited in 1838.

But in 1842 it was re-established by an Order in Council, dated January 15, then by an act of Parliament, dated December 2, and subjected to minute formalities ;* then, after numerous abuses, reduced to the single port of Calcutta, beginning from January 1, 1844, and intrusted to government. From 1834 to 1847, 94,004 Coolies were introduced into Mauritius, which formerly employed only 23,000 slaves in field labor.† The colony, during this time, exceeded the statistics of production anterior to emancipation, carried from 73,000,000 pounds of sugar, in 1832, to 80,000,000 pounds, in 1846, but by spending 17,493,340 francs, burdening itself with an enormous debt,‡ exposing itself to fearful immorality,§ and becoming an Asiatic instead of an African colony. The other principal colonies followed this example somewhat slowly. Jamaica received, in 1844, 250 Indians, Guiana 556, and Trinidad 220; these numbers increased during the two following years : || —

	1845.	1846.
Jamaica	1,735	2,515
Guiana	3,497	4,120
Trinidad	2,083	2,076

Guiana also received 2,548 in 1847, and Trinidad 1,024, but the operation was then discontinued. It was inter-

* *Revue coloniale*, 1843, III. p. 559.

† *Ibid.*, 1845, VII. p. 205; 1847, XII. p. 354; 1848, I. p. 168. The Coolie costs from 10*s*. to 14*s*. per month.

‡ The expenses for the annual introduction of 6,000 immigrants were estimated, in 1844, at £50,000 (*Revue coloniale*, 1845, VII. p. 475). Now 6,000 per year scarcely sufficed to make up for the deaths and departures; the real expense was from 180 to 250 fr. per head. *Ibid.*, 1849, p. 143.

§ From 1834 to 1839, of 25,468 Coolies, there were 727 women; of the 40,318 introduced from 1842 to 1844, 453 women; of the 5,092 introduced in 1845, 646 women; in all, of 94,004 Indians, 13,284 women.

|| *Revue coloniale*, 1847, XIII. p. 154; 1848, I. p. 170.

rupted with respect to Jamaica, in 1846, by the Legislative Assembly.

The *Chinese* immigration, attempted after the example of Java, and authorized in 1842 by Lord Stanley,* did not develop to any great extent.

The *African* immigration, reduced within narrow limits, produced insignificant results. In 1847, Lord Grey permitted immigration from every part of the African coast, especially from Kroo, but still prohibited redemption. The colonies did not receive, therefore, more than 7,000 or 8,000 African immigrants, free or liberated, from 1840 to 1847.† If to this number be added about 14,000 natives of Madeira,‡ received in 1846 and 1847, it is seen that, before 1848, immigration had not brought into the eighteen slave colonies other than Mauritius more than 30,000 immigrants, which does not mean 30,000 effective laborers. Thus, therefore, if Mauritius be excepted, the 3,200,000 quintals produced by these colonies in 1847, inferior only by 400,000 quintals to the average product of 1814 and 1815, were really very nearly the same as the product of the labor of the former slaves.

The colonists demanded that immigration *by way of redemption* should be authorized. The abolitionists still maintained, some, that this operation was a return to the slave-trade; others, that it was the best means of discouraging it.§ The government resisted, and it did rightly, for

* *Revue coloniale,* 1843, p. 514.

† 1840 – 1842 3,045
1844 – 1845 1,390
1846 . . . . from 3,000 to 4,000
(*Revue coloniale*, 1848, I. p. 173.)

‡ Guiana 9,750
St. Vincent 1,762
Antigua 1,068
Small colonies 1,945

§ In an excellent work on African emigration (*Revue coloniale*, January, 1858), M. Delarbre affirms that Sir Robert Peel was of this opinion. On reading the

it thus forced the colonies to seek elsewhere the diminution of the net cost, to multiply machinery, and to take pains to retain the freed negroes in the fields by treating them better, instead of completing their estrangement from labor by an overwhelming competition.

They will show themselves broader when, exposed to foreign rivalry by the reduction of tariffs, they will have need of more favors.

But, except at Mauritius, immigration does not assume vast proportions.

The total number of immigrants introduced into the English colonies of the West Indies and Mauritius, from the abolition of slavery to the end of 1849, is 179,223,* and in this number Mauritius represents 106,638 ; there remain, therefore, for the other colonies, but 72,585, thus apportioned : —

Guiana	39,043
Jamaica	14,519
Trinidad	13,356
Grenada	1,476
St. Vincent	1,197
Antigua	1,075
Dominica	732
St. Lucia	665
Nevis	427
St. Christopher	95

From 1849 to 1855, the colonies received 31,861 new immigrants, of whom 19,519 were for Guiana, while the island of Mauritius alone received 76,342 immigrants.†

On grouping these immigrants according to nativity, we

speech delivered by this illustrious orator, July 27, 1846, we see that he speaks only of *free* laborers, and that he declares that he *has not great confidence in the introduction of free labor*. *Ibid.*, 1846, IX. p. 361.

* Report of the Committee of Emigration, March, 1850. *Revue coloniale*, 1850, V. p. 220.

† *Revue coloniale*, 1858, XIX. p. 178.

see that the English colonies had received, at the end of 1855, an aggregate of 235,999 immigrants, of which

27,906	were	Africans,
26,533	"	Madeirians,
2,107	"	Chinese,
151,191	"	Indians.

This table proves several important points : —

1. England has held a firm hand in persisting to interdict the immigration of *ransomed* Africans ; in twenty years, its colonies have only received about 1,000 annually, all *free* or *liberated* Africans ; and this is so true, that, although it may be presumed that fraudulent transportations have evaded the orders of government, the African immigration from Sierra Leone has ceased to figure in the official statistics since 1853, because the captures have diminished, and the Africans are no longer willing to emigrate.*

2. It is true that England had, in her East Indian possessions, a resource which was not at the disposal of other nations. More than 150,000 immigrants, out of 235,000, are of this origin.

3. Mauritius absorbs more than half the immigration ; less than 100,000 immigrants are left for the other colonies.†

Now, at Mauritius, the production of sugar has tripled, while its population has quadrupled ; a part of the agricultural force has therefore been renewed, and a large number of the former slaves have changed occupation. But in the other colonies, an increase of less than 100,000 immigrants in the face of the former slave population, which attained the number of 703,677 persons, is truly insignificant. It is evident, therefore, that in the West Indies the principal element of labor is, and will long be, the black population.

* From 1841 to 1851, 14,113 sailed from Sierra Leone. *Revue coloniale*, 1852, VIII. p. 291.

† *Revue coloniale*, 1854, XII. p. 456.

The public opinion that consists in believing that, since emancipation, immigration alone has rescued labor, is a prejudice, as is formally declared by the English Committee of Immigration, in its report presented to Parliament in 1853.*

The success of emancipation, said Lord Stanley in 1842, has been complete *as to the principal end of the measure*; the same thing may be said of immigration. The success has been complete as to the principal end of the measure, which was the lowering of wages and the increase of production, the progress of which will be presented in the following chapter; but it is equally true that, in the moral point of view, immigration has been, and is, a scourge, not only at the epoch when it was an unwatched enterprise of private speculation, but even after the intervention of the government. Admirable indeed are all these regulations by which humanity strives to protect, by the most minute precautions, the life and liberty of the most degraded of beings, — of a poor Indian, or a wretched negro; but, in practice, how are these regulations executed? The colonists of Mauritius address themselves to the commercial houses of Calcutta,† and the latter employ Indians, known by the name of *duffadars*, a sort of traffickers in men, or crimpers, who speculate on the laborer, speculate on the merchant, and, by more or less disgraceful manœuvres, procure for the colonists what workmen? — vagabonds, strollers of the bazaar, the offscourings of the population.

It is impossible to induce Indian women of an honorable class and irreproachable morality to quit their native soil. All the reports agree that, in consequence, the relations between the sexes have the most marked character of degradation; that concubinage is becoming more frequent and more open, and that the passions which result from it

* *Revue coloniale*, 1858, XIX. p. 165.
† *Ibid.*, 1844, III. p. 458.

lead to fatal quarrels and bloodshed.* It was hoped that at Mauritius the number of women would reach 50 per cent in 1860; but in 1851 there were still seven men to two women.

In the other colonies, vices and crimes have likewise entered in with the immigrants.

Upon the whole, the result of the English experiment as to immigration is as follows.

The only moral and effective immigration would be that of families; but with family, a man is unwilling to quit his country; without family, he roves from place to place instead of settling. In families, immigration is expensive; without families, it must be constantly begun anew. It is an experiment useful to production, prejudicial to civilization. After half a century of population, the colonies will have a surcrease of population, which will be a great advantage; but this population will be wretched, mongrel, and vicious, if not recruited from other sources, or formed into families.

Now of all immigrants, which is the best? The one who settles most willingly, labors best, becomes civilized most speedily, and most easily establishes the family relation, is the African; the Indian cannot replace him. But how obtain African *families?* In the colonies, by the widespread influence of the Christian religion; in Africa, by the foundation of extended settlements, where free and converted families can establish themselves by degrees. Until this is done, immigration will be void, if confined to Africans already free; distrusted, if procuring them by the way of purchase.

But, without speaking of the future, we will confine ourselves to verifying from the past these two results, fitted to gladden the hearts of the partisans of the abolition of slavery.

* *Revue coloniale*, 1858, XIX. p. 165.

In the first place, the slaves who have become free are, wherever they labor, better workmen and more moral men than all the immigrants that are compared with them; in the second place, although their labor may have diminished, especially at Jamaica, Guiana, and Trinidad, nevertheless the immigration into the English colonies, with the exception of the island of Mauritius, has been inconsiderable, and to the labor of the former slaves is due almost the whole of the present production.

We shall now see what production in the English colonies has become since the Act of Emancipation.

§ 2. Production, the Sugar Law, Commercial Freedom.

Prior to the epoch when slavery was abolished in the English colonies, their condition was far from prosperous, and the inquiry instituted in 1832* established that this distress, aggravated by the uncertainty which weighed on property, through the influence of the debates on emancipation, dated back to more real and profounder causes, the gravest of which was the debasement of prices, resulting from the excess of production. The net cost of sugar was estimated at 30 fr. 20 c. per 100 pounds, including the freight, but without calculating anything for the interest of the capital; and the selling price at 29 fr. 60 c.; thus making a deficit of 60 c. The sum of the colonial products being greater than the consumption of the mother country, it had been necessary to confront competition in other markets with products less burdened with expenses. The measures for ameliorating the condition of slaves and the abolition of the slave-trade had at once raised the cost and the maintenance of laborers. The continuance of the restrictions imposed on importations by the colonial sys-

* *Rapport sur les questions coloniales*, by M. Jules Lechevallier, Tom. II. p. 331. Report made in the English Parliament, April 10, 1832.

tem, the interdiction of refineries, and the establishment of high duties, embarrassed the colonies. The inquiry revealed an almost universal distress, and the committee concluded on the removal of several prohibitions, and on a considerable reduction of duties.

To those who pretend that these evils had been caused by the abolition of the slave-trade, it may be answered that a preceding inquiry, instituted in 1807,* before this measure, had revealed the same distress. Only it was true, that the maintenance of this traffic preserved to foreign colonies a disgraceful advantage to the detriment of those that abstained from it.

The English colonies, at the time of emancipation, received the advantages and endured the burdens of the system of reciprocal monopoly, known under the name of the *Colonial Compact.* Obliged to receive English products under the English flag, they carried to the mother country nearly the whole of their products, by favor of a prohibitory tariff. Colonial sugar especially paid a duty of 24*s.* *per quintal* only, while foreign sugar had to pay a duty of 63*s.* This tariff was not changed for ten years after emancipation; the first modification, in fact, was in 1844. Thus the whole period of apprenticeship, and the first six years of freedom, were passed under favor of a protective duty.

The average quantity of sugar imported annually from the West Indies † during the six years preceding emancipation had been 3,965,034 quintals.‡ During the four years of apprenticeship, it was 3,058,000 quintals; during the first year of freedom (1839), 2,824,000 quintals; during the

* See, in the same document, the Report of the Committee of 1807, p. 287.

† Speech of Lord Stanley, 1842.

‡ If we take the average of four years (1831-1834), it is only 3,841,837 quintals; if we take the average of twenty years (1814-1834), only 3,640,712 quintals. These averages are taken, in turn, as the standard in the official tables.

second (1840), 2,210,000 quintals; and during the third (1841), 2,151,117 quintals.

From this minimum the figures again ascended, and reached: —

In 1842	2,473,715 quintals.
1843	2,503,577 "
1844	2,444,811 "
1845	2,847,698 "

But under the influence of this diminution of quantity, the prices rose from 119 fr. 50 c. in 1831, and 134 fr. 70 c. in 1834, successively to 143 fr. 90 c., 162 fr., and even to 185 fr. 60 c. in 1840.

So that the gross income of the colonies increased, since, according to the calculations of Lord Stanley, the sale produced, during the six years prior to emancipation, an average of 26,600,000 fr.; for the four years' apprenticeship, 31,115,000 fr.; for the first year of freedom, 32,650,000 fr.; and for the second year of freedom, 29,120,000 fr.

In his memorable report of 1843 on the colonial questions in France,* M. Broglie presents the same calculations, with other elaborations, which he sums up as follows: —

"A reduction of *one fourth* in the importation of sugar produced by slave colonies, a reduction of *one third* in the importation of rum and coffees; — such are the facts which at present correspond to the introduction of free labor into these colonies.

"The colonists, taken as a whole, have received the indemnity, sold at a higher price, and obtained a gross revenue superior to that which they obtained before."

If we examine the production of each colony, we see that at Mauritius, where immigration was, and continued to be, in great activity, the figures were, from the first year of freedom, higher than before.

* P. 28.

SLAVERY.

1814–1834 . . . . 538,954 quintals.

APPRENTICESHIP.

1835–1838 . . . . 549,872 quintals.
1839 . . . . . . 618,705 "
1810 . . . . 545,007 "
1841 . . . . . . 696,652 "
1842 . . . . 676,237 "
1843 . . . . . . 477,124 "
1844 . . . . 540,515 "
1845 . . . . . . 716,338 "

Almost all the loss falls on Jamaica, Guiana, Grenada, St. Vincent, and Tobago. On the contrary, Antigua, Barbadoes, Dominica, St. Christopher, St. Lucia, and Trinidad are progressing. At Montserrat, Nevis, and Tortola the statistics are unimportant.

But during the same time the production of the East Indies rises from 109,596 quintals to 1,103,181 quintals.

Here is the general table: —

Places of Importation.	Period of Slavery, 1831–1834.	Period of Apprenticeship, 1835–1838.	Period of of Liberty, 1839–1845.	1846.	1847.
	Quintals.	Quintals.	Quintals.	Quintals.	Quintals.
Antigua	180,802	143,878	189,406	102,644	249,201
Barbadoes	356,254	409,354	314,501	302,496	469,022
Dominica	54,214	35,660	45,497	52,700	65,451
Grenada	193,156	161,308	87,161	76,931	104,952
Jamaica	1,343,506	1,040,070	646,255	572,883	751,416
Montserrat	22,283	11,032	11,842	5,316	7,657
Nevis	47,950	28,510	26,523	26,714	41,833
St. Christopher	92,079	79,823	101,336	91,022	149,096
St. Lucia	57,549	51,427	57,070	63,566	88,370
St. Vincent	204,095	194,228	127,364	129,870	175,615
Tobago	99,579	89,332	52,962	38,822	69,240
Tortola	16,863	12,036	6,180	6,786	8,285
Trinidad	316,338	295,787	292,023	353,293	393,537
The Bahamas	4	175	832	3,356	
Guiana	857,165	935,849	542,907	325,756	635,622
Total average	3,841,837	3,508,469	2,501,859	2,152,155	3,209,297
Mauritius	536,134	549,872	618,906	845,304	1,193,849
East Indies	109,596	244,630	1,103,181	1,425,114	1,418,682

We are astonished at the disparity of the figures; we had expected to see the same cause produce everywhere the same effects. If they differ, it is probable that they are not all due to the same cause. In fact, on entering into details, we ascertain that the diminution of one fourth in the products is explained, apart from the influence of emancipation, by a succession of bad seasons, the abandonment of numerous plantations by the owners themselves, encumbered with debts or discouraged, the absolute lack of capital or credit wherewith to pay wages, and the unfriendly behavior of many of the planters, especially at Jamaica, towards their former slaves, as much as by the tendency of the latter to go to dwell in towns and to form villages.*

Taking general results, we see, therefore, that, in 1845, that is, during the first ten years of freedom, production was not ruined in the English colonies by the emancipation of the slaves. It increased in a few, and diminished in a few others. The total average reduction was one fourth.

But wealth results much less from the quantity produced than from the net cost and selling price of the product.

Now has the net cost been raised by emancipation? Probably it has; nevertheless, this point is strongly contested, especially in so far as it concerns Jamaica. Is it really true that wages have attained an exorbitant rate?† If this be true, what are we to blame for it?

* Report of M. de Broglie, pp. 30 – 42.

† The opinion of Lord Elgin, Governor of Jamaica, in his report of 1846, is as follows: "I cannot admit that the rate of wages has been exorbitant; except in a few instances where the scale has been established by the planters themselves, labor has never cost more than 1*s.* 6*d.* per day." At Barbadoes, wages were 10*d.* per day; at Antigua, from 9*d.* to 1*s.*; at St. Christopher, 1*s.* 4*d.*; at Guiana, 1*s.* 4*d.*; at Trinidad, 2*s.* 1*d.*; in the small colonies, 6*d.* (*Revue coloniale*, 1843, p. 13.) It must not be forgotten that distress and complaints in Jamaica are of long standing. From 1772 to 1792, 177 estates were sold for debt, 55 abandoned, 92 occupied by creditors, and the clerk's office had witnessed the record of 80,121 executions. In 1807, 65 plantations had been abandoned during the past six years. In 1812, the Assembly declared to the king, that "the distress was so great that it could no longer increase." "Ruin is imminent," wrote the

Is it the desertion of labor that has caused wages to rise? Is it the lack of money to pay them? Is it the folly of planters who have accorded exorbitant wages in order to monopolize laborers? Is it the ill-will of other planters, who have estranged the free negroes, especially by exacting high rents for the cabins and gardens of which they had peaceable possession, or by paying them irregularly for their labor? We will grant that all these causes have acted at once; there is no doubt that, under their disastrous influence, the lack of hands and the lack of money, the net cost at first increased perceptibly, and a considerable number of proprietors were reduced to the necessity of ceasing cultivation. But in any case this excessive rise did not last long, and after a few years the *net cost* diminished by degrees, especially in the colonies where the immigration of new laborers aroused competition with the freed negroes.

By way of compensation (and herein doubtless lay the chief cause of the distress of the English colonies) the *selling price*, — also very high during the first years, as we have seen, since it rose in 1840 to 185 fr. 60 c. per metrical quintal, a price which had not been reached since 1815, — the *selling price* fell, despite the progress of consumption, in proportion as the introduction of foreign sugars came to compete with colonial sugars in the market of the mother country; the high prices attracted this competition, and the changes in the tariff opened the door to its admission.

It may be affirmed that, if the same protective tariff had secured the sale of colonial sugar at high prices a few years longer, production would have rapidly revived, and the colonists would have really had nothing of which to complain.

But this was precisely the epoch at which England en-

planters to Parliament in 1832. Such was the position of affairs under the system of slavery, monopoly, and premiums. (*Revue coloniale*, 1847, XII. p. 281; XIII. p. 317.)

tered upon the path of her great economical reforms. In studying the results of the emancipation of the slaves in the English colonies in the point of view of production, it is proper not to forget these most important facts, which complicate investigations.

England attempted two bold experiments at the same time,—the freedom of slaves and the freedom of trade. These two kinds of freedom passed from public opinion into Parliament, from books into the laws, from minds into facts, almost at the same moment. It was from 1820 to 1831 that commercial liberty was personified in Mr. Huskisson, and it was in 1823 that Mr. Buxton made the first motion for the abolition of slavery. When, after the death of George IV. and the accession of William IV. (June, 1830), Lord Grey came into office with the Whigs, the commercial reform made new progress in 1831 and 1832, and it was precisely in 1831 that Mr. Robinson, called to power by Mr. Canning with Mr. Huskisson, and become Lord Goderich, proposed the emancipation of the slaves belonging to the crown, and in 1833 Lord Stanley presented the Emancipation Bill in the House of Commons.

From the beginning, the most ardent partisans of commercial liberty had proposed an exception in favor of the products of the colonies, — an exception justified by the social crisis through which they had to pass, and moreover by the propriety of not encouraging the slave-trade and slavery, after having done so much to abolish them. When a celebrated radical, Deacon Hume, proposed in 1840 an inquiry upon the tariffs of importation, he himself declared that this exception was equitable and necessary.

But the impulse in favor of commercial freedom daily became more irresistible, and the Abolitionist opinion itself was divided. The question was indeed curiously complicated. Interests were not less divided than opinions.

The colonies had need, on the one hand, of *commercial*

freedom, in order to buy at a lower price the products furnished them by England, and, on the other, of *protection*, in order to sell at a higher price, and thus indemnify themselves for the losses which had naturally followed emancipation.

England owed protection to these distant communities which it had just shaken to the centre, and at the same time owed cheap living to its internal population. It was asked wherefore the planters of Jamaica, already indemnified, deserved more favor than the agriculturists and freeholders of Great Britain, who were greatly affected by the corn-laws; wherefore the negroes of Barbadoes or Essequibo deserved more interest than the indigent laborers of Manchester or Bolton; now the one needed that sugar should be at a high price, the others that it should be at a low price.

England wished to multiply exchanges, but it could not do this without opening its territory to the products of the entire universe; yet, notwithstanding, to favor slave labor was to contradict the lofty views which had inspired the great Act of Emancipation.

The treasury, deprived of considerable revenues by commercial reforms, needed to regain new resources by the increase of consumption; but the ruin of the colonies menaced it on the other side with graver losses.

There was not a single one of the interests involved in this complicated question that was not in contradiction with itself, and such great difficulties explain the waverings of public opinion. Nevertheless, Parliament and public opinion held firm in the debate in favor of the colonies.

When, in the beginning of 1841, the Whig Cabinet proposed to lower the duty on foreign sugar * from 63*s*. to 36*s*., the committee of the British and Foreign Antislavery Society energetically protested against it, and demanded a postponement at least. The West India Corporation

* We speak only of sugar, since this is the principal product.

protested on its side by a long petition ; but in a general convention of the Abolitionists,* on the 14th of May, the Assembly, drawn on by O'Connell, loudly declared that free labor was less expensive than slave labor, that there was no reason to fear competition, and that, in the interest of emancipation itself, it was desirable that Great Britain, in multiplying her relations with slave states, should preserve over them the influence of her policy.

Other orators demanded that the government should reduce the duties on sugar produced by free labor, whether foreign or colonial, but should continue to exclude sugar produced by *servile* labor. The Abolitionists were thus divided into three opinions upon the one question.

The same dissensions were manifested when the question was carried to the House of Commons.

Lord John Russell, Lord Palmerston, Mr. Labouchère, Mr. Hume, and Mr. Macaulay sustained the project of the Chancellor of the Exchequer, Mr. Baring.

Lord John Russell drew an ingenious parallel between the condition of the freed negroes, numbering 5,800 small freeholders at Jamaica, peaceable and happy at Barbadoes, laborious and moral at Antigua, filling the churches and schools at Guiana, erecting chapels at their own expense and providing for the wants of their sick at Trinidad, and the wretched life of the workingmen of the manufacturing towns of England, exposed to famine or beggary. "We have done all that our generosity permitted us to do," said he, "for the inhabitants of these distant regions. I do not believe that we are justified in making their interests the object of our exclusive attention, when the people are suffering in this country, and lacking the most imperative necessaries of life."

Mr. Labouchère showed the consumption rising or falling with the rise or fall of prices.

* Abstract, etc., III. p. 513.

Price of Sugar.		Consumption.
1836	40*s*. 9*d*.	16.58 lbs. per head.
1837	34*s*. 5*d*.	18.38 "
1838	33*s*. 7*d*.	18.42 "
1839	39*s*. 4*d*.	17.00 "
1840	48*s*. 7*d*.	15.28 "

Mr. Hume recalled the fact, that the sale of tea and coffee had increased 80 per cent in twenty years (1820–1840), thanks to the diminution of the price, while the consumption of sugar had increased but 15 per cent, by reason of the high price.

Mr. Macaulay exclaimed pungently: "What sort of a principle of morality, humanity, and justice is this, which permits us to dress ourselves in the cotton and inhale the tobacco produced by slave labor, and forbids the addition of sugar and coffee arising from the same source?"

"The Brazilian slave," said Lord John Russell before, "will find himself no happier because the fruit of his labor will be consumed by Germans instead of Englishmen."

Lord Stanley replied, that, if a million quintals of Brazilian sugar should take the place of a million quintals of colonial sugar, foreign slave labor would be evidently encouraged, and English free labor discouraged; and that the prosperity of the colonies should not be destroyed at the very moment when it was affirmed that it was reviving.

Sir Robert Peel won over the House by a speech worthy of a statesman.

"I am concerned," said he, "about the moral and social condition of your empire, where you have just attempted the greatest, the most hazardous, and, I admit with lively satisfaction, the most happy reform of which the civilized world could offer an example, and I cannot disguise from myself the consequences which may ensue in these countries, still shaken by so violent a concussion, from the adoption of a measure which would be equivalent to the impossibility of continuing there the cultivation of sugar. . . . . .

"If our colonies were not sufficient for our supply, we should be obliged to raise the prohibition; but in time the East Indies will make up the deficiency of the West Indies. . . . . . But the East Indies are in fearful distress, desolated by famine, pestilence, and want; wages there are 2½*d.* per day, the laborer lives on rice, and dies when rice fails him.

"Now when we reflect that the English nation is responsible for the moral and physical lot of these populations, can it be alleged that considerations of a higher order oblige us to prefer the sugar obtained by the slave labor of Cuba to the production of this national country, whose inhabitants are dying with hunger for lack of work?

"You are told that it is necessary to furnish to free labor an occasion of proving its superiority over slave labor. . . . . But is this a moment for our colonies to sustain such a struggle, when emerging from the crisis which they have just passed through?

"If the desire of having cheap sugar leads you to protect slave labor, say so once for all, and foreign nations will understand you; but do not say that it is your intention, by admitting products of this origin, to destroy the slave-trade and slavery, for no one in the world will believe you.

"It is pretended that the conduct of foreign nations does not concern us, that we should not set ourselves up as reformers of humanity. . . . . . I reject this selfish doctrine, in the name of the nation. We have dearly bought the right to speak to the peoples of earth with authority on this question; let us not descend from the high position which we have taken in offering ourselves as an example to nations."

The amendment of Lord Sandon against the ministerial scheme was passed May 18, 1841, by 317 votes against 281, and the duty on foreign sugar was not lowered.

The same efforts were renewed the following year, both in and out of Parliament.

In a new general convention of the Abolitionists,* which held twelve sessions at London, some (of whom Mr. Cobden was one) repeated that, by diminishing the duties, the prices would be diminished, and the consumption, and consequently the production, increased. Others maintained that the admission of foreign sugars would complete the ruin of the English colonies, and encourage servile labor at Cuba and Brazil.

These last arguments again prevailed in Parliament at the sequel of two extended inquiries, prescribed by the two Houses.†

The equalizing of the duties on sugars of every origin, demanded by Mr. Ewart, and the reduction of the duties on foreign sugars to 34*s.* (the colonial sugars paid 24*s.*) proposed by Mr. Hawes, and combated by Sir Robert Peel, were also rejected by a majority of more than thirty votes.

Notwithstanding, the commercial treaty with Brazil, which secured to this country the treatment of the most favored nations, expiring in November, 1844, and the production of the English colonies reviving but slowly, the Tory ministry resolved to attack Parliament by another tariff bill.‡

It adopted the idea put forward by the Abolitionists, of making a distinction between free and servile labor, and admitting the products of the first while continuing to exclude those of the second. From November 1, 1844, English colonial sugars were to pay 24*s.* per quintal; sugars produced by free labor, 34*s.*; all others, 63*s.*§

Defended by Sir Robert Peel and Mr. Gladstone, this tariff was adopted on the 17th of June by a majority of twenty-two votes.

This law, logical and moral in appearance, was imprac-

* *Revue coloniale*, 1843, p. 14.

† Abstract, published by the Secretary of the Navy, Vol. III.

‡ *Revue coloniale*, 1844, III. pp. 193, 271, 423, 547.

§ Coffees of every production were admitted with the same duty (Tariff of June 17, 1844).

ticable and defective. How was it possible to distinguish between certain free countries and certain slave countries? Java, Siam, Manilla, and China were pointed out as the former; * but a system of compulsory labor differing little from servitude prevails at Java, while in China and Siam are polygamy, the sale of children, and other crimes more heinous than slavery.

How refer to certificates of origin? How excommunicate sugars and receive coffees? The total consumption of the world being equal to its total production, to close England to the sugar of Brazil was to open to this sugar other markets, to change the market and not the tariff, to dissatisfy a great country, and displease without injuring it. Lord John Russell avenged himself for his defeat of 1840 by heaping censure on the new bill, "which," he said, "established a pulpit in every custom-house," and predicting that its partisans would find it impossible to stop at it, but would be forced to return to the reduction which he had proposed four years before, and even to exceed this after having opposed it.

The colonies and West India Corporation complained by forcible addresses, and uttered cries of distress in advance. In the protest of Jamaica was remarked the first wish for commercial freedom. The tariff satisfied no one, and encountered inextricable difficulties in its application.

On the 14th of February, 1845, Sir Robert Peel proposed a new tariff, reducing the duty on English sugars from 24*s.* to 14*s.* for raw sugars, and from 24*s.* to 16*s.* for clayed sugars, and the duty on foreign *free* sugars from 34*s.* 6*d.* to 23*s.* 4*d.* for raw sugars, and from 34*s.* to 28*s.* for clayed sugars. This was a reduction of from 6*s.* to 10*s.* on both, leaving a differential duty of from 9*s.* to 11*s.* in favor of the colonies. The exclusion of *slave* sugars was maintained.

* A treaty connected England with the United States; but it is known that this nation consumes more than 50,000 tons of sugar beyond what it produces.

It was calculated that the consumer would gain 16 c. per pound by this tariff, and that the treasury would lose by it 32,500,000 francs.* This law is dated March 7, 1845. In the following three months, the consumption increased almost double, — an increase which was due, moreover, rather to the growth of comfort, than to the fall or introduction of foreign sugar; for very little was brought in, the prices were maintained, and the colonial producers profited almost entirely by the reduction.† The partisans of free trade could therefore maintain, with some reason, that a larger reduction might be attempted. On their side, the representatives of the colonies justly complained of the continual changes of tariffs, and begun to propound the question in its true terms; — either absolute monopoly or absolute liberty; protect our products, or free us from the obligation of receiving yours.

On returning to power, the Whig ministry proposed, July 20, 1846,‡ through the organ of Sir John Russell, a new tariff on the following bases: —

The maintenance of the duty of 14*s.* on English sugars;

The gradual reduction of the duty on foreign sugars;

The complete equality of duties from July 5, 1851;

No distinction between *free* sugar and *slave* sugar.

This was an economical revolution from the threefold stand-point of the interest of the colonies, the interest of the treasury, and the interest of emancipation.

The new leader of the Tory party, Lord George Bentinck, so suddenly restored to public life, from which he was about to be as suddenly snatched by death, the old representative of religious interests, Sir Robert Inglis, and the witty and fiery orator, Mr. D'Israeli, attacked the bill with rare vivacity in the House of Commons; but the solid

* *Revue coloniale*, 1845, V. p. 183; VI. p. 125.

† *Ibid.*, 1846, VIII. p. 294.

‡ *Ibid.*, IX. p. 280.

speeches of Lord John Russell and Lord Grey, and, above all, the imposing and unexpected authority of Sir Robert Peel in favor of a measure entirely different from the laws which he had himself proposed, carried the vote by a majority of a hundred and thirty voices.

In the House of Lords, where Lord Brougham presented a petition of the aged Clarkson against the law, and opposed it with the co-operation of Lord Stanley and the Bishop of Oxford, it was passed by a majority of eighteen voices, through the influence of Lord Clarendon.

If we dare venture on a decision among opinions sustained by such defenders, it seems as if both sides were partly right and partly wrong.

It is clear that, by permitting Cuban and Brazilian sugars to compete with the sugars of the West Indies, compulsory labor was encouraged and free labor discouraged.

"Some three slaves are employed in producing a hogshead of sugar," said Sir Robert Inglis, forcibly; "these three slaves are the survivors of nine Africans torn from their country. Thus, for every ton of sugar of this production imported into England, the House will have caused the capture, massacre, or sufferings of nine of our fellow-beings, and these, multiplied by 20,000, the number of hogsheads expected to be imported, produce a total of 180,000 individuals, on whom a Christian assembly will have, in cold blood, inflicted the greatest possible injury."

"The nation which has made a gift to humanity of £20,000,000, will consent, in pursuance of the same end, to pay a penny a pound more for its sugar, and this humble tribute will be pleasing to God," exclaimed Lord George Bentinck.

But, to favor the products of the colonies, it was necessary to protect them by a high duty against *all* competition It was truly chimerical to make a distinction between free sugar and slave sugar, yet receive cotton from the United

States and copper from Cuba. "Lord Stanley's opinions on this matter," said Lord Clarendon, wittily, "are like a thermometer; they rise to boiling heat when sugar from Cuba is in question, and fall to the freezing-point when the question is of cotton from South Carolina."

If England had broadly accepted the principles of commercial freedom at this very hour, an exception of a few years in favor of sugar would have been comprehensible. This had been until then maintained by the illustrious promoter of the Corn Laws, Sir Robert Peel.

"What!" it was said, "have you not promised that free labor should cost less than compulsory labor?" "Yes," replied Lord Brougham, justly, "all circumstances being equal; but they are not so. Take two countries, both placed in the same habitual conditions of climate and territory, and place slaves in the one and freemen in the other: there is not the least doubt that free labor will stifle slave labor in the end, the freeman laboring with more interest and intelligence. But this is not the case here; the struggle is between a country which possesses free labor, without having recourse to any means of keeping up the supply, and another which employs compulsory labor, renewing it through the slave-trade."

A protection continued a few years longer would have been, therefore, a just exception. At least, it would have been prudent not to adopt a tariff which, through the difference of net cost, created a veritable advantage in favor of Brazilian sugars.*

But if the Whig ministry had decided on this exception, the Tory ministry, on returning to power, would have overthrown the new commercial policy entire; it was better to renounce the exception, — this was the fear and the argument of Sir Robert Peel. Mr. D'Israeli warmly reproached him for sacrificing the colonial empire, £50,000,000, the

* See the calculations of M. Colquhoun, *Revue coloniale*, 1846, X. p. 214.

most sacred principles, and his own convictions, to the question as to who would be seated in eight days on the ministerial benches. But the majority, composed of the Whigs and the wrecks of the Tory party, followed Sir Robert Peel.

At least they should have been logical, and gone to the full extent of liberty by breaking the colonial compact. This was demanded, in a sensible and courageous speech, by a colonist, M. Bernal. "It is my firm design," said he, "to redouble activity and energy, to triumph over competition. The times and men belong wholly to freedom of trade; it is in vain that the colonists seek to resist it. . . . . . But is it just that the colonies, whose interests are sacrificed to these principles, should not be permitted to profit by the advantages which this freedom can secure to them?"

From this day, these prayers became more ardent and more definite in the publications of the colonists and the protests of the colonies.* The unlimited freedom of the ports, the full liberty of immigration, loans for its encouragement, the entrance of the spirituous liquors of the colonies under the same duty as those fabricated in the mother country, the free use of sugar in English breweries and refineries, the abolition of entrance duties on colonial products imported into all other English possessions, — such was thenceforth the programme of the demands of the colonies.

"I think," Sir Robert Peel had said, "that, the bill once passed, the Cabinet will not lose sight of its rigorous duty of furnishing to the colonists the means of sustaining the competition which has been aroused against them." This counsel was followed.

On the 22d of January, 1847, the Chancellor of the Exchequer, Mr. Wood, proposed the reduction of the duty on spirituous liquors, and the free use of sugar in refineries instead of malt.†

* *Revue coloniale*, X. pp. 214, 231.

† *Ibid.*, 1847, XI. p. 75. The experiments made at this time proved that

But such had been the effect of the sudden reduction of duties which unfortunately coincided with a year of drought, that the exportation of the East Indies fell from 2,911,503 quintals in 1845, to 2,422,573 ; to this diminution of 500,000 quintals corresponded a fall from 146 fr. 80 c. to 118 fr. 50 c., and even to 107 francs. The colonies multiplied meetings, memorials, and petitions ; the Chamber of Commerce of Kingston convoked an assembly of delegates from all the colonies at the island of St. Thomas.* The Governors called the attention of government to the universal distress and alarm of the inhabitants. Agitation took possession of England, and when, February 7, 1848, Lord George Bentinck proposed the formation of a committee to inquire into the state of public opinion, the Cabinet did not oppose the proposition.

The committee, by its report dated May 29, 1848, recommended the establishment, for six years, of a protective duty in favor of colonial sugar.†

Lord John Russell opposed this project, and, with a bold logic, taking a step forward towards commercial freedom, instead of the step backward that was proposed, presented a bill, which was adopted, and of which the following were the bases : —

1. A new reduction of duties on colonial sugars from 24*s.* to 13*s.*, and eventually to 10*s.*, without a corresponding diminution for foreign sugars. 2. The equality of duties for all sugars, fixed at 10*s.*, from July 1, 1854. 3. The opening of a loan of £500,000 in favor of the colonies.

This was a momentary protection, and a large encouragement to consumption, ending at a fixed date in free competition. The loan was to serve thenceforth to favor the

sugar could be mixed with malt, or even combined alone with hops, without injuring the quality of the beer.

* *Revue coloniale*, 1847, XII. p. 463; 1847, XIII. p. 335.

† *Ibid.*, 1848, 1849, I. p. 6.

immigration of new laborers; but immigration by means of redemption remained positively interdicted, as Lord John Russell, Mr. Labouchère, and Sir Robert Peel affirmed with a common voice.

A last effort was attempted, May 3, 1850, by the Abolitionist party, aided by the Protectionist party. Sir E. Buxton proposed to the House of Commons to "declare that it was unjust and impolitic to expose the sugar of the British colonies to competition with the sugar of slave countries."

Mr. Hume proposed to add, that the government "should put an end to the difficulties which hindered the colonies from procuring *free* laborers in Africa or elsewhere."

Sir John Pakington and Mr. Gladstone again maintained that colonial commerce should form an exception to the principles of free exchange. But the Chancellor of the Exchequer repeated to Mr. Buxton, that all distinction between the product of free labor and that of servile labor was impracticable. He added, that the competition of servile labor in the English market was inconsiderable and constantly decreasing.†

He showed that, in spite of exaggerated fears, the importation of West Indian sugar had increased enormously during ten years.‡ He congratulated himself, above all,

* *Revue coloniale*, 1850, IV. p. 335.

† 1846, 1847,	Colonial sugar	227,000 tons.
" "	Sugar of slave countries	61,000 "
1840–1850,	Colonial sugar	282,000 "
" "	Sugar of slave countries	36,000 "

	1840–1844.	1845–1849.
‡ Antigua	177,727 quintals.	180,737 quintals.
Barbadoes	290,873 "	402,927 "
Trinidad	282,000 "	385,000 "
St. Christopher	89,000 "	107,000 "
St. Lucia	55,000 "	70,000 "
Guiana	522,000 "	572,000 "
Jamaica	602,000 "	665,000 "
Mauritius	591,000 "	907,000 "
East Indies	3,925,000 "	5,072,000 "

that the consumption of sugar in England was rising from year to year.*

Such results, and the general tendency of politics at this moment, left to the proposition small chance of success. It was rejected by a majority of forty-one votes.

From this moment, the application of the system of commercial freedom to the colonies was irrevocably won. Its enemies counted vainly on the return to public affairs of a protectionist minister, who was assailed with petitions. Fate decreed that each of the ancient adversaries of freedom should arrive successively at power, and that each should make his retraction. On the 12th of March, 1842, Sir John Pakington, then Minister of the Colonies, refused to discuss a petition and motion tending to the revision of the tariff of sugars.† The most earnest complaints of the colonies, and a curious petition from the negroes, complaining of being the victims of the legislation of 1846,‡ remained without effect on Mr. D'Israeli. Become Chancellor of the Exchequer, he made, December 3, 1852, this decisive declaration : § —

"Since last year, English production has increased 1,250,000 quintals, and foreign production has decreased 600,000 quintals. Call me traitor, call me renegade, if you will, but I should like to know if there is a single member of this assembly, to whatever bench he may belong, that would be willing to propose a differential duty to sustain a branch of trade, pretended to be languishing, which at this moment dictates the law for the market of the mother country."

*	1840	15 lbs. per head.
	1841-1844	17 "
	1845	20 "
	1846	21 "
	1847	23 "
	1848-1849	24 "

† *Revue coloniale*, 1853, X. p. 386.

‡ *Ibid.*, 1852, VIII. p. 459.

§ *Ibid.*, 1852, IX. pp. 156, 310.

Become in turn Chancellor of the Exchequer, Mr. Gladstone replied, April 18, 1853, to the demand for a reduction on colonial sugars: * "It is quite impossible for the government to entertain the slightest hope that the demand will be received."

The year 1852 thus saw all sugars attain the same tax, and all parties rally to the same opinion.

Nothing more was left to the colonies than to invoke for themselves the principle of commercial freedom, and to deal the last blows to the dismantled edifice of the colonial compact. Their wishes agreed on this point with the doctrines of the free-tradists, and it was by the logical coalition of their efforts that, in June, 1849, was obtained the repeal of the *Navigation Laws*, beginning from January 1, 1850. This most important measure, almost immediately adopted by Sweden, Holland, and Belgium, and in part by the United States, had to encounter the ardent opposition of the ports; † but it resulted in lowering the freight, and was thus a perceptible relief to the colonies.

Other measures, which it would take too long to detail, were taken to suppress the custom duties of entry of the colonies, and, twenty years after freedom of labor had been proclaimed, freedom of products and freedom of transportation appeared as its result. It is at this date that we should take our stand to ascertain what has been the influence of those two great events — the act of 1834 and the bill of 1846 — on colonial production.

The progress of the consumption of sugar in England from 1801 to 1858 was enormous.§

The average from 1801 to 1814 was 1,423,759 metrical

* *Revue coloniale*, 1853, X. p. 80.

† *Ibid.*, 1851, VI. p. 461. See especially the speech of Lord Granville, p. 470, and the Letters of Mr. Lindsay, VII. pp. 68, 192, 437.

‡ *Histoire de la réforme commerciale en Angleterre*, by Henri Richelot. Letters of Lord Grey on the Colonial Policy, *Revue coloniale*, June, 1860.

§ Annals of Outside Trade, March, 1860, pp. 44, 45.

quintals, of 51 kilogrammes. It rose to about 2,000,000 metrical quintals in the ten years which preceded emancipation (1824 – 1834), and continued to stand at nearly the same figure during the ten years which followed it (1834 – 1844). Under the influence of the reduction of tariffs, it attained ten years after, in 1854, 4,166,203 metrical quintals. In 1859, lastly, it amounted to 4,510,000 metrical quintals.

On comparing this progress with the growth of the population,* we ascertain the average quantity of sugar consumed per head, which in 1814 was 8 kilogrammes 900 grammes, to be, in 1854, 15 kilogrammes 850 grammes.†

The treasury has found its account in this progress, by reason of the lowering of tariffs. Instead of 63*s.* per quarter on foreign sugar, and 24*s.* per quarter on colonial sugar, it now receives but 10*s.* per quarter, whatever the production; yet notwithstanding, its receipts, the maximum of which had been, under the old tariff, 125,000,000 fr. in 1828, and 130,000,000 fr. in 1844, fell below 100,000,000 francs after the reform of 1846, only to rise again erelong, and to attain 153,000,000 fr. in 1859, a figure which it had never exceeded.

	fr.	c.	
During this time the average price of the metrical quintal,‡ which was (including duties) . .	185	60	in 1814
had risen to	231	0	" 1815

* 1814 . . . . 17,256,000 inhabitants.
1858 . . . . 28,681,000 "

† The consumption of tea has followed a corresponding and still greater progression. It was 10,678,568 kil. in 1801. In 1858, it attained 32,860,355 kil. The proportion was 0.608 kil. per head in 1801, and 1.014 kil. per head in 1858.

‡ Price in entrepôts: —

	fr.	c.
1814	120	40
1824	78	10
1834	73	70
1844	83	90
1854	53	0
1858	69	50

	fr.	c.		
and stood afterwards at	166	0	in	1825
	134	30	"	1835
	146	80	"	1845
This same price fell, after the reforms, to . . .	85	40	"	1848
and even reached the minimum of	79	50	"	1853
to remain a very little time under 100 fr., standing at	103	10	"	1858

Thus, in England, all have been gainers; first, the consumer, then even the treasury.* The producer has also been the gainer, since he receives a less profit, but on a greater quantity and with a lower duty.

But what producer has profited by this progress? Is it not the foreign producer? Has not the colonial producer been sacrificed to him?

The answer requires that, instead of considering the quantities *consumed,* we should take account of the quantities *imported,* both for consumption and for re-exportation, and that we should distinguish between the different productions.†

Doubtless *foreign* sugar has the largest share in the growth of consumption in England, and how can we be surprised at it, since the almost prohibitive impost which burdened it has been lowered from 63*s.* to 10*s.* per quarter? Until the first reduction, the importation of *foreign*

* The custom-house system of England is so well combined, and wealth is so widely diffused in this country, that the revenue of the customs attained 626,000,000 fr. in 1859; and of this amount, four articles of luxury — sugar, tea, tobacco, and wine — produced more than five sixths, the rest not exceeding 89,000,000 fr.

Sugar	153,000,000 fr.
Tea	135,000,000
Tobacco	139,000,000
Wines and brandies	110,000,000
Total	537,000 000 fr.

† We borrow these figures from the remarkable work of Henri Richelot, *Histoire de la réforme commerciale en Angleterre,* Vol. II. pp. 484, 485. The author has been kind enough to communicate to us the unpublished statistics which complete his tables for the years prior to 1851. (See Appendix.)

sugar, despite the abolition of slavery, despite the progress of the population and of consumption, made but slow progress. In 1831, it was 507,547 quintals; in 1835, it fell below 200,000, and rose again to 777,900 quintals in 1844. After the reform of 1846, the importation of foreign sugar attained, in 1847, 2,408,981 quintals, fell back in 1852 to 1,058,961 quintals, but to double, then triple, and amount in 1858 to 3,630,915 quintals, more than seven times the figure of 1831.

The progress of the East Indies has been almost as rapid. They represented but 296,679 quintals in 1837, and amounted to 1,585,430 quintals in 1851, the amount having more than quintupled. The quantity has diminished under the influence of the recent events, but was still 1,181,368 quintals in 1857, and 794,309 quintals in 1858.

We find the same progress in the island of Mauritius. Its production did not much exceed 500,000 quintals before emancipation; ten years after (1844) it was the same; ten years later (1854) it amounted to 1,662,190 quintals, having tripled; since diminished, it remains above 1,000,000 quintals.

As to Guiana and the Antilles, as we have already said, the decrease of production, by reason of the abolition of slavery, was from one fourth to one half during the first ten years; but it had already so far revived at the end of this period, as to give serious reason to hope a speedy return to the former figure, when the tariff reform intervened.

In fact, the production in 1834 was 3,844,243 quintals; it had risen in 1845 to 2,854,010 quintals. At the same time, the price which was, including duty, 134 fr. 30 c. in 1834, rose to 143 fr., 162 fr., 167 fr., even to 185 fr. 60 c. during the first years, and was still 146 fr. 40 c. in 1845; so that the producers received more for a less quantity. The larger introduction of foreign sugar caused the importation to fall again in 1846 to 2,147,363 fr.; and it may be affirmed that, by not continuing a necessary protection a few years longer, the English government arrested the serious tendency to revival of colonial business. Notwithstanding, the complaints were exaggerated, for the production speedily returned to the figures of 1845, and higher. In 1847 it rose again to 3,199,821 quintals, attained 3,795,311 in 1848, and, remaining nearly at the same level, was still 3,499,171 quintals in 1858. Let us remember that the average was 3,640,712 quintals from 1814 to 1834; this is nearly the same figure.

It would be well to distinguish one by one the importations of the nineteen colonies; but, since 1852, the official tables of English commerce make no distinction of the share of the different West India islands in the general importation, only separating Guiana and the West Indies.

Now the statistics of 1852 still presented a great diminution at Jamaica. Guiana rose towards the figures anterior to 1834, and attained them in 1854. The increase was notable at Barbadoes and Trinidad; at Antigua, St. Vincent, and Grenada there was almost a parity between the two epochs; and the importation had increased, taken as a whole, in the other small West-Indian possessions. (See the detailed table in the Appendix.)

In twenty-five years, the English colonies, after two ordeals as grave as the abolition of compulsory labor and that of the protective tariff, have returned to nearly the exact statistics of their production before these two ordeals. The first diminished the quantity produced, but raised the price; the second increased the quantity produced, but diminished the price. The second injured the colonies more than the first; but, without separating them, who could have believed in good faith that two such radical attempts would not have cost more dearly?

CHAPTER IV.

RESUME.

During the years which separated emancipation in the English possessions from emancipation in the colonies of France, the advocates of these colonies did not cease to repeat, some that England had acted from a selfish motive, in order to ruin all the other colonies by excluding their products from her market; others, that this great experiment had ended in failure. These two assertions, which mutually refute each other, are repeated to satiety in the United States; they are the commonplaces of every speech in favor of slavery.

The first is unjust, the second incorrect. It is by a voice from the United States that England has been most eloquently avenged for the reproach of selfishness.

"Other nations," exclaims Channing, in his admirable Letter to Clay (August 1, 1837) on the Annexation of Texas, "have acquired immortal glory by the heroic defence of their rights; but there never before has been an example of a nation which, disinterestedly, and in the midst of the greatest obstacles, has espoused the rights of others, the rights of those whose only claim was that of also being men, the rights of the most fallen of the human race. Great Britain, under the weight of an unparalleled debt, with overwhelming taxes, has contracted a new debt of $100,000,000 to give liberty, not to Englishmen, but to degraded Africans. This was not an act of policy, it was not the work of statesmen. Parliament has done nothing but to record the edict of the people. The English naiton, with one heart and one voice, under a powerful Christian impulse, and without distinction of rank, sex, party, or communion, has decreed the freedom of the slave. I know of no more sublime, more disinterested act related in history. In the course of ages, the maritime triumphs of England will occupy a narrower and narrower place in the annals of humanity. This moral triumph will fill a broader and more brilliant page."

Let us repeat it, to the eternal glory of England, the abolition of slavery was not a calculation, neither has it been a failure.

A social revolution has been attempted at once in nineteen countries, dispersed between the Caribbean Sea, the southern extremity of Africa, and the entrance to the Indian Ocean, having neither the same climate, nor the same institutions, nor the same social state, and placed many thousand leagues from the handful of legislators who wrote their fate in a daring law. In the most extended of these countries, Jamaica, 300,000 slaves were face to face with 35,000 whites. Since the commencement of this century, five formidable insurrections had spread incendiarism and slaughter, the last of which, only two years before emancipation, had been followed by the execution of more than five hundred negroes. Another, Guiana, occupied by only 16,000 whites, offered 6,400 square miles as a refuge to more than 80,000 negroes. "This event, so formidable at first sight," wrote M. de Broglie,* and we can repeat it seventeen years after him, "the summons to freedom of 800,000 slaves on the same day, at the same moment, has not caused in all the English colonies the tenth part of the disturbance ordinarily caused among the most civilized nations of Europe by the smallest political question that agitates minds ever so little."

* Report, p. 8.

The harm produced by emancipation is reduced to the incontestable ruin of a certain number of colonists, and the momentary and inevitable suffering of all. It is worthy of note that the colony which resisted most, Jamaica, suffered most. The colony which most promptly resigned itself, and made efforts to renew the methods, stock, and *personnel* of manufacture — Mauritius — scarcely suffered at all, and its wealth is to-day doubled, nearly tripled. The aggregate production of the other colonies has again reached the amount prior to 1834. There is no doubt that it would have surpassed it if the commercial reform had not complicated the results of the abolition of slavery.

But, while according to these evils the regret which they deserve, how compare them for an instant with the blessings which date from these two great measures for England, for the colonies themselves, and for humanity?

Nearly a million of men, women, and children have passed from the condition of cattle to the rank of rational beings. Numerous marriages have elevated the family above the mire of a nameless promiscuousness. Paternity has replaced illegitimacy. Churches and schools are opened. Religion, before mute, factious, or dishonored, has resumed its dignity and liberty. Men who had nothing have acquired property; lands which were waste have been occupied; inadequate populations have increased; detestable processes of culture and manufacture have been replaced by better;* a race reputed inferior, vicious, cruel,

* We speak of the progress which was not entered upon before emancipation, — the substitution of the plough for the hoe, the use of the harrow, the importation of machinery, the improvement in the planting of the cane, central mills, lastly, the surveying or laying down of railroads at Jamaica, Guiana, Barbadoes, and Trinidad. "The advantages resulting from the use of agricultural implements are incalculable," was written from Antigua in 1845. "The colony has already, this year, with less than 10,000 hands, gathered crops almost equal to those for which Bourbon has employed 30,000,000 laborers." — *Revue*

lascivious, idle, refractory to civilization, religion, and instruction, has shown itself honest, gentle, disposed to family life, accessible to Christianity, eager for instruction. Those of its members who have returned to vagrancy, sloth, and corruption are not a reproach to their race as much as to the servitude which had left them wallowing in their native ignorance and depravity; but these are the minority. The majority labor, and show themselves far superior to the auxiliaries which China and India sends to the colonists. In two words, wealth has suffered little, civilization has gained much; such is the balance-sheet of the English experiment.

By an indirect effect of the same event, the colonial policy is wholly transformed. The first statesmen of England have changed their opinion on the utility of the colonies and the manner of governing them. The freedom of labor has been followed by freedom of trade, and even by political freedom. Of all the reasons which caused the settlement of the colonies, — gold, the shipping, commerce, power, — a single one subsists, or at least prevails, — the interest of civilization. The colonies were destined for the wealth, they serve above all the greatness, of the mother country.

To whom reverts the honor of having abolished slavery in the English colonies?

The government, the different ministers, without distinction of party, did much. They may be reproached with two mistakes, — they did not take effective measures to secure labor during the first years; they did not continue long enough the protection necessary to colonial products; but they accorded a large indemnity, they facilitated credit, they kept a firm hand over immigration, that it should not degenerate into a new slave-trade; above all, they sent to

coloniale, 1845, p. 433. Similar facts have been pointed out in almost all the reports of the Governors to the English government. But it is necessary to be brief.

the colonies firm, conciliating, capable, and upright Governors, a Marquis of Sligo, a Carmichael Smyth, a Nicolay, an Elgin, worthy representatives of the Goderiches, the Glenelgs, the Stanleys, and the Greys.

But listen to this solemn testimony of the Duke de Broglie : * —

"We do too much honor, in fact, to the English government, and we would wrong her too much, in attributing the abolition of the slave-trade and the abolition of slavery on her part either to lofty views of wisdom and foresight or to Machiavellian combinations ; on this point, the English government has neither gone in advance of the times nor directed events ; it has limited itself to maintaining the *statu quo*, so long as it has not been forced from it ; it has resisted for fifteen years the abolition of the slave-trade, for twenty-five years the abolition of slavery ; it has defended all the intermediate positions step by step, and has only yielded, in each occasion, to necessity.

"We would also do too much honor to the philosophy and philanthropy of England in assigning them the chief part in this great enterprise. Philosophers and philanthropists have, doubtlessly, figured gloriously in the number of the combatants ; but it is the religious spirit which has borne the heat and burden of the day, and it is to this that reverts, before everything, the honor of success. *It is religion that has truly freed the negroes in the English colonies ;* it is this which raised up, in the beginning of the struggle, the Clarksons, the Wilberforces, Granville Sharps, and so many others, and armed them with indomitable courage and unshaken perseverance ; it is religion which has progressively formed, first in the nation, then in Parliament itself, that great Abolition party which goes on swelling from day to day, infiltrating itself, as it were, into all parties, calling them all, and the government first of all,

* Report, p. 117.

to account; and it is this party which, profiting during forty years by every event and every circumstance, successively carried the abolition of the slave-trade in 1807; inspired through its representatives, in 1815, the declarations of the Congress of Vienna, and later those of the Congress of Verona; dictated in 1823 the motion of Mr. Buxton, the resolutions of Mr. Canning, and the circular of Lord Bathurst; hurled in 1831 on the colonies the Order in Council of November 2, thus rendering the abolition of slavery inevitable in 1832, and the maintenance of apprenticeship impossible in 1838. . . . . .

"The Abolition party has been no more sparing of pains in the colonies than in the mother country; it has covered them with churches, chapels, missions, and congregations, belonging to all of the dissenting sects of England, thus exciting a salutary emulation in the clergy of the Established Church. In laboring to render emancipation necessary at London, it has labored to render it possible and easy in the West Indies; it has prepared the way, cleared and ploughed the soil, put aside or surmounted the obstacles. Ministers of the Established Church, Methodists of all sects, Presbyterians, Moravians, missionaries of the Society of London, priests of the Catholic Church, Baptist missionaries, all vying with each other, have penetrated into the workshops, bearing to the negroes the light and consolation of the Gospel, admitting to their various communions the different quarters of their respective abodes, placing themselves face to face with the masters as the protectors of the slaves, face to face with the civil authorities as intercessors for this oppressed class, and becoming by this means the masters of hearts, the arbiters of wishes, and the true guardians of the public order.

"There happens thus, in the English colonies, something analogous to what happened formerly in the Roman empire, when this empire was marching with giant strides towards its decline. Above a narrow, antiquated, oppressive community, constituted solely for the profit of the ruling class, has been formed, by the cares and under the protection of the ministers of religion, a Christian community, composed solely of the weak, the poor, and the oppressed; a community still ignorant, but progressive, and which was found standing, when the hour of affranchisement sounded, ready to fall into its ranks, and recognize the voice of its leaders."

But how have religious men set to work to win so magnificent a victory? I will leave the answer to one of the most illustrious soldiers of the same cause in France, Count de Montalembert.

"Cast a glance on the immortal lessons given us by England! See these four victories, as difficult as legitimate, which have been won there in less than twenty years, without revolution, without subversion, *without costing a single drop of blood,* without causing any other tears than those of joy to flow, solely by the natural working of those admirable institutions which we possess in part, although we know not how to use them.

"These four victories are: —

"1. Catholic Emancipation (1829);

"2. Parliamentary Reform (1830);

"3. The Abolition of Slavery (1833);

"4. Freedom of the Corn Trade (1846).

"Let it be remarked, that none of these pacific victories, which we point out with envy and admiration to our fellow-citizens, has inflicted excessive or lasting injury on the vanquished cause. The Anglican Church has regained new life since Catholic emancipation; the aristocracy has risen up more strongly than ever since the abolition of the rotten boroughs, and we may be sure that English agriculture will lose nothing by the abolition of its monopoly; in ten years, no one will doubt it. It is the peculiarity of lawful and pure victories not to drive to despair, not to crush, not even to humiliate the vanquished.

"Admire, above all, the peaceful and sublime memory of *the abolition of colonial slavery.* Therein was at stake only a great moral interest, a reform to be won slowly and laboriously over the most deeply-rooted habits and inveterate prejudices: — it has triumphed. Far from bringing back any material profit, this reparation of the greatest of iniquities was to cost the English nation £20,000,000 as an indemnity to the owners of the negro slaves: — it has been paid. The first authors of this great reparation have had to struggle, not only against routine, but also against politics, against commerce, against the merchant-shipping, against the arts and manufactures, against all the most powerful elements of British greatness: — they have conquered them. They have had to oppose to all these united forces only the single force of moral and religious sentiment: — it has sufficed. They have never recoiled, never doubted themselves; and, after thirty years of labor, disappointments, and calumnies, on the day fixed by the eternal decrees, God has crowned them with success, and with a glory so pure and beautiful, that my French and Catholic heart cannot console itself for seeing it snatched from France and the Church."

Can there be a lesson more sublime, and better worth remembrance? Ah, may we never forget it! What power destroyed slavery in England? Religion. By the aid of what weapon? Liberty.

BOOK THIRD.

COLONIES OF DENMARK, SWEDEN, AND HOLLAND.

I. DANISH COLONIES.

DENMARK possesses three islands in the West Indies:

St. Croix, purchased of France, in 1733, for 738,000 livres, and which has two cities, Christianstadt and Frederickstadt;

St. John, occupied by the Danes in 1687;

St. Thomas, which has no other important feature than its French port.

Fallen into the hands of the English in 1807 and 1808, they were restored to Denmark by the peace of 1814.

St. Croix possessed in 1835, according to an official census, 161 plantations, 142 sugar-mills, and 19 provision warehouses, and was peopled by 26,681 inhabitants, of whom 6,805 were free (1,800 Europeans), 19,876 slaves.

St. Thomas numbered 22 plantations, and 14,022 inhabitants, of which 8,707 were free (5,315 Europeans), 5,315 slaves; St. John, 2,475 inhabitants, of which 532 were free (107 Europeans), 1,943 slaves.

There was, therefore, a total of 43,178 inhabitants, 16,034 freemen against 27,144 slaves.*

This population is divided into seven creeds: the Catholic, which embraces about 13,000 souls; the Lutheran, the religion of the state, which numbers but about 6,000; the

* *Revue coloniale*, 1843, pp. 291, 495; 1845, p. 257; 1846, p. 209; 1847, p. 193; 1848, pp. 157, 422.

Anglican Church, 10,000; the Moravians, 10,000; the Calvinists, Methodists, and Jews, which share the remainder.

The decay of the Danish colonies, the ruin of the colonists, and the sufferings of the slave population, made lamentable progress subsequently to 1814.

A general officer of the Danish Marine, M. Dahlerup, despatched by his government in 1841, declared that at St. Croix sixty plantations had been abandoned to the state for lack of being able to repay its advances. Heavy mortgages burdened the greater portion of the other plantations. At the same epoch, the *Fœderlandet* journal affirmed that, of 151 plantations, 76 belonged to non-residents of the colony, that 16 had reverted to the state, and that 60 had fallen into the hands of creditors. The mortality increased grievously. From 1807 to 1815, 7,000 individuals out of 26,000 had died, and the deaths almost every year exceeded the births. It was the same at St. John. This result was due in part to the extinction of family feelings in the heart of the slaves, who took no care of the aged and children, and in part to the excessive labors with which they were overburdened, despite the regulations decreed in 1810, but rarely executed. The slaves made the most desperate efforts to escape.

The exportation of sugar from St. Croix had not diminished with the number of the population, which proves that the labor imposed on the slaves had increased: —

1815 – 1824 (ten years)	25,400,000 lbs.
1825 – 1833 (nine years) . . .	24,100,000
1834 – 1841 (eight years)	21,400,000

The culture of sugar, moreover, became daily less productive, on account of the exhaustion of the soil, which is remarked in all slave countries.

Happily, the Danish government, still inspired by the generous spirit which procured Christian VII. the honor of being the first sovereign of Europe to abolish the slave-trade

(Ordinance of March 16, 1792), early resolved to pave the way for emancipation and to ameliorate the condition of the slaves, as it had reserved itself the right to do, shortly after the capture of St. Croix, by a royal edict dated February 3, 1755.

More happily still, it found in Major-General Van Scholten, Governor-General of the Danish West Indies, an intelligent and resolute man, who, by a wise and firm guidance, knew how to pave the way for and hasten the hour of freedom.

Until 1845, the measures taken were in view of ameliorating the condition of the slaves. From this epoch, which was that of the abolition of slavery by England, all the measures tended undeviatingly to emancipation. It was hoped at first to succeed in it by degrees through partial emancipation, and a royal rescript, dated November 22, 1834, commanded the government to establish obligatory redemption and the legal right of slaves to acquire property, to interdict the public sale of slaves and the separation of children, at an early age, from their parents, to constitute an exceptional jurisdiction for disputes between masters and slaves, and to frame a statute on the labor, maintenance, and discipline of slaves, and another on vagrancy.

During this time, the Danish government negotiated with England, with a view to obtaining lower duties after emancipation on the importation of the sugars of its colonies.

Surrounding himself with committees chosen from among the most honorable planters, the Governor-General put into execution all the orders which were intrusted him. Obligatory redemption was established, dating from November 22, 1834. A general regulation of May 7, 1838, determined the hours of labor, the discipline to be exercised in it, and the cares due the slaves, and a committee was appointed to regulate the food, lodging, and holidays. The words *not free* thenceforth replaced that of slave. The government council was placed in possession of the special jurisdiction. The observance of Sunday was imposed (December 20, 1836).

An ordinance on vagrancy, and the institution of a house of correction, appeared May 10, 1838 ; ten days previously, another ordinance had prohibited the sale of slaves in the public markets. Eight schools were established, and the co-operation of the different clergy in the work of moral education was warmly sought.

A statute of May 1, 1840, ratified the most important of these provisions, — a statute remarkable in two points of view.

Animated by the best intentions towards the slaves, it nevertheless still authorized the punishment of the lash, even inflicted upon women, while abolishing " blows with the tamarind or any other tree upon the naked body " (Art. 11) ; and the punishment of solitary imprisonment on bread and water, but for forty-eight hours at most. Sad vestiges reproaching the abominations of the former system !

It approved the minute regulations made concerning the height of the cabins, the hour of opening the mills, the ringing of bells for rising and for meals, the driving of the mules, the cutting of grass, the length of the stick of the driver, the furnishing of *cats-o'-nine-tails* by the police-officers at a suitable price. Thus, to intervene in all cases where abuses could creep in, regulations must intervene in everything ; they must anticipate everything ; the masters in turn become the real slaves ; the law is everywhere master, where it is not everywhere violated. An exact type, borrowed from the system of slavery, of what would be the pretended universal foresight of the system of socialism !

It may be thought that it would have been simpler to leave all this to the good-will and well understood interests of the colonists. Was this possible ? We are about to judge.

The government, forbearing to make any decision on the

concession of a free day to the slaves, had commissioned the Governor to make arrangements in this respect with the planters.

At St. John, the latter consented with tolerable willingness. The planters of St. Thomas refused all concession. Lastly, at St. Croix, 63 plantations, employing 6,801 slaves, resisted. Happily, the crown possessed 16 plantations; 81 belonged to Englishmen; a majority could, therefore, be formed, and 98 plantations, employing 10,023 slaves, adhered to the proposition of the Governor. A compromise measure was proposed, and sanctioned by the statute of March 23, 1844, prescribing the observance of Sunday, according Saturday to the slaves, releasing the masters from a poll-tax, and developing the schools.

On the same occasion, the planters gave expression to their opinion on emancipation; namely, that *partial* emancipation was baleful, because the ransomed would be their best workmen, and that *general* emancipation was impossible, until education had rendered the slave worthy and capable of freedom.

The usual conclusion, — to do nothing, to wait, and count on time to avert an importunate solution.

Providence sent to the slaves other succor than this suspicious good-will.

From the time that the English government allowed the entrance of foreign sugars, one of the principal fears was removed. The decay, moreover, had reached that point, that a slave at St. Croix brought in less than the interest of what he was worth, so that an indemnity might be considered by the planters as a profit.

Lastly, the measures of Governor Van Scholten had effected a better moral condition, without being able to arrest the depopulation. European public opinion, convulsed by the example of England and the projects of France, was re-echoed even in Denmark. There is no cause for surprise, therefore, that when, in 1846, a deputy, M. David, proposed immediate and simultaneous emancipation, in consideration of an indemnity to the states, assembled at Rotschild, the proposition was welcomed with sympathy. After a favorable report, the Assembly of the States, by a majority of 37 votes against 19, demanded in due form of the government to present a bill having for its object *complete emancipation.* They did not enter upon the question of indemnity, which was estimated at 2,000,000 Danish dollars, or from £ 10 to £ 12 per slave, a price analogous to that fixed by England for the similar colonies of Antigua and Tortola.

On the 28th of June, 1847, the birthday of the queen-dowager, who had warmly solicited emancipation, King Charles VIII. rendered a decree which abolished slavery, but postponed for twelve years the cessation of the masters' power, and declared free all children born in the interval.

But this decree, which at once gave and retained freedom, caused an agitation in the Danish West Indies, which the reaction of the events in France of February, 1848, carried to its height. The negroes, persuaded that the decree of their emancipation had arrived, but was withheld from them by their masters, repaired peaceably and without arms to the city, to assure themselves of the truth. In the face of this manifestation, which might become sanguinary, the Governor proclaimed immediate emancipation, July 3, 1848.

The planters resisted ; the militia sided with them. A collision took place, and ten or twelve negroes were killed. The revolt became general ; troops sent by the Governor of Porto Rico slew one hundred and thirty-one negroes, and the former slaves, subdued, were subjected to the severest punishment. But these unhappy events rendered the return to obedience still more impossible. The king of Denmark confirmed the emancipation, and the planters, who would have done better to have yielded to it with good grace, were happy to owe the maintenance of order to General Van Scholten, while the slaves owed to him their liberty.

II. SWEDISH COLONIES.*

The Isle of St. Bartholomew, ceded in 1784 to Sweden by France, in exchange for the right of depositing merchandise in the port of Gothenburg, and re-exporting it without paying duties, owes some importance to maritime wars, during which its port, freely open to the commerce of all nations, did a vast amount of business. But arid, not furnishing grass enough in the suburbs of the city of Gustavia for the pasture of the fifteen or twenty horses of its principal inhabitants, it scarcely deserves the name of colony. The number of its inhabitants in 1833 was estimated at 1,700, of which 531 were slaves in 1846.

In 1844, King Oscar notified the States of his desire to decree the abolition of slavery. In 1846, the Legislature placed at the disposal of the government 50,000 francs annually for the successive redemption of the 531 slaves and their complete liberation.

What has been the result of the abolition of slavery in these little possessions?

We have found it impossible to procure the statistics of their production; but all know that St. Thomas has become a wealthy and important entrepôt, and that St. Croix is a flourishing colony. For the last ten years, no sound of disorder or distress has been echoed from these little communities.

What we have said is sufficient to demonstrate that here, as elsewhere, slavery produced no good, and its abolition has produced no harm. A hail-storm, a hurricane, the change of a degree of temperature, would have exercised a more injurious and lasting influence than the happy liberation of 25,000 or 30,000 human beings, unjustly subjugated.

* *Revue coloniale*, 1844, II. 482, 1845, January and July, 1846, X. p. 210.

III. DUTCH COLONIES.

While the abolition of slavery is as yet in the United States but a distant hope, the realization of which, though approaching, is subordinate to the sanguinary chances of an interminable war, a generous, intelligent, and free nation, Holland, has just peacefully annihilated slavery in its American colonies by a law bearing date August 8, 1862.

It is well known that the Dutch are the possessors in Asia of the finest colonies in the world. There this people, so small in territory, but so great in character, this people of 3,000,000 Europeans, has succeeded in extending its rule over a population of 20,000,000 inhabitants, and obliging them to labor without subjecting them to slavery. It is true that the colonial system of the Dutch East Indies is open to sharp criticism. Left in dependence on the Mahometan native chiefs, and burdened with taxes, the Javanese, it must be confessed, are far from a fortunate race; and the part of the Board of Trade (Handel-Maatschappy) which, since 1819, has bought, transported, resold, and traded in virtue of a monopoly, is not strictly in conformity to the rules everywhere followed in the relations of nations. But this is not the place to examine this system, the results of which, it must be admitted, are magnificent. Before the establishment of the system to which the Governor, Van den Bosch, attached his name, Holland sent to its possessions a subsidy, which, in 1826, amounted to 80,000,000 francs. Thirty years after, in 1856, Holland received, on the contrary, from her East Indian colonies, a subsidy exceeding 63,000,000 francs.* These are the only colonies which enrich their metropolis. At the same time, slavery has no share in their products. Labor is compulsory, but the laborer is free; he may found a family, receives wages,

* *Revue maritime et coloniale*, p. 119, September, 1862.

is at liberty to change his residence; he is the debtor of the government, the slave of no one. Slavery, which existed there, as everywhere, before the settlement of the Europeans, was long maintained; but only domestic, not field slavery. The custom of having slaves, either negro or Indian, for coachmen, cooks, etc., was continued, though diminishing by degrees, until one of the best Governors of the East Indies, and one of the best Ministers of the Dutch colonies, M. Rochussen, secured the adoption of the law of May 7, 1859, which, making good the promise contained in a previous law, dated September 2, 1854, destroyed slavery in the Dutch East Indies, from January 1, 1860.

But if Holland no longer had slaves in her large possessions, she still retained them in her lesser ones; that is, in the colony of Guiana or Surinam, and in the islands of Curaçoa, Saba, St. Eustachius, Araba, Bonaire, and St. Martin, — small islands forming a part of the West Indies, — and in her stations on the west coast of Africa, of which St. George d'Elmina is the chief. The number of slaves in Surinam is estimated at 34,000, in a statement presented in 1861 by the ex-Minister of the Colonies, M. Loudon, making, with that of the small islands, a total of 45,272.

Emancipation was made the subject of debate by a royal message, dated December 17, 1851. Between English and French Guiana, where there were no longer any slaves, it seemed difficult to preserve them at Surinam. The colony itself demanded that the question should be resolved. But it was ten years under discussion; bill after bill, amendment after amendment, was proposed; the patience of the unfortunate slaves was wellnigh turned as a weapon against them, to maintain them in the bonds which they knew not how to break for themselves, as had been feared, by insurrection or flight to the neighboring colonies. Public opinion, the Chambers, and government, happily persevered,

More thorough investigation only confirmed the facts collected by the indefatigable defenders of emancipation, among whom it is just to cite M. Julius Wolbers, the author of a remarkable history of Surinam. The history of all slaveholding peoples is fatally always the same; it may be summed up in these words of the statement of the reasons of the Dutch statute, depicting the condition of the little islands of Curaçoa, St. Eustachius, etc.: "No progress, no use of improvements in agriculture, the intellectual, social, and religious state of the slave population falling more and more into decay." *

It would take too long to sum up the extended discussion called forth in the first and second Chambers by the bill, ably supported by the present Minister of the Colonies, M. Uhlenbeck; to set forth the report presented by a commission, composed of MM. Hugenholtz, Delprat, Cool, Mackay, and Dullert; and to cite the various opinions and amendments offered by the most distinguished and marked men, such as MM. Van Zuylen van Nievelt, Blom, Van Bosse, and Van Lynden, — we would gladly quote all the names commended by so noble an action. But it is not without interest to present the general economy of the law; voted by a majority of forty-five votes against seven, after long deliberation, by the representatives of so practical and prudent a people, thirty years after the experiment of England, fifteen years after that of France, it gives realization of a progress in what may be termed the art of emancipation.

There are two laws, one for Surinam, the other for the small islands. The stations on the coast of Africa, the territory and population of which are, it is true, very imperfectly defined, are unfortunately not in question.

Both laws are the repetition of the same provisions, and may be analyzed as follows: —

* *Memoire van Toelichting*, No. 4, p. 20.

The 45,000 slaves of Holland are free from July 1, 1863.

An indemnity is secured to the owners. This is fixed, at Surinam, at 300 florins (630 fr.) per head, without distinction of age, sex, or kind of labor; and at the small islands, at from 200 to 250 florins, except at St. Martin's, where the slaves have been free in point of fact since the French emancipation, but where no indemnity had been accorded: here the indemnity is fixed at 150 francs. The average indemnity in the French colonies was 530 francs; in the English colonies, 630 francs. This last figure is adopted as a basis in the Dutch colonies. The total expense will be 15,000,810 florins (33,201,000 fr.).

This sum includes a subsidy of 1,000,000 florins, to be apportioned in premiums for the encouragement of the immigration of new laborers, to replace the freedmen who may at first refuse field labor, to lessen wages by competition, and to stimulate the progress of agriculture. The Danish government has just offered the government of the United States to receive and transport, at its own expense, 3,000 fugitive slaves to its colonies of St. Thomas, St. Croix, and St. John, — 3,000 fugitive slaves who have taken refuge in the Northern States. 3,800 of these freed laborers have been already sent to South Carolina (Port Royal, Ladies' Island, etc.); and a remarkable report recently addressed by Mr. Pierce to the Secretary of the Treasury, Mr. Chase, attests the partial success of this attempt at colonization. Perhaps the Dutch colonies, in this moment of transition, may also profit by this abundant resource.

For ten years, the freedmen are to be subjected to a surveillance exercised by salaried public functionaries, who are forbidden to have any interests in the colonies. Free to choose their residence, their occupation, and their patron, the freedmen will not be free to choose idleness, but are bound to contract an engagement of labor for from one to three years on the plantations, and from three months to a year in the towns, or to prove an occupation by the pur chase of a license. During the first two years only, the government may even limit their choice to the district of their present abode, — a somewhat exorbitant measure, which is at least compensated for by an amendment of M. Van Bosse, by which the government is at liberty to exempt any freedman from surveillance who may show himself worthy the favor. This intermediate system is free from some of the objections of the apprenticeship of 1834, which it became necessary to abolish in 1838, as was opportunely recalled by M. Van Zuylen van Nievelt, in demonstrating that this mixed system resulted only in irritating both the quasi masters and quasi slaves, the one uncertain of their property, the others disquieted for their liberty.

A civil state, a name, schools, culture, and the right to property, are at once secured to the slave; this is to place before him, provided he attain them, the four degrees which separate servile from social life, — the family, religion, instruction, and property. Take these away, and he is a brute. Add these, and he is a man. And after the transitional ten years, the Dutch law unequivocally declare him an inhabitant and citizen (Acts 22, 23), very different from those laws of the Northern States which, after according him liberty, refuse him equality.

Thus, therefore: 1. Immediate emancipation; 2. Preliminary indemnity; 3. Surveillance, with compulsory labor; 4. Immigration at the public expense; 5. Religious and moral education; — such are the bases of the law of August 8, 1862. They are very nearly borrowed from the memorable report of 1845, by which the illustrious Duke de Broglie has taught all legislators the peaceful and practical method of elevating human beings from dependence to liberty.

Forty-five thousand men! Thirty-three million francs! It is very little, — scarcely more than what is wasted and expended in a single day's strife between the North and the South! I am persuaded that the king of Holland must have signed with heart-felt joy this unpretending law, which sets so many unhappy beings at liberty, gives to our century a spectacle which it has rarely tasted, — that of a progress accomplished without violence, — and at length effaces from the name of Holland a stain which rests now upon the name of but a single Christian nation in Europe, yet the most obstinate, the first and last in the practice of the slave-trade and slavery. This nation is Spain.*

* *Journal des Débats*, Sept 20, 1862.

APPENDIX.

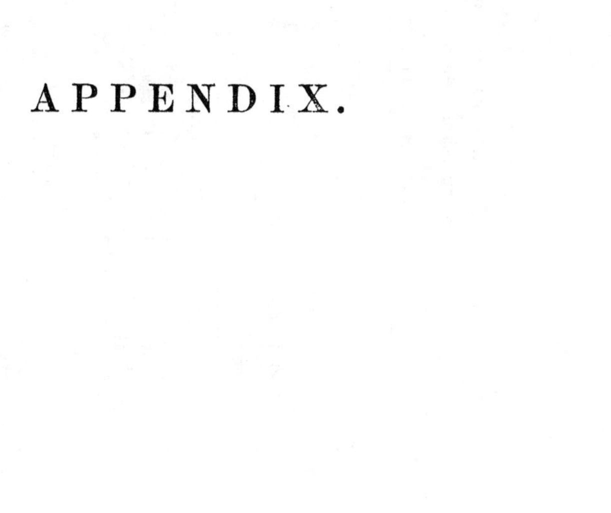

TABLES A AND B.

VALUE OF IMPORTATIONS AND EXPORTATIONS BEFORE AND AFTER 1848.

(From statements published in the *Revue coloniale.*)

Table No. 1.

IMPORTATIONS BEFORE 1848.

	1847.	1846.	1845.	1844.	1843.	1842.	1841.
	Francs.						
Martinico	22,841,091	21,542,939	20,661,375	22,679,912	21,066,338	17,919,090	20,696,100
Guadaloupe	21,339,190	19,857,687	24,974,370	26,166,861	18,296,458	16,661,782	17,365,875
Guiana	2,878,828	2,971,689	2,575,164	2,891,706	3,462,006		
Bourbon	15,647,096	17,250,733	17,015,753	19,494,323	20,011,791		
	62,706,205						

EXPORTATIONS.

	1847.	1846.	1845.	1844.	1843.	1842.	1841.
Martinico	18,323,921	16,185,432	18,127,978	19,588,527	15,054,021	13,581,010	15,601,500
Guadaloupe	20,420,522	14,769,945	18,294,370	17,943,151	13,782,542	16,948,797	17,365,875
Guiana	1,622,919	1,648,171	1,812,882	1,821,610	1,739,019	2,000,000	2,000,000
Bourbon	12,620,602	16,221,660	15,921,660	15,276,923	15,869,295		
	52,987,964						

AGGREGATE MOVEMENT.

	1847.	1846.	1845.	1844.	1843.	1842.	1841.
Martinico	41,165,012	37,789,353	38,789,353	42,268,439	36,120,359	31,500,100	36,197,600
Guadaloupe	41,759,713	34,627,632	43,268,106	44,410,012	32,079,000	33,610,580	34,818,000
Guiana	4,501,747	4,619,861	4,388,046	4,713,317	5,201,025	5,499,871	
Bourbon	28,267,698	33,472,393	32,982,225	34,776,246	35,881,086		
	115,694,170						

Quinquennial average, 1843 – 1847		
	Martinico	39,226,503 fr.
	Guadaloupe	39,228,912
	Guiana	4,081,799
	Bourbon	33,074,648

Table No. 2.

IMPORTATIONS FOR 1848–1858.

	1848.	1849.	1850.	1851.	1852.	1853.	1854.	1855.	1856.	1857.	1858.
	Francs.										
Martinico	14,153,733	16,524,306	17,930,076	21,536,567	25,625,695	27,050,495	28,909,910	25,836,624	23,833,540	22,696,221	22,613,325
Guadaloupe	11,980,480	12,494,115	12,741,735	17,596,014	19,157,895	16,048,311	22,950,177	23,512,552	23,671,375	22,470,671	20,632,877
Guiana	2,253,205	2,721,314	2,682,167	3,097,726	4,276,703	6,030,906	5,725,886	5,490,901	7,103,063	6,420,789	6,899,312
Bourbon	10,569,375	11,552,739	16,079,252	17,766,418	20,910,489	28,472,455	31,747,750	39,614,318	28,309,904	32,229,543	43,107,415
	38,956,793										93,252,929

EXPORTATIONS.

	1848.	1849.	1850.	1851.	1852.	1853.	1854.	1855.	1856.	1857.	1858.
Martinico	9,212,554	10,891,782	9,737,676	13,580,971	14,594,544	16,344,433	18,636,070	16,399,439	20,186,613	24,830,093	20,862,304
Guadaloupe	8,873,539	10,229,298	8,155,932	11,885,027	10,183,897	10,372,363	15,823,903	15,934,902	15,147,176	23,319,277	19,070,428
Guiana	1,143,515	1,032,326	1,131,191	731,660	1,380,242	1,380,952	1,285,885	1,274,845	958,553	961,272	746,484
Bourbon	9,107,507	10,428,646	11,936,256	11,136,763	13,939,032	21,856,675	28,881,893	37,161,923	29,677,084	33,130,125	38,423,669
	28,337,115										79,102,885

AGGREGATE MOVEMENT.

	1848.	1849.	1850.	1851.	1852.	1853.	1854.	1855.	1856.	1857.	1858.
Martinico	23,306,287	27,416,088	27,667,752	35,117,538	40,220,239	43,394,928	47,545,980	42,236,063	44,020,153	47,526,314	43,475,629
Guadaloupe	20,854,020	22,724,413	20,897,667	28,481,041	29,341,792	30,947,875	38,774,080	39,447,454	38,818,551	45,789,948	39,703,305
Guiana	3,396,720	3,753,920	3,813,359	3,829,386	5,606,945	7,411,858	7,011,771	6,765,746	8,061,617	7,382,062	7,645,796
Bourbon	19,676,882	21,981,385	28,015,508	28,903,181	34,849,521	50,329,130	60,629,643	76,776,241	57,986,988	65,359,668	81,531,084
	67,233,909										172,355,814

		1848–1852.	1853–1857.	Decennials. 1848–1857.
Quinquennial averages	Martinico	36,676,505	51,546,959	44,111,732
	Guadaloupe	28,461,649	39,904,671	34,183,159
	Guiana	4,427,460	7,954,376	6,190,917
	Bourbon	34,708,672	72,324,705	53,516,693

TABLE

COMPARATIVE

In actual values, of the Importations and Exportations of the French Colonies French Commerce, published by the Administration of

Table No. 3.

Years.		Martinico.	
		Francs.	Francs.
1848	Importations of all productions	12,211,716	24,806,221
	Exportations of all destinations	12,594,505	
1849	Importations . . .	20,281,048	35,392,773
	Exportations	15,111,725	
1850	Importations . . .	18,367,676	31,155,436
	Exportations	12,787,760	
1851	Importations . . .	27,082,160	44,364,770
	Exportations	17,282,610	
1852	Importations . . .	26,070,220	47,663,324
	Exportations	21,593,104	
Totals for five years, from 1848 to 1852		. . . .	183,382,524
Quinquennial averages . .		. . . . .	36,676,505
1853	Importations	25,558,832	44,204,739
	Exportations	18,645,907	
1854	Importations	27,737,500	48,925,973
	Exportations	21,188,473	
1855	Importations	24,901,774	46,942,247
	Exportations	22,040,473	
1856	Importations	30,277,174	60,360,432
	Exportations	30,083,258	
1857	Importations	27,352,510	57,301,406
	Exportations	29,948,896	
Totals for five years, from 1853 to 1857		. . . .	257,734,797
Quinquennial averages . . .		. . . .	51,546,959
Totals for ten years, from 1848 to 1857		. . . .	441,117,321
Decennial averages		. . . .	44,111,732

C.

CONDITION,

during the Decennial Period 1848 - 1857, *according to the General Tables of Metropolitan Customs and the States of Local Customs.*

GUADALOUPE.		GUIANA.		BOURBON	
Francs.	Francs.	Francs.	Francs.	Francs.	Francs.
10,415,876 11,684,400	22,100,276	1,848,311 2,129,907	3,978,218	10,361,094 13,349,957	23,711,051
13,672,339 13,943,827	27,616,166	2,929,447 1,485,655	4,415,102	13,979,612 16,616,684	30,596,296
14,292,925 11,005,549	24,298,474	2,561,965 1,517,328	4,079,293	18,247,354 18,920,777	37,168,131
19,168,391 13,438,546	32,606,937	2,834,107 1,223,635	4,057,742	21,079,741 15,007,081	36,086,822
21,637,007 14,149,383	35,686,390	4,276,703 1,330,242	5,606,945	22,278,786 23,702,326	45,981,112
. . . . .	142,308,243 28,461,649	. . . . .	22,137,300 4,427,460	. . . . .	173,543,412 34,708,672
18,761,523 11,556,056	30,317,579	5,676,152 1,703,173	7,379,325	26,046,747 23,073,481	49,120,228
22,270,194 18,435,481	40,705,675	5,979,406 1,433,545	7,412,951	30,615,944 31,748,068	62,364,012
22,778,433 19,924,845	42,703,278	5,912,360 1,284,901	7,197,261	37,607,507 34,271,080	71,878,587
23,793,290 15,774,056	39,567,346	6,234,114 4,495,551	10,729,665	33,671,020 45,005,550	78,676,570
25,400,362 20,829,113	46,229,475	5,580,779 1,471,897	7,052,676	42,140,612 54,443,518	99,584,130
. . . . .	199,523,353 39,904,671	. . . . .	39,771,878 7,954,376	. . . . .	361,623,527 72,324,705
. . . . .	341,831,596 34,183,159	. . . . .	61,909,178 6,190,917	. . . . .	535,166,939 53,516,693

TABLE D.*

COLONIAL SUGAR.

Table No 4.

Years.	Average Price per 100 kilog. on the Paris Exchange.		Average Duty affecting the Year, tenths included.	Remainder.	To be deducted for Average Costs of Transportation.	Real Net Cost at the Entrepôt.	Quinquennial Average of Net Cost.
	Nominal Price.	Real Price.					
1819	156.37	141.10	49.50	91.60	3.00	88.60	88.60
1820	162.41	146.58	49.50	97.08	3 00	94.08	
1821	151.65	136.87	49.50	87.37	3.00	84.37	
1822	139.19	125.61	49.50	76.11	3.00	73.11	91.91
1823	187.15	168.91	49.50	119.41	3.00	116.41	
1824	159.64	144.11	49.50	94 61	3.00	91.61	
1825	181.70	164.00	49.50	114.50	3.00	111.50	
1826	161.32	145.59	49.50	96.09	3·00	93.09	
1827	172.13	155.35	49.50	105.85	3.00	102.85	99.70
1828	168.50	152.07	49.50	102.57	3.00	99.57	
1829	159.54	144.01	49.50	94.51	3.00	91.51	
1830	155.03	139.90	49.50	90.40	3.00	87.40	
1831	142.60	128.72	49.50	79.22	3.00	76.22	
1832	149.10	134.57	49.50	85.07	3.00	82.07	80.49
1833	144.97	130.89	49.50	81.39	3.00	78.39	
1834	144.97	130.89	49.50	81.39	3.00	78.39	
1835	139.01	125.49	49.50	75.99	3.00	72.99	
1836	141.70	129.82	49.50	80.32	3.00	77.32	
1837	130.80	118 09	49.50	68 59	3.00	65.59	67.73
1838	126.25	113.97	49.50	64.47	3.00	61.47	
1839	119.00	107.18	42.90	64.28	3.00	61 28	
1840	138.75	125.27	42.90	82.37	3.00	79.37	
1841	129.75	117.13	49.50	67.63	3.00	64.63	
1842	124.75	112.63	49.50	63.13	3.00	60.13	64.25
1843	122.75	110 03	49.50	60.53	3.00	57.53	
1844	124.25	112.13	49.50	62.63	3.00	59.63	
1845	128.50	115.98	49.50	66.48	3.00	63.48	
1846	129.25	115.68	49.50	66.18	3.00	63.18	
1847	124.80	112.68	49.50	63.18	3.00	60.18	59.73 } 68.80
1848	116.30	104.98	49.50	55.48	3.00	52.48	
1849	122.33	111.86	49 50	62.36	3.00	59.36	
1850	138.34	124.86	49.50	75.36	3.00	72.36	
1851	132.58	119.75	44.82	74.93	3.00	71.93	
1852	125.17	113.00	40.97	72.03	3.00	69.03	69.10
1853	116.93	105.56	41.80	63.76	3 00	60.76	
1854	128.74	116.22	41.80	74.42	3.00	71.42	
1855	130.11	117.44	43.70	73.74	3.00	70.74	
1856	144.93	130.85	45.60	85.25	3.00	82 25	
1857	153.27	138 34	45.60	92.74	3.00	89.74	77.57
1858	137.75	124.37	46.80	77.57	3 00	74.57	
1859	136.04	122.76	49 20	73.56	3.00	70.56	

* I am indebted for these tables to the friendly kindness of one of the first sugar manufacturers of France, the Honorable M. Kolb-Bernard, deputy of Lille.

INDIGENOUS SUGAR.

Years.	Average Price per 100 kilog. on the Paris Exchange.		Average Duty affecting the Year, tenths included.	Remainder.	To be deducted for Average Costs of Transportation.	Real Net Cost to the Manufacturer per 100 kilog.	Quinquennial Averages of Net Cost.	
	Nominal Price.	Real Price.*						
1830†	147.70	133.32	0.00	133.32	3.00	130.32		
1831	132 08	119.20	0.00	119.20	3.00	116.20		
1832	132.22	119.35	0.00	119.35	3.00	116.35	121.96	
1833	142.00	128.22	0.00	128.22	3.00	125.22		
1834	138.20	124.72	0.00	124.72	3.00	121 72		
1835	128.20	115.73	0.00	115.73	3.00	112.73		
1836	130.74	118.01	0.00	118.01	3.00	115.01		
1837	wanting	0.00	0.00	0.00	0.00	0.00	105.74	
1838	121.75	109.93	5.50	104.43	2.50	101.93		
1839	120.25	109.53	13.75	95.78	2.50	93 28		
1840	141.25	127.47	22.00	105.47	2.50	102.97		
1841	130.25	116.48	27.50	88.98	2.50	86.48		
1842	124.25	112.23	27.50	84.53	2.50	82.03	87.59	
1843	123.00	111.08	27.50	83.58	2.50	81.08		
1844	130.00	118.18	30 25	87.93	2.50	85.43		
1845	131.75	118.92	35.75	83.17	2.50	80.67		
1846	130.50	117.82	41.25	76.57	2.50	74.07		
1847	120.75	109.03	46.75	63.28	2.50	60.78	64.78	
1848	112.25	101.33	49 50	51.83	2.50	49.33		
1849	123.00	111.08	49.50	61.58	2.50	59.08		
1850	132.76	119.81	49.50	70.31	2.50	67.81		
1851	127 51	115.09	49.50	65.59	2.50	62.09		
1852	120.68	108.92	49.50	59 42	2.50	56.92	61.04	64.62
1853	118.67	107.81	49.50	58.31	2.50	55.81		
1854	129.43	116.82	51.75	65.07	2.50	62.57		
1855	130.09	117.41	54.00	63.41	2.50	60.91		
1856	140.77	127.05	54.00	73.05	2.50	70.55		
1857	148.53	134.06	54.00	80.06	2.50	77.56	68.05	
1858	134.21	121.13	54.00	67.13	2.50	64.63		
1859	136.38	123.09	54.00	69.09	2.50	66.59		

The average of the first six years, dating from 1830, and amounting to 121 fr. 96 c. per 100 kilog., compared with the average of the last fifteen years, dating from 1845 and amounting to 64 fr. 62 c. per 100 kilog., represents the margin of the abatement of price on indigenous sugar in consequence of improvements in the manufacture.

It is proper to take an average extended over a great number of years, for the second period, in order to compensate for all the commercial accidents and abnormal rises and falls produced in this period by various circumstances.

The diminution of the net cost has not followed a regular progress in the period from 1845 to 1859, because during the last years all the elements of manufacture increased in price; as labor, the beet-root, carbon, charcoal, bone-black, etc.

* The real price is deducted from the nominal price after a deduction of 2 per cent for tret, 5 per cent for tare, and 5 per cent for discount.

† The price of indigenous sugar did not begin to be quoted on 'Change until 1830.

STATISTICS OF THE ENGLISH COLONIES IN AMERICA. 1855.

Names of the Colonies.		Population.	Budget.	No. of Vessels.	Amount of Importations.	Amount of Exportations.
			Francs.		Francs.	Francs.
The Barbadoes	1605	100,000	1,723,450	838	16,119,600	19,758,250
The Bermudas	1611	80,000	408,075	206	4,063,900	1,025,500
St. Christopher	1623	23,000	378,800	406	2,402,425	3,616,050
Antigua	1625	35,000	679,250	665	4,812,625	7,731,525
Nevis	1628	10,000	85,275	237	493,200	974,400
Montserrat	1632	7,000	87,500	134	192,600	499,650
Virgin Islands	1648	8,000	37,775	784	91,525	204,975
Jamaica	1655	361,400	7,980,275	488	22,487,675	25,208,025
Newfoundland	1663	75,000	3,161,225	1,077	28,820,000	28,556,300
Hudson's Bay and Vancouver *	1668					
Barbadoes *	1684					
Bay of Honduras	1714	3,794	364,625	116	6,137,150	11,564,775
Nova Scotia *	1759					
Canada	1763	1,015,000	28,825,000	2,622	225,538,150	176,177,875
Prince Edward's Island	1763	71,502	754,825	962	6,712,900	3,618,300
Dominica	1763	18,660	194,400			
St. Vincent	1763	26,200	432,800	320	2,812,325	2,547,800
Grenada	1763	21,000	398,100	324	2,144,500	2,283,600
The Bahamas	1783	27,519	726,725	332	4,818,775	2,791,750
New Brunswick	1784	193,800	3,458,825	3,442	35,783,250	20,659,525
Tobago	1794	13,200	214,525	76	934,500	1,184,675
Trinidad	1797	39,400	2,016,425	657	13,863,350	9,699,975
English Guiana	1803	99,710	6,375,200	693	22,150,400	33,296,795
St. Lucia	1815	25,230	372,100	157	1,387,850	1,374,500
Falkland Islands	1833	420	161,750	53	527,500	465,000
Totals		2,205,315	58,826,925	14,589	402,294,700	352,238,245

* Not found included in the Statistical Tables.

SUGARS IMPORTED

FROM ALL SOURCES INTO THE UNITED KINGDOM, SINCE 1851, ACCORDING TO THE OFFICIAL DOCUMENTS.

Years.	From foreign Countries.	General Importation in English Quintals.					From foreign Countries and the Colonies. General Total.
		Mauritius.	East Indies.	Guiana.	West Indies.	Total.	
	Francs.	Francs.	Francs.	Francs.		Francs.	Francs.
1851	2,261,281	1,000.269	1,585,430	3,085,554		5,671,253	7,932,534
1852	1,058,961	1,122,064	1,303,885	3,411,851*		5,837,800	6,896,761
1853	1,942,321	1,252,269	1,225,378	584,345	2,279,977	5,341,969	7,289,290
1854	3,198,102	1,662,190	784,966	898,240	2.568,866	5,914,262	9,112,364
1855	2,301,275	1,363,132	732,055	761,093	2,166,578	5,022,858	7,324,133
1856	2,069,453	1,647,257	1,226,847	672,554	2,145,129	5,696,787	7,761,240
1857	3,065,182	1,184,329	1,181,368	804,480	2,155,337	5,325,514	8,390,696
1858†	3,630,915	1,086,501	794,309	773,825	2,725,246	5,379,881	9,010,796

* Since 1852, the official tables of English commerce make no distinction, in the general importation, between the different West India Islands, which at this time are, Guiana included : —

Demerara	747,640 metrical quintals
Barbadoes	743,012
Jamaica	511,259
Trinidad	483,857
Antigua	185,662
St. Vincent	176,593
Grenada	125,008
All the other English possessions in the West Indies	438,820

† In 1859 and 1860 the importation of *colonial* sugar has greatly increased, while that of *foreign* sugar has diminished. (*Revue coloniale*, Jan. and Feb. 1861, p. 100.)

APPENDIX TO PAGE 306.

Dicunt quia die quadam, cum advenientibus nuper mercatoribus multa venalia in forum fuissent collata multique ad emendum confluxissent, et ipsum Gregorium inter alios advenisse ac vidisse inter alios pueros venales positos, candidi corporis ac venusti vultus, capillorum quoque forma egregia. Quos cum aspiceret interrogavit, ut aiunt, de qua regione vel terra essent adlati. Dictumque est quod de Britannia insula, cujus incolæ tales essent aspectus. Rursus interrogavit utrum iidem insularii Christiani, an paganis adhuc erroribus essent implicati. Dictumque est, quod essent pagani. At ille intimo ex corde longa trahens suspiria: "Heu, proh dolor! inquit, quod tam lucidi vultus homines tenebrarum auctor possidet, totaque gratia frontispicii mentem ab interna gratia vacuam gestat!" Rursus ergo interrogavit quod esset vocabulum gentis illius. Responsum est quod *Angli* vocarentur. At ille: "Bene, inquit, nam et *angelicam* habent faciem, et tales angelorum et cœlis decet esse cohæredes." "Quod habet nomen ipsa provincia de qua isti sunt adlati." Responsum est quod *Deiri* vocarentur iidem provinciales. At ille: "Bene, inquit, Deiri, *de ira eruti*, et ad misericordiam Christi vocati, 'Rex provinciæ illius quomodo appellatur.'" Responsum est quod *Aella* diceretur. At ille, alludens ad nomen, ait: "*Alleluia*, laudem Dei creatoris illis in partibus oportet cantari." Accidensque Pontificem Romanæ et apostolicæ sedis, nondum enim erat ipse Pontifex factus, rogavit ut genti Anglorum in Britanniam aliquos verbi ministros, per quos ad Christum converterentur, mitteret? seipsum paratum esse in hoc opus, Domino cooperante, perficiendum, si tamen Apostolico papæ hoc ut fieret, placeret. Quod dum perficere non posset, quia etsi Pontifex concedere illi quod petierat voluit, non tamen cives Romani, ut tam longe ab urbe recederet, potuere permittere; mox ut ipse pontificatus officio functus est, perficit opus diu desideratum, alios quidem prædicatores mittens, sed ipse prædicationem ut fructificaret suis exhortationibus et precibus adjuvans.*

* This text from the venerable Bede, *Hist. Eccles. Gent. Anglor.* Lib. II. c. 1, is cited in the Letters on Domestic Slavery, by Mgr. England, Bishop of Charleston, Letter IX. p. 144, Vol. III.

Cambridge: Stereotyped and Printed by Welch, Bigelow, & Co.

www.ingramcontent.com/pod-product-compliance
Lightning Source LLC
LaVergne TN
LVHW011150110826
845150LV00006B/1205

* 9 7 8 1 4 2 5 5 4 6 9 9 1 *